# Indigenous Peopl

MW01135469

During the Second World War, indigenous people in the United States, Australia, New Zealand and Canada mobilised en masse to support the war effort, despite withstanding centuries of colonialism. Their roles ranged from ordinary soldiers fighting on distant shores, to civilians capturing Japanese prisoners on their own territory, to women working in munitions plants on the home front. R. Scott Sheffield and Noah Riseman examine indigenous experiences of the Second World War across these four settler societies. Informed by theories of settler colonialism, martial race theory and military sociology, they show how indigenous people and their communities both shaped and were shaped by the Second World War. Particular attention is paid to the policies in place before, during and after the war, highlighting the ways that indigenous people negotiated their own roles within the war effort at home and abroad.

**R. Scott Sheffield** is Associate Professor of History at the University of the Fraser Valley. He is the author of *The Red Man's on the Warpath: The Image of the 'Indian' and the Second World War*.

**Noah Riseman** is Associate Professor of History at the Australian Catholic University. His first book, *Defending Whose Country? Indigenous Soldiers in the Pacific War*, was shortlisted for the 2013 Chief Minister's Northern Territory History Award. He is also the co-author of *Defending Country: Aboriginal and Torres Strait Islander Military Service since 1945* and *Serving in Silence? Australian LGBT Servicemen and Women*.

# Indigenous Peoples and the Second World War

## The Politics, Experiences and Legacies of War in the US, Canada, Australia and New Zealand

**R. Scott Sheffield**
*University of the Fraser Valley*

**Noah Riseman**
*Australian Catholic University*

**CAMBRIDGE**
UNIVERSITY PRESS

# CAMBRIDGE
## UNIVERSITY PRESS

University Printing House, Cambridge CB2 8BS, United Kingdom

One Liberty Plaza, 20th Floor, New York, NY 10006, USA

477 Williamstown Road, Port Melbourne, VIC 3207, Australia

314-321, 3rd Floor, Plot 3, Splendor Forum, Jasola District Centre, New Delhi - 110025, India

79 Anson Road, #06-04/06, Singapore 079906

Cambridge University Press is part of the University of Cambridge.

It furthers the University's mission by disseminating knowledge in the pursuit of education, learning and research at the highest international levels of excellence.

www.cambridge.org
Information on this title: www.cambridge.org/9781108440745
DOI: 10.1017/9781108341172

First published 2019
First paperback edition 2020

*A catalogue record for this publication is available from the British Library*

ISBN 978-1-108-42463-9 Hardback
ISBN 978-1-108-44074-5 Paperback

# Contents

vi    Contents

Conclusion                                        301

# Figures

# Tables

# Foreword

In 1942 journalist Richard L. Neuberger published an article in the *Saturday Evening Post* stating that a Nazi propaganda radio broadcast predicted an 'Indian uprising' should Native Americans be asked to fight against the Axis. The broadcast, according to Neuberger, also asked the rhetorical question: 'How could the American Indians think of bearing arms for their exploiters?'[1] I asked a good friend, Leipzig University instructor Frank Usbeck, to look into Neuberger's assertion. Professor Usbeck could not find a reference to this particular broadcast in German archives, so it might very well be that Neuberger was engaging in a bit of propaganda of his own. The question, however, lingered on.

*Indigenous Peoples and the Second World War* does much to answer this question and many more. R. Scott Sheffield and Noah Riseman, both talented historians, have crafted a detailed comparative study of Native peoples – Native Americans of the United States, First Nations peoples of Canada, the Māori people of New Zealand and the Indigenous peoples of Australia and the Torres Strait Islands – and their service in the militaries of four settler colonial states during World War II. Although the different Indigenous servicemen and women, of course, served in different capacities and in different theatres of the war, their experiences before, during and following their return home were remarkably similar. Quite often they served in very specific combat roles. Each of the four groups was stereotyped as possessing military skills or propensities useful to the combat missions of the various states. Indigenous service personnel entered the military during World War II often in greater numbers than their proportional populations and performed their duties with devotion and courage. It appeared to 'prove' the notion that if oppressed people can fight against the Axis, the entire war effort was a just cause.

All was not as this idea seemed. In all four settler colonial states, Native peoples questioned the fact that as second-class or even non-citizens

---

[1] Richard L. Neuberger, 'On the Warpath', *Saturday Evening Post* 215 (24 October 1942): 79.

with little in terms of civil rights, why indeed should their people risk their lives in service of those that took their lands, suppressed their cultures and left them as the poorest of each nation's poor. Additionally, some Indigenous nations questioned conscription as illegal because of the fact that many of their people were simply not full citizens of their particular settler colonial states. Other Native nations asked that their young men be exempted from military service as conscientious objectors based on religious beliefs or because of historic treaty provisions. These protests were either ignored or explained away as the complaints of a vocal minority.

Indigenous peoples largely volunteered or accepted the draft on an individual basis and except for an all-Māori battalion (primarily under the command of non-Māori officers), special units in northern Australia and Alaska, and the Comanche and Navajo Code Talkers, they were integrated into regular military units. On the other hand, Indigenous servicemen were often put into dangerous combat situations because of non-Native stereotyping. They were placed generally in 'non-technical' military occupations meaning infantry, reconnaissance and commando duties based on the idea that they were warriors, trackers, hunters and scouts by birth. They thus saw more than their share of combat.

The authors make excellent use of oral histories found in the archives of the four settler-colonial states. The readjustment of the Indigenous servicemen and women was not altogether satisfactory, according to those who returned home following the war. Many were dissatisfied with their homecomings because settler state policies regarding their peoples remained unchanged or were in fact markedly worse. For example, Native Americans returned to the United States to face a policy shift from relative political and cultural autonomy to forced assimilation. Policymakers in the United States argued that because Native Americans fought valiantly in the war or aided the war effort at home, they wanted to become fully assimilated into the larger American society. With that as an excuse, the government began the policy of relocating Native Americans from their reservations to major metropolitan centres and terminating Native American tribal governments.

Across all four countries, many servicemen returned from combat with severe emotional and physical trauma. Combat situations promote a kind of solidification of group ethos of mutual aid. They often returned to a disjointed, individualised society that was exactly the opposite of the group cohesion that combat produces. In some cases, they were aided by the settler state in readjusting to civilian life. On the other hand, readjustment came as a result of tribal healing and honouring ceremonies and simple kinship compassion in what has been called the social absorption of wartime trauma. Often the veterans saw themselves as warriors fighting for their own land and peoples rather than as soldiers in service of the larger nation-state. Sheffield and Riseman do a remarkable job of integrating the narratives of the different groups' experiences into this study.

What follows, all in all, is a rigorously researched and highly readable study. The authors have taken into account the different backgrounds of these peoples with perception and detail. As the reader will discover, Sheffield and Riseman have put together a very fine and much-needed study in answer to the question of why and how Indigenous peoples served in the militaries of culturally repressive settler colonial states.

EMERITUS PROFESSOR TOM HOLM
*University of Arizona*
*Tucson, Arizona*

# Acknowledgements

This book is the product of years of research we have both been conducting independently and collaboratively across continents, grants and, of course, time zones. We first met in 2013 in Saskatoon, Saskatchewan, at the Native American and Indigenous Studies Association annual conference, when we both participated in a panel on the global history of Indigenous military service in the twentieth century. We hit it off right away (well, almost right away – there was that embarrassing moment when Noah was not wearing his glasses so did not recognise Scott and gave an awkward look as they passed in the corridor). Two years later, Noah hosted a conference in Melbourne entitled 'Brothers and Sisters in Arms: Historicising Indigenous Military Service'. It was over dinner that Scott proposed to Noah: he had been working on a book on comparative and transnational Indigenous Second World War service since 2007, but he could not complete it alone. Would Noah join him? After a bit of to-ing and fro-ing, Noah agreed and a fantastic partnership was born. We can both confidently say that it has been amazing working with each other, including the many overnight emails, Skype chats, and our now-biennial catch-ups on alternating continents.

Of course, the research and writing journey is always a product of an intellectual community that surrounds the authors. Along the way, we have had significant intellectual, financial and editorial support. First and foremost we must thank P. Whitney Lackenbauer, who was heavily involved in the genesis and early shaping of this project. While other commitments prevented him from continuing with the project, Whitney remained an enthusiastic supporter through to the end, providing us with primary source documents and critical information and insights across the book. In particular, he provided access to existing and forthcoming work of his pertaining to Arctic defence in both Canada and Alaska, which informed especially parts of Chapters 4–6. Without the groundwork laid by Whitney, this book could not have come to fruition. The two readers, Tom Holm and Ann McGrath, provided fantastic feedback that really reshaped how we approached the manuscript. Ann's comments about gender, in particular, really challenged us to interrogate some of the gendered structures affecting women and their roles during the war. Tom Holm's work has, of course, been ground-breaking in this field, and we are honoured that he agreed to write the book's foreword.

Initial funding for this project came in the form of a Canadian Social Sciences and Humanities Research Council Grant in 2008. Additional funding for part of this project was available from an Australian Research Council Linkage grant LP120200327: 'Serving our country: a history of Aboriginal and Torres Strait Islander people in the defence of Australia'. In addition, Scott was consistently and generously supported by the University of the Fraser Valley through course releases, student research funding and travel support. We were fortunate to work with a capable and dedicated army of undergraduate, graduate and postdoctoral research assistants in conducting this wide-ranging research. These included: University of the Fraser Valley undergrads, Kimberly Unruh, Anastasia Lownie, Sarah Sewell and Kelsey Siemens, and Australian Catholic University graduate, Julien Varrenti-Osmond; grad students, Adrienne MacDonald (MA, University of Waterloo) and Hayley Brown (PhD, Victoria University of Wellington); and postdoctoral fellows Jamie Shanks and Timothy Winegard. At Cambridge University Press, thanks go to Executive Publisher Michael Watson for supporting this book, and to editorial assistant Lisa Carter for her work converting the manuscript to print.

Academic colleagues from across the globe have provided mentorship and valuable feedback over the course of this project. We are indebted to our friends and colleagues who work in this field and who have encouraged us on this journey: Claudia Orange, Bob Hall, Monty Soutar, Timothy Winegard and the above-mentioned P. Whitney Lackenbauer and Tom Holm. Noah also extends thanks to his colleagues on the 'Serving Our Country' project: John Maynard, Mick Dodson, Allison Cadzow, Joan Beaumont, Craig Greene, Kate MacFarlane and Sam Furphy. We have both been supported by many colleagues in our respective institutions. From UFV, thanks are particularly extended to Robin Anderson, Chris Leach, Barbara Messamore, Sylvie Murray, Geoff Spurling, Alisa Webb, Steven Schroeder, Brad Whittacker, Adrienne Chan, and Jacqueline Nolte. From Australian Catholic University, thanks as always go to colleagues Shurlee Swain, Nell Musgrove, Naomi Wolfe, Maggie Nolan, Melissa Bellanta, Hannah Forsyth, Fiona Davis, Mark Chou, Michael Ondaatje, Ellen Warne, Doseena Fergie and Linc Yow Yeh. Thanks also to Noah's colleagues at other institutions whose intellectual contributions and friendship have made this book possible: Pat Grimshaw, Richard Trembath, Claudia Haake, Kat Ellinghaus, Phil Deloria, Victoria Haskins,

Rachel Standfield, Shirleene Robinson, Ara Keys, Patty O'Brien, Cath Bishop and Tristan Moss. Scott similarly thanks Paul D'Arcy, Giselle Byrnes, Richard Hill, Peter Stanley and Russell McGregor, whose conversations and friendship all helped a northern hemisphere scholar find his feet down under.

On a personal level, it is never just the authors who produce a book such as this, but also the loved ones who come along for the ride through no fault of their own. Noah sends his final gratitude to all of his friends and family across both sides of the Pacific, and of course to loving partner Michael. Noah may not always express it well, but he loves Michael more than anything, and his career would not be where it is without his ongoing support. Scott could not have sustained himself through this decade-long process without the love and emotional support of his boys, Jordan and Liam and his amazing spouse, Kirsten. This work is first and foremost a tribute to them.

Sections of Chapter 4 have previously been published in:

R. Scott Sheffield, 'Indigenous Exceptionalism under Fire: Assessing Indigenous Soldiers and Combat during the Second World War', *Journal of Imperial and Commonwealth History* 45, no. 3 (2017): 506–24. www.tandfonline.com/toc/fich20/current

Sections of Chapter 8 have previously been published in:

R. Scott Sheffield, 'Veterans' Benefits and Indigenous Veterans of the Second World War in Australia, Canada, New Zealand and the United States', *Wicazo Sa Review* 32, no. 1 (Spring 2017): 63–79.

Indigenous readers are advised that this book contains the names and images of persons who are deceased.

# Abbreviations

| | |
|---|---|
| AIF | Australian Imperial Force |
| ANZ | Archives New Zealand |
| ANZAC | Australian and New Zealand Army Corps |
| AWAS | Australian Women's Army Service |
| AWM | Australian War Memorial |
| BIA | Bureau of Indian Affairs (and its predecessor agencies; USA) |
| CMF | Citizen Military Forces (Australia) |
| DAB | Dependants' Allowance Board (Canada) |
| IAB | Indian Affairs Branch (Canada) |
| ICC | Indian Claims Commission (USA) |
| LAC | Library and Archives Canada |
| LOC | Library of Congress |
| MWEO | Maori War Effort Organisation |
| NAA | National Archives of Australia |
| NAIB | North American Indian Brotherhood (Canada) |
| NARA | National Archives and Records Administration (USA) |
| NCAI | National Congress of American Indians (USA) |
| NCO | Noncommissioned officer |
| NORFORCE | North West Mobile Force |
| NRMA | National Resources Mobilisation Act (Canada) |
| NTSRU | Northern Territory Special Reconnaissance Unit |
| NZEF | New Zealand Expeditionary Force |
| PCMR | Pacific Coast Militia Rangers |
| POW | Prisoner of war |
| PTSD | Post-traumatic stress disorder |
| RAAF | Royal Australian Air Force |
| RAF | Royal Air Force (UK) |
| RAN | Royal Australian Navy |
| RCAF | Royal Canadian Air Force |
| RCN | Royal Canadian Navy |

| | |
|---|---|
| RN | Royal Navy (UK) |
| RNZAF | Royal New Zealand Air Force |
| RNZN | Royal New Zealand Navy |
| RSL | Returned Services League (as named at the time of the Second World War) |
| SJC | Special Joint Parliamentary Committee (Canada) |
| SRO | State Records Office of Western Australia |
| TSLI | Torres Strait Light Infantry Battalion |
| VLA | Veterans' Lands Act (Canada) |
| WAAAF | Women's Auxiliary Australian Air Force |
| WAAC and WAC | Women's Army Corps (and its predecessor names; USA) |
| WASP | Women Airforce Service Pilots (USA) |
| WAVES | United States Naval Reserve (Women's Reserve) |

# Introduction

The Indigenous warrior has long captivated Western imaginations. As vicious savages impeding the march of civilisation or loyal allies fighting alongside settlers, the be-feathered Indian, fierce Māori and elusive Aborigine were entrenched in the popular consciousness of Canadians, Americans, New Zealanders and Australians by the nineteenth century. Although pre-1939 Indigenous-settler relationships differed substantially across these four countries, each Indigenous population responded when the Second World War broke out by declaring their support for the cause and volunteering to serve. Thousands of Native Americans, Māori, Aboriginal and Torres Strait Islander Australians and First Nations men and women fought overseas or served at home in settler military forces, sometimes in segregated Indigenous units but more often as individuals integrated into massive settler military organisations.[1] Most Indigenous veterans recall experiencing respect and acceptance from their comrades in arms, something unimaginable before the war. At the same time, on the home front Indigenous families, communities and leadership offered voluntary, monetary and symbolic aid to national war efforts. Many men and women also found employment opened up as departing soldiers and wartime economic expansion created lucrative opportunities that would make the war years, in some ways, the best of times. Each Indigenous population's varied and extensive wartime contributions won admiration and appreciation from the settler nations. The result was a ripe, if ephemeral, climate for Indigenous policy and legislative reforms in the immediate post-war years. While Indigenous wartime energies and post-war lobbying produced some important reforms, the direction of change largely followed settler desires rather than Indigenous aspirations.

---

[1] We use the term 'Indigenous' to refer to Māori, Aboriginal and Torres Strait Islander, Native Americans and First Nations. The term 'Aboriginal' is often used in both Canada and Australia. To avoid confusion, when we refer to Aboriginal people, we specifically mean the Indigenous people of mainland Australia and Tasmania. We refer to Canada's Indigenous peoples specifically as First Nations and, where relevant, Inuit or Métis.

In the decades that followed, Indigenous contributions to the Second World War were largely forgotten. Aboriginal and Torres Strait Islander, Native American, Māori and First Nations veterans often languished without recognition, respect or adequate veterans' benefits. These circumstances began to change in parallel with the broader political resurgence of Indigenous peoples in all four countries since the 1970s. Veterans and their communities sought recognition for their service and sacrifices, agitated for restitution of grievances regarding pay or benefits and demanded inclusion in national and local ceremonies and monuments of remembrance. These striking parallels in historical experiences cry out for transnational and comparative examination. They also highlight the continuing relevance and political significance of wartime service in contemporary discussions about the place of Indigenous peoples in these settler societies.

This book explores Indigenous contributions and experiences in the Second World War in a transnational and comparative manner. This approach allows us to reflect on why these ostracised peoples chose to engage in the war effort. Without a sense of belonging or even basic citizenship rights in Australia, Canada and parts of the United States, Indigenous individuals were less personally invested in the well-being of the settler society and state – a crucial precursor for the sense of obligation to defend the larger collective. Yet thousands of Indigenous men and women chose to serve, and questions still swirl around why and what this choice meant, both to themselves and to settler societies during and after the war. Issues of citizenship, belonging and identity became more visible, their boundaries even redefined by the wartime roles assumed by Indigenous peoples. The sacrifices of Indigenous service personnel produced moral capital to demand change, leading to post-war policy reform and new legislation that set the stage for relationships between Indigenous peoples and settler societies/states through to the present.

## Settler Colonialism

Whilst historical ideas about settler societies have long roots in the twentieth century, it is really since the 1990s that historians have examined the structures associated with what is now popularly referred to as settler colonialism.[2] Settler colonialism specifically describes situations where the main purpose of colonisation was to transplant persons from the home country into a new territory. As Patrick Wolfe writes, in settler colonies, 'the colonizers came to stay, expropriating the native owners of

---

[2] Lorenzo Veracini, "'Settler Colonialism': Career of a Concept," *The Journal of Imperial and Commonwealth History* 41, no. 2 (2013): 313–333.

the soil, which they [colonizers] typically develop by means of a subordinated labor force (slaves, indentures, convicts) whom they import from
elsewhere'.[3] Donald Denoon argues the 'fact that settler societies resem-
ble one another in several respects, is not a consequence of conscious imitation, but of separate efforts to resolve very similar problems'.[4] Indeed,
James Belich similarly asserts that Anglo settler societies emerged from a
so-called 'settler revolution' in the nineteenth century. Cyclical patterns
of population boom, followed by busts and then new economic exports
combined with a recolonising of ties to the metropole, led to exponential
growth in the population and wealth of these societies.[5] The eventual
outcomes of settler colonialism are 'societies in which Europeans have
settled, where their descendants have remained politically dominant over
indigenous peoples, and where a heterogeneous society has developed in
class, ethnic and racial terms'.[6]

In contrast to other colonial states – where the primary aim of colonisation was to exploit Indigenous labour – in settler states, Indigenous
people en masse were only intermittently useful and often were an
impediment to settler aspirations. The goal of the settler state – capitalist
land acquisition – required technological, ideological and social methods to exclude Indigenous peoples from the settler state.[7] Patrick Wolfe
summarises this relationship between settlers and indigenes as a 'cultural logic ... of elimination [which] seeks to replace indigenous society
with that imported by the colonisers'.[8] In most places, the prospect of
eliminating Indigenous presence was not a stated doctrine. Instead, as a
cultural 'logic', any government policies, even those espoused allegedly
to help Indigenous people, still had underpinnings to preserve the settler
states' interests over Indigenous vitality and sovereignty.

At the time of the Second World War, all four settler societies studied in this book – Australia, Canada, New Zealand and the United
States – were implementing assimilation policies over their Indigenous

---

[3] Patrick Wolfe, "Land, Labor, and Difference: Elementary Structures of Race," *The American Historical Review* 106, no. 3 (2001): 868.

[4] Donald Denoon, "Understanding Settler Societies," *Historical Studies* 18 (1979): 518.

[5] James Belich, *Replenishing the Earth: The Settler Revolution and the Rise of the Anglo-World, 1783–1939* (Oxford: Oxford University Press, 2009).

[6] Daiva Stasiulis and Nira Yuval-Davis, "Introduction: Beyond Dichotomies – Gender, Race, Ethnicity and Class in Settler Societies," in *Unsettling Settler Societies: Articulations of Gender, Race, Ethnicity and Class*, ed. Daiva Stasiulis and Nira Yuval-Davis (London: Sage Publications, 1995), 3.

[7] Patrick Wolfe, *Traces of History: Elementary Structures of Race* (London; Brooklyn: Verso, 2016), 15.

[8] Patrick Wolfe, *Settler Colonialism and the Transformation of Anthropology: The Politics and Poetics of an Ethnographic Event* (London; New York: Cassell, 1999), 27. See also Patrick Wolfe, "Settler Colonialism and the Elimination of the Native," *Journal of Genocide Research* 8, no. 4 (December 2006): 387–409.

populations and were highly racialised societies. They had also developed, to varying degrees, mythologies surrounding settlement, nationhood and relationships to empire, especially the British Empire for Australia, New Zealand and Canada. As Lorenzo Veracini argues, the settler society was premised on the violent dispossession of Indigenous peoples, yet the settler consciousness also disavowed that violence. By focusing instead on notions of taming frontiers and developing democratic traditions, the very idea that the land was previously inhabited disappeared from the settler consciousness and justified settler claims of sovereignty.[9] The Second World War, too, was a powerfully affirmative experience for these settler societies' mythologies but also a contested place with Indigenous peoples. The democratic nature of the societies, the citizen-basis of the defence forces, and the 'good war' crusade all fed nationalist mythologies in Australia, Canada, New Zealand and the United States. The good war crusade also provided grounds for Indigenous people to challenge and contest settler mythologies and/or to assert their own sovereignties. This was, and remains, the locus of the moral leverage and the significance of Indigenous participation in the conflict.

## Historiography

This book builds on the existing national historiographies of Indigenous Second World War service in all four countries. As Riseman argues, all four national historiographies have witnessed significantly growing interest in Indigenous military histories since the 1990s. Prominent scholars of the Second World War include:

| | |
|---|---|
| CANADA: | R. Scott Sheffield, P. Whitney Lackenbauer, Grace Poulin |
| NEW ZEALAND: | Monty Soutar, Wira Gardiner, Claudia Orange |
| UNITED STATES: | Tom Holm, Jeré Bishop Franco, Alison Bernstein, Kenneth Townsend, William C. Meadows, Al Carroll |
| AUSTRALIA: | Robert Hall, Noah Riseman, Elizabeth Osborne[10] |

All of these scholars provide critical foundational work and pose broadly similar arguments in their national contexts: notwithstanding some countries' efforts to restrict military service, Indigenous peoples overwhelmingly supported the war effort as servicemen and servicewomen as well as on the home front. For those who served in regularly enlisted units, military service was an experience of equality – often for the first time in their lives. Upon their return home, veterans were discontented with

[9] Lorenzo Veracini, *Settler Colonialism: A Theoretical Overview* (Basingstoke, UK: Palgrave Macmillan, 2010), 75–86.
[10] Noah Riseman, "The Rise of Indigenous Military History," *History Compass* 12, no. 12 (2014): 901–911.

the return to inequality and this presaged battles for civil rights and self-determination in the 1960s–70s. Almost all of these scholars have interpreted Indigenous experiences within a national – rather than a global, comparative or transnational – framework. An advantage to this national approach is that it facilitates a clear narrative and analysis of the policy issues, politics, Indigenous perspectives and national impacts of Indigenous service. National or local histories provide the opportunity to focus on particular aspects of military service, such as recruitment policies, labour or remote regions, as well as the (re)actions of specific Indigenous communities.

Memorialisations of war have gained increasing civic importance in all four states, particularly since significant anniversaries such as the fiftieth-anniversary ceremonies of D-Day and VE-Day in 1994–5 and the seventy-fifth anniversary of the ANZAC Gallipoli landing in 1990. These events catalysed a broad revival of interest in veterans and military history amongst the Allied nations of both the First and Second World Wars, which historian Jay Winter refers to as the 'memory boom'.[11] In all four countries existing Indigenous veterans groups, as well as newly emerging ones, capitalised on the climate of recognition – a process accelerated in Australia and, to a lesser extent, New Zealand, by the centenary of the First World War. From an academic perspective, studies of Indigenous military history only emerged between the mid-1980s and the 2000s. Before then, scholars of military history tended to focus more on operations or generalised histories of soldier experiences. Researchers in Indigenous history focused primarily on themes like trade/exchange, dispossession, frontier conflict and child removal. Indeed, these were the very matters at the heart of Indigenous people's own struggles for recognition, justice, restitution and self-determination. Essentially, the area of twentieth-century Indigenous military history fell through the cracks, situated between these two historical fields. Now, driven both by Indigenous communities and historians – and sometimes with the support of veterans' affairs departments – previously forgotten Indigenous military service is on the public and political agenda in all four settler states.

Many of the national histories have, as a result, developed a 'forgotten warrior' trope that sought to salvage Indigenous military contributions from their historical purgatory and foster greater recognition within settler societies.[12] While such scholarship has revealed a broad historical

[11] Jay Winter, *Remembering War: The Great War between Memory and History in the Twentieth Century* (New Haven, CT: Yale University Press, 2006).
[12] See P. Whitney Lackenbauer and R. Scott Sheffield, "Moving Beyond 'Forgotten': The Historiography on Canadian Native Peoples and the World Wars," in *Aboriginal People and the Canadian Military: Historical Perspectives*, ed. P. Whitney Lackenbauer and Craig Leslie Mantle (Kingston, ON: Canadian Defence Academy Press, 2007): 209–232;

landscape surrounding Indigenous military service and its meanings to both the settler states and Indigenous communities, it has tended to adhere to binaries: settler versus Indigenous objectives, enlistment as assertion of citizenship/sovereignty versus participation as collaboration with colonial states, Indigenous loyalty versus opposition, Indigenous loyalty versus state perfidy, racial discrimination versus equality. We acknowledge that some of our earlier work was shaped by and subscribed to many of these dichotomies. Of course, such narratives are important because they can elucidate general patterns, trends and macro-histories of Indigenous peoples in the Second World War. Even so, such binary constructs are not always sensitive to the nuanced diversity of responses across Indigenous and non-Indigenous communities, over-simplifying a tremendously complex history.

Rather than construct this book in a way that feeds that binary perspective, we seek to comprehend Indigenous interactions and relationships with the war and state as contested processes, constantly negotiated over ever-shifting terrain. Indigenous attitudes and experiences of the war were not static and their identities and attitudes shifted in particular times and contexts. As relationships with(in) the wartime settler states changed, so too did the nature of Indigenous roles in the conflict. Indigenous peoples consistently sought to exercise as much control as possible over their wartime contributions, though the amount of influence they exerted varied enormously from state to state, community to community and issue to issue. Many Indigenous people had little capacity to be heard (especially in Australia and Canada), but by comparison, Māori were able to gain substantial autonomy over their war effort. Indigenous actions or reactions were also situational and tailored to the challenges/opportunities before them. Some communities that strongly encouraged voluntary enlistments, for instance, could just as vigorously oppose and even resist the effort of the settler state to conscript their young people. Some communities could obtain tangible rewards out of being in the war effort, such as Native American or First Nations communities that allowed their land to be used for military purposes while others were coerced into working for the armed forces, as in parts of northern Australia. Such examples caution against essentialising or reifying particular experiences beyond a specific context.

Importantly, our book owes a debt to the work of scholars in all four countries and builds upon their foundations. Each of these national

---

Elizabeth Rechniewski, "Remembering the Black Diggers: From 'the Great Silence' to 'Conspicuous Commemoration'?," in *War Memories: Commemoration, Recollections, and Writings on War*, ed. Renée Dickason and Stéphanie A. H. Bélanger (Montreal: McGill-Queen's University Press, 2017), 388–408.

literatures has developed independently and exhibits different strengths. New Zealand has a strong tradition built upon unit histories, especially the 28th Maori Battalion. The United States contains excellent national surveys which link the war years to civil rights and fundamental shifts in US Indian policy. There is also a significant subset of the historiography focusing on code talkers. Australia has a strong tradition of community-based studies, particularly about remote parts of northern Australia and the Torres Strait. Canadian literature's strength lies in its diversity of approaches. Each country's scholarship can inform and enhance under-standings in other countries, raising questions or developing analytical approaches not undertaken elsewhere. This is one of the key benefits of and principal aims of this book: to lift each country's experience out of its domestic silo for collective transnational examination, comparison and cross-fertilisation.

The little transnational or comparative work undertaken in this field thus far has only dipped the proverbial toe into potentially deep waters. Riseman has used case studies of the Navajo Code Talkers, Papua New Guineans and the Yolngu people of Arnhem Land, Australia to extrap-olate histories of how settler governments exploited Indigenous knowl-edge and skills for military purposes.[13] Sheffield's work on Indigenous veterans' post-war access to benefits and settler society perspectives on Indigenous peoples during the war has revealed the potential value of such an approach.[14] These studies, though, have been limited in their scope and focus. Timothy Winegard's study *Indigenous Peoples of the British Dominions and the First World War* has begun the project of more broadly examining the experiences of Indigenous participation in the First World War.[15] Our book represents an extension of that transnational methodology to the Second World War.

## Transnational and Comparative History

Transnational and comparative analysis in the field of Indigenous-settler relations has exploded in the new millennium and holds great promise

[13] Noah Riseman, *Defending Whose Country? Indigenous Soldiers in the Pacific War* (Lincoln: University of Nebraska Press, 2012).
[14] R. Scott Sheffield, "Veterans' Benefits and Indigenous Veterans of the Second World War in Australia, Canada, New Zealand and the United States," *Wicazo Sa Review* 32, no. 1 (Spring 2017): 63–79; and "Rehabilitating the Indigene: Post-war Reconstruction and the Image of the Indigenous Other in Anglo-Canada and New Zealand, 1943–48," in *Rediscovering the British World*, ed. Phillip Buckner and R. Douglas Francis (Calgary: University of Calgary Press, 2005), 341–360.
[15] Timothy Winegard, *Indigenous Peoples of the British Dominions and the First World War* (New York: Cambridge University Press, 2012).

for helping us to see the patterns, commonalities and anomalies across these relationships. Historian Ann Curthoys suggests transnational histories 'are less concerned with comparison, and more with tracing patterns of influence and networks of connection across national boundaries, perhaps ignoring the nation altogether'.[16] Comparative history is equally as valuable, if for different reasons. George Fredrickson recognises the value of comparative history to 'inspire a critical awareness of what is taken for granted in one's own country, but it also promotes a recognition that similar functions may be performed by different means'.[17]

Book-length comparative analyses of settler-Indigenous histories have been more common than transnational investigations. The purpose of comparative analysis is to assess what is unique within and what is common across national boundaries.[18] Scholars such as Margaret Jacobs, Ann McGrath and Katherine Ellinghaus have produced prominent texts focusing on intimacy and welfare while Penelope Edmonds, Miranda Johnson, Julie Evans, Patricia Grimshaw, David Philips and Shurlee Swain have drawn useful comparisons of political-legal regimes and cross-cultural relations.[19] Such comparative histories enable separation of the local elements from the broader structural factors operating in the global phenomenon of British colonialism. Even in these texts, though, much of the comparative work is really parallel national histories where the actual comparison is reserved primarily for introductions and conclusions. An additional value of comparative analysis, as Andrew Armitage notes, is that it opens a door to scholars who otherwise struggle

---

[16] Ann Curthoys, "Does Australian History Have a Future?" in *Challenging Histories: Reflections on Australian History*, *Australian Historical Studies* 33, special issue no. 118 (2002): 145–146.

[17] George Fredrickson, "From Exceptionalism to Variability: Recent Developments in Cross-National Comparative History," *The Journal of American History* 82, no. 2 (September 1995): 604.

[18] See Theda Skocpol and Margaret Somers, "The Uses of Comparative History in Macrosocial Inquiry," *Comparative Studies in Society and History* 22, no. 2 (April 1980): 174–197.

[19] Margaret Jacobs, *A Generation Removed: The Fostering and Adoption of Indigenous Children in the Postwar World* (Lincoln: University of Nebraska Press, 2014); Margaret Jacobs, *White Mother to a Dark Race: Settler Colonialism, Maternalism, and the Removal of Indigenous Children in the American West and Australia, 1880–1940* (Lincoln: University of Nebraska Press, 2009); Ann McGrath, *Illicit Love: Interracial Sex & Marriage in the United States and Australia* (Lincoln: University of Nebraska Press, 2015); Katherine Ellinghaus, *Taking Assimilation to Heart: Marriages of White Women and Indigenous Men in the United States and Australia, 1887–1937* (Lincoln: University of Nebraska Press, 2006); Miranda Johnson, *The Land is Our History: Indigeneity, Law and the Settler State* (New York: Oxford University Press, 2016); Penelope Edmonds, *Urbanizing Frontiers: Indigenous Peoples and Settlers in 19th-Century Pacific Rim Cities* (Vancouver: University of British Columbia Press, 2010); Julie Evans et al., *Equal Subjects, Unequal Rights: Indigenous Peoples in British Settler Colonies, 1830–1910* (Manchester: Manchester University Press, 2003).

to extricate themselves from the national paradigm.[20] As a practitioner, not only does getting outside the national box enable one to learn about another country's historical narrative and historiographical debates, but it also grants scholars an outsider's eye with which to reassess their own national story. Comfortable and uninvestigated assumptions are laid bare by new questions and potentially productive and novel lines of enquiry suggested by the work of scholars in a different context.

Transnational approaches are increasingly becoming more common in settler-Indigenous histories. Gary Magee and Andrew Thompson have argued that 'Part of the attraction of focusing on settler societies as a way of writing transnational history is that their ideas and institutions stemmed from common roots; they also faced similar problems, especially with respect to indigenous populations'.[21] Many of these texts break down chapters into case studies of particular nations to show how particular ideas or concepts manifested across time and place. Stuart Banner's *Possessing the Pacific*, Marilyn Lake and Henry Reynolds' *Drawing the Global Colour Line*, Patrick Wolfe's *Traces of History* and Penelope Edmonds' *Settler Colonialism and (Re)conciliation* are examples of this approach: brilliant concepts, parallel history chapters of differing locales/case studies from different Indigenous peoples, bookended by an introduction and conclusion that extrapolate some fascinating comparative insights.[22] Less common, and more challenging, is to organise the book thematically, to provide consistent transnational and comparative synthesis of secondary and primary source material across two or more national histories. That is the approach taken in Cecilia Morgan's *Building Better Britains?*, James Belich's *Replenishing the Earth*, Angela Woollacott's *Gender and Empire*, Tracey Banivanua-Mar's *Decolonisation and the Pacific*, and Kenneth Coates' *A Global History of Indigenous Peoples*.[23] This is also

---

[20] Andrew Armitage, *Comparing the Policy of Aboriginal Assimilation: Australia, Canada, and New Zealand* (Vancouver: University of British Columbia Press, 1995), 7.

[21] Gary Magee and Andrew Thompson, *Empire and Globalisation: Networks of People, Goods and Capital in the British World, c. 1850–1914* (Cambridge: Cambridge University Press, 2010), 25.

[22] Stuart Banner, *Possessing the Pacific: Land, Settlers, and Indigenous People From Australia to Alaska* (Cambridge, MA: Harvard, 2007); Marilyn Lake and Henry Reynolds, *Drawing the Global Colour Line: White Men's Countries and the Question of Racial Equality* (Carlton, VIC: Melbourne University Publishing, 2008); Wolfe, *Traces of History: Elementary Structures of Race*; Penelope Edmonds, *Settler Colonialism and (Re)conciliation: Frontier Violence, Affective Performances, and Imaginative Refoundings* (Basingstoke: Palgrave Macmillan, 2016).

[23] Cecilia Morgan, *Building Better Britains? Settler Societies within the British Empire 1783–1920* (Toronto: University of Toronto Press, 2016); James Belich, *Replenishing the Earth: The Settler Revolution and the Rise of the Anglo-World, 1783–1939* (New York: Oxford University Press, 2009); Angela Woollacott, *Gender and Empire* (New York: Palgrave Macmillan, 2006); Tracey Banivanua-Mar, *Decolonisation and the Pacific:*

the approach we take in this book. Indeed, we engage a blend of transnational and comparative history because such a mixed-methods approach best elucidates the complex histories of Indigenous military service. We do not carefully delineate one approach from the other necessarily, nor have we structured chapters for rigid comparison. Transnational analysis predominates, and typically, we draw comparisons when and where the subject matter and interpretation make it appropriate or insightful. In practice, we shift between transnational and comparative approaches seamlessly.

There is a risk that this approach, employing such broad lens, might be criticised for homogenising Indigenous experiences. Augie Fleras and Jean Leonard Elliott's book on settler-Indigenous relations notes this: 'In painting a picture with such broad brush strokes, the challenge is to avoid homogenization and excessive generalization. Yet the task of simplifying complex matters for the sake of clarity or space is daunting.'[24] We acknowledge Fleras and Elliott's caution, but like them, our transnational approach in the thematic chapters requires exploration of common patterns and careful generalisations, without permitting mention of every anomaly across the four countries. For every pattern or trend we analyse, there are exceptions across and within nations, as Indigenous nations and settler regimes operated differently at local levels. Moreover, there was no uniformity within Indigenous nations or settler institutions, with particular personalities playing significant roles to shape individual and collective experiences. To address that level of detail across four countries would produce an unwieldy and unreadable text, but more importantly, it would miss the purpose of transnational analysis to provide a broader backdrop that more localised research cannot otherwise glimpse. Crucially, such caution is not a rationale to disavow or turn away from such work; Wendy Kozol asserts: 'transnational perspectives do not so much supplant as work in dialogue with theoretical approaches … [and] utilize historical methods and methodologies that have proven effective in studies of local or national contexts within a framework that encourages new perspectives on major global events and processes like war, migration, or neocolonialism'.[25] One purpose of a book like this is to

---

*Indigenous Globalisation and the Ends of Empire* (Cambridge: Cambridge University Press, 2016); Kenneth Coates, *A Global History of Indigenous Peoples: Struggle and Survival* (Basingstoke: Palgrave Macmillan, 2004).

[24] Augie Fleras and Jean Leonard Elliott, *The Nations Within: Aboriginal-State Relations in Canada, the United States and New Zealand* (Toronto: Oxford University Press, 1992), x.

[25] C. A. Baylyl, Sven Beckert, Mathew Connelly, Isabel Hofmeyr, Wendy Kozol, and Patricia Seed, "AHR Conversation: On Transnational History," *American Historical Review* 111, no. 5 (December 2006): 1462.

provoke such a dialogue with scholars working in different national and local contexts across and beyond these four countries.

Isabel Hofmeyr suggests that 'Another way in which transnationalism can open up new vistas is by directing our attention to "in-between" areas'.[26] She refers to geographical in-between spaces, but in our case, this is also relevant to conceptual or topical in-between areas, such as the in-between nature of the study of Indigenous military service and wartime participation, long positioned between the mutually indifferent solitudes of Indigenous and military history. Different national historiographies have begun to fill this in-between in different ways, and a transnational approach enables us to draw from each to bridge the void more effectively. Our intent is not to measure the benevolence or oppression of one state versus another subjectively. As Deborah Montgomerie argues, we 'need histories that do more than congratulate administrations that preferred the legalisms of colonization by treaty or land purchase over the extra-legal methods of conquest and occupation'.[27] Such practices have a long tradition in both Canada and New Zealand, where such self-serving comparisons have become part of the mechanisms by which they distinguish their settler identities from their American and Australian neighbours, respectively. Acknowledging genuine differences in the degree of colonial impact is not necessarily an exercise in awarding points for good behaviour, so long as it is framed and directed at understanding how and why similar and different relationships, administrative and legislative structures and historical processes developed.

## Martial Race Theory

Numerous military sociologists have written about the interrelationships between minorities, militaries and civilian society. Morris Janowitz argues that Western military service since the American and French Revolutions has been constructed as a duty of citizenship with attendant entitlements and privileges for veterans.[28] Yet service personnel from marginalised social groups – whether they be the working class, women, gays and lesbians or racial and ethnic minorities – have not always had equal opportunities within the military or equal access to veterans' benefits. The ground-breaking work of Warren Young analyses three possible patterns that describe the links between racial minorities' treatment

[26] Ibid., 1454.
[27] Deborah Montgomerie, "Beyond the Search for Good Imperialism: The Challenge of Comparative History," *New Zealand Journal of History* 31, no. 1 (1997): 160.
[28] Morris Janowitz, "Military Institutions and Citizenship in Western Societies," *Armed Forces and Society* 2, no. 2 (1976): 185–204.

in militaries and civilian life: discontinuous, continuous or parallel. He describes the discontinuous situation occurring if the minority group's status in the military is substantially different from its position in civilian society. Continuous patterns signify when their status in the military matches their treatment in civilian society while a parallel model is mostly similar but with some variations. Young argues that while many racial minority groups have tried to leverage their military service for civil rights, the continuous and parallel patterns of treatment are most common. This means that, generally speaking, minority groups' status within armed forces either mirrors their position in civilian society or is mostly similar with some minor variations.[29] In other words, if a minority is treated unequally and subject to discrimination in civilian society, they are likely to be treated unequally within the military as well.

Young's analysis, and similar studies by scholars such as Ronald Krebs, focuses primarily on minorities such as African-Americans in the United States, Quebecois in Canada and Druze in Israel.[30] Indigenous peoples in the Second World War Anglo-settler societies represent a different case. For a variety of reasons, militaries which had clear policies towards larger minority groups (e.g., African-Americans) often overlooked Indigenous peoples. While there may have been discriminatory policies in relation to their enlistment, as in Australia, once in the services there tended not to be specific rules or regulations differentiating Indigenous from white service personnel. Thus, as this book will elaborate, Indigenous personnel often saw military service as an egalitarian experience – a discontinuous pattern from their pre-war civilian lives.

What also sets Indigenous peoples apart from other racial and ethnic minorities in the settler states is their smaller population and the way that governments/militaries often constructed these particular peoples as martial races. Cynthia Enloe defines martial race theory as one 'usually applied by outsiders to flag certain ethnic groups in a society as somehow inherently inclined towards military occupations, possessing some characteristic so embedded in its physical makeup – its "blood" – that it passes beyond being simply a cultural – that is, an ethnic – predilection'.[31] Discourses about martial peoples date back to ancient times; as Europeans colonised various parts of the globe in the modern era and formulated new discourses about race, they continually constructed

[29] Warren Young, *Minorities and the Military: A Cross-National Study in World Perspective* (Westport, CT: Greenwood Press, 1982), 248–252.
[30] Ronald Krebs, *Fighting for Rights: Military Service and the Politics of Citizenship* (Ithaca and London: Cornell University Press, 2006).
[31] Cynthia Enloe, *Ethnic Soldiers: State Security in Divided Societies* (Athens, GA: The University of Georgia Press, 1980), 39.

different Indigenous peoples as martial races. Such categorisation was constantly shifting and unstable, as a particular race could be deemed 'martial' when it suited the needs of a European power and weak at other times.[32] According to Enloe, state elites judged both ethnic military proclivities and how loyal they were to the state, based largely on stereotypes. Consequently, a minority group with supposedly high martial abilities, but considered politically unreliable, would be unlikely to receive training or weaponry that might be turned on the state. Politically reliable groups, whether or not they had genuine military traditions, would be more likely to be permitted to carry arms.[33]

Enloe's analysis focuses on the ways that colonising powers deployed supposed martial races as ethnic soldiers to advance European imperial projects. The Second World War represents a different circumstance where these nominally democratic societies constructed military forces largely purpose-built for that conflict only. Moreover, these citizen-based militaries were fighting other world powers, rather than being sent to pacify Indigenous resistance to colonialism. The crusade-like justification of the conflict – in defence of democracy, freedom, equality – potentially undermined crass ethnic calculations on the part of settler state politicians and officials. Instead, this citizen ethos entwined in the national war effort, when combined with ethnic 'other' military service, was more likely to unsettle and challenge elites and dominant settler societies.

Even so, martial race discourse *did* persist to varying degrees in these settler societies at the time of the Second World War and therefore deserves attention. As Tom Holm argues, 'U.S. elites have been more and more willing to view Indians – no matter what proportion of them are well trained and experienced militarily – as being a "safe" minority rather than a tangible threat to the Euroamerican status quo.'[34] Such observations are applicable as well in Canada, New Zealand and Australia. Twenty years after Holm's observation, Winona LaDuke elaborated, stating that Native American communities in the United States have become thoroughly militarised. She argues that across the twentieth century, processes of economic deprivation, colonial domination and racism led to a situation where Native Americans now – as during the Second World

---

[32] Heather Streets, *Martial Races: The Military, Race and Masculinity in British Imperial Culture, 1857–1914* (Manchester: Manchester University Press, 2010), 4.
[33] Cynthia Enloe, *Police, Military and Ethnicity: Foundations of State Power* (New Brunswick, NJ: Transaction Books, 1980), 142.
[34] Tom Holm, "Patriots and Pawns: State Use of American Indians in the Military and the Process of Nativization in the United States," in *The State of Native America: Genocide, Colonization, and Resistance*, ed. M. Annette Jaimes (Boston: Smith End Press, 1992), 354. See also "The Militarization of Native America: Historical Process and Cultural Perception," *The Social Science Journal* 34, no. 4 (1997): 472.

*Figure I.1*  Private Mary Greyeyes, Cree, from Muskeg Lake, Cree Nation, Canadian Women's Army Corps, with Harry Pall, Piapot First Nation, 29 September 1942 (DND/LAC/PA-129070).

War – have the highest rates of military enlistment of any ethnic group in the United States.[35] They have essentially become dependent on the US military; high enlistment rates among Māori in New Zealand suggest military service has similarly become an important employment path.

One reason that recruitment of Indigenous service personnel has been so successful in the United States, Canada and New Zealand across much of the twentieth century is because the martial race construct was a settler distortion of Indigenous warrior traditions (Figure I.1). Anthropologist and historian William Meadows distinguishes between martial race constructs and Indigenous self-identities as military societies where many cultural and kinship practices revolve around warrior traditions.[36] Indeed, many First Nations, Native American and

---

[35] Winona LaDuke, *The Militarization of Indian Country* (East Lansing: Michigan State University Press, 2013).
[36] William Meadows, *Kiowa, Apache, and Comanche Military Societies: Enduring Veterans, 1800 to the Present* (Austin: University of Texas Press, 1999).

Māori groups have adapted service in settler militaries as a contemporary way to practice their longstanding warrior traditions. As historian Al Carroll points out, we must be cautious not to deny Indigenous people's agency and to see them merely as pawns of state militaries: 'Natives are not foolish or being used by the nation-state; the choices Natives make to be in the military are perfectly rational and in line with longstanding cultural values.'[37] Even so, as LaDuke and Holm point out, traditional Indigenous understandings of both the warrior and war are different from the goals and operation style of modern settler militaries. LaDuke particularly distinguishes between traditional 'demonstration[s] of bravery and skill as opposed to the demonstrations of immense force that are intrinsic to America's military prowess'.[38] The settler idea of martial race and Indigenous ideas of warrior societies both significantly inform this book. Martial race ideas infiltrate some government and military officials' attitudes towards how to employ Indigenous servicemen, such as the Maori Battalion or the Navajo Code Talkers, as well as popular media portrayals of Indigenous military exploits. Ideas of the warrior society and rites of passage inform many of the First Nations, Māori and Native American behaviours during the war. In our analysis, we are careful to discern the ways these cultural constructs shaped the attitudes, actions and reactions of both Indigenous and non-Indigenous actors.

### Book Layout

The book is divided into three sections. The two chapters in Part I introduce readers to basic national narratives about Indigenous populations, settler-Indigenous relations and the Indigenous role in the world wars, providing essential context for readers unfamiliar with any of these four settler states. These chapters cannot be comprehensive national histories given their brevity and are thus massive exercises in what to leave out, as much as what to retain. Readers wanting more detail will find direction to additional sources in the notes. Chapter 1 provides a brief survey, covering settler-Indigenous relationships post-contact, the development of colonial administration and policy and the evolving status of Indigenous populations until the turn of the twentieth century. In addition, we foreshadow some of the issues the later chapters address: settler-Indigenous conflict and/or alliance and settler perceptions of martial qualities of

---

[37] Al Carroll, *Medicine Bags and Dog Tags: American Indian Veterans from Colonial Times to the Second Iraq War* (Lincoln: University of Nebraska Press, 2008), 2. See also Holm, "Patriots and Pawns," 358.

[38] LaDuke, *The Militarization of Indian Country*, 3. See also Holm, "Patriots and Pawns," 354–357.

Indigenous populations. Chapter 2 turns to Indigenous military service prior to and during the First World War, Indigenous affairs in the inter-war period and a quick summary of the key historical milestones of the Second World War for the settler nations. The latter is important because the national complexities of the war differ in terms of when, where and why the different settler nations deployed. Additionally, the national narratives of diverse policy developments vis-à-vis Indigenous populations and the war can be more easily followed.

Part II is organised into five thematic chapters that weave transnational and comparative analysis of the wartime experiences throughout. This is done to avoid the parallel histories approach so common in transnational and comparative work. Each chapter takes a specific prominent theme or aspect of the shared Indigenous experience of the Second World War. These include Chapter 3 – voluntary service, Chapter 4 – life and combat in settler militaries, Chapter 5 – mobilisation of Indigenous knowledge, language and culture, Chapter 6 – the home front, and Chapter 7 – conscription and the limits of engagement. Part III similarly inter-twines comparative and transnational analysis to explore the transitional period at the end of the war and its short- and long-term impacts on Indigenous returned service personnel, their families and their communities. Chapter 8 addresses the home front shift to peacetime, soldiers' return home and their access to veterans' benefits, and Chapter 9 focuses on post-war policy reform.

Within these chapters, we have not sought to be comprehensive in our coverage but rather to explore the issues, patterns and anomalies that transnational and comparative examination throws into relief. The results bring insights from each national historiography to the collective group, and in so doing, provide different ways of viewing events, actors, rationales and meanings. This will challenge some historical interpretative elements in various national narratives, reaffirm others and generally provoke new questions and lines of enquiry for scholars in each country.

*Part I*

# Context

# 1 Indigenous Peoples and Settler Colonialism to 1900

The first encounter between Christopher Columbus and the Taino happened in a particular place (San Salvador) at a specific time (12 October 1492). Yet, that encounter set a precedent that had ripple effects for both Europeans and Indigenous peoples – effects felt well into the twentieth- and twenty-first centuries. The early interactions between Europeans and Native Americans left lasting impressions on both sides, and those impressions would inform behaviours during subsequent encounters. Though Indigenous peoples – from present-day northern Canada all the way south to Tierra del Fuego were diverse in their social organisation, economies and lifestyles, Europeans would come to meet them with preconceived notions that would continue to layer in, comparing groups, passing judgements on different nations and, at the same time, homogenising conceptions of an Indian 'other'. European explorers and colonisers expanded beyond the Americas into the Pacific, drawing on their experiences with Native Americans as they encountered other Indigenous peoples. As 'knowledge' of Indigenous peoples grew, it reinforced Europeans' ideas of their own superiority and destiny to control lands inhabited by Indigenous peoples. Over the course of 400 years, the Europeans' justifications changed from Christian notions of condemning Indigenous paganism to theological ideas about the Great Chain of Being through to pseudo-scientific racism and its accompanying racial hierarchies. These were mere intellectual constructions to explain and legitimise what was already happening on the ground: Europeans expropriating Indigenous land and wreaking physical, economic and social devastation in their wake.

Of course, how colonialism operated varied across time and place, and recent historiography of colonialism has explored how Indigenous-European relations were complex processes that were not always clear-cut, white coloniser versus Indigene. There were times when Europeans and Indigenous people worked together, fought alongside one another, shared land and resources, cohabited urban spaces, forged intimate relations and even grew to rely on each other in willing, productive and

19

co-dependent manners. Recent historiography examining these nuances within settler colonialism has sought to destabilise the binaries of the frontier and coloniser versus colonised, whilst still showing the ways that colonialism has operated as a structure rather than an event.

The purpose of this chapter is to provide an introductory overview to the colonial histories of Native Americans, First Nations, Aboriginal and Torres Strait Islander people and Māori from first contact until the turn of the twentieth century. While acknowledging the diversity of colonial experiences, settler colonialism is a useful overarching lens to juxtapose these histories. Patrick Wolfe articulates three stages of settler colonialism, which may overlap chronologically and geographically, as confrontation, carceration and assimilation. Confrontation was characterised by invasion, disease, massacre and tribal warfare; carceration entailed 'protection' or segregation of Indigenous people onto reservations where government and missionaries attempted to train them in Christianity and agriculture; finally, assimilation emphasised 'practical education', adequate reserves and policy guided by anthropologists. Wolfe ties all of these strategies to a logic of elimination; whereby, colonisers sought to eliminate Indigenous people, whether through death, violence, relocation or cultural assimilation.[1] Historians looking at Indigenous responses to settler colonialism have traditionally emphasised aspects such as resistance, collaboration, accommodation or adaptation. In a recent article, Hannah Forsyth and Altin Gavranovic bring these concepts together, considering them mutually operating strategies that were proactive as much as reactive, constituting Indigenous people's own logic of survival.[2]

This chapter provides brief overviews of the logic of elimination and the logic of survival in the four settler states. It is organised thematically around the three stages of settler colonialism, acknowledging that these did not happen at the same time across or even within the nations. Given the scope of this chapter and the diversity of Indigenous nations within the four settler states, the intention is not to go into great detail about each particular country, nor to provide comprehensive references; instead, this chapter draws on the broad themes with a few high-profile, indicative examples that highlight the macro-histories of Indigenous peoples, which would continue to influence Indigenous and settler attitudes during the Second World War, including constructs of martial races.

---

[1] Patrick Wolfe, "Nation and MiscegeNation: Discursive Continuity in the Post-Mabo Era," *Social Analysis: The International Journal of Social and Cultural Practice*, no. 36 (1994): 99–102.

[2] Hannah Forsyth and Altin Gavranovic, "The Logic of Survival: Towards an Indigenous-Centred History of Capitalism in Wilcannia," *Settler Colonial Studies*, 8, no. 4 (2018): 464–488.

## Confrontation

Western science and Indigenous knowledge have different explanations for the first presence of Indigenous peoples. New archaeological evidence suggests that Aboriginal Australians arrived via Southeast Asia and a land bridge from present-day Papua New Guinea at least 80,000 years ago. Archaeologists remained divided over the evidence of the earliest human habitation in the Americas; many insist that arrival was earlier than 20,000 BCE, while some have argued for dates of 30,000 to 50,000 BCE. In New Zealand, it is believed the Māori arrived via canoe, after hundreds of years of migrations, populating Polynesia between 1200 and 1400 CE.[3] Māori traditions also include the migration, referencing Kupe as the first Māori to encounter Aotearoa (New Zealand) after a long voyage from the land of Hawaiki. Following Kupe, a migration of seven canoes came and settled in Aotearoa. Indigenous peoples in North America and Australia, by contrast, usually explain how the people were created on and from the land. For instance, the Kulin Nations around present-day Melbourne refer to the creator spirit Bunjil the Eagle, while the Abenaki people of Atlantic Canada and New England describe how Gluskonba created humans out of stone. Regardless of which version of history one subscribes to, one certainty in all four places is that there was a great longevity of inhabitation before Europeans arrived on the scene.

After the Spanish conquests of the 1500s, it would be the French and British who would colonise most of eastern North America. Even before Europeans set foot in these and other territories, waves of European disease – particularly smallpox and influenza – travelled along Indigenous trade routes and decimated the populations. Native Americans and First Nations were responding to shifting intertribal power dynamics and reconfiguring their societal structures and thus would have their own motives to build alliances with the European newcomers. The French came first to Canada with a series of failed settlements in the 1530s–40s. In 1608, they established a permanent settlement at Quebec and ushered in 162 years of trade and small-scale settlements. The fur-trade orientation of the French settlement was designed to connect with pre-existing Indigenous trade systems, and First Nations continued to reshape their own economies to capitalise on the opportunities. Other settlers were Catholic missionaries, who initially met with minimal success in converting First Nations. While the French maintained generally constructive relations with surrounding Algonquian-speaking nations and the

---

[3] Atholl Anderson, "Origins, Settlement and Society of Pre-European South Polynesia," in *The New Oxford History of New Zealand*, ed. Giselle Byrnes (Melbourne: Oxford University Press, 2009), 21–46.

Iroquoian-speaking Huron, they introduced muskets and aligned themselves in intertribal wars against other groups such as the Haudenosaunee
(League of Five Nations).

After a few failed settlements in the late 1500s, the British joined
the colonisation game starting with Jamestown, Virginia, in 1607 and
Plymouth, Massachusetts, in 1620. At both sites, the British later confronted challenges adapting to the climate and environment, and it was
only with the intervention of Native Americans that they were able to
survive and transform the land to enable economically viable agriculture. Local Native Americans were keen to use the newfound colonisers and their technology in their own intertribal rivalries, but within a
few years of arriving, British settlers' desire for more land sparked wars
against the local Native American populations. The first Powhatan War
broke out around Jamestown in 1610, the Pequot War erupted in southern Massachusetts in 1636, and King Philip's War tore apart the region
in 1675–76. Over the next 140 years, there would be similar patterns
across British North America: encroachment into new land, alliances
with some Native American nations, conflict ranging from widespread
raiding to major pitched battles. The repetition of war, treaty and disease
across centuries enabled settlers gradually to occupy more of the coast
and penetrate inland.

Out of these shifting cycles of conflict developed two important traditions: First, amongst many Indigenous nations, traditions of fighting as
allies of particular imperial or settler nations became increasingly important to their self-definition. In so doing, these Native Americans and
First Nations were adapting their own warrior traditions to the changed
geopolitical circumstances while making active choices to secure the best
economic and political outcomes for their people. Second, long experience fighting against or alongside Indigenous warriors embedded in
the minds of Europeans the generalised notion of Indigenous North
Americans as 'warrior' peoples. This image was dichotomous – there was
the image of the noble warrior but also of the primitive, brutal, savage
who only understood violence. These depictions could operate simultaneously and even be used to differentiate between Indigenous allies
versus enemies. Settlers also mobilised images of the savage 'other' to
justify their own brutality and frontier violence. These cultural notions
of the 'other' would merge with colonial experiences across the globe
and nineteenth-century concepts of race, crystallising understandings
of martial ability and aggression as inherently 'in the blood' of certain
peoples: the martial race. By the late nineteenth century, the idea of the
martial indigene grew particularly strong in settler constructs of First
Nations, Native Americans and Māori.

Within Australia, myths of peaceful settlement meant that Europeans did not apply the martial race ideology so much to Aboriginal and Torres Strait Islander people. Australia's colonisation was far from peaceful, though, witnessing similar patterns of encroachment, resistance, reprisals and occupation. Dutch explorers had sailed along Australia's north and west coasts since the early 1600s, and Abel Tasman reached as far as present-day Tasmania and even New Zealand in 1642. English sailors came to the north and west coasts from the late 1600s, and their impressions of Aboriginal people significantly influenced later explorers. Perhaps most famous was William Dampier's 1699 observation that 'The inhabitants of this country are the miserablest people in the world.'[4] In 1769 then-Lieutenant James Cook was the first European to stop in New Zealand, mapping the two islands and befriending Māori on the north coast at the Bay of Islands. Cook was also the first European to reach and map the east coast of Australia. The French were exploring Australia and New Zealand around the same time, and on Cook and botanist Joseph Banks' advice to solidify British claims to the region, the British government established a penal colony in New South Wales.

On 26 January 1788, the British First Fleet made landfall at Port Jackson, present-day Sydney and founded a penal colony. At first, the relations with the local Eora people were a mixture of curiosity and friendliness, transforming quickly to hostility when the Europeans began chopping down trees.[5] Despite Governor Arthur Phillip's orders, to try 'by every possible means to open an intercourse with the natives, and to conciliate their affections, enjoining all our subjects to live in amity and kindness with them', it did not take long for enmity to emerge on both sides.[6] Most settlers viewed Aboriginal people as inferior savages, seeing the land as terra nullius or land belonging to no one because the Aboriginal people did not visibly till the soil or have, from European perspectives, any permanent settlements (recent research from Bruce Pascoe has highlighted the falseness of these perceptions[7]). The year 1790 witnessed the first punitive expedition sent to hunt Aboriginal people as vengeance for an attack on a settler, a practice that would continue in other parts of Australia well into the 1920s. The first site of warfare was against the Darug people along the Hawkesbury River north

---

[4] See Nick Brodie, *1787: The Lost Chapters of Australia's Beginnings* (Richmond, VIC: Hardie Grant Books, 2016).

[5] Inga Clendinnen, *Dancing with Strangers* (New York: Cambridge University Press, 2005).

[6] Quoted in Richard Broome, *Aboriginal Australians: A History since 1788*, 4th edn. (Crows Nest, NSW: Allen & Unwin, 2010), 22.

[7] Bruce Pascoe, *Dark Emu: Black Seeds, Agriculture or Accident?* (Sydney: Magabala Books, 2014).

and west of Sydney from 1795; violence flared there sporadically until Aboriginal resistance was finally quashed in 1816. Resistance figures such as Pemulwuy organised small bands to raid settlements such as Parramatta, but ultimately the British muskets were able to subdue such leaders.

Treaties were one major difference between Australia and the experiences of Canada, the United States and Aotearoa/New Zealand. Treaties as a practice began in British North America in the mid-1600s as a method to broker peace. While peace treaties continued, over time, the model was adapted to negotiate settler access to Indigenous lands while guaranteeing Indigenous rights to particular lands for living, hunting and possibly a set of colonial protections and annuities or goods.[8] Because ever-increasing numbers of settlers regularly breached treaties, new conflicts often resulted. Perhaps the most significant turning point in Indigenous-settler relations came in the aftermath of the British defeat of French power in North America in 1760. British leadership believed that it no longer had any obligations to sustain productive relations with Indigenous peoples in North America, provoking an angry reaction from a newly consolidated Indigenous confederacy in the Great Lakes-Ohio River country.[9] Galvanised by the Odawa chief, Pontiac, an uprising swept British garrisons and settlers from the region west of the Appalachian Mountains, exposing Britain's limited ability to project its military power into the interior.[10] To regain a peaceful equilibrium in the region, the British issued the *Royal Proclamation of 1763*, which regulated settler relations with Indigenous people and decreed most lands west of British or French settlement to be Indian country off limits to further colonisation. Settler discontent over this proclamation became one causal factor leading to the American Revolution a decade later.

In the wake of the American Revolution, both sides of the new border between the United States and what was to become Canada continued treaty-making, but treaties took a new approach after the *Proclamation of 1763*. Rather than treaties being about friendship and confirming de facto land arrangements, treaties became primarily land cession instruments, extinguishing Indigenous nations' title and transferring Indigenous

---

[8] J. R. Miller, *Compact, Contract, Covenant: Aboriginal Treaty-Making in Canada* (Toronto: University of Toronto Press, 2009).

[9] Richard White, *The Middle Ground: Indians, Empires, and Republics in the Great Lakes Region, 1650–1815*, 2nd edn. (Cambridge: Cambridge University Press, 2010).

[10] Matthew Ward, "'The European Method of Warring is Not Practiced Here': The Failure of British Military Policy in the Ohio Valley, 1755–1759," *War in History* 4, no. 3 (1997): 247–263.

lands to the state.[11] Treaty-making continued in the United States until 1887 as settlers moved ever westward and eastward from new Pacific Coast settlements from the mid-1800s and in British North America – confederated as Canada in 1867 – until 1921. Regularly, settler authorities made Native Americans and First Nations sign treaties that they clearly did not understand, or settlers made verbal promises that were not included in the written documents. Sometimes authorities signed treaties with 'chiefs' who were not recognised as such by Indigenous nations, but still, governments enforced the treaties. In Australia, because of the racialist ideas deeming Aboriginal people so low as not to own land, colonial authorities would not negotiate treaties and even refused to recognise colonists' attempts to do so.

New Zealand also had a treaty experience, with only one agreement designed to cover all iwis (tribes). After Cook's visits, British and French explorers frequented New Zealand, and by the early 1800s, missionaries, whalers and sealers were also setting up small-scale settlements. Māori had their moments of hostility against Europeans, but generally, they welcomed them for the trade opportunities and increasingly for muskets. There followed a complex series of inter-iwi wars in the 1820s and early 1830s, when armed with the new technology, old and new enmities wrought war and devastation across Aotearoa.[12] Europeans dubbed these conflicts the 'Musket Wars', a technological determinism that fit their assumptions of the 'fatal impact' of colonisation on Indigenous societies. This construct of these conflicts has been convincingly overturned by Angela Ballara, who argues that the wars of the 1820s–30s fit within Māori social, cultural and military norms.[13] The fighting ended in the late 1830s with the onset of war weariness, old and new dispute resolution mechanisms and relative equilibrium of firearms. Out of a population of 100,000, as many as 20,000 Māori died in the Musket Wars, severely weakening some iwis while greatly enhancing others and forever changing the demographic landscape of Aotearoa. As the 1830s drew to a close and British land speculators turned to New Zealand for settlement possibilities, the colonial office decided to stake a claim to New Zealand and ensure orderly colonisation.

On 6 February 1840, representatives of the British Crown convened with roughly forty Māori chiefs at Waitangi to negotiate and sign a treaty.

---

[11] Miller, *Compact, Contract, Covenant*, 66; Olive Patricia Dickason, *A Concise History of Canada's First Nations*, 4th edn. (Toronto: Oxford University Press, 2006), 102–106.
[12] See R. D. Crosby, *The Musket Wars: A History of Inter-Iwi Conflict 1806–1845*, 2nd edn. (Auckland: Reed, 2001).
[13] Angela Ballara, *Taua: 'Musket Wars', 'Land Wars', or Tikanga? Warfare in Māori Society in the Early Nineteenth Century* (Auckland: Penguin, 2003).

Afterwards, representatives travelled around the North and South Islands to secure another 500 signatures on copies of the document. The British understood this Treaty of Waitangi as a transfer of sovereignty over Aotearoa to the Crown, transforming Māori into British subjects and, in exchange, confirming Māori possession of their own lands. In the Māori written version of the treaty, as there was no literal translation of the word sovereignty, the authors used two terms. The treaty granted the British Crown kāwanatanga – a distant and perhaps loose governorship – while Māori leaders would retain their rangatiratanga, chiefly powers and authority – a problematic difference and hazy boundary – that has led to physical and legal conflicts over the treaty's meaning even to the present day. For the next hundred years, Pākehā (non-Māori) largely ignored the treaty; it was not until the centenary that the Treaty of Waitangi was res-urrected in Pākehā popular consciousness and retroactively transformed into the founding document of New Zealand.[14]

After the signing of the Treaty of Waitangi, British immigration and settlement expanded rapidly. Under the treaty, only the Crown could purchase land from Māori and then sell it on to settlers. British initially tended to found settlements at the request of Māori, who benefited from the establishment of a Pākehā town in their vicinity and who remained confident in their autonomy and power. But these settlements grew beyond the ability of the Māori to control. Settler authorities quickly developed pretensions about extending their authority into the Māori world, and the cycles of confrontation already witnessed in the United States, Canada and Australia emerged in New Zealand as well. Beginning at the Bay of Islands in 1845–6, there was a series of conflicts eventually known collectively as the New Zealand Wars. These conflicts flared espe-cially in the early 1860s, by which time the demographic balance had tipped with Pākehā surpassing Māori in population. Conflicts of varying intensity erupted across the west, central and northeast North Island throughout the decade in Taranaki, Wanganui, Waikato, the Bay of Plenty and the Urewera mountains.

In the larger conflicts of 1860–1 and 1863–4, the wars pitted Māori against British imperial and settler forces. A number of prominent iwis, such as Wanganui, Te Arawa and Ngati Porou, developed strong alliance (kupapa) traditions in the wars against Māori prophet leaders. These later battles were sometimes virtually inter-Māori events with little settler involvement. Here, too, as in North America, Māori fought settler forces to a standstill, and battling against or beside settler and imperial troops,

---

[14] Claudia Orange, *The Treaty of Waitangi* (Wellington: Allen & Unwin in association with Port Nicholson Press, 1987).

settlers solidified the idea of the great Māori warrior in settler popular culture as well as in Māori traditions. The instability and violence did not fully subside until the early 1870s.

Amidst the violence and dispossession in all four settler societies were also sexual relations across the frontier. Generally, these were relationships between white men with Indigenous women, and these were complex cases ranging from intimate and loving, to ephemeral or commercial and even rape and sexual slavery. In some early encounters, Indigenous men may have offered Indigenous women as wives, or indeed, the women exercised their agency and presented themselves to settler men in exchange for goods, status or as a means to incorporate white men into their kinship networks. In North America, it had long been a practice to adopt captured members of an enemy group into a tribe, and Native Americans and First Nations extended this practice to adopt captured white men, women and children into their nations. Yet the stories of sexual violence are also prevalent; while white authorities regularly expressed anxieties over Indigenous men claiming white women, more common were settlers or traders such as whalers and sealers who would force themselves on Indigenous women. From the violent to the loving, evidence of the multifaceted dimensions of interracial sexual encounters included the rise of venereal disease (such as syphilis and consequent falling birth rates), the birth of new mixed-race communities (such as at the bottom of New Zealand's South Island, in Bass Strait off the coast of Tasmania) and the rise of the Métis as a distinct Indigenous people of mixed European-Indigenous descent in the Canadian west.

The patterns of encounters from curiosity, misunderstandings, frontier violence, and shifting power relations constantly repeated across Canada and the United States in the 1600s–1880s, in New Zealand from the 1840s to 1870s and in Australia from 1788 to 1920s. The nature of warfare in all four countries varied, but some common patterns and tactics developed. After initial numerical superiority, settlement usually shifted the demographics against Indigenous peoples. The greatest advantages that settler military forces had were numbers and resources, and it was these more than any technology that consistently overcame Indigenous resistance in North America or the Antipodes. To these approaches, others were added such as enlisting the help of Indigenous allies, police or scouts, conducting total war against Indigenous people's livelihoods and communities, the use of poisons and possibly bacterial vectors to kill their foes and intermittent mass killings of entire communities.

Indigenous peoples often responded by adopting European weapons and capitalising on their knowledge of the land, their greater mobility and traditional military styles to fight guerrilla campaigns to great effect.

Māori differed in their development of sophisticated fortification structures known as pa, which they adapted to thwart even modern artillery
and used to decimate attacking British and settler forces. Australian
Aboriginal peoples differed again in that they resisted settler encroachment fiercely, but, as Henry Reynolds argues, they 'dealt with Europeans
as though they too were Aborigines. Their violence was judicial rather than
martial, seeking revenge rather than military victory'.[15] Indigenous people
did have their victories over settler police and military forces, but in the
long term, the encroaching settler wave was so large and so powerful that,
whether it took decades or centuries, Indigenous resistance was gradually
overwhelmed. The logic of survival necessitated other techniques to adapt
to the ever-changing realities wrought by settler colonialism.

## Carceration

Indigenous people had been adapting to and accommodating settlers
from the moment of first contact: sometimes enthusiastically, sometimes
reticently and sometimes at the barrel of a gun. As the balance of power
shifted, the latter two became more common, and the War of 1812 effectively marked settler dominance in the northeast of North America, subsequently enabling legislative instruments to enforce physical removal
and segregation on reserves on both sides of the United States–Canadian
border.

Also influencing the movement towards segregation in all four states
was the rise of humanitarianism. This was a movement of mostly middle-
class evangelical Protestants who had been part of the anti-slavery cause,
and who, from the 1830s in the British Empire and 1870s in the United
States, turned their attention to the treatment of Indigenous peoples on the
frontiers. Humanitarians were not trying to stop colonisation, and indeed,
they often considered colonisation and the death of the Indigenous peoples to be an inevitable part of God's plan. The idea was that Indigenous
races should at least die in peace instead of simply being massacred.
In Britain, an 1837 Select Committee on Aborigines recommended the
establishment of settlements where Indigenous peoples could be protected from settler violence and converted to Christianity.

Though humanitarians pushed for carceration in all four settler states,
reservations and reserves had their origins well before the 1830s when,
in the United States and Canada, the Crown, state, and colonial governments negotiated treaties recognising particular tracts of land for Native

---

[15] Henry Reynolds, *The Other Side of the Frontier: Aboriginal resistance to the Europeans invasion of Australia* (Sydney: University of New South Wales Press, 2006), 83–84.

American possession. When Native Americans lost control of their land, whether through war or signing it away in a treaty, they often had no choice but to relocate to other territories. In 1824, the US government set up the Office of Indian Affairs (rebadged the Bureau of Indian Affairs in 1947 and referred to as the BIA in this book) to manage land and treaty negotiations. As the federal government exerted more control over Native Americans from the 1830s, the BIA became the main instrument to implement its policies – often in concert with the Army when there was resistance.[16]

The major turning point in the United States was the 1830 Indian Removal Act, which authorised the executive to negotiate arrangements to relocate most Native American nations east of the Mississippi River into Indian Territory (present-day Oklahoma), with the promise to be left alone forever. Notwithstanding legal challenges, letters protesting removal and even Supreme Court rulings against the law, President Andrew Jackson forced the majority of eastern Native American nations to relocate. The most infamous case of removal was the Trail of Tears where approximately 4,000 out of 15,000 Cherokees died en route to Indian Territory between 1838 and 1839. Over the ensuing decades to 1887, similar removal practices occurred across the west in the aftermath of frontier conflicts and treaties. What emerged, solidified under the 1851 Indian Appropriations Act, was a reservation system whereby Indian nations would be contained within tracts of land. Usually, this land was not arable, hence, not being desirable for settlers and sometimes the reservations would be away from a group's traditional lands.

In Canada, as well, the territorial boundaries of reserves had their origins in the treaty system. After confederation, the Canadian Parliament assumed authority over Indian affairs and between 1871 and 1921 negotiated a series of eleven numbered treaties as part of its orderly approach to carceration. The Numbered Treaties were similar to the Treaty of Waitangi in that they led to local chiefs ceding sovereignty over vast swaths of territory covering most of the interior of Canada, from northwestern Ontario west to the Rocky Mountains and north into the Northwest Territories. Where these treaties differed from Waitangi was that chiefs were also signing away their land ownership with treaty provisions setting aside relatively tiny reserves for exclusive Indigenous use. Even though they would have rights such as hunting and fishing protected off the reserves, they still did not have ownership or sovereignty over the reserves, which were held in trust by the Crown for an Indian band.

---

[16] See Claudia Haake, *The State, Removal and Indigenous Peoples in the United States and Mexico, 1620–2000* (New York & London: Routledge, 2007), 11–39.

The Numbered Treaties usually presaged white settlement, so the removal was not necessarily immediate or as violent as in the American west. While Canadians at the time and since have been self-congratulatory for this, it was less a product of their virtue than of the almost total dearth of European emigrants choosing Canada prior to 1900. As a result, Canada had time to complete treaty signing, confine First Nations to reserves, disperse resistant Métis and establish a legal and policing system prior to large-scale settlement in the early twentieth century.

The Treaty of Waitangi did not mandate reserves for Māori, yet segregation in rural areas and land expropriation still happened. Because Māori were legally equal to Pākehā, settlers would need to use different measures from authorities in North America. During the 1860s, the Parliament established the Native Land Courts to provide a structure and a sense of legal legitimacy to the process of dismantling Māori communal land tenure.[17] The courts divided Māori lands into blocks with individualised owners or shareholders, facilitating the fragmentation and sale of previously communally held Indigenous lands. Māori participated in the courts and land sales for several reasons: for some, it enhanced their mana by affirming their rights to certain property; for others, it prevented their land from being sold by other Māori while an increasing number sought funds necessary to address growing indebtedness. By the end of the nineteenth century, Māori lands constituted a mere 17 per cent of the total land mass, and by 1920, there was less than one million acres of usable land.[18]

Australia had no treaties and colonial authorities never recognised any form of Aboriginal or Torres Strait Islander land tenure, but still, authorities in the different colonies established protectorates and reserves to segregate and 'protect' Aboriginal people. The motives for the reserves were twofold: first was in response to the humanitarian outcry over settler violence, but the second was the pragmatic effect that reserves had, like in the United States and Canada, of ending Indigenous resistance. The latter motive is most pronounced in the case of Tasmania. In the 1820s and 1830s, settlers and palawa people were embroiled in a conflict known as the Black War. Changing tack, the governor dispatched a settler named George Augustus Robinson on the so-called friendly mission.

---

[17] James Belich, *Making Peoples: A History of the New Zealanders* (Auckland: Penguin, 1996), 258.

[18] Michael King, *The Penguin History of New Zealand* (Auckland: Penguin Books, 2003), 256–58; Tom Brooking, "'Busting Up' The Greatest Estate of All: Liberal Maori Land Policy, 1891–1911," *New Zealand Journal of History*, 26, no. 1 (1992): 78. It should be noted that Māori still retained about 5 million acres all told, but leased more than three million to Pākehā, and not all of what remained was arable.

Robinson travelled across Tasmania, guided by local Aboriginal people such as Truganini, convincing about 100 surviving palawa to relocate to Wybalenna on Flinders Island. Between 1835 and 1876, the population withered as disease and the harsh environmental conditions in Wybalenna and then subsequent relocation at Oyster Cove slowly killed all of the carcerated Aboriginal Tasmanians. A mythology emerged that Truganini was the last Aboriginal Tasmanian, but in fact, the palawa community did survive from another population of Aboriginal women abducted by sealers and settled on Cape Barren Island.[19]

The Tasmanian experience of the Black War and the Friendly Mission convinced humanitarians of the need to segregate and protect Aboriginal people as well as the inevitably of their extinction as a race. In the late 1830s, other colonies established protectorates to guard Aboriginal populations against settler predation and to encourage them into a sedentary agricultural existence, often under the Christian guidance of allied missionaries. By the late 1850s, most of the protectorates had been shut down as futile experiments. Thus when self-government arrived in most colonies during the 1850s, they inherited little in the way of Aboriginal policy beyond annual distributions of blankets and some police units of dubious utility as protection for Aboriginal populations.

In the 1860s, a new wave of protection, normally driven by missionaries, began the establishment of Aboriginal reserves in Victoria, New South Wales and South Australia. Beginning in Victoria in 1869, New South Wales in 1883, and mirrored in other colonies from the 1890s, Aborigines Protection Boards became the state instruments to oversee administration of Aboriginal reserves and with legal authority over every aspect of residents' lives. The reserves were sites where superintendents, usually missionaries, exerted strict control over Aboriginal residents. They banned the use of Aboriginal languages, preached Christianity, prohibited traditional spiritual practices and focused on training on men for farm labour and women as domestic servants. Missionaries tended to write off adults as a lost cause but pinned their hopes on Aboriginal children being raised as good Christian workers. Yet, the living conditions on reserves were often crowded and unsanitary, with waves of disease, such as tuberculosis, sweeping through and killing residents.

Reservations and reserves in the United States and Canada similarly had poor conditions, exacerbating the population declines until the turn of the twentieth century. After confederation, First Nations residing on

---

[19] Henry Reynolds, *Fate of a Free People* (Ringwood, VIC: Penguin Books Australia, 1995); Murray Johnson and Ian McFarlane, *Van Diemen's Land: An Aboriginal History* (Sydney: University of New South Wales Press, 2015).

reserves gradually devolved to a category of legal wardship, essentially disenfranchising them and placing them under the control of the Department of Indian Affairs.[20] Parliament consolidated all existing legislation with a single centralised act that came to be colloquially termed the Indian Act of 1876, which defined those with 'Indian Status' (a person of Indian blood who belonged to a particular tribe or band). This instrument would henceforth be the principle mechanism shaping First Nations' relationships with the state. Though initially designed to facilitate the voluntary civilising and assimilation of First Nations people, administrators progressively gained more power and arbitrary control over their charges through to the 1920s.[21] In 1871, the United States likewise passed a law declaring Native Americans to be wards of the state, thus reducing the need for tribal consent. These situations in Australia, the United States and Canada thus essentially gave Indigenous people a legal status similar to children.

Notwithstanding the harsh conditions and strict controls akin to prisons exerted by missionaries, superintendents, protection boards, the BIA or Canada's Department of Indian Affairs, Indigenous peoples adapted to survive on reserves and worked to preserve or even develop new traditions. Elders still passed down knowledge to young people when beyond the watchful eye of missionaries. For instance, Aboriginal residents became adept at sport including cricket and Australian Rules football, itself possibly an adaptation of an Aboriginal pastime from Victoria called Marn Grook.[22] Navajos actually developed fry bread, now seen as a staple of their food culture, during the three-hundred-mile forced relocation in 1864 known as the Long Walk.[23] West Coast First Nations sustained potlatch traditions following the government ban on the cultural practice in 1884, initially by ignoring the law, and, once it began to be vigorously enforced in 1921, by conducting altered ceremonies in secrecy.[24] Māori and numerous other Indigenous groups developed, with the help of missionaries, their own written languages. These examples of the innovation and adaptive logic of survival also marked a significant

[20] Dickason, *A Concise History of Canada's First Nations*, 159.
[21] John Tobias, "Protection, Civilization, Assimilation: An Outline History of Canada's Indian Policy," in *As Long as the Sun Shines and the Water Flows: A Reader in Canadian-Native Relations*, ed. Ian A. L. Getty and Antoine Lussier (Vancouver: University of British Columbia Press, 1983), 39–55; E. Brian Titley, *A Narrow Vision: Duncan Campbell Scott and the Administration of Indian Affairs* (Vancouver: University of British Columbia Press, 1986).
[22] See Chris Hallinan and Barry Judd, "Duelling Paradigms: Australian Aborigines, Marn-Grook and Football Histories," in *Indigenous People, Race Relations and Australian Sport*, ed. Chris Hallinan and Barry Judd (London and New York: Routledge, 2014), 61–72.
[23] Jen Miller, "Frybread," *Smithsonian Magazine* (July 2008), www.smithsonianmag.com/arts-culture/frybread-79191/.
[24] Douglas Cole and Ira Chaikin, *An Iron Hand Upon the People: The Law Against the Potlatch on the Northwest Coast* (Vancouver: Douglas & McIntyre, 1990).

thorn in the racialist discourse of mid- to late-1800s settler societies: it turned out that Indigenous people were not all dying off.

## Assimilation

At its most basic, assimilation refers to the process by which an individual or social group becomes a part of a larger collective group. For Indigenous peoples, assimilation has negative connotations because of the ways it has been deployed as a discourse and policy designed to eliminate their cultures. The discourses and policies implementing assimilation ranged from ideas of biologically absorbing Indigenous people into the white race over generations, through to wiping out their culture and thus being Indigenous in appearance but European on the inside. Even though assimilation emerged in popular discourse in the late 1800s (in Australia not until the 1930s), from the moment of first contact there were proto-assimilationist projects in operation in the different settler states. For instance, in 1814 Governor Lachlan Macquarie opened the first boarding school for Aboriginal children in Parramatta, Sydney, called the Native Institution. Missions were always a site of assimilation because of the efforts to convert Indigenous people to Christianity and, concurrently, stop their own practices.

Legislation and government policies of assimilation began first in Canada in earnest. Even before confederation, the colony of Canada was legislating the definition of who an Indian is as well as ways to restrict the numbers with Status and to legally unmake a Status Indian though a policy known as 'enfranchisement'. Paternalism amongst lawmakers shaped the policy so that a Status woman who married a non-Status Indian lost her status, as did any subsequent children. Increasingly, as Canada developed its highly centralised administrative structure for managing its relationships with First Nations, during the latter 1800s and early 1900s, assimilation came to shape everything the Department of Indian Affairs did: It developed residential schools under its education policy; it banned cultural practices like the Sun Dance and potlatch to extinguish stubborn Indigenous cultural expressions; it imposed elected band councils and chiefs to supplant Indigenous governance; and, ultimately, even attacked Indian reserves themselves as a barrier to assimilation, removing hundreds of thousands of acres by 1920s. By the 1920s, Indian Affairs even gained the power to forcibly enfranchise a Status Indian. These reforms met stiff resistance because they were reshaping traditional tribal structures, attempting to hasten the breakdown of those political and cultural systems and replace them with Western liberal individualism.[25]

[25] Dickason, *A Concise History of Canada's First Nations*, 182–183.

In the United States, the Dawes Act of 1887 ushered in the assimilation era. Under this law, BIA officials would work to enrol recognised members of Native American nations. The reservations would then be broken into individual allotments for each of the enrolled members. The idea behind allotment was to break down collective, tribal governance and hasten the assimilation of Native Americans as individual farmers. Of course, an added benefit of allotment was that now, as individual landowners, Native Americans could be encouraged to sell their allotted lands to speculators, leading to the so-called checkerboarding of reservations. Interestingly, as Katherine Ellinghaus has noted, there was never a legal definition of Indianness based on blood quantum until the 1934 Indian Reorganization Act – that which marked the end of this assimilation era. Yet, officials drawing up the tribal rolls from the 1890s onwards were invariably drawing on a racial discourse of blood quantum.[26] Such practices of defining who was and who was not Indian had a similar effect as the status issue in Canada: severing certain Indigenous individuals from access to their communities and limiting their access to entitlements.

In Australia, while assimilation generally did not come into play until the 1930s, from the late 1800s, Victoria, and then other colonies, laid the groundwork through adopting racial discourse into law. Victoria in 1886 was the first place to distinguish so-called 'half-castes' from Aboriginal people. With exceptions, those Aboriginal people of mixed descent under the age of thirty-four were to be kicked off the reserves to fend for themselves in white society. Thenceforth, Aboriginal people of mixed descent were to be apprenticed out at age thirteen and not allowed to return to the reserves. Of course, just because the legislation now said that Aboriginal people of mixed descent were no longer Aboriginal did not mean that Indigenous or non-Indigenous society saw them that way. Aboriginal communities did not distinguish based on blood quanta, yet this was forced upon them from colonial authorities. Outside the reserves, settlers still saw mixed-descent people as racial inferiors and discriminated in employment, housing and general daily life. Other states adopted similar legislation and regulations differentiating Aboriginal people of mixed descent.

The other major component of the assimilation program in Australia, intricately tied to the mythology of blood quanta, was child removal. Racialist ideas assumed that Aboriginal children of mixed descent were 'part-white' and therefore stood a better chance at functioning in white

[26] Katherine Ellinghaus, *Blood Will Tell: Native Americans and Assimilation Policy* (Lincoln: University of Nebraska Press, 2017).

society – if the system could encourage the 'white half' and remove children from any native influences. Beginning in Victoria in 1869, the various state protection legislations established and appointed a Chief Protector of Aborigines as guardian over all Aboriginal children. The 1886 Victorian legislation gave more authority to the Chief Protector to remove Aboriginal children from their families for their own good. The guardianship and removal provisions were in place in every state by 1909, and across Australia, the state protection boards and chief protectors forcefully removed Aboriginal children from their families at any age ranging from birth through to their teens. In some states, the children were sent to reformatories or industrial schools; in others, they were segregated in different dormitories; in others, they were sent to separate reserves or missions.

From the 1930s, child removal became intricately tied to new assimilation policies, and after the Second World War, practices of child removal persisted but with some shifts towards sending children to foster care or to be adopted. The goal of child removal was explicitly to separate Aboriginal children from their kin and culture and to train them as a working underclass of manual labourers and domestic servants. The separated children regularly reported cases of physical and sexual abuse, and intergenerational removals and traumas have persisted until the present day. It is estimated that between 1909 and 1969 between one out of every three and one out of every ten Aboriginal children was forcefully removed, and there is no Aboriginal family that has not experienced at least one removal. The removed children are collectively known as the Stolen Generations.[27]

The notion of separating children from their communities and culture was not unique to Australia. Missionaries in all four settler societies ran schools that tried to stop Indigenous children from speaking their languages and limit cultural transmission. In the assimilation era, though, the United States and Canada established more formal, federally funded boarding schools for Indians. The US government established a school system for Native Americans in the 1860s and founded the first boarding school at Carlisle, Pennsylvania, in 1879. Other schools followed in the eastern states and then in the west, with the aim to encourage Native American children in the ways of Western individualism, agriculture, discipline, Christianity and trades. Schools banned all forms of Native

[27] Australia, Human Rights and Equal Opportunity Commission, National Inquiry into the Separation of Aboriginal and Torres Strait Islander Children from Their Families, *Bringing Them Home: Report of the National Inquiry into the Separation of Aboriginal and Torres Strait Islander Children from Their Families* (Sydney: Human Rights and Equal Opportunity Commission, 1997).

American culture, including dress, long hair, language and other traditional practices. Living conditions at these schools were poor, with physical and sexual abuse and disease running rampant.[28] In Canada, day
schools on reserves had been common across the more settled east of the
country, but from the 1880s residential and industrial schools prolifer-
ated across the west and north, usually drawing First Nations children
long distances from their reserves or traditional territories. Like in the
United States, these schools were under-funded, over-crowded and the
reports of poor conditions were rife.[29] In the United States, the laws did
not force Indigenous children into these schools, and in the early years,
parents often resisted sending their children to the schools.[30] Over time,
though, authorities misled parents to compel them into sending their
children away. In Canada, police officers combed reserves to seize children to send them to residential schools. Often children left to a school
at age five and returned at sixteen or seventeen having never seen their
families in the interim.

Motivated by the humanitarian impulses of the mid-nineteenth
century, and pushed by Māori families and communities who valued
literacy, the New Zealand colonial government established a separate
school system for Māori children in 1867. Their intent was much the
same as school systems in the other settler societies: to teach the finer
points of civilisation and eventually to speed the process of assimilation.
There was little uniformity across the system, and different personalities,
interpretations and expectations meant these schools varied widely and
their impact proved a blend of constructive and assimilationist.[31] Māori
families were usually the ones who requested a school in their area,
helped pay for them and often had some degree of influence through parent committee participation. When the separate Māori system was dismantled in 1968, many Māori lamented, as their children subsequently
struggled in the Pākehā school system.[32]

---

[28] Zuzanna Buchowska, *Negotiating Native American Identities:The Role of Tradition, Narrative
and Language at Haskell Indian Nations University* (Poznań, Poland: Uniwersytetu im.
Adama Mickiewicza w Poznaniu, 2016), 56–62.

[29] John Milloy, *A National Crime: The Canadian Government and the Residential School
System, 1879–1986* (Winnipeg: University of Manitoba Press, 1999); Canada, The Final
Report of the Truth and Reconciliation Commission of Canada, Canada's Residential
Schools:The History, Part I – Origins to 1939, Vol. 1 (Montreal and Kingston: McGill-
Queen's University Press, 2015).

[30] J. R. Miller, *Shingwauk's Vision:A History of Native Residential Schools* (Toronto: University
of Toronto Press, 1996).

[31] Judith Simon and Linda Tuhiwai Smith, eds., *A Civilizing Mission? Perceptions and
Representations of the New Zealand Native Schools System* (Auckland: Auckland University
Press, 2001), 3.

[32] Maxine Stephenson, "Closing the doors on the Maori Schools in New Zealand," *Race
Ethnicity and Education* 9, no. 3 (September 2006): 307–324.

Assimilation policies and practices persisted in some form or another well into the later twentieth century. As in other eras, the Indigenous populations resisted and adapted, whether through hiding their children, refusing to send them away to a boarding school, or moving to urban locations where they had more autonomy to live their own lives. Indigenous people did not wholly reject working with(in) white society, for they saw value in education. The main difference was that while they were interested in participating in white society, they wanted it to be by choice, on their own terms and not at the cost of their own cultures and traditions. In the 1960s, such ideas cohered under the umbrella of self-determination and integration, rather than assimilation.[33] By the turn of the twentieth century, in Canada, New Zealand and the United States, there were even a small number of Indigenous people who were able to attain higher education, participate in the professions and advocate for Indigenous rights through the political system. In New Zealand, especially, where the legal system was more open to Māori as equals, they would have an impact on preserving Māori interests.

### Conclusion: Legal Status Circa 1901

Across the four-settler states, at the turn of the century, the legal status for Indigenous peoples varied. Perhaps at the bottom, in terms of rights and recognition, was Australia. When the nation federated on 1 January 1901, the Australian Constitution made only two references to Aboriginal people: they were not to be counted as part of the population in the census, and the states would have all powers over Indigenous affairs (except in the territories, which were the reserve of the Commonwealth government). States that did not yet have protection boards would form them in the next decade, and the Commonwealth Electoral Act 1902 would disenfranchise the majority of Indigenous Australians. Indigenous people essentially had no rights whatsoever over either themselves or recognition to land. Southeast and southwest Australia were in the carceration phase of settler colonialism while settlers were only beginning to explore the northern and interior frontiers with the accompanying violence constitutive of confrontation.

In Canada, the distinction between Status and non-Status became only more pronounced at the turn of the century. Those on reserves had limited rights to self-government, but only subject to approval by increasingly authoritarian Indian Agents and senior officials in Indian Affairs. Ideas about enfranchisement determined eligibility for citizenship rights

---

[33] Russell McGregor, *Indifferent Inclusion: Aboriginal People and the Australian Nation* (Canberra: Aboriginal Studies Press, 2011).

such as the vote. Under the Indian Act, a person who essentially severed their ties with their community and moved off the reserve could become enfranchised and gain the rights and freedoms of citizenship. The high personal cost of enfranchisement in abandoning a First Nations' identity meant very few individuals voluntarily took it up. Assimilation policies were dominant across most of the southern areas of Canada from coast to coast, affecting First Nations and Métis. State officials were only beginning encounters with Inuit people in the North; though, these meetings usually lacked the same violent patterns witnessed in the south earlier.

In the United States, longstanding juridical and treaty rights gave Native Americans slightly more rights to self-government on their reservations than in Canada. This was despite the intentional process of trying to break down the reservations into individual allotments. Under the US Constitution, 'Indians not taxed' were not considered citizens, and a series of court cases in the 1880s confirmed that those Native Americans citizen to a tribal nation were not also US citizens. As such, only the small number of Native Americans who left the reservations and participated as taxed members of American society had the same rights as other citizens, including the vote (if they were male). The last formally recognised massacre of Native Americans happened at Wounded Knee on the Lakota Pine Ridge Indian Reservation in 1890. Neglect was a common factor in Indian affairs at the turn of the century: government neglect on reservations, at boarding schools and the subsequent poor living conditions nationally for Native Americans. The flipside of neglect, though, was that, notwithstanding assimilation policies, Native Americans on reservations – particularly larger, more remote ones – had some autonomy. In Alaska, as in northern Canada, most Inuit, too, were isolated and only encountering settler society in small numbers of fishermen, explorers and gold prospectors. Hawai'i, which would play a significant role in the Second World War, had just been conquered by the United States and was experiencing a shift in power. In the early twentieth century, the influx of Japanese, Filipino and other immigrants would transform Kanaka Maoli (Native Hawai'ians) into a minority population.

Only in New Zealand did Indigenous people, at least under the law, retain equal rights. Māori not only had the vote (including women from 1893) and access to education and the social welfare system, but the parliament also had four reserved seats for Māori under the Maori Representation Act of 1867, which had also removed the individual property requirement for Māori electors. Sophisticated parliamentary leaders, in the form of James Carroll, Apirana Ngata and others, worked from the turn of the century to the 1940s from within the colonial establishment, often in cabinet positions. James Carroll served as Minister of

Native Affairs from 1899 until 1912 and even served briefly as acting Prime Minister in 1909 and 1911.

Thus, as the twentieth century dawned, the historical relations between Indigenous people and settlers – both on the ground and with government agencies – significantly guided the behaviours, actions and decisions of Indigenous people. This is not to say that they only reacted to settler and government actions. Rather, the logic of survival meant that Indigenous agency and autonomy would have to manoeuvre within, or challenge when feasible, the frameworks set by the settler states. The twentieth century would witness new technologies, new ideologies – including those of race and human rights – and new types of wars. First Nations, Māori, Native Americans and Aboriginal and Torres Strait Islander Australians would have to continue adapting, accommodating and deciding what roles they would play when such occasions arose.

# 2    Indigenous Peoples and Settler Militaries, 1900–1945

By the early twentieth century, with exceptions, Indigenous peoples had largely transitioned from autonomous nations to subjugate and subordinate minorities, whether wards or citizens. Through this evolution, continuity survived in some of the alliance traditions developed from the 1600s to 1880s. These had become part of the array of survival strategies adopted by such communities to strengthen their own political situations and, increasingly, to manage their dealings with settler states. Henceforth, when Indigenous men and women went to war, it would be as soldiers in settler armies rather than independent warriors of autonomous nations. The new century would provide ample opportunities for such Indigenous military service, particularly in the world wars that would involve all four of these settler states.

The precedents actually predate the Great War, involving smaller colonial conflicts such as the Spanish-American War (1898), Philippine-American War (1899–1902) and the Second Anglo-Boer War (1899–1902). None of these could match the scale and salience of the First World War for establishing or entrenching Indigenous war service in settler militaries as an important reality. Each side's collective memories and interpretation of the war experience shaped subsequent relationships between Indigenous peoples and settler states, casting long shadows and shaping events when global war again broke out in 1939. This chapter explores this early twentieth-century era and its implications for Native Americans, First Nations, Māori, Aboriginal and Torres Strait Islander Australians during the Second World War. Finally, this chapter surveys the Second World War experience, in brief, providing an overview of the respective nations' dominant war histories both at home and abroad.

## From Indigenous Warriors to Indigenous Soldiers

In order to unravel the motivations for Indigenous voluntarism, we need to consider the long historical context of Indigenous people allying themselves with, or fighting on behalf of, settler societies.

Considered in these contexts, Indigenous voluntarism does not appear aberrant, but rather an outgrowth of a lengthy tradition of collaborative war service. Almost like military service, in the mid to late 1800s, the various Australian colonies established native police forces, which were renowned for their brutal pacification of resistance on the frontiers.[1] There were various segregated scout units along the American western frontiers and Native Americans served on both sides in the American Revolution and Civil War.[2]

By the First World War, US military officials determined that Native American servicemen should be integrated with mainstream units where the tradition of military service on behalf of the United States continued. In comparison, while there were fewer opportunities for Canadian First Nations to renew allegiance with the British Crown through military service during the nineteenth century, oral traditions sustained Indigenous connections to past military relationships.[3] Alliance traditions rapidly developed during Māori-Pākehā cooperative military activity in the New Zealand Wars and had significant long-term repercussions on Māori-Pākehā relations and on Māori military service in the world wars.

Around the turn of the twentieth century, Indigenous men across the four countries began formally to enlist and fight as soldiers of settler society expeditionary forces. In the United States, integrated Native American soldiers served with Theodore Roosevelt's 'Rough Riders' in Cuba and with American forces in the Philippines and China.[4] Other Apache scouts worked with the US Army in pursuit of Pancho Villa during the Mexican Revolution.[5] The British Dominions had begun sending contingents of their volunteer soldiers to partake in imperial military campaigns in Africa as early as 1885. More important for all three Dominions was the Second Anglo-Boer War, 1899–1902, to which each sent substantial contingents. While the British were increasingly keen for Dominion troops, Imperial authorities were not eager for Indigenous

[1] Jonathan Richards, *The Secret War: A True History of Queensland's Native Police* (St Lucia: University of Queensland Press, 2008).

[2] See Thomas Dunlay, *Wolves for the Blue Soldiers: Indian Scouts and Auxiliaries with the United States Army, 1860–90* (Lincoln and London: University of Nebraska Press, 1982); Mark van de Logt, *War Party in Blue: Pawnee Indian Scouts in the United States Army, 1864–1877* (Norman: University of Oklahoma Press, 2010).

[3] See Carl Benn, *The Iroquois in the War of 1812* (Toronto: University of Toronto Press, 1998); P. Whitney Lackenbauer, et al., *A Commemorative History of Aboriginal People in the Canadian Military* (Ottawa: Department of National Defence, 2010).

[4] Thomas Britten, *American Indians in World War I: At Home and at War* (Albuquerque: University of New Mexico Press), 25–26.

[5] James Shannon, "With the Apache Scouts in Mexico," *Journal of the United States Cavalry Association* XXVII, no. 114 (April 1917): 539–557.

soldiers to be amongst them.[6] Despite many offers of service from First Nations' communities across Canada, the government largely followed London's lead and privileged European-Canadians. John Brant-Sero, a Mohawk, ran afoul of this policy:

I have just returned from South Africa, disappointed in many respects, though I do not wish these lines to be understood as a grievance. I went to that country from Canada hoping that I might enlist in one of the mounted rifles; however, not being a man of European desent [sic], I was refused to do active service in Her Majesty's cause as did my forefathers in Canada ... I was too genuine a Canadian.[7]

Nevertheless, a few First Nations' men managed to skirt the rules.[8] In New Zealand, too, Māori community and parliamentary leaders made numerous offers of Māori men to New Zealand and Imperial governments. Premier Richard Seddon even planned to send the Sixth Contingent half-filled with Māori soldiers, but all such efforts were to no avail in the face of Imperial opposition. The raising of such expeditionary forces for overseas conflicts provided important precedents for the Dominions and the United States, as well as for Indigenous communities when a major European war broke out in 1914.

### The Great War

The Great War brought Indigenous military service on a much vaster scale and of a far higher profile than at any time previously. In Australia, this was not so much reinvigorating existing traditions of service as birthing a new precedent – the inclusion of Aboriginal men in the Australian Imperial Force. By contrast, the war provided North American and New Zealand Indigenous populations with the inspiration and opportunity to proclaim anew, to settler societies and to themselves, their loyalty to the country and/or Crown and demonstrate their martial vitality as a people. In New Zealand, Māori leaders proclaimed:

[The] Maori Race of Te Aotearoa and Te Waipounamu had a reputation for bravery in his fights of ancient days and also during the wars against the White Race.

[6] Carman Miller, *Painting the Map Red: Canada and the South African War, 1899–1902* (Montreal and Kingston, Canadian War Museum and McGill-Queen's University Press, 1993); Ian McGibbon, ed., *The Oxford Companion to New Zealand Military History* (Auckland: Oxford University Press, 2000); Henry Reynolds, *Unnecessary Wars* (Sydney: NewSouth Publishing, 2016); John Maynard, "'Let us go' ... it's a 'Blackfellows War' – Aborigines and the Boer War," *Aboriginal History* 39 (2015): 143–162.
[7] Quoted in John Moses, with Donald Graves and Warren Sinclair, *A Sketch Account of Aboriginal Peoples in the Canadian Military* (Ottawa: DND Canada, 2004), 61.
[8] Timothy Winegard, *For King and Kanata: Canadian Indians and the First World War* (Winnipeg: University of Manitoba Press, 2012), 37–38; McGibbon, *Oxford Companion to New Zealand Military History*, 296.

Wherefore during the first days of the present war, the people of both islands waited to hear the voice of the Maori people calling 'Let the Maori Race also go to put out the fire that is raging afar off'. They did not have to wait long ... The most important feature is this, the voice of such a small race is heard crying out to be allowed to enter the war of great nations, of the world.[9]

Among North American Indigenous populations, the Great War offered a chance for renewal, not only of traditions of military alliance but also of a warrior ethos in those communities that retained this cultural imperative. Especially among North American plains Indigenous peoples, the war offered opportunities that had been scarce in the aftermath of settlement on reserves. L. James Dempsey argues that warriors' status as knowledge-bearers was significant for the performance of ceremony. Yet, the decades of peace meant that young men could not fulfil the requirements to become warriors just as the population of Elders was dwindling, leaving gaps in the social life of the plains nations.[10] Thomas Britten argues that Native Americans volunteered for a variety of important and compelling reasons, including the same ones as other racial and ethnic groups: patriotism, to protect their country, notions of democracy and liberty. Of course, how such motivations drove Native Americans differed from other ethnic groups.[11] The diverse rationales and influences on Indigenous participation are worth emphasising, and the notion of variability within nations applies across the individual Indigenous experiences of the war.

Whatever the reasons, Indigenous men volunteered or were drafted in the thousands to serve in the national expeditionary forces of all four settler states. Estimates suggest that by the First World War's end, approximately 2,816 Māori, 1,000 Aboriginal Australians, 4,050 Canadian First Nations and between 12,000 and 12,500 Native Americans had served.[12] Initially, though, the Dominion military establishments proved unwilling to accommodate Indigenous desires to participate. In New Zealand, authorities expressed the British government's wish that Māori not partake in wars between white races.[13] In Australia, revisions to the Defence Act in 1909 added the stipulation that 'Persons who are not substantially of European origin or descent' were to be exempted from

---

[9] Chris Pugsley, *Te Hokowhitu a Tu: The Maori Pioneer Battalion in the First World War* (Auckland: Reed Publishing, 1995), 20.

[10] L. James Dempsey, *Warriors of the King: Prairie Indians in World War I* (Regina: Canadian Plains Research Centre, 1999), 47.

[11] Britten, *American Indians in World War I*, 63.

[12] Duncan Campbell Scott, *1919 – Report of the Deputy Superintendent General for Indian Affairs: The Indians and the Great War – House of Commons Sessional Paper No. 27* (Ottawa: King's Printer, 1920); Britten, *American Indians in World War I*, 84.

[13] Pugsley, *Te Hokowhitu a Tu*, 20.

compulsory training.[14] Although these provisions related to *compulsory* service, authorities were quick to apply them to voluntary enlistment as well. Nevertheless, as historian John Maynard has recently uncovered, the majority of Aboriginal servicemen still managed to enlist in the early years of the war.[15] Most were light complexioned, so-called 'half-castes'. In May 1917, the Army loosened its racial barriers expressly to permit 'half-castes' with one white parent to enlist, leading to another boost in Indigenous recruitment, especially from Queensland.[16] A similar pattern of loosening constraints in 1915 emerged in New Zealand and Canada, with the sailing of the first Māori contingents in February and September and the Canadian Army's sanctioning of Indian enlistment in December.[17] The United States entered the war only in 1917, but Native Americans experienced their own challenges in the draft and volunteering due to the ambiguities surrounding their citizenship status. The American military was segregated between black and white; Native Americans, not easily placed in this dichotomy, usually were integrated into white units.

In all four countries, the First World War was a gendered experience; none of the four countries had separate women's services in that conflict, though women could serve as nurses. Only one Aboriginal Australian woman is known to have served, and she actually served with Canada's No. 41 Ambulance Train.[18] From the United States, there were fourteen known Native American women who served in the Army Nursing Corps, two of whom served overseas.[19] Given the (relatively) wider educational opportunities available for Indigenous women in the other settler nations,

[14] Australia, Defence Act 1909, section 138(1)(b).

[15] John Maynard, "The First World War," in *Serving Our Country: Indigenous Australians, War, Defence and Citizenship*, ed. Joan Beaumont and Allison Cadzow (Sydney: NewSouth Publishing, 2018), 76.

[16] Noah Riseman, "Enduring Silences, Enduring Prejudices: Australian Aboriginal Participation in the First World War," in *Endurance and the First World War: Experience and Legacies in New Zealand and Australia*, ed. David Monger, Katie Pickles and Sarah Murray (Newcastle upon Tyne: Cambridge Scholars Publishing, 2014), 178–195; Rod Pratt, "Queensland's Aborigines in the First AIF," in *Aboriginal Peoples and Military Participation: Canadian & International Perspectives*, ed. P. Whitney Lackenbauer, R. Scott Sheffield and Craig Leslie Mantle (Kingston, ON: Canadian Defence Academy Press, 2007), 223; David Huggonson, "Aboriginal Diggers of the 9th Brigade, First AIF," *Journal of the Royal Australian Historical Society*, 79, no. 3–4 (1993): 219.

[17] Pugsley, *Te Hokowhitu a Tu*, 85; Winegard, *For King and Kanata*, 53, 60–61.

[18] Sophie Verass, "The fascinating life of WWI's only serving Indigenous woman, Marion Leane Smith," *National Indigenous Television*, 25 April 2017, www.sbs.com.au/nitv/article/2017/04/25/fascinating-life-wwis-only-serving-indigenous-woman-marion-leane-smith.

[19] William Meadows, "Native American 'Warriors' in the US Armed Forces," in *Inclusion in the American Military: A Force for Diversity*, ed. David E. Rohall, Morten G. Ender, and Michael D. Matthews (Lanham, MD: Lexington Books, 2017), 98.

presumably, there were also a small number of female Māori and First Nations' nurses, though histories to date have not addressed this topic.

The shape of Indigenous military service took distinct forms for some soldiers. Māori served within segregated contingents at Gallipoli that later were consolidated into the Maori Pioneer Battalion, a combat engineer unit that served with distinction on the Western Front. Almost 2,700 Māori served and 1,070 became casualties.[20] The Canadian military, too, flirted with the idea of segregated First Nations infantry and labour units. One of these, the 107th Battalion, saw action after converting to a pioneer battalion but was subsequently broken up in an engineering reorganisation.[21] Otherwise, most First Nations men served as individuals amongst many settler units, with a few serving in segregated lumber and other labour units.[22] While Aboriginal soldiers fought and died with their settler comrades, they never took their place in the ranks of the national heroes. Native Americans served in regular US military units as individuals, though a number of units of varying sizes contained concentrations or even majorities of Indigenous soldiers.[23] Regardless, scholars suggest that Native American soldiers were killed in action at a much higher rate than the 1 per cent average for the American Expeditionary Force, perhaps 5 per cent, with some communities such as the Pawnee suffering 14 per cent killed from their young men that served.[24] The war service of Native Americans managed both to alter Americans' perceptions of Indigenous people while also reinforcing long-standing martial race and warrior stereotypes.

For the Dominions, especially, national mythologies emerged out of the First World War experience. In Australia and New Zealand, this is known as the Anzac mythology – deriving from the Australian and New Zealand Army Corps. The ANZACs first landed at Gallipoli in present-day Turkey on 25 April 1915, part of a larger force aiming to secure control of the Dardanelles and knock the Ottoman Empire out of the war. The Gallipoli Campaign was a disaster, yet amidst the adversity the ANZACs, so it was said, fought bravely against the odds and forged the bonds of mateship with one another. As the ANZACs became popularised in the press, the Anzac legend emerged and would continue to dominate much of Australian and, to a lesser extent, New Zealand

[20] Timothy Winegard, *Indigenous Peoples of the British Dominions and the First World War*, 230–231.
[21] Stephen Bell, "The 107th 'Timber Wolf' Battalion at Hill 70," *Canadian Military History* 5, no. 1 (Spring 1996): 73–78.
[22] Winegard, *For King and Kanata*, 6.
[23] Britten, *American Indians in World War I*, 74–75.
[24] Russell Barsh, "American Indians in the Great War," *Ethnohistory* 38, no. 3 (Summer 1991): 278, 298; Britten, *American Indians in World War I*, 82.

ideas of masculine nationalism for the next 100 years.[25] There were
Aboriginal and Māori soldiers within the ranks of the ANZACs, but
the Anzac legend did not include them. Instead, the ANZAC identity
has generally been a white conception of heterosexual, hegemonic masculinity, used by politicians, ex-servicemen and pundits alike to define
membership within the Australian nation.[26] Mark Sheftall argues, 'that
the type of narrative represented by the Anzac legend was peculiar to
Australia and New Zealand only in name ... and in very specific characteristics'.[27] Canada, too, developed a comparable 'mythic version' of its
war experience, for similar cultural and nation-building reasons and subsequently vested symbolically in the victory and national memorial built
upon the crest of Vimy Ridge.[28] In the United States, while there was
some mythology around the 'Dough Boy' soldiers who went to Europe
to defend democracy, the myths did not develop into such an enduring nationalist tradition because the United States already had enduring
mythologies dating back to the American Revolution.

While much of the literature and the popular memory of Indigenous
people during the Great War speaks of their voluntarism, military service and collaboration with settler societies, it is worth remembering
that many Indigenous communities remained indifferent or hostile to
the state or participating in its defence. Within the living memory of
many peoples, they had been autonomous entities, sometimes bitterly
embattled with the expanding colonial society. The scars of historic battles encumbered wartime relations in New Zealand where the traditionally allied Māori iwis provided the recruits for the Māori contingents
and Pioneer Battalion, and those who had fought settler forces in the
1860s–70s and suffered land confiscations remained aloof and hostile to
any role in the Pākehā's war. Princess Te Puea emerged as a leading figure
amongst Kingite iwi in the Waikato–Tainui region and remained resolute in leading passive resistance when the state imposed conscription on

25 See Marilyn Lake and Henry Reynolds, *What's Wrong with Anzac? The Militarisation
of Australian History* (Sydney: University of New South Wales Press, 2010); Carolyn
Holbrook, *Anzac: The Unauthorised Biography* (Sydney: NewSouth Publishing, 2014).
26 See Graham Seal, *Inventing Anzac: The Digger and National Mythology* (St Lucia: University
of Queensland Press in association with the API Network and Curtin University of
Technology, 2004); Frank Bongiorno, "Anzac and the Politics of Inclusion," in *Nation,
Memory and Great War Commemoration Mobilizing the Past in Europe, Australia and New
Zealand*, ed. Shanti Sumartojo and Ben Wellings (Oxford: Peter Lang AG, 2014), 81–97.
27 Mark Sheftall, "Mythologising the Dominion Fighting Man: Australian and Canadian
Narrative of the First World War Soldier, 1914–1939," *Australian Historical Studies* 46,
no. 1 (March 2015): 81–99.
28 Jonathan Vance, *Death So Noble: Memory, Meaning and the First World War* (Vancouver:
University of British Columbia Press, 1997); Tim Cook, *Vimy: The Battle and the Legend*
(Toronto: Allen Lane, 2017).

these resistant Māori communities in 1918. More than 100 men were gaoled for refusing to serve during this resistance, which created a potent legacy of bitterness.[29]

Conscription became a lightning rod for Indigenous opposition in Canada as well when it was imposed in August 1917. There, though, loud protests managed to secure a limited exemption for Status Indians from overseas combat service in early 1918.[30] Even before this, many First Nations responses to the war were characterised more by indifference than enthusiastic participation.[31] The United States instituted a draft in 1917 with all men, ages twenty-one to thirty-one, required to report to local boards, including Native Americans, but only those with citizenship were actually liable. The BIA administered the registration process because of pragmatic challenges and the complications of uncertain citizenship status, which generated confusion and frustration in many Native American communities. Draft resistance was relatively uncommon and widely dispersed but could be intense in some communities.[32] Australia held two plebiscites on introducing conscription, both of which failed. Even if they had passed, the provisions of the Defence Act, presumably, would have excluded Aboriginal people from conscription.

### Interwar

While service in the First World War had won Indigenous soldiers recognition and inclusivion among their comrades, much of this was lost in translation when they returned to civilian life. The one exception to this broader pattern was the gradual granting of citizenship to Native Americans, which had clear connections to their Great War service.[33] Citizenship as status, granted by legislation in 1919, 1923 and then 1940, did not mean equal rights for Native Americans. Eleven states continued to restrict Native Americans from voting until the 1940s and 1950s, and citizenship did not grant religious freedom, civil rights or economic opportunity.[34] Otherwise, Aboriginal Australians, First Nations and Māori fell back into existing racial, social and economic structures

---

[29] Michael King, *Te Puea: A Life* (Auckland: Reed, 2003, first published in 1977), 88–97.

[30] Winegard, *For King and Kanata*, 92–103. Order-in-Council, P.C. 111, passed by the War Cabinet, created this limited exemption in January 1918, based primarily on Status Indians' lack of the federal franchise.

[31] Robert Talbot, "'It Would be Best to Leave Us Alone': First Nations Responses to the Canadian War Effort, 1914–1918," *Journal of Canadian Studies* 45, no. 1 (Winter 2011): 90–120.

[32] Britten, *American Indians in World War I*, 66–71.

[33] Ibid., 181.

[34] Al Carroll, *Medicine Bags and Dog Tags*, 116.

that marginalised them and often muffled their voices in the countries for which they had risked so much. Indeed, in Australia, repatriation schemes such as land grants or annuities generally precluded Aboriginal participation or the state protection regimes usually restricted Aboriginal people and even their families' access.[35] In New Zealand, while Māori had the same entitlements as Pākehā veterans, the communal nature of Māori land ownership meant that few were eligible to take up land grants.[36]

Nevertheless, some Indigenous men continued, where permitted, serving through the interwar years in regular military forces or in militia, National Guard or Territorial service. The close camaraderie and decline of racial prejudice experienced in military service during the Great War was less evident in peacetime. The Royal New Zealand Navy in 1936 sent a note to the Minister of Defence reminding him that though 'the New Zealand [Naval] Division cannot refuse to accept a Maori provided, he is up to all requirements ... it is very unusual to find in the Navy individuals who are not the sons of European Parents ... [and] so far as is known no Maori boys have ever succeeded in reaching the high standard of those boys actually selected'.[37] The New Zealand Army was likewise unenthusiastic about Māori service even as it set about expanding the Territorial Force in 1939; as one report noted, the 'better type of European – the type of man we want in the Territorials – will not join up in a platoon which includes Maori'.[38]

More broadly, the trends in the relations between Indigenous populations and settler states moved in diverging directions during the interwar years. The United States and New Zealand both witnessed substantial policy disruption and change, particularly in the 1930s with the Indian New Deal and the election of the Labour Party, respectively. The American assimilation policies crafted under the Dawes Act were still in place, though less prominent by the 1920s. Still, speculators continued to target land where there was suspected mineral or oil wealth, leaving Native American reservations vulnerable under allotment. In 1933, President

---

[35] Riseman, "Enduring Silences, Enduring Prejudices," 188–193; Patricia Grimshaw and Hannah Loney, "'Doing Their Bit Helping Make Australia Free': Mothers of Aboriginal Diggers and the Assertion of Indigenous Rights," *Provenance: The Journal of Public Record Office Victoria* 14 (2015): 3–16.

[36] Ashley Gould, "From Taiaha to Ko: Repatriation and Land Settlement for Maori Soldiers in New Zealand after the First World War," *War & Society* 28, no. 2 (2009): 49–83.

[37] Memorandum from Naval Secretary, 17 April 1936, ANZ, N 1 308 13/3/1 Personnel – Recruiting – Entry Maoris 1920–37.

[38] Memorandum for: The Honourable Minister of Defence, 31 July 1939, ANZ, AD1, 226-19-7, vol. 1, 1935–1941.

Franklin Roosevelt appointed John Collier as the Commissioner of the BIA, ushering in a decade of significant reform. Collier introduced the Indian New Deal, legislated under the Indian Reorganization Act of 1934. Among the Indian New Deal reforms, the most significant was the end to allotment, return to communal ownership of Native American reservation land (held in trust by the US government) and the implementation of self-government on Native American reservations. Of course, Collier has come under criticism as well. For instance, to be eligible for self-government, tribes had to develop governing structures operating within a Western framework, and Collier subscribed to essentialist ideas of Indianness. Even so, Collier's reforms represented a significantly more enlightened approach to Indian affairs and a hiatus from assimilation policies.[39]

New Zealand governments changed several times through these decades, but in most of them, Māori influence was present indirectly through sympathetic Pākehā leaders like Gordon Coates or Michael Savage or directly through Māori cabinet ministers. Whether inside or outside the Pākehā state, according to James Belich, 'Protest and co-operation, engagement and disengagement, and a mix of each, were among their strategies; and [James] Carroll, Ratana, Te Puea and, above all, [Apirana] Ngata, were among their leaders.'[40] The results were uneven, but they produced positives for Māori in land claims settlements, state-supported agricultural development, improving public health and social welfare and enhanced rights, especially after the advent of the Labour government in 1935.

By contrast, the interwar years were less dramatic, bipartisan and more a 'muddling through' period where assimilation policies accelerated in Canada and Australia. In Canada, the aftermath of the Great War witnessed the high-water mark of increasingly coercive assimilation policies in the early 1920s, which had greatly damaged both the relationship with First Nations and the economic, cultural and political well-being of their communities. Through the later 1920s and 1930s, a more custodial administration developed. First Nations people, largely segregated, unheard and ignored by a Canadian populace distracted by its own challenges during the Depression, struggled to survive. In Australia, through the course of the war, all remaining states had established protection regimes akin to those discussed in the previous chapter. By the 1930s, realising both that Aboriginal people were not dying out and concerned

---

[39] Rebecca Robbins, "Self-Determination and Subordination: The Past, Present, and Future of American Indian Governance," in *The State of Native America: Genocide, Colonization, and Resistance*, ed M. Annette Jaimes (Boston: South End Press, 1992), 87–121.

[40] James Belich, *Paradise Reforged: A History of the New Zealanders* (Auckland: Allen Lane, 2001), 206.

about the rising population of Aboriginal people of mixed descent, state chief protectors turned their attention more aggressively toward assimilation. The most extreme example of this was in Western Australia where the notorious Chief Protector A.O. Neville proposed crude eugenic ideas of 'breeding out the black' over a few generations. At the first Commonwealth-State Native Welfare Conference in 1937, representatives of all states except Tasmania came together to discuss a coherent approach to Indigenous affairs. Following Neville's lead, the conference determined: 'that the destiny of the natives of aboriginal origin, but not of the full blood, lies in their ultimate absorption by the people of the Commonwealth, and it therefore recommends that all efforts be directed to that end'. Furthermore, the practice of child removal, already in place since the late 1800s, would continue to play a role to facilitate this assimilation agenda.[41]

Indigenous people continued to resist assimilation and other discriminatory treatment during the interwar period. In the United States, organisations such as the Mission Indian Federation formed, attacking the BIA, denouncing allotment policy, condemning mistreatment of Indian children in boarding schools and also building strategic alliances with white allies.[42] In Australia, the 1920s and 1930s marked the formation of the first Aboriginal rights organisations, including the Australian Aboriginal Progressive Association, Australian Aborigines' League, Native Union and Aborigines' Progressive Association. These organisations all, in their respective states, advocated for the abolition or reform of the protection boards, end to segregation, equal treatment under the law and an end to child removal. The interwar years saw some Indigenous activism in Canada as well, especially in the early 1920s with the ongoing bitter battle over Aboriginal land rights in British Columbia and the formation of the League of Indians in Ontario, the first Indigenous organisation with national aspirations.[43] Canadian Indigenous political organisations struggled through a nadir in the late 1920s and 1930s. Māori political action was primarily directed through hapu and iwi avenues around land consolidation, development and compensation during the interwar years. Pan-tribal or super tribal groups like the King Movement or the Ratana Church were active and vocal critics of the Pākehā state, but both would

---

[41] Australia, Human Rights and Equal Opportunities Commission, *Bringing Them Home*, 25–150.

[42] John Maynard, "On the Political 'Warpath': Native Americans and Australian Aborigines after the First World War," *Wicazo Sa Review* 32, no. 1 (2017): 49.

[43] Paul Tennant, *Aboriginal People and Politics: The Indian Land Question in British Columbia, 1849–1989* (Vancouver: University of British Columbia Press, 1990); Peter Kulchyski, "A Considerable Unrest: F.O. Loft and the League of Indians," *Native Studies Review* 1, no. 1–2 (1988): 95–117.

make an alliance and work with the Labour governments of the later 1930s.[44]

A commonality across many of these Indigenous rights organisations was the presence of either First World War veterans or families of veterans and deceased soldiers. In addition, these organisations regularly invoked war service in their calls for Indigenous rights. For instance, at the 1920 Convention of Mission Indians of Southern California, Chief Red Fox reflected that 'our people have fought under the stars and stripes for American freedom, why can't we as a people enjoy all that freedom'.[45] In 1938, Aboriginal activist William Cooper wrote to the prime minister:

... at least a thousand Aborigines were among the first to enlist in the defence of the British Empires in the 1914–18 war and for which Empire they gave their lives.

It was a thankless task for them, no thanks being given for the valuable services rendered. We get no encouragement, and the result of this neglect appears to be that we are looked upon as a useless race and greatly misrepresented thereby.[46]

The First World War and Indigenous people's post-war shattered dreams thus weighed heavily just as conflict was stirring again. These experiences would influence how Indigenous communities responded once again.

### Second World War

The German invasion of Poland, followed by the British declaration of war in early September 1939, brought the Dominions into a global confrontation for the second time in a generation. Australia accepted Britain's declaration as its own, but New Zealand almost immediately, and Canada a week later issued their own declarations of war. Just over two years later, the United States was drawn into the maelstrom of war in the wake of Japan's attack on Pearl Harbor. All four countries rose to the challenge of a total war that would demand much of each society in blood, sweat and resources. In each case the effect was broad, deep and transformative, constructed as a coming-of-age story for the Dominions and as the emergence of the United States as a superpower. Each stretched itself to build huge military forces while simultaneously ramping up the wartime economy. Men and women in the hundreds of

---

[44] Richard Hill, *State Authority, Indigenous Autonomy: Crown-Maori Relations in New Zealand, 1900–1950* (Wellington: Victoria University Press, 2004), chapter 5.

[45] Quoted in Maynard, "On the Political 'Warpath,'" 56.

[46] William Cooper, Secretary, Australian Aborigines' League, to the Prime Minister, Joseph Lyons, 31 March 1938, reproduced in Bain Attwood and Andrew Markus, *Thinking Black: William Cooper and the Australian Aborigines' League* (Canberra: Aboriginal Studies Press, 2004), 92–93.

thousands donned uniforms and often shipped out for distant shores to take the fight to their enemies. Booming economies, short of labour, opened their doors to those usually on the fringes of the workforce: women, ethnic minorities and Indigenous peoples. In many ways war galvanised and drew together these societies in a spirit of wartime solidarity and national crusade, loosening previous sociocultural constraints around race, gender and class. Darker or less savoury episodes, like the wholesale incarceration of those of Japanese, Italian or German ancestry, were creatively left out of this upbeat narrative. These parallel experiences were evident in varying degrees in what remains the 'good war' for Americans, Australians, Canadians and New Zealanders.

While there were many parallels, each country engaged in the war in different ways, shaped by their histories, geographies and capabilities. For instance, Canada's war was almost entirely Europe-Atlantic focussed, with relatively few of its people or military resources involved in the Pacific theatre, in spite of its long exposed western coast. Though its peacetime military was tiny and largely ill-equipped in 1939, it would build up a substantial overseas ground force of five divisions, with total enlistments topping 700,000. Canada's soldiers initially defended Britain and were not heavily engaged until 1943 when significant forces fought in the Italian campaign and, thereafter, in Normandy and Northwest Europe. In addition to this, Canada invested heavily in building the Royal Canadian Air Force (RCAF) and the Royal Canadian Navy (RCN) from minuscule pre-war cadres to the fourth largest air force and navy in the world by VE-Day. New Zealand shipped the bulk of its military assets to fight in the Mediterranean theatre, including 104,000 men with the 2nd New Zealand Expeditionary Force (2NZEF), which fought extensively throughout North Africa, Greece, Crete and Italy. An under-strength 3rd NZ Division did see limited service in the Pacific, when the country found itself on the edge of the Pacific War and thus directly threatened. Australia's war was like a play in two acts. Act 1 saw the 2nd Austrian Imperial Force (2AIF) largely deployed to the Mediterranean theatre alongside their Kiwi cousins, until Japan's entry into the war. Act 2 began with the Australian government pulling all its troops back to Australia in early 1942 and expanded its forces to a peak of 476,000 to defend its imperilled north and eventually drive Japanese forces from Papua New Guinea and Indonesia. Thus its war was, by turn, both European and Pacific in nature.

Only the United States had the population and immense resources to pursue the Second World War on both European and Pacific fronts simultaneously, with more than twelve million under arms by 1945. The American effort in Europe focused primarily on North Africa in 1942–3, followed by the invasion of Italy and the D-Day landing at Normandy in June 1944.

From that foothold in France, US and Allied forces drove into Germany, meeting Soviet forces at the Elbe River on 25 April 1945, two weeks before Germany surrendered on 8 May 1945. In the Pacific Theatre, American forces halted the Japanese advance at Midway, the Battle of the Coral Sea and Guadalcanal in 1942–3, then turned the tide through a strategy of island-hopping toward Japan. The atomic bombs dropped on Hiroshima and Nagasaki on 6 and 9 August 1945 brought the Pacific War to an end, with Japan formally surrendering on 15 August 1945. The American war experience, for ground, air and sea forces was thus more diverse than for any of the Dominions, but for each, the war effort represented very nearly a maximum possible as a proportion of the population.

Within the broader war story of each settler state, Indigenous populations experienced their own war in ways that varied in nature, scope and intensity. In the United States, Native Americans were presented with the institution of the draft before the country even entered the conflict. While some tribes opposed compulsory service, the majority appear to have viewed their inclusion in the national draft as a symbol of inclusion and citizenship. By November 1941, nearly 42,000 Indigenous men, aged 21–35, had registered, almost two-thirds of eligible Native American males.[47] At the same time, thousands were already voluntarily enlisted and serving prior to Pearl Harbor. This robust response to the national call to arms was sustained through the war, with roughly 25,000 Native American men and women from reservations in uniform. Almost all of these enlisted and served as individuals within mainstream military units; although, there were secret experiments with segregated communication units such as the Marine Corps' Navajo Code Talkers. As a result, most Native Americans found their military service a powerfully acculturative experience, though many also experienced cultural reaffirmation and renewal. Native Americans served in every branch and theatre of war in which American forces were engaged, earning promotions and citations for bravery. These were the most visible manifestations of a broader sense of acceptance and respect Native American service people felt from their comrades while in the military.

In Canada, there was initial uncertainty about whether First Nations people could serve in the military, but this quickly gave way to broad acceptance of Indigenous recruits, at least in the Army. The RCAF and RCN both retained racial restrictions in their recruitment policies that denied recruits not 'of pure European descent and of the white race'.[48]

---

[47] Kenneth Townsend, *World War II and the American Indian* (Albuquerque: University of New Mexico Press, 2000), 61.

[48] See Machlachlan to Camsell, 18 March 1941, Directorate of History and Heritage (hereafter DHist), 112.3H1.009/D293 and DHist, 75/347, 25-04-1939.

Reaction to military service varied widely across the country, from First Nation to First Nation; most supported voluntary service, with some communities achieving high enlistment rates and others providing almost no recruits. Canada did enact conscription initially just for home defence in the summer of 1940, but the length of service and where conscripts could be sent was gradually extended and made more dangerous as the war progressed. Almost uniformly, First Nations peoples opposed conscription, with protest and some resistance across the country for the duration of the war. In 1944, conscription was finally extended to shipping thousands of conscripts to the front lines in Europe; the government extended a limited exemption to a minority of First Nations in a select few treaty regions. As in the American case, First Nations were integrated into Canadian units rather than kept separate, and many recalled the experience as the first and last time in their lives when they felt respected and equal.

*Figure 2.1* Lieutenant-General Sir Bernard Montgomery investing Corporal H. E. Brant of the Hastings and Prince Edward Regiment with the Military Medal. Catanzaro, Italy. 13 September 1943 (Capt. Frank Royal/DND/LAC/PA-130065).

In Australia, the Second World War experience was much an echo of the First World War, but with some variations after Japan's entry. Regulations initially adopted rules against enlisting people not 'substantially of European origin or descent', but of course interpretations of this clause on the ground meant that some men managed to enlist. After the attack on Pearl Harbor and the direct threat to Australia, these rules remained in place but local recruiters, for the most part, ignored them when presented with an able-bodied person. This war did include auxiliary women's services, so Indigenous women, too, served, and like the men, they served in integrated units. Where there were variations from the First World War was in the north; there the Japanese threatened a sparsely populated region in which Aboriginal and Torres Strait Islander people made up a significant proportion of the few residents. The Army created two formal Indigenous units – the Torres Strait Light Infantry Battalion and Northern Territory Special Reconnaissance Unit – to defend the Torres Strait and Arnhem Land respectively while Indigenous residents also contributed informally through labour camps, coast watching and patrols. By war's end, an estimated 4,000 Aboriginal people and 850 Torres Strait Islanders had served in the armed forces, and this does not include the hundreds more who contributed in the north in non-enlisted capacities.

Māori men and some women would step forward in support of the New Zealand war effort in extremely large numbers, some 16,000 all tolled.[49] The Māori total includes the more than 3,600 men who served overseas with the 28th (Maori) Battalion, as well as other active service personnel, Territorial soldiers and members of the Home Guard. Political leaders from many Māori communities pressed the New Zealand government to create a segregated combat unit for them, building on the precedent of the Maori Pioneer Battalion during the Great War. The 28th (Maori) Battalion was the result: initially led by mostly Pākehā officers, the Battalion was increasingly commanded by Māori officers and fought extensively through North Africa and the Mediterranean with the 2nd NZ Division. During its hard-fought campaigns, it earned wide acclaim in New Zealand and elsewhere for its tremendous record of battlefield success. Māori recruitment officers controlled enlistment for this unit, and they were successful in raising sufficient reinforcements to ensure that Māori remained exempt after New Zealand instituted conscription in 1940. This was essential after the bitter divisiveness of conscription for Waikato Māori in 1918 and enabled greater unity amongst Māori in

---

[49] See "Māori and the Second World War: Page 3 – Achievements," *New Zealand History*, available from www.nzhistory.net.nz/war/maori-and-the-second-world-war/achievements.

*Figure 2.2*  Maori Battalion prepare to leave Rotorua during World War II. A man and a woman hold hands in the foreground. John Pascoe Collection, Alexander Turnbull Library.

the Second World War. While Māori served throughout the New Zealand forces, both at home and abroad, the 28th Maori Battalion became the face of their wartime contributions and the subsequent popular memory of the Māori war effort.

The home front experiences across these four Indigenous populations and the post-war transitions share enough parallels that they need not be canvassed here separately. For those Indigenous people that remained on the home front during the war a series of prevalent themes emerge, including a decline of overt prejudice, expanding economic opportunities, mobility and urbanisation and the intrusion of settler state and militaries into heretofore remote sheltered regions. Indigenous individuals, families and communities faced difficult decisions about whether they wished to engage in the settler war effort and, if so, in what fashion and to what degree. This voluntarism and collaboration was sometimes contrasted by Indigenous protest and resistance to particular government measures. Authorities also expressed anxieties about Indigenous women moving to cities and entering the workforce, with concerns about their sexuality especially heightened with the American presence in Australia, New Zealand and parts of Canada. On the whole, the home front efforts of Indigenous peoples garnered publicity and appreciation from settler society and governments. The consequence of Indigenous military and civilian contributions to the cause was a post-war political climate open to policy reform in Indigenous affairs in each of these countries. Though the timing, nature and significance of the legislative and policy change varied, the war helped in shifting attitudes and expectations on both Indigenous and settler sides of these relationships. These changes set the shape of Indigenous-settler relations and negotiations through the latter half of the twentieth century.

### Conclusion

This brief survey across the four countries showcases how the Indigenous experiences of, and contributions to, the Second World War in the United States, Canada, Australia and New Zealand arose out of a long historical context. Settler colonialism continued to operate as a structure in all four states with assimilation policies being the dominant (though not exclusive) discourse on the eve of the Second World War. Meanwhile, the logic of survival led Indigenous people to continue adapting to, and at times, challenging the settler colonial states in the fight for their own cultural survival. Part of that adaptation included joining settler military engagements overseas, whether they be the Spanish-American War, Anglo-Boer War or, more significantly, the First World War. These were not the first times that Indigenous peoples served with settler armed forces, but this was the first time that Indigenous people served in significant numbers and overseas. First World War service exposed Indigenous men, in particular, to equal treatment in the armed forces, galvanising a new generation of activists to fight for equal citizenship rights in its aftermath. The disappointments of the interwar period would have a profound effect on those and other Indigenous people when faced with another, even larger conflict against fascism. Just as the Allied governments would approach the Second World War conscious of the lessons of the First World War and interwar period in mind, so too would Indigenous people. The Second World War did not occur in a vacuum; as the war began, Indigenous people went in fully aware of the legacies of settler colonialism and their earlier war service and how they responded to the war would shape their destinies for the rest of the twentieth century.

*Part II*

# The War Years, 1939–1945

# 3 Engagement

## Indigenous Voluntary Military Service

Through the 1930s, Australians, Canadians, New Zealanders and Americans confronted economic hardships in their own communities and looked out with foreboding at the gathering storm clouds over Europe and Asia. Even before events in Poland brought tensions to a head in September 1939, each Dominion had begun calling out reserves and guarding strategic points. In all four settler societies, many Indigenous populations also took note of the rising international tensions and the talk of war. The Canadian Press wire service ran a story in mid-September 1939 about some Cree trappers from the isolated Norway House region who arrived at a fur trader's post. A number of them, 'clustered around the trader's radio Sept. 3 would not at first even believe the broadcast stating that Great Britain was at war with Germany. "You white people have been talking about war for four years and it has never come," one native said'.[1] Even if Indigenous people could not learn of the international situation via media, many still noted the heightened anxiety and activity in the settler societies surrounding them. Indigenous communities and individuals soon faced the question of how they should respond, discussing and debating these issues within communities, families and individual minds.

Indigenous reactions to the war varied tremendously in all four countries: in the degree of support for the national cause, in the nature of contributions made, in the reasons for, and extent of, opposition or protest and in aspirations for their people during, and after, the war. This chapter addresses the most visible symbol of Indigenous involvement: voluntary military service. It explores two key themes. First is the nature and shape of the military service that Indigenous individuals performed, which varied substantially across and within the four settler nations. Whilst some recruitment policies enabled them to enlist, others purposefully excluded particular Indigenous groups; some countries established

---

[1] "Indians did not believe war on," *Calgary Herald*, 15 September 1939, 11.

all-Indigenous units, but the majority of Indigenous soldiers, sailors or air personnel were integrated into mainstream units.

The second aspect that this chapter examines is the decision to volunteer for war: Why did Indigenous young people offer themselves for service, particularly given their relatively marginalised status? Deciding how to respond to the onset of conflict and shifting demands of settler society was often difficult and divisive within Indigenous communities. For some young men and women, the choice was an intensely personal one, but family, clan or tribal influences and pressures could play a part as well. Economic, cultural and political factors, as well as historical precedents of alliances and service in settler societies' expeditionary forces, help to explain the extent and persistence of Indigenous voluntarism.

## The Nature of Indigenous Military Service

The overarching patterns of formal military service performed by Aboriginal and Torres Strait Islander people, Māori, First Nations and Native Americans were statistically similar. In the broadest terms, a significant proportion of the Indigenous population in each country served in the military forces, and the overwhelming majority of them voluntarily enlisted (see Table 3.1). While statistics are harder to come by for women, estimates of their enlistment across the respective women's services are: United States 800[2]; Canada 100 Status Indian and Métis[3]; Australia fewer than 100[4]; and New Zealand, unknown.

There are interpretive problems in trying to discern too much from such numbers. Comparing the higher proportion of Native American enlistments against Aboriginal and Torres Strait Islander enlistments or the higher percentage of Ma¯ori volunteers than First Nations may hint at some measure of relative enthusiasm on the part of the Indigenous population or the particular military forces. On the other hand, so many factors shaped such numbers, and with such variability, that this is of little practical

---

[2] Townsend, *World War II and the American Indian*, 177–178; Jeré Bishop Franco, *Crossing the Pond: The Native American Effort in World War II* (Denton: University of North Texas Press, 1999), 65; 73.

[3] See Grace Poulin, *Invisible Women: WWII Aboriginal Servicewomen in Canada* (Thunder Bay, ON: D.G. Poulin, 2007), 25.

[4] We base this estimate on Jan "Kabarli" James' count of fewer than fifteen Second World War Aboriginal women from Western Australia, which generally had lower enlistment rates of Aboriginal people than eastern states. See Jan "Kabarli" James, *Forever Warriors* (Perth: Scott Print, 2010); Noah Riseman, "Escaping Assimilation's Grasp: Aboriginal Women in the Australian Women's Military Services," *Women's History Review* 24, no. 5 (2015): 758.

Table 3.1. *Indigenous enlistment and population figures*

| Country | Indigenous population | Total indigenous enlistment | Percentage of indigenous population | Percentage that volunteered |
|---|---|---|---|---|
| Australia[a] | 76,000 | Approx. 4,000 Aboriginal + 850 Torres Strait Islanders | 5% | 100% |
| Canada[b] | 125,946 | Approx. 4,300 Status Indians + unknown non-Status, Métis and Inuit | 3% | >70% |
| New Zealand[c] | 115,000 | Approx. 16,000 | 14% | 100% |
| United States[d] | 345,252 | Approx. 25,000 | 7% | Unknown |

[a] Population includes Aboriginal, 'part-Aboriginal' and Torres Strait Islander people as of June 1944.
[b] Population for Status Indians drawn from the 1944 census and printed in the Indian Affairs Branch Annual Report, 1945, 150. The percentage of greater than 70 per cent volunteered is based on the authors' estimate, derived from decades of research in Canadian First Nations' enlistment and conscription.
[c] Population figure is from 1945: "Historical Population Estimates Tables," *Stats NZ Tatauranga Aotearoa*, available from www.stats.govt.nz/browse_for_stats/population/estimates_and_projections/historical-population-tables.aspx.
[d] Total population figures is for 1940 and drawn from Alison Bernstein, *American Indians and World War II: Toward a New Era in Indian Affairs* (Norman: University of Oklahoma Press, 1991), 3. No source provides any sense of the relative ratio of draftees to volunteers.

value in understanding Indigenous motivations. Moreover, as Chapters 5 and 6 explore, in all four countries there were examples of Indigenous people participating in defence activities without having enlisted.

The figures in Table 3.1 derive from official recruiting numbers, often based on incomplete records and complicated by both arbitrary and vague definitions of Indigenous status. Rarely did military recruiting documents in any of the four countries note race or ethnicity (beyond black or white in the United States). As a result, the numbers are approximate at best. For instance, the Indian Affairs Branch of the Canadian government developed an official number of 3,050 Status Indian volunteers, but their figures were compiled from dozens of reports by overworked Indian Agents based on news they heard from First Nations communities in their often vast agencies. Not all agents reported, and not all were equally diligent or capable of collecting the needed information. In Western Australia, the Commissioner of Native Affairs still had confirmed records of only seventy-three men as late as 1946, while the other state Indigenous affairs bureaucracies did not keep figures.[5] Jan 'Kabarli' James' genealogy research in 2010 counted at least 410 Aboriginal servicemen and women from Western Australia.[6] The current national estimate of approximately 4,000 Aboriginal people and 850 Torres Strait Islanders derives from subsequent lists compiled by the Australian War Memorial through Indigenous community networks.

Importantly though, each jurisdiction's definition of who constituted an Indigenous person shaped the official numbers. In the United States, as Bernstein notes, there was no official definition of Indians except for those living on or near reservations. Such figures were always problematic, and they did not account for those Native Americans of mixed background or who were not on tribal rolls.[7] In Canada, the Indian Act defined a Status Indian as a 'male person of Indian blood reputed to belong to a particular band', and their spouse and dependents – with the federal Indian Affairs Branch having significant control over band lists.[8] Those who had lost Status through marriage or enfranchisement, as well as non-Status Indians and Métis, were not under the Branch's jurisdiction. Likewise in Australia, there was disagreement over the classification of Aboriginal people of mixed descent, with different states using different measures of blood fraction, often applied unevenly.[9]

The lack of numerical and categorical clarity, combined with a lack of military records, has forced scholars to construct estimates or to fall back on period officials' numbers of uncertain accuracy. Jeré Bishop Franco, for instance, estimates that 20,000 off-reservation Indians served in addition to the official figures of the Bureau of Indian Affairs for a total of 44,500.[10] The political utility of the memory of Indigenous war service gives contemporary significance to higher estimates and oft-repeated claims of rates higher than other segments of the population. From a historical perspective, the macro statistics need to be used with caution, and even then, they simply cannot provide the detail needed to elucidate the meaning, nature and extent of Indigenous service.

The most difficult obstacles to Indigenous voluntarism were racial barriers in settler military recruitment policies, which could be eclectic and unevenly applied. Indigenous Australians and Canadian First Nations faced the most rigid colour lines. After some initial confusion that saw a few

---

[5] Commissioner of Native Affairs to Secretary, The Fighting Services Association, 10 April 1946, State Records Office (hereafter SRO) WA, Acc 993-529-40 #12.
[6] James, *Forever Warriors*.
[7] Bernstein, *American Indians and World War II*, 10–11.
[8] Indian Act, Statues of Canada, 1876.
[9] Broome, *Aboriginal Australians*, 197–198.
[10] Franco, *Crossing the Pond*, 62.

Aboriginal and Torres Strait Islander men successfully enlist, the chiefs of the Australian naval, air and general staffs met 15 February 1940 to clarify their policies regarding the enlistment of aliens and 'British Subjects of Non-European Descent in Australia Defence Forces'. The committee determined that in all three services, 'eligibility to enlist or to serve is subject to the condition that a person must be of pure or of substantially European origin or descent'. The admission of Aboriginal and Torres Strait Islander personnel was thus deemed 'undesirable in principle', though it was noted that a 'departure from this principle is justified in order to provide for the specials needs of any Service during the war'. This decision all but slammed the door for the majority of Aboriginal and Torres Strait Islander recruits early in the war.[11] The Royal Australian Air Force (RAAF) would remain somewhat more open to non-European recruits in order to meet its heavy manpower commitments to the British Commonwealth Air Training Plan, as well as the needs for the defence of Australia.[12] According to an internal analysis of war recruiting measures, there were 'a number of aboriginals among the many who served as volunteers in the AIF who resented the imputation that they were not fit to serve in a combatant arm and it is a fact that very few did serve as non-combatants'.[13]

While the wording never changed in legislation or any of the recruitment policies of the three services, the situation changed radically with Japan's entry into the war. The Minister for the Army, F. M. Forde, described the regulations to a fellow member of parliament in March 1942 in the following terms:

... in deciding whether or not a person with some aboriginal blood is or is not substantially of European origin or descent, medical officers (who are described in the Defence Act as the judges in this matter) will be guided by the general suitability of the applicant, and by the laws and practices of the State or Territory in which the enlistment takes place.[14]

This loosening of the colour line and sheer urgency of personnel needs left medical officers with wide discretion through 1942 and 1943. The Army thus increasingly accepted people of Aboriginal and mixed ancestry as well as Torres Strait Islanders.

---

[11] Military Board Proceedings, Agendum no. 214, 1940, 30 July 1940, National Archives of Australia (hereafter NAA) A2653, 1940/M214. British Subjects of Non-European Descent in Australia Defence Forces.

[12] Robert Hall, *Fighters from the Fringe: Aborigines and Torres Strait Islanders Recall the Second World War* (Canberra: Aboriginal Studies Press, 1995), 155–156; Robert Hall, *The Black Diggers: Aborigines and Torres Strait Islanders in the Second World War* (Sydney: Allen and Unwin, 1989), 14–15.

[13] Notes for Australian Military Recruiting 1939–45, Australian War Memorial (hereafter AWM) 834-1-1, 7.

[14] F. M. Forde to J. J. Clark, 12 March 1942, NAA MP508/1, 275/701/556.

In Canada, the Royal Canadian Navy (RCN) and Royal Canadian Air Force (RCAF) had race restrictions in their recruitment policies at the outbreak of war. Both initially required volunteers to be '... of pure European descent and of the white race', though the RCAF also stipulated recruits 'must also be the sons of parents both of whom are (or, if deceased, were at the time of death) British subjects or naturalised British subjects'.[15] The burden of proof, where there was any doubt of nationality, rested with the volunteer.[16] This wording drew from British Royal Air Force (RAF) recruiting regulations, which accounts partly for the similar wording also later adopted in the Australian forces. Dominion naval and air forces particularly planned to operate and fight in a highly integrated way with their parent forces, the Royal Navy (RN) and RAF. The pressures to conform certainly need to be accounted for in understanding such strict racial policies. Interestingly, the RCAF quickly removed First Nations people from those barred by the colour line, making them effectively honorary Europeans for recruitment purposes.[17] The RCAF dropped its colour line for good in September 1942.[18] The RCN followed suit in March 1943, though there are indications that it continued such restrictions in practice.[19] These policies constrained the options for First Nations such as Stó:lō recruit, Wes Sam:

A lot of my white friends got into the air gunners and that's where I wanted to go too, but when I tried out I was rejected. All my white friends were accepted, but I was rejected. So I thought I'd try to get in through the back door, and I was told 'try the army.' So I did, and the army accepted me so fast I never even got to go home to visit my family – straight to the barracks.[20]

The result of such policies meant that the numbers of First Nations who served in the RCN or RCAF were minuscule. According to the 1942–3 Indian Affairs Annual Report, only twenty-nine Status Indians served in the Air Force, and nine were in the RCN (even with the colour line in effect).[21] As of 15 February 1943, total First Nations enlistment had

---

[15] DHIST, 75/347, 25-04-139.
[16] Maclachlan to Camsell, 18 March 1941, DHIST, 112.3H1.009/D293, and DHIST, 75/347, 25-04-1939.
[17] R. Scott Sheffield, "'... in the same manner as other people': Government Policy and the Military Service of Canada's First Nations, 1939–1945" (MA Thesis, University of Victoria, 1995), 28; Hollies to OIC, RCAF Recruiting Centre, Montreal, Libraries and Archives of Canada (hereafter LAC) RG 24, Vol. 3307, no. H.Q. 282-1-2 v.2).
[18] Scully to Edwards, 27 September 1942, NAC, RG 24, vol. 3302, file # 280-1-2 v.2.
[19] DHIST, P.C. 1986, N.S. 30-2-12; DHIST, Historical Section Army H.Q. Report no.71, p. 10.
[20] Keith Thor Carlson, "Stó:lō Soldiers, Stó:lō Veterans," in *You are Asked to Witness: The Stó:lō in Canada's Pacific Coast History*, ed. Keith Thor Carlson (Chilliwack, BC: Stó:lō Heritage Trust, 1996), 131.
[21] Department of Mines and Resources, *Annual Report* (Ottawa: 1942 and 1943).

reached approximately 1,800, giving a stark indication of how difficult it was for Canadian Indigenous men to enlist in the RCN and RCAF.[22]

By contrast, the recruiting policies of American and New Zealand militaries erected relatively few racial barriers to Indigenous recruits. The literature on Native American enlistment pays little heed to any distinctions between the various military services, implying that access was relatively open across the board. Nevertheless, Bernstein's breakdown of the roughly 25,000 Native American service personnel suggests an uneven pattern: 21,767 served in the Army, 1,910 in the Navy, 874 in the Marines and 121 in the Coast Guard (with no reliable numbers for the Army Air Force).[23] It is difficult to determine whether the preponderance of Native Americans in the Army was a result of their desire to serve with the Army and how much was due to structural factors inhibiting access to other options. Confusion was initially evident in the United States amongst government and military officials due to some ignorance regarding the citizenship status of Native Americans, though this does not seem to have slowed the rate of volunteering.[24] The US military segregated white and black troops, and Native Americans did not fit within this binary. In most circumstances, they served integrated into white units, but there were instances when Native Americans were assigned to black units. In Mississippi, for instance, discretion determined placement of Choctaw men based on their skin complexions.[25] Such decisions – whether to exclude or where to assign Indigenous service personnel – were a continuing exercise of settler power over Indigenous peoples.

Of the four settler societies, New Zealand was arguably the most inclusive with the least overt racism and prejudice directed at Indigenous minorities. Moreover, the existence of the high-profile Maori Battalion, and Māori control over their own recruitment, might suggest New Zealand was free of racial barriers in its recruitment. This was not in fact the case. Only a minority of Māori men that went overseas served in the 28th (Maori) Battalion while thousands of others served in other non-Māori Army units, the Royal New Zealand Navy (RNZN), Royal New Zealand Air Force (RNZAF) or in Territorial and Home Guard units in New Zealand. Accurate figures are difficult to obtain, but in a report on gratuities being paid to deceased Māori service personnel, the assistant legal officer, Army HQ, estimated deceased Māori outside the Maori Battalion as 174 (with 626 deaths on the Battalion list, for about

[22] T. R. L. MacInnes to Edith Doran, 15 February 1943, LAC, RG 10, Vol. 6764, file #452-6, pt.2.
[23] Bernstein, *American Indians and World War II*, 40.
[24] Franco, *Crossing the Pond*, 46.
[25] Bernstein, *American Indians and World War II*, 41.

800 overall). The accuracy of this figure is uncertain, but it provides a rough sense of proportion for the sizable number of Māori serving outside the confines of the 28th Battalion.[26] Both the RNZN and RNZAF wrestled with the issue of Māori personnel, especially given the relatively small size of their forces and thus heavy reliance upon and integration with Britain's RN and RAF.

New Zealanders' imperial patriotism factored in as well. Undoubtedly, the British Commodore commanding the New Zealand Squadron expected a favourable response when he complained to the Naval Secretary about Māori listed among potential recruits in January 1939:

it is not desirable or practicable to mess ratings of different races together in H. M. Ships, where conditions are so cramped ... I am also of the opinion that it is most undesirable to start a precedent in H. M. Ships whereby a member of a native race, however distinguished, might, by reason of seniority or advancement, be placed in charge of white personnel.[27]

The reply of the Naval Secretary, E. L. Tottenham, made the RNZN Board position explicitly clear:

the position is that the New Zealand Division [of the Royal Navy] cannot refuse the application of a Maori, provided there are vacancies, and provided that the candidate satisfies the physical and mental requirements and is selected as suitable for entry into the service. The general practice of New Zealand is based on the tradition of equality of status, consequently the introduction of regulations tending to abrogate the practical effect of that tradition for Naval purpose could not be contemplated.[28]

As the war progressed, though, integrated service proved increasingly awkward for the RNZN. Commanders struggled with where to post Māori sailors, as they were seemingly not welcome in Britain and were deemed especially problematic in Britain's colonial postings in the Pacific, Middle East and India. Interestingly, there was always a desire to keep knowledge of this from Māori recruits.[29]

The RNZAF likewise began the war enlisting 'good types of Maoris', but by 1943, the 'colour question has become acute problem with Maoris posted India and Middle East'.[30] In response, air officials sought to transfer Māori air and ground personnel in those theatres either to the United Kingdom or

---

[26] Minute – Maori Deceased Gratuities, Asst. Legal Officer, 14 October 1946, AD1 344-3-30 – Gratuity – Deceased Maori Servicemen.

[27] Commodore to Naval Secretary, 19 January 1939, Archives New Zealand (hereafter ANZ) N1 309 13-3-1.

[28] E. L. Tottenham to the Commodore, 1 February 1939, ANZ, N1 309 13-3-1.

[29] Personnel, Recruiting Entry of Maoris, ANZ, N1 309 13-3-1.

[30] Telegram, Air HQ to NZLO Air Ministry, 15 December 1939 and telegram, Air Dept to RNZAF HQ, 3 May 1943, ANZ, Air 1 762 33-20-4, pt. 1.

to New Zealand for continued service, where their race was not deemed troublesome to imperial authorities. Māori personnel numbers quickly exceeded the limited requirements in New Zealand, and fit men were encouraged to transfer to the 28th (Maori) Battalion. RNZAF command rescinded the order permitting Māori enlistment in the Air Force in June 1943, closing the door to Māori recruits.[31] Some continued to serve, and some men of mixed ancestry enlisted subsequently, though their skin colour was noted in their files, potentially limiting their service utility.[32] It is a curiosity that the pattern of Indigenous service in New Zealand is the reverse of the other three countries where the opportunities and avenues of service open to Indigenous people generally expanded as the war progressed.

### Rejecting Enlistees

Beyond rigid colour lines, Indigenous volunteers could still encounter impediments to military service: regulatory requirements that were typically more difficult to overcome for Indigenous populations. Rates of rejection faced by hopeful Indigenous recruits were often higher than the national average. The United States was an exception, with Indian rejection rates statistically in-line with the white population at around one-third. Kenneth Townsend notes that some states with large Native American populations had higher rejection rates: in Arizona, white rejection rates were 27 per cent while the rejection rates for Native Americans and blacks were 45 per cent and 46 per cent, respectively.[33] Franco suggests that after education levels, the next largest rationale for rejection of Native American personnel was health related, with 37 per cent failing the physical exam nationally (as opposed to 32 per cent for the white population).[34] The major ailments were trachoma (8 per cent) and tuberculosis (5 per cent), but local rates could be quite varied.[35]

High rates of tuberculosis in Indigenous populations were particularly likely to prevent Indigenous young people from successfully enlisting.

---

[31] Minute No. 181 from Air Commodore, 25 August 1943 and Memo from Director of Mobilisation, 11 June 1943, ANZ, Air 1 762 33-20-4, pt. 1.

[32] Minute Sheet, Director of Operations 20 September 1943, ANZ, Air 1 762 33-20-4, pt. 1.

[33] Townsend, *World War II and the American Indian*, 64, 66–67.

[34] Franco, *Crossing the Pond*, 59.

[35] R. Scott Sheffield, "'Of Pure European Descent and of the White Race': Recruitment Policy and Aboriginal Canadians, 1939–1945," *Canadian Military History* 5, no. 1 (Spring 1996): 8–15; Michael Stevenson, "The Mobilisation of Native Canadians During the Second World War," *Journal of the Canadian Historical Association* (1996): 212.

One Canadian newspaper reported the difference in deaths, per hundred thousand population, in Canada was 732 for Status Indians versus 51 for the general populace.[36] The result was that Indigenous men and women were more likely to fail a medical examination for enlistment or, potentially, once in the services. A report of the New Zealand Mobilisation Branch noted that during the 'early stages of the war, wastage in Maori drafts owing to medical unfitness was considerably above that of Europeans, but during the latter years of the conflict, this state improved a good deal'.[37] In another example, an incomplete nominal roll of seventy-five Aboriginal men who successfully enlisted in the Army in Western Australia included ten subsequently discharged due to medical unfitness.[38] An additional five were discharged as 'unlikely to become efficient soldiers' and six more for disciplinary issues: 'services no longer required', or 'unfit for further military service'. Overall, such high rates of medical rejection were an indictment of settler state administration of Indigenous populations, but for would-be Indigenous volunteers, health failings often proved an insurmountable barrier to military service.

Other than the United States, rejection rates are only vaguely evident in reports or in anecdotal accounts. In Canada, the variability between First Nations communities was huge. Some, such as the Cape Croker Ojibwa in Ontario, were reported as having fifty-three men and women enlisted and only three rejected due to health from a 1943 population of 471.[39] On the other hand, a mobile recruiting unit was sent to Moose Lake in Northern Manitoba where they examined over forty Indigenous men and rejected all but two, who went south only to be returned home at a later date – a 100 per cent rejection rate.[40]

Education levels, too, were far lower than among settler society. This was less concerning for Army service, which usually had low

---

[36] "The Original Canadians," *Saint John Telegraph-Journal*, 15 July 1946. The paper mistakenly reported 732 deaths per thousand population, but the actual statistic was per hundred thousand.

[37] Report on the Mobilisation Branch, 1939–45, 3, ANZ WAII 21 62C-CN115.

[38] Nominal Roll – Natives Enlisted in the Army, undated (likely 1946), SRO WA, Acc 993-529-40 #21. This roll is well short of the total number for Western Australia, with an estimate of about 300 cited by the Acting Commissioner of Native Affairs in 1947, Acting Commissioner to Mr. K. W. Growcott, 1 September 1947, SRO WA, 135–147.

[39] "Their Braves Gone to War, Cape Croker's Indian Women and Children Carry On," photo collection, *Globe and Mail*, 23 October 1943; "Bruce Peninsula Reserve Does Bit To Put Every Victory Loan Over Top," *Globe and Mail*, 23 October 1943. By war's end, Cape Croker had recorded seventy-eight voluntary enlistments according the IAB, Voluntary Enlistments by province and reserve, 15 January 1945, LAC, RG, vol. 6764, file 452-6 pt. 2.

[40] Sheffield, "'… in the same manner as other people'," 35. See also correspondence for this incident in LAC, RG 10, Vol. 6769, file# 452-20, pt. 5.

educational minimums. For the more technical naval and air forces, the educational requirements for completed high school or matriculation were quite demanding, even by settler society standards when many left school at grade seven or eight. John Barrington highlights that in 1938, the percentage of Māori reaching Standard 6 (approximately twelve years old) was only 3.4 per cent from native schools and 3.1 per cent from boarding schools; this compares with 10.1 per cent of Pākehā in boarding schools. Only in 1939 did more than 50 per cent of Māori in Standard 4 continue on to Standard 6.[41] Similarly, in Canada during the interwar years, over 75 per cent of First Nations' children attained an educational level of grade three or less.[42] In Australia, the states all ran separate education regimes, but most Indigenous people's education occurred on missions or reserves and not necessarily by qualified teachers. In New South Wales there was a formal structure of segregated schools for Aboriginal children, which tended to employ substandard teachers.[43]

Another common reason for rejections is because volunteers were underage. This is not dissimilar to many young non-Indigenous men and women who, caught up in the patriotic war fever, were keen to enlist. Testimonies from across all four countries, though, reveal that many men or women rejected for being underage either returned when they were older or went to a different recruiter and lied about their age. What seems clear is that systemic barriers blocked many Indigenous men and women from successfully enlisting and that the overall numbers and per capita rates of enlistment might have been much higher.

Though we do not often consider the impact on those individuals denied access to military service, it could be bitter or even devastating. This was apparent when a Sydney paper published a story about the rejection of three Aboriginal men who had passed their first fitness screening and travelled to Sydney for the next stage in their enlistment, only to be rejected. One of the three, Sendy Togo, protested: 'I am anxious to serve Australia, but, without any examination or explanation I am sent back – a thousand mile journey for nothing.'[44] In New Zealand, Thomas Pereki Pohatu (known as Lyon) and his future

41  John Barrington, *Separate but Equal? Māori Schools and the Crown 1867–1969* (Wellington: Victoria University Press, 2008), 208.
42  Jean Barman, Yvonne Hebert and Don McCaskill, *Indian Education in Canada, Volume I: The Legacy* (Vancouver: University of British Columbia Press, 1986), 18.
43  Amanda Barry, "Broken Promises: Aboriginal education in South-eastern Australia, 1837–1937" (PhD thesis, School of Historical Studies, University of Melbourne, 2008).
44  *Sunday Sun*, 4 January 1942, cited in Mahdi Neilson, "Hiatus or Catalyst? The Impact of the Second World War on Aboriginal Activism and Assimilation, 1939–1953" (BA [Honours] Thesis, ANU, 2008), 16–17.

brother-in-law, Rangi Ria, were both sent home diagnosed with tuber-culosis and his sister, Bebe, recalled that 'Lyon was more angry than anything. He was always a soldier man and had been in the territori-als here in Manutake.' As a result, Rangi's younger brother Rapiatu (Darcy) remembered, the two 'were really down. They were supposed to get seen by the doctor, but they didn't bother. My brother took to the drink for a while.'[45]

In Australia, many Aboriginal men and women were angered at being denied the right to serve. Herbert John Milera, who had actually served in the First World War, wrote a letter of complaint to Prime Minister John Curtin in January 1942, stating: 'I was told "We have received orders that no more aboriginals should be taken in any part of the Australian Army." We Dark Men are now Black Bald [sic] right throughout the Commonwealth. So much for that lot.'[46] Even among those Aboriginal people who did manage to enlist early in the war, many were subse-quently discharged. Of twenty-six men from Lake Tyers, Victoria, who had enlisted in July 1940, eighteen had been discharged by March 1941. The men who returned were angry and disillusioned, remarking 'we have no King and no country', and their hostile feelings resonated more widely. The manager of Lake Tyers claimed for a time that the settle-ment was 'a community on strike and threats of violence against the Management were of daily occurrence [sic]'.[47]

While the overarching pattern of structural factors tended to limit Indigenous options for voluntary enlistment, it was possible for oppor-tunities to arise as well. For example, one of the reasons that so many Indigenous men and women served in the forces was the insatiable man and womanpower needs. The fact that the armies usually suffered heav-ier casualties than the other services meant that those low standards for minimum age, education, health and family status were incrementally lowered as wartime demands forced the hand of senior army officials. Similar urgent demands for personnel to meet its quotas under the British Commonwealth Air Training Program also partially explains the anomaly of the RAAF, which formally remained more open to Aboriginal Australian volunteers than was the case in the other Australian military branches (at least early in the war) or for the air forces of any of the other three settle states.

---

[45] Interviews with Bebe Ria and Darcy Ria, quoted in Monty Soutar, *Nga Tama Toa: The Price of Citizenship: C Company 28 (Māori) Battalion 1939–1945* (Auckland: David Bateman, 2008), 59.
[46] Herbert John Milera, letter to Prime Minister John Curtin, January 1942, NAA MP508/1, 50/703/12.
[47] Hall, *The Black Diggers*, 20.

## Segregated versus Integrated Service

A key final factor shaping the nature of military service for would-be Indigenous recruits was whether they would be funnelled into segregated units or integrated into regular army, naval and air units. The concept of segregated Indigenous units was raised, often by Indigenous leaders and debated to greater or lesser extent in all four settler societies. Sometimes publicly discussed, sometimes conducted quietly in official internal communications, settler societies wrestled with the potentially thorny and uncomfortable topic. Indigenous interest in segregated service, as well as their relative political influence, interacted with the variety of competing agendas among the several military and governmental agencies involved in the decision-making processes. The results were decidedly varied within and between these four countries: Canada barely flirted with the notion; Australia and the United States both leaned toward integrated service but conducted notable experiments in segregation; while New Zealand bowed to Māori demands for a segregated infantry battalion, partly based on the precedent of the First World War.

Indigenous leaders in all four countries requested segregated units. In Australia, Aboriginal activist William Ferguson responded to the outbreak of war by conveying the following message to Prime Minister Robert Menzies:

> In times of National crisis, when the Mother Country is facing the world in a fight for freedom, it behooves every member of the community to join together in the common cause. It is this which urges me to write to you, on behalf of the Aborigines of Australia, requesting that instead of Aborigines enlisting in the AIF that we be allowed to form an Aboriginal Division.[48]

In the Canadian west, Joe Dreaver, a Great War veteran and Chief of the Mistawasis Cree, made a public call for an 'All-Indian Battalion' in March 1940.[49] Similar calls were made in the United States,[50] but only the Māori garnered state acquiescence to a mainstream military segregated Indigenous unit. Politically influential Māori harnessed vocal and fairly widespread Māori support and drew on the precedent of the Maori Pioneer Battalion in the Great War to win over Pākehā authorities.[51] The primary goal for Indigenous political leaders seeking

[48] W. Ferguson to Prime Minister Menzies, 8 July 1940, NAA MP508, 82/712/1310. See a similar request for a segregated battalion in a letter from the Secretary of the Committee of Aboriginal Citizenship to the Minister for the Army, 7 January 1942.

[49] *Saskatoon Star-Phoenix*, 5 March 1940.

[50] Bernstein, *American Indians and World War II*, 40–41.

[51] Ranginui Walker, *He Tipua: The Life and Times of Sir Āpirana Ngata* (Auckland: Penguin, 2005), 339, 343–348; Wira Gardiner, *Te Mura O Te Ahi: The Story of the Maori Battalion* (Auckland: Reed, 1992), 23; Hill, *State Authority, Indigenous Autonomy*, 184.

segregated units was the heightened profile and visibility of a larger collective entity, and the political influence promised by such enhanced public awareness. Many settler authorities were uncomfortable with, indifferent to or outright opposed the segregation of Indigenous service personnel.[52]

Not all suggestions for segregated units came from Indigenous people; others originated from settler citizens or government officials. The rationales for such units varied, but two are prevalent. For instance, one initiative in Saskatchewan, advocated by a newspaper editor and a militia colonel in a cable to the Canadian Minister of Defence, stated: '... we believe raising of several all-Indian platoons would give much impetus to closing phase recruiting campaign anxious to raise at least one platoon to have attested in presence prime minister King here July 8 story and pictures would have national appeal'.[53] In this case, the units were designed primarily for enhancing recruitment amongst First Nations people, though it is clear the editor especially saw a propaganda opportunity with broader potential to inspire, encourage, and/or shame other Canadians. A similar request from an Australian veteran of the Boer War and the First World War, L. M. McMaugh, points to the other dominant rationale for segregated units: the perceived 'racial' abilities and bushcraft that Indigenous people were believed to possess. McMaugh recommended the Australian military should employ Aboriginal people on defence works in the Northern Territory: 'Native tribes have a secret code for signalling, and can glean what is happening at extraordinary [sic] long distances. With instruction, he is also a good rifle shot. He would also be employed in making depots, emplacements, erecting, water conservation, road making, etc.'[54]

Some government administrators, especially those involved in Indigenous affairs, viewed military service as an ideal assimilative tool.[55] The Indian Affairs Branch in Canada was decidedly cool to the notion of segregated service, even if it might encourage First Nations recruiting because it undermined what they saw as the value of Indigenous military participation. According to the Director, Dr. H. McGill, from 'the standpoint of the Indian himself and the effectiveness of his service in the Armed Forces, we are not at all sure that an Indian battalion would

[52] Hall, *The Black Diggers*, 9.
[53] Telegram, D. B. Rogers to T. A. Crerar, 30 June 1941, LAC, RG 10, VOl.6764, file# 452-6, pt. 2.
[54] L. M. McMaugh to Minister for Defence, 17 May 1939, NAA MP431/1, 929/19/912.
[55] R. Scott Sheffield, *The Red Man's on the Warpath: Images of the Indian and the Second World War* (Vancouver: University of British Columbia Press, 2004), 48; Noah Riseman, "Aboriginal Military Service and Assimilation," *Aboriginal History* 38 (2014): 155–178.

be of much value.'[56] There was a single RCAF field directive to transfer 'as many American Indians as possible' into the RCAF 421 'Red Indian' Squadron that does not seem to have been enforced; other than this instruction, Canadian military officials were largely uninterested in segregated units.[57] BIA Commissioner Collier took an opposite view after the draft was initiated in 1940. He initially supported special separate Native American units – even an all-Indian division – under BIA control. He advocated segregation largely as a cultural protection tool, in keeping with the broader Indian New Deal agenda. The American Secretary of War, Henry Stimson, opposed any segregation of Indian soldiers and blocked Collier's efforts.[58]

Across Australia, the various state Aboriginal administrations had not fully implemented assimilation policies as yet, so the official opposition to segregation in Australian military service originated from different roots. In Western Australia, for example, the Commissioner of Native Affairs, Walter Bray, had such a limited belief in the capabilities of Aboriginal people that he lamented any form of military service:

In many cases it is now clear that the enlistment of natives into the Services was inadvisable. Enlistment has unsettled them and I am doubtful of the effect when natives are discharged. Their wives and children have migrated to the city and environs, and they mostly live in hovel conditions. Moreover, the uniformed natives are mostly spending their unusual revenue on drink and gambling, and most assuredly there will be an aftermath.[59]

Such a negative perception of a people was unlikely to see value, military or otherwise, in a unit formed wholly of such individuals. In response to the Premier of New South Wales' suggestion that 'a special unit of aborigines be formed', Prime Minister John Curtin replied that 'in light of experience, that the disabilities associated with the formation and maintenance of such a unit would be out of all proportion to its value as a combatant force, and that as a non-combatant unit it would be even less effective'.[60] Often it only took a single individual to block such suggestions. For instance, in the summary notes of a conference dealing with the Northern Territory Force, 28 December 1942, under the heading, 'Formation of Bn. Of Aboriginals', was the statement that the 'views of the Comd. N.T. Force are concurred in here and it is not proposed to

---

[56] Director to Hill, 19 August 1942, LAC, RG 10, Vol.6764, file 452-6, pt.2.

[57] Field Liaison Bulletin No. 17, 1 September 1943, DHIST, file S.2-1-2.

[58] Bernstein, *American Indians and World War II*, 22–23; 40–41.

[59] Letter from the Commissioner to the Deputy Director-General of Manpower, Perth, 15 March 1943, SRO WA, Acc 993-38-1940.

[60] Prime Minister to the Premier of New South Wales, 18 March 1942, NAA MP508/1, 275/701/556.

recommend the formation of this unit'.[61] One exception in the mainstream Army was an experiment in 1940 at the Lake Tyers Aboriginal Reserve, 326 kilometres southeast of Melbourne, where twenty-six Aboriginal men were recruited with the idea of creating an Aboriginal platoon.[62] Military officials did not train them adequately and were dubious of their value, so the experiment ended within a matter of months, dubbed a failure.[63]

The lack of official enthusiasm for segregated Indigenous units in Australia, Canada and the United States did not prevent experimentation with more specialised, finite, and/or ad hoc segregated service. Wartime needs and crises after the rapid Japanese advance had the power to overcome the broader scepticism of Indigenous-only units, especially for military officials. Local military authorities in northern Australia and northwest North America raised an assortment of nontraditional mainstream units as well as semi or unofficial Indigenous units. These units will be addressed in Chapter 5.

Only in New Zealand did circumstances permit the creation of an explicitly segregated Indigenous unit along standard military lines and incorporated fully into the order of battle as a part of settler military forces. Māori, through the work of MPs Apirana Ngata, Paraire Paikea and Eruera Tirikatene, wielded relatively significant influence with the Labour government in 1939. Ngata and Paikea's sales pitch to the government was full Māori support for the national war effort, in exchange for a Māori combat unit and exemption from conscription. To ensure sufficient recruits for a Māori battalion, special Māori recruitment officers were created who would know best how to encourage Māori enlistment.[64] It helped that Pākehā officials recalled the divisiveness and resistance amongst some Māori during the Great War and were eager to avoid a repetition damaging national unity and the war effort. It is clear, though, that the New Zealand Army and government had no initial plan for the inclusion of a Māori unit, as the 2nd NZ Division was already assigned the standard complement of nine (Pākehā) infantry Battalions. A formal announcement of the formation of a Māori battalion did not occur until 4 October 1939, when it was decided to attach the 28th (Maori) Battalion to 2nd NZ Division as an extra battalion, rather than to replace an existing Pākehā battalion. Māori already enlisted in gen-

---

[61] Summary Notes of Conference, 28 December 1942, NAA A2653, 1943/M2. There was willingness to permit some 'half-castes' into the militia in Darwin. See NAA A659 1939/1/129.

[62] Hall, *Fighters from the Fringe*, 83.

[63] Lake Tyers Manager's report for period ended 31 July 1940, NAA B356, 54.

[64] ANZ, AD1, 226/19/7 vols. 1–2.

eral service would have the choice of transferring to the 28th (Maori Battalion) once formed or continuing in their present force.[65] More details about the Maori Battalion are also in Chapter 5.

Even though segregation appears to have won a central place in Māori military participation during the Second World War, it was far from total or uncontested. Nor should official acquiescence to the 28th Battalion be read as broad acceptance, as some Pākehā officers were ambivalent about the efficacy and impact of segregation. In 1942, when segregation of Māori was extended to Territorial and Home Guard units stationed in New Zealand, the Central Military District Commandant proclaimed: 'it would be better for the Maori to serve with a unit nearer to his home town, and to emphasize this brotherhood between the two races than to emphasize a difference by the formation of separate Maori and Pakeha units'.[66] Interestingly, in this case, the Maori War Effort Organisation's determination for segregation, and the autonomy and Māori command positions it produced, steamrolled the officer's concerns. Thus Māori influence over the nature of their voluntary service proved remarkably strong, gaining much greater settler state and military acquiescence.

## Message and Meaning of Indigenous Voluntary Service

Whilst government and military policies clearly influenced the extent and manner of Indigenous enlistment, of course, such policies would be meaningless if Indigenous recruits were not ready to serve. Almost as soon as the ink was dry on declarations of war in each country, and sometimes before, young Indigenous men and women were lining up at recruitment centres to offer themselves for service. In New Zealand, Rangi Logan, a well-educated young man, enlisted immediately when war was declared. He was training in the Artillery when offered the chance to transfer to the 28th (Maori) Battalion, which he took.[67] In the small Canadian prairie town of Cardston, two Kanai men from the neighbouring Blood Indian Reserve were the first enlisted on the rolls.[68] In Australia, Leonard Waters' obsession with flying led him to attempt enlistment in the RAAF when war broke out, though being only seventeen years old he was unsuccessful.[69]

[65] ANZ, AD1 226-19-7, vol. 1.
[66] District Commandant to Army HQ, 4 August 1942, ANZ, AD1 1117 209-3-57.
[67] Gardiner, *Te Mura O Te Ahi*, 5.
[68] "First Local Volunteers For Army Service Leave Here For Training," *Cardston News*, 14 September 1939, 1.
[69] Hall, *Fighters from the Fringe*, 157–163.

The United States was distinct because it remained out of the conflict until December 1941, but it was expanding its military service during the period 1939–41, including the establishment of selective service. By the eve of American entry into the war, nearly 42,000 Native Americans of eligible age had registered for selective service, constituting nearly two-thirds of eligible Native American men. Moreover, as Kenneth Townsend points out, more than 60 per cent of the 4,500 Native Americans already in the military before Pearl Harbor were volunteers and the number of enlisted Native Americans nearly doubled afterward.[70] For example, Native Americans such as Navajo man Keith Little enthusiastically volunteered. Little recalls:

> Me and a bunch of guys were out hunting rabbits with a .22. We had a
> rabbit cooking down in the wash, and somebody went to the dorm
> [at boarding school], came back and said:
> 'Hey, Pearl Harbor was bombed!'
> One of us asked, 'Where's Pearl Harbor'
> 'In Hawaii.'
> 'Who did it?'
> 'Japan.'
> 'Why'd they do it?'
> 'They hate Americans. They want to kill all Americans.'
> 'Us, too?'
> 'Yeah, us too?' Then and there, we all made a promise. We were, most
> of us, 15or 16, I guess. We promised each other we'd go after the
> Japanese instead of hunting rabbits.[71]

How do we explain such spontaneous outbursts of voluntarism among Indigenous populations in each of these four countries?

Given the rich and lengthy history of Indigenous military service in all four settler societies, it should not have surprised anyone when these populations volunteered in similar fashion during the Second World War. Gunditjmara man Reg Saunders, from western Victoria, noted that he had 'merely followed in the footsteps of hundreds of other Aboriginals in World War I. The men that I grew up with – you know, my school mates' fathers and that – they were nearly all soldiers or involved in the military. So I thought it was just a normal thing.'[72] Three Calves, a Blackfoot Elder, called to the young men on his reservation, saying: 'Go and fight as your forefathers did ... our Great White Father is calling us to help. We

---

[70]  Townsend, *World War II and the American Indian*, 61.
[71]  Keith Little, in Bruce Watson, "Jaysho, moasi, dibeh, ayeshi, hasclishnih, beshlo, shush, gini. (World War II voice code)," *Smithsonian* 24, no. 5 (August 1993): 34–43.
[72]  Reg Saunders, in Hall, *Fighters from the Fringe*, 64.

must go.'[73] Indigenous women, too, could draw on family traditions of service. Newspaper reports of Native American or First Nations women who enlisted usually drew connections to famous ancestral chiefs or other male figures such as fathers or brothers currently serving. One such article from 1944 mentions Women's Army Corps (WAAC) June Doctor, in relation to her three brothers from the Tonawanda Reservation and the Thompson family of Cataraugus Reservation having five children in the services, including daughter Mae in the Army Nurses Corps.[74] A *Winnipeg Tribune* article talks about Mary Greyeyes' enlistment into the Canadian Women's Army Corps (CWAC) only in the context of the male Indian councillor – a veteran of iconic First World War Battle of Vimy Ridge – bestowing his blessing to her.[75]

Sometimes fathers or uncles who served in the Great War were encouraging the younger generation to enlist, such as Plains Cree Chief, Joe Dreaver. A veteran of the First World War, he drove eighteen men from his reserve community, including three sons, into Saskatoon to enlist a month after Canada's declaration of war.[76] In New Zealand, responding to an announcement of some northern Māori favouring service in home defence only, the following telegraph arrived at the Prime Minister's office:

THE SPIRIT OF THE ARAWAS AND ASSOCIATE TRIBES THROUGHOUT AOTEAROA FLAME AT DEEDS OF WANTON AGGRESSION AND PRAY NAY DEMAND THAT THEY BE ALLOWED TO AGAIN RECROSS THE SEAS TO STAND SHOULDER TOUCHING SHOULDER WITH THEIR WHITE BROTHERS SHARING WITH THEM EQUALITY OF SACRIFICE IN DEFENDING THE SAME IDEALS THEY FOUGHT FOR 25 YEARS AGO ... GOD SAVE THE KING.[77]

Not all communities or individuals shared such outspoken determination, but many Māori, Aboriginal and Torres Strait Islander Australians, First Nations and Native Americans would offer themselves at recruiting centres.

In Australia, before the July 1940 rules stipulated that enlistment was restricted to persons 'substantially of European origin or descent', a policy

---

[73] Townsend, *World War II and the American Indian*, 77.

[74] "Six Nations Send Youth on Warpath," *Buffalo Courier Express*, 2 January 1944, National Archives and Records Administration (hereafter NARA) RG 75, Records of the Bureau of Indian Affairs, Scrapbook of Newsclippings Relating to World War II, 1944, Box 1, Entry 998A.

[75] Poulin, *Invisible Women*, 27.

[76] Janice Summerby, *Native Soldiers, Foreign Battlefields* (Ottawa: Veterans Affairs Canada, 1993), 22. See also *Saskatoon Star Phoenix*, 14 October 1939, 3.

[77] Tai Mitchell to Honourable Peter Fraser, 16 September 1939, ANZ, AD1 226-19-7, vol. 1, 1935–1941.

vacuum on Indigenous enlistment enabled some Aboriginal Australians to enlist. Examples include Joseph Mye of Pimpana, Queensland, who was enrolled under 'the impression that an aboriginal was a natural born British subject'.[78] A document from 1941 from a public servant, attempting to clarify rules surrounding Australian Indigenous enlistment, read: 'A full blooded aboriginal is therefore required to render only non-combatant service, but a half-caste could be required to perform combatant duties if the medical authorities considered that he was substantially of European origin or descent.'[79] It was the confusion surrounding such policies that enabled an estimated 300–400 Aboriginal and Torres Strait Islander men and women to enlist prior to Pearl Harbor. Some of these individuals feigned being Italian or Māori (who were allowed despite being non-European) or, in other circumstances, local medical officers interpreted the confusing regulations to permit Aboriginal men of mixed descent (so-called 'half-castes' or 'quadroons'). Indeed, as Stewart Murray writes, 'The recruiting officer never looked up to see who I was or what colour I was.'[80] According to an internal post-war analysis of Australian war recruiting measures, 'Persons who were not substantially of European origin, especially our own aborigines, gave a little trouble, but only because they wanted to serve, and never because they wanted to claim exemption.'[81]

In Canada, Indian Affairs officials, like the Indian Commissioner for British Columbia, were unclear whether 'in view of their being wards of the Government, any special sanction is necessary' for Status Indians to enlist.[82] Subsequently, recruitment officials generally accepted Indigenous recruits, though there were brief periods in certain military districts where individual officers refused Status Indians on their own initiative.[83] Less confusion seems to have been evident regarding Indigenous eligibility to volunteer in New Zealand.

One of the most profound questions arising from Indigenous peoples' Second World War military service is why they offered themselves in the service of settler states that had dispossessed, oppressed and

---

[78] City Hall Recruiting Depot to Area Brigade Major, 22 July 1940, AWM, 1187, Enlistment of Aborigines and Half-castes in AIF 1940–1.

[79] J. T. Fitzgerald, Secretary, to R. S. Vincent, Esq, MLA, 24 July 1941, NAA MP508/1, 323/723/972.

[80] Stewart Murray, in Alick Jackomos and Derek Fowell, *Forgotten Heroes: Aborigines at War from the Somme to Vietnam* (South Melbourne: Victoria Press, 1991), 48.

[81] Notes for Australian Military Recruiting 1939–45, AWM 834/1/1, 7.

[82] Commissioner McKay to the Secretary of Indian Affairs, 13 September 1939, LAC, RG 10, Vol. 6764, file#452-6, pt. 2.

[83] District Recruiting Orders, M.D. 10, LAC, RG 10, Vol.6768, #452-20, pt. 4; Sheffield, "Of Pure European Descent and of the White Race," 12–13.

marginalised their people for generations. This is a difficult question to answer because every individual had his or her own individual motivations to serve. Interestingly, many oral history testimonies or written accounts from Indigenous veterans do not discuss their explicit reasons to enlist. Instead, the idea of joining up almost seems self-evident to the veterans because the Second World War was a total war that touched all aspects of society. Yet what is striking is how historians, ourselves included, seem to place so much importance on the question of 'why'. This retrospective emphasis on uncovering Indigenous peoples' motivations comes out of historians' and Indigenous people's desires to make sense of war service in the context of colonialism. Much of the importance of (re)claiming Indigenous war histories has been part of political agendas to position Indigenous peoples as active citizens in the respective nation-states, and uncovering their motivations is central to the claims-making process for civil and Indigenous rights.

Among the common threads weaving through Indigenous responses to the war was that military service offered the promise of economic security after a decade of depression. The Great Depression hit each of these settler societies hard. The Indigenous land base had been systematically whittled away through the nineteenth and early twentieth centuries, to the extent that the growing Indigenous populations could not come close to supporting themselves from their remaining fragments. In Canada and New Zealand, large-scale Indigenous land loss came to an end around 1920; in the United States, it continued until the Indian New Deal reforms of 1934.[84] In Australia, on the other hand, the interwar period represented an era of what historian Heather Goodall refers to as a 'second dispossession'.[85]

These dispossessions across the four settler nations were problematic not only because they severed Indigenous cultural ties to land but also because Indigenous populations were less mobile than settler populations and thus more dependent on their lands. Most Indigenous communities resembled the situation in the United States where the sad fact was that reservations were not economically viable in a capitalist economy. Unsustainable practices had led to the depletion of soil quality, timber and range, and the majority of Native Americans did not have the finances necessary to purchase equipment, livestock or fertiliser

---

[84] Titley, *A Narrow Vision*, 16, 20–22, 40–42; Belich, *Paradise Reforged*, 192; Ellinghaus, *Blood Will Tell*.

[85] Heather Goodall, *Invasion to Embassy: Land in Aboriginal Politics in New South Wales, 1770–1972* (St. Leonards, NSW: Allen & Unwin in association with Black Books, 1996), 115–258; Richard Broome, *Aboriginal Victorians: A History since 1800* (Crows Nest, NSW: Allen & Unwin, 2005), 185–285.

needed to produce economically viable agriculture.[86] As a result of land insufficiency, many Indigenous people had been forced to seek marginal wage labour in settler society economies. They were usually stuck on the fringe of the workforce, finding casual or seasonal work where they could and often for less pay than workers of European extraction earned. Indigenous reserves and communities were often located far from settler urban centres and employment opportunities. This meant people gravitated to what were often the only options in the primary industries of agriculture, forestry, mining and fishing.

Even if they were not employed in marginal positions or in seasonal industries, Indigenous people often suffered racial marginalisation – the first fired and last rehired. The cumulative effects were evident in the statistics of average wages in the United States where, in 1939, Native American men living on reservations earned about $500 per year, as opposed to the national median for American males, which sat at $2,300.[87] As Dakota soldier Shirley Quentin Red Boy explained: 'Back then everybody was poor, and everybody was scratching out a living, like chickens scratching for food.'[88] Wilfred John Henry, a Canadian Métis soldier, undoubtedly speaks for many Indigenous servicemen and women in his recollections:

Well I joined [the army] to make money; $1.10 a day, which was better than the 50 cents I'd been getting hauling wood into town. On top of that, there were free clothes, and free board and room. So I joined up because it would help my folks out. Their conditions weren't very good and I could give them half my pay, and they wouldn't have to feed me or buy me clothes. I told my dad that the money I sent home was to go to his machinery. I enlisted because I couldn't stand him not having any money. He was still hauling wood into town for 50 cents a cord.[89]

Native American man Lawrence Leslie Byrd specifically mentions the money to support himself and his family: 'They paid me $21 a month, and I remember that was all in $2 bills. So they gave me ten $2 bills and a $1 bill. And I still had money to send home to Mom.'[90] Under such circumstances, even the relatively low pay of a private, combined with clothing, a roof over their head, three meals a day, dependents' allowances and a sense of purpose was very appealing.

[86] Bernstein, *American Indians and World War II*, 15.
[87] Ibid.
[88] Interview quoted in Elise Boxer, "Citizen Soldiers: Fort Peck Indian Reservation's Company B, 1940–1945" (MA Thesis, Utah State University, 2004), 18.
[89] Wilfred John Henry, in *Remembrances: Métis Veterans*, ed. Dave Hutchinson (Regina, SK: Gabriel Dumont Institute of Metis Studies & Applied Research, 1994), 55.
[90] Lawrence Leslie Byrd, Library of Congress (hereafter LOC) AFC/2001/001/00666.

Interestingly, while men often joined for economic reasons, across the settler societies, women's economic statuses varied. Australia was one extreme where Indigenous women's employment was generally relegated to unskilled work as domestic servants. Women like Betty Pike (nee Ray) had been doing such employment, but in 1943, she was kicked out of a cousin's home and was unemployed. She recalls: 'Well what was I to do? I hit on this idea I'll go and join up in the Air Force. I did ... This was all 1943, the war is already going on. I was underage. If I didn't join up then I had nowhere to go.'[91] In other places such as Canada, though, Indigenous women could sometimes find work in semi-skilled positions that paid more than the military. First Nations woman Jannet Foulds had been working as a nurse trainee in Saskatchewan, earning $60 per month. She was unimpressed with 'Army pay $1.10 per day with increases of fifty cents for trades pay.'[92] Canadian Ojibwe woman Joan Martin had worked as a waitress before joining the army and noted that they 'weren't paid very much, less than working in Nipigon [Ontario] as a waitress'.[93] Such examples reveal that for women, like men, there were more dynamics at play than just sheer economics when they decided to enlist.

For many young Indigenous men and some women from New Zealand, the United States and Canada, cultural structures within their communities encouraged their participation or valued participation in military activities and the warrior status thereby conveyed. Albert Smith, a Navajo Code Talker, said that he enlisted because 'this conflict involved Mother Earth being dominated by foreign countries. It was our responsibility to defend her.'[94] In New Zealand, Māori notions of mana pushed some to enlist, especially in iwi with strong traditions of alliance with Pākehā. Rangi Logan, a Ngati Porou NCO, was struck by this: 'They really went at it so enthusiastically that where a whanau [family] didn't have a young man of appropriate age, well it's a matter of family honour that the whanau must be represented, so we had men as young as fifteen in the Battalion.'[95] One volunteer later explained that 'all their history had been steeped in the religion of war, and the training of the Maori child from his infancy to manhood was aimed at the perfection of the warrior-class, while to die in the pursuit of the War God Tumatauenga was a sacred duty and a manly death'.[96] Townsend notes while the end to American

[91] Betty Pike, interview with Noah Riseman, 12 April 2011, Melbourne.
[92] Jannet Foulds, quoted in Poulin, *Invisible Women*, 65.
[93] Joan Martin, quoted in Ibid., 70.
[94] Townsend, *World War II and the American Indian*, 77.
[95] Soutar, *Nga Tama Toa*, 38.
[96] Ibid., 35.

frontier wars was a positive, community practices and ceremonies were under threat because men did not have the same opportunities to earn the warrior status. Combat in the Second World War, as an extension of the First World War, was an opportunity for men especially to earn the prestigious warrior status as their ancestors had since time immemorial.[97] Similar practices were recorded amongst Canadian Plains First Nations, such as 'some of the young Bloods who had joined the army and been overseas with the Expeditionary Force made sure, when they came back, that they could join the Old Warriors Society'.[98] The adaptation of modern military service to continue warrior traditions constitutes what historian Tom Holm refers to as the 'nativization' of the military.[99]

While the fulfilment of a warrior status was important in many Indigenous communities, this was by no means universal, and it is important to guard against slipping into the essentialised stereotyping of Indigenous peoples as 'warlike' or inherently aggressive. Such notions had captivated settler societies and had become intertwined in constructs of the 'Indian' in North America and the 'Māori' in New Zealand.[100] In many other Indigenous communities in all four countries, there was little or no cultural veneration for the warrior or success in conflict. For instance, most Coast Salish people in the Pacific Northwest traditionally saw warriors as necessary but problematic individuals. Such figures were viewed as volatile or dangerous and often ostracised, living separately or on the margins of their communities.[101] Pueblo peoples of the American southwest, such as the Zuni and Hopi, likewise held little regard for combat or those who undertook such actions. It is worth noting, though, that during the Second World War, cultural notions surrounding the concept of 'warrior' spread across Indigenous communities through what Al Carroll calls 'intertribal syncretism, where tribal nations without any or much of a significant warrior tradition first began to imitate the warrior ethos of other tribes'.[102]

Australia sits slightly apart from the other case studies because Aboriginal and Torres Strait Islander peoples did not have comparable notions of 'warriors'. Certainly, there are traditions around manhood initiations, and this is also not to say that Indigenous Australians never had warfare before Europeans arrived. Such conflicts tended to be about

---

[97] Townsend, *World War II and the American Indian*, 78.
[98] Frederick Niven, "Civilized Warfare," *Saturday Night*, August 30 1941, 25.
[99] Holm, "Patriots and Pawns," 358–361.
[100] See for example, Sheffield, *The Red Man's on the Warpath*; Franchesca Walker, "Descendants of a Warrior Race: The Maori Contingent, New Zealand Pioneer Battalion, and Martial Race Myth, 1914–19," *War & Society* 31, no. 1 (2012): 1–21.
[101] Carlson, "Stó:lō Soldiers, Stó:lō Veterans," 133.
[102] Carroll, *Medicine Bags and Dog Tags*, 115.

payback when someone from one clan violated laws of another. The pre-
colonial warfare tended to be limited and contained within kinship and
law.[103] There was no connection between manhood initiation and warfare, though, which differentiates Aboriginal and Torres Strait Islander
Australians from the other Indigenous peoples of North America and
New Zealand. Even so, what is intriguing is that many Indigenous
Australians today have adopted the language of warriors to describe
their military service and colonial resistance fighters. In an article drawing connections between these men, entitled 'Warriors then … Warriors
still', Noongar filmmaker Glen Stasiuk describes them all as warriors
'exud[ing] rare courage and fighting qualities'.[104]

Beyond economic or specific cultural imperatives, many Indigenous
recruits articulated concepts of ideological affinity with the larger
cause, loyalty, and/or patriotism in explaining their decisions to volunteer. Commitment to democracy was a motivator for some Indigenous
enlistees, such as Navajo man Cozy Stanley Brown: 'The Anglos say
"Democracy", which means they have pride in the American flag. We
Navajos respect things the same way they do.'[105] Many Indigenous people
developed their own clear sense of the purpose of the war and believed
in the fight against fascism. In one anonymous letter to Canada's Indian
Missionary Record, one individual argued that Indians needed to 'stand
up and fight for what we believe is a righteous and a just cause. We therefore take it upon ourselves to share the burdens of our white brothers,
even though it means war, and to do our utmost to overcome what may
threaten to take away all that is dear to us.'[106] Native American veteran
Oscar Alvin Goodwin recollects a sense of civic duty: 'All I was thinking
about is getting in service … I went to my mother and told her that I
had to go to service. I wasn't doing enough for my country delivering
telegrams, which was very important, but I told her that, you know, that
I had to do some more than that for my country.'[107]

'Patriotism' can sometimes be a problematic concept to apply to
Indigenous peoples given their experience of colonisation and continuing

[103] John Connor, "Traditional Indigenous Warfare," in *Before the Anzac Dawn: A Military History of Australia before 1915*, ed. Craig Stockings and John Connor (Sydney: NewSouth Publishing, 2013), 8–20.
[104] Glen Stasiuk, "'Warriors then … Warriors still': Aboriginal Soldiers in the 20th Century," *Journal of Australian Indigenous Issues* 7, no. 3 (2004): 3–13.
[105] Cozy Stanley Brown, "Code Talker: Pacific Theater, World War II," in *Navajos and World War II*, ed. Broderick H. Johnson (Tsaile, Navajo Nation, AZ: Navajo Community College Press, 1977), 61.
[106] James Dempsey, "Alberta's Indians and the Second World War," in *For King and Country: Albertans and the Second World War*, ed. K. W. Tingley (Edmonton: Provincial Museum of Alberta, 1995), 41.
[107] Oscar Alvin Goodwin, LOC AFC/2001/001/56155.

marginalised status. Indigenous patriotism may have looked distinct in some ways from settler patriotism, but the notion of patriotism motivating men and women to sign up for military service transcends nations and cultures. Roger Reese's work on Soviet motivations in the Second World War draws useful conceptual relationships between patriotism, voluntarism and military service. Reese argues that Russian soldiers' willingness to volunteer, be conscripted and fight did not necessarily mean that they supported the Stalinist system or the socialist project. Rather, he claims:

it is feasible for individuals to fight for a country whose leadership they do not like or whose policies negatively affect them ... Therefore, individuals can fight for their country despite mental reservations about the government and the economic and social systems. In fact, people can fight for their country with the hope that their efforts will change the social and political order.[108]

There are significant parallels here to the Indigenous motivation because military service was not an endorsement of colonialism or deference to the settler state.

Patriotism could, for many Indigenous people, have meanings toward their own nations in addition to or instead of the settler state. Navajo man Cozy Stanley Brown succinctly proclaimed that his 'main reason for going to war was to protect my land and my people'.[109] Another anonymous Navajo Code Talker explains: 'during World War II, we were fighting for *our country. Then,* we were being attacked – as close as Pearl Harbor! The enemy was headed this way and we had to stop them. If someone is trying to take something away from us, we fight back. If this is what you call *patriotism,* then we are very patriotic!'[110] For some, fear for their families and traditional territories lay at the root of their volunteering. Peter Gladue wrote a passionate letter after being rejected when he tried to enlist, expressing his sincere concern for the dangers the war presented to everyone in Canada, including Indigenous peoples:

Today and on is our chance to save our children their lives is beyond to help of winning this big flame of fire coming toward us in a world war. Today every stitch of everything is needed. And beyond, all Indian of Canada of all points should now look in future if they love their children and their lands, to help winning this terrible war. A man is fit for war should now go and stop this big flame of fire

---

[108] Roger Reese, *Why Stalin's Soldiers Fought: The Red Army's Military Effectiveness in World War II* (Lawrence: University Press of Kansas, 2011), 17.

[109] Cozy Stanley Brown, quoted in Peter Iverson, *Diné: A History of the Navajos* (Albuquerque: University of New Mexico Press, 2002), 182.

[110] In Doris Paul, *The Navajo Code Talkers* (Philadelphia: Dorrance and Company, 1973), 111.

coming to burn our children their lives. And any one not fit to go should help on every penny to help those people are fighting for us all.[111]

Reading the views of Indigenous voluntarism expressed at the time, one is unable to escape the feeling that enlisting was an inherently political act. Volunteering for military service was public, visible and rich in symbolic meaning in democratic societies. A prime example is Creek woman Laughing Eyes, who enlisted in the Women's Army Corps in May 1942. The *New York Times* showed a picture of the moment, describing her as: 'dressed for a war dance, in tribal outfit complete from beaded band around her straight black locks to white buckskin dress and bright colored Indian blanket as shawl'. When asked why she was signing up, Laughing Eyes, who already had a brother in the Navy, retorted: 'Don't you think I have more right to join than some of the other women?'[112] One reading of this exchange is to see Laughing Eyes as asserting sovereignty. She was signing up to the US Army but as an Indian woman who had the right to defend her country, drawing on her culture to assert a distinct role for American Indians within the Second World War.

This is not to say that every Indigenous young person that set foot in a recruiting office did so as a political crusader or that voluntary enlistment's political utility was uniform or clear-cut. In fact, the political nature of voluntarism was situational, varied and fluid, even within individual countries, and the political messages conveyed by Indigenous peoples were, if even noted by settler societies, often altered or lost in translation. Nevertheless, the potential political nature of Indigenous voluntarism was evident across all four countries.

At the tribal or organisational level, invoking ties to the Crown or state was a significant political act to position Indigenous people as allies with(in) the settler state, defending shared territories.[113] Only one day after war was declared in September 1939, the Secretary of the Tuwharetoa Trust Board, Puataata A. Grace, and Hoani te Heuheu sent a telegram to the New Zealand Prime Minister and another letter to the Native Department assuring both 'that the leaders and Tuwharetoa tribe as a whole will be behind the Government and the Great British

---

[111] "Indian Says All Should Help In War to End 'Flame of Fire'," undated news clipping, LAC, RG 10, Vol. 6764, file 452-6, pt. 2.

[112] Lucy Greenbaum, "10,000 Women in U.S. Rush To Join New Army Corps," *New York Times*, 28 May 1942, 5.

[113] R. Scott Sheffield, "Canadian First Nations and the British Connection during the Second World War," in *Fighting with the Empire: Canada, Britain and Global Conflict, 1867–1947*, ed. Steven Marti and Will Pratt (Vancouver: University of British Columbia Press, in press).

Empire in every possible way in the trial and danger now confronting us all'.[114] In another example, a prairie First Nation appended the following letter to an $850 donation to the Canadian Red Cross from band funds: 'We the Blackfoot tribe of Indians desire to show our loyalty to Canada and to the Empire by our humble bit to help in the struggle for freedom against tyranny. Canada has, and always shall be, our home. The outlook of the Indian is purely Canadian in its nature and character.'[115] Invoking Indigenous people as allies also represented an assertion of sovereignty. In one such example, a Navajo Tribal Council Declaration of 3 June 1940 stated: 'Now, therefore, we resolve that the Navajo Indians stand ready as they did in 1918, to aid and defend our Government and its institutions against all subversive and armed conflict and pledge our loyalty to the system which recognizes minority rights and a way of life that has placed us among the greatest people of our race.'[116] This positioning of themselves as the 'first peoples' was an astute way to assert both membership and autonomy within the settler society.

In Australia, loyalty to the Crown and British Empire was also a justification to challenge the military's colour bar. For instance, a 1940 letter from the Australian Aborigines League to the prime minister protested the regulations against Aboriginal enlistment:

Of course we always discriminate between natives who are primitive or semi-civilised as apart from those who are civilised. For the latter we have always sought full citizenship, which now includes the right to fight for King and Empire. I would like to be assured that the latter category are not to be debarred, and if it has been your intention to do so, I protest and ask for some amendment.

Another letter from the Australian Aborigines League stated: 'the Aboriginal population is intensely loyal to the Empire and the volunteering of the native men is for this reason. They are capable, they have good initiative, and I am informed by those training them that they will make excellent soldiers.'[117]

Indigenous organisations and governments often recognised that military participation could provide political leverage to those seeking to secure improved civil or sovereign rights. In Canada, the long-standing Nisga'a Land Committee directly linked their loyalty to their decades-long battle for recognition of their Aboriginal title to their traditional

---

[114] Letter from Secretary to the Under Secretary, Native Department, 4 September 1939, MA 1 Acc W2459 19-1-239.
[115] "Indian Assist Red Cross Drive," *Calgary Herald*, 3 August 1940.
[116] Iverson, *Diné*, 179.
[117] A. P. A. Burdeau to the Prime Minister, 7 July 1940, NAA A2653, 1940/M214.

territories in a letter to the Prime Minister: 'to show our loyalty to our country contributing $25 ... To protect our tribal rights and to strengthen his Majesties [sic] Forces ... We also pray that there always be an England and final victory.'[118] Few so eloquently connected service to enhanced citizenship rights as did the Kanai chiefs of the Blood Reserve in southern Alberta:

why should we be asked to go when we only live in the empire and are not a part of it. We are only wards of the government and have no voice in controlling the affairs of government but are asked to submit like children and take full responsibility with those who are fortunate to be full citizens and subjects of the King ... Surely if our young men are good enough to wear the King's uniform and take their place with others, they should have full right to say with the others when and where Canada should fight.[119]

In New Zealand, Māori politician Apirana Ngata published the booklet *The Price of Citizenship* in 1943. In it he declared:

Has he [the Māori soldier] proved a claim to be an asset to his country? If so, he asks to be dealt with as such. An asset discovered in the crucible of war should have a value in the coming peace. The men of the New Zealand Division have seen it below the brown skins of their Maori comrades. Have the civilians of New Zealand, men and women, fully realised the implications of the joint participation of Pakeha and Maori in the last and greatest demonstration of citizenship?[120]

The Kanai chiefs and Ngata explicitly invoked the military-citizenship nexus about which military sociologists have written extensively. Ronald Krebs argues that because armed forces epitomise democratic nations' discourses of civic virtue, racial minorities have often invoked their military service as a significant claim to citizenship rights. Moreover, through participation in the military, minorities can often 'test' how the state would respond to calls for civil rights.[121] Arguments connecting Indigenous service to citizenship rights found fertile ground among some segments of the settler society. One example from Australia is a letter from the Aborigines' Uplift Society: 'Aborigines are enlisting, with our encouragement, without any promise of amelioration and they will continue to enlist but it does seem to us that the fact that on acceptance they will be accorded a full Australian status should decide the matter in respect

---

[118] Peter Calder to McKenzie [sic] King, 6 March 1941, LAC, RG 10, Vol. 6763, file 452-5 BC.
[119] Chief Shot Both Sides, et al., to the Minister of Defence, 3 September 1942, LAC, RG 10, Vol. 6769, file 452-20, pt. 5.
[120] Apirana Ngata, *The Price of Citizenship* (Wellington: Whitcombe & Tombs Limited, 1943), 18.
[121] Krebs, *Fighting for Rights.*

to those whose wavering is brought about by the fact that they are now refused an Australian Status.'[122] In 1940, the Commonwealth Cabinet even considered a memo from the Department of the Interior passing on requests it had received to grant citizenship rights to all Aboriginal men who had enlisted in the AIF.[123] As both Krebs and Warren Young point out, though, often nations' willingness to call on racial minorities for military service in times of crisis does not eventuate in the granting of civil rights.[124] Chapters 8 and 9 will analyse in more detail the extent to which Indigenous people's assertions of military citizenship achieved enduring civil rights reforms after the war.

While Indigenous nations or organisations may have had political reasons to assert support for the war effort, for most individual servicemen and women the notion of king, country or civic duty was far removed from their decisions to join the war. Reg Saunders explicitly rejected any connection to empire: 'I don't owe any allegiance or loyalty to the Queen of England. They tried to bloody destroy me, and my family, my tribe, my people. So I'm a bit like the Irish. I love my country very much and I like the people in Australia, so my loyalty was purely Australian.'[125] Others joined for more personal political reasons. One such was Thomas Prince, from the Scantebury Reserve in Manitoba. 'All my life', Prince explained, 'I had wanted to do something to help my people recover their good name. I wanted to show they were as good as any white man.'[126] These considerations provide an insight into another motivation for military service and, in Prince's case, his many daring exploits in uniform: he did not seek an anonymous role but to be the example to change attitudes by his actions.

Voluntarism may well have arisen from a complex blend of tradition, economic need, deep-seated cultural imperatives or of grand notions of patriotism, but at its heart it was an intensely personal choice and we must leave room for idiosyncratic individual rationales. The bulk of Indigenous volunteers were young males between sixteen and twenty-five years of age and, like young males the world over, impulsiveness rather than careful consideration may have shaped many decisions to enlist. Though smaller in number, the majority of Indigenous servicewomen, too, were aged between eighteen and twenty-two and single. Henry Beaudry, from the Sheepgrass First Nation, was a young man who left his

[122] A. P. A. Burdeau to the Prime Minister, 30 June 1940, NAA A2653 1940/M214.
[123] Memorandum for Cabinet, from Minister of the Interior, 4 October 1940, NAA A6006 1941/01/24.
[124] Young, *Minorities and the Military*.
[125] Hall, *Fighters from the Fringe*, 64.
[126] McKenzie Porter, "Warrior: Tommy Prince," *Maclean's* 65, no. 17 (1 September 1952).

*Figure 3.1*   Sergeant Tommy Prince (R) M.M., 1st Canadian Parachute Battalion, with his brother 1, Private Morris Prince, at an investiture at Buckingham Palace, 12 February 1945 (C.J. Woods/DND/LAC/ PA-142289).

reserve to work for a farmer in spring 1941. In May, he went to the town of Paynton and saw a sign at the Post Office: 'Join the army and see the world'. He decided to do so: 'I went to the post office and just … signed my name. That same evening I was in a train going to Saskatoon.'[127] In New Zealand, Harry Mackey, recalled: 'I was in Rotorua one Saturday and met Whiu Te Purei and two other Ngati Porou chaps. They asked me to go to the pub with them. I refused saying I was going to the drill hall to enlist. They talked it over for a while then said they'd come with me and enlist also.'[128] Such tales are an important corrective to tendencies to portray Indigenous voluntarism as solely political or economic.

There was also the promise of adventure, the chance to travel to exotic far-off lands in a time when only the wealthy few had such opportunities. According to one Māori woman from Rangitukia, the young men in her community were encouraged to enlist, 'not to fight, but rather for the adventure and the opportunity to travel'.[129] Gilbert Horn, Sr. grew up on the Fort Belknap Indian Reservation in Montana, and he succinctly recalls: 'I wanted to know what was beyond the reservation boundary.'[130] Sioux man William Irons lived in Fort Yates, North Dakota, when he enlisted for a sense of adventure: 'Well my brother, he was already over in Australia. And it gets kind of boring around the places where I was raised up in the prairies. And I went down and joined.'[131] Even women, such as Canadian Ojibwe Joan Martin, attest to enlisting because they 'wanted a little adventure'.[132] Perhaps the allure of a snappy uniform and the admiring glances it might draw from the opposite sex were part of the equation, as it was for Navajo man Eugene Crawford. He listened to the sales pitch of the Marine recruiter in 1942, but what 'did it for me was the dress uniform on the poster. Crisp white hat and gloves, brass buttons against the deep blue material, boy he looked sharp! I wanted a uniform just like that.'[133]

Numerous veterans' testimonies across all four settler societies describe joining with their friends, both Indigenous and non-Indigenous. Indeed, Aboriginal man Harold Stewart recalls, 'I didn't join because I was patriotic. I joined because my mates had gone. And I make no apology – I'm not giving the Army a pat on the back for that one, or the government.'[134]

---

[127] P. Whitney Lackenbauer et al., *Aboriginal Peoples in the Canadian Military*, 189.
[128] Quoted in Soutar, *Nga Tama Toa*, 40, ft#36.
[129] Quoted in Ibid., 39.
[130] Gilbert Horn, Sr, LOC AFC/2001/001/24257.
[131] William D. Irons, LOC AFC/2001/001/17531.
[132] Joan Martin, quoted in Poulin, *Invisible Women*, 69.
[133] Sally McClain, *Navajo Weapon: The Navajo Code Talkers* (Tucson: Rio Nuevo Pub., 2002), 38. See also Riseman, *Defending Whose Country?* 191–192.
[134] Harold Stewart (When the war came to Australia), 21 February 1991, AWM, F04051.

Dana McGovern, on hearing news of the impending draft, opted to re-enlist in the National Guard unit on the Fort Peck Reservation: 'if I was going to go, I was going to go with guys that I know from Company B. Bob Mitchell [who] lived across the street over here ... [was] the same age as I am. We both said we'd join Company B and go with them and [then] we'd know everybody.'[135] Women, too, often joined with their friends. Twenty-year-old Gunditjmara woman Alice Lovett was working as a domestic servant in Melbourne when she went walking with a friend through the city in 1941. Her friend went into the recruiting centre, and while Alice was waiting:

[T]his recruiting officer came out and said, 'Come over here and join your friend. Come on, come and see what she's going to do'. After a lot of coaxing I walked over and went in and he said, 'You've only got to sign here. Only sign here, you mightn't get in' ... Mary failed her medical, but they passed me and away I went down to Rosebud for training.[136]

Men also experienced the pressure of peers challenging one's masculinity, mana or courage. The sheer number of men enlisting could isolate those who did not sign up. Alaskan Native Roy Daniel Bailey was still in high school in Sitka, Alaska, when the war broke out. He recalls that by early 1942, he was the only boy left in his class: 'You feel the odd being the only boy in a class full of girls. Nothing against girls, but the desire to be with the boys and be also in the military is one of the reasons why ... I volunteered at seventeen.'[137] Arnold Reedy, thirty-eight years of age and with five children, would not normally have qualified. Yet he wrote passionately to Apirana Ngata, making the case for those such as himself who were outside the qualifications:

My family is a sizeable one with considerable land holdings but not one member has enlisted yet. Therefore, I signed up to put to rest the murmurings of the many young men [about our family] so that they might ask why this burden is being left to us to carry, to those like me to enlist ... When they [the young men] have consumed liquor on Saturday nights they are tough, but when it comes to take one's name to the place where the manliness of a person is seen [the recruiting office] they are slow to come forward.[138]

Native American Leonard Clarkson's testimony effectively describes how both external and internal pressures of masculinity – not necessarily distinct to Indigenous peoples – could influence men to enlist: 'Lack of other teenagers, after Pearl Harbor, it was just a natural inclination to get

---

[135] Quoted in Boxer, "Citizen Soldiers," 22.
[136] Alice Lovett, in Jackomos and Fowell, *Forgotten Heroes*, 38.
[137] Roy Daniel Bailey, LOC AFC/2001/001/44446.
[138] Soutar, *Nga Tama Toa*, 40–41.

*Figure 3.2* 1941 portrait of Aboriginal servicewoman, Aircraftwoman Alice Lovett of the Women's Auxiliary Australian Air Force (centre), and two civilian Aboriginal friends: Mary King (left) and Eileen Watson (right). Courtesy Australian War Memorial, accession number P01651.004.

involved. That was in 1942. Also, I had visions of becoming a hot pilot in the air force, as most young guys did. I took the examination, and I was accepted as an air force cadet.'[139]

No doubt for some volunteers, military service provided an escape, whether from an unhappy relationship, a difficult home environment, or a smothering settler administrative regime and lack of opportunity in their own communities. Shirley Quentin Red Boy was one such person: 'I was sixteen and I had an abusive father. He'd wake me up early in the morning, to get horses. He'd kick me to get me awake … he was abusive to me so I signed up for the B Company [National Guard] and told them I was eighteen. So I got away from him. I got away from the pain and anguish.'[140] Bill Edwards from western Victoria recalls volunteering as an escape from boredom:

I got sick of working cows so I went to Warrnambool and joined up. That was in 1941. But I was under age, I was only sixteen, so they give me a discharge. So I roamed around the countryside and to the mission and up and back again. I got sick of it and I joined up again. I put my age up, went back to Warrnambool and joined up.[141]

Queensland Aboriginal woman Oodgeroo Noonuccal was motivated by the access to educational opportunities in the forces:

You see, Aboriginals weren't entitled to any extra concessions of learning and it was the Army that changed the whole things around. They said if you join the Army, you are going to go into the 'dimwits' course and you can learn. So, [one of the reasons] I joined the Army was it was the only way I could learn … I would be allowed to learn.[142]

Leonard Waters was motivated by his childhood fascination with flying; in his words:

When the war broke out in '39, I couldn't get into it quick enough. As a matter of fact I tried to enlist in the Air Force before I turned 17. I would have liked to have gone into aircrew straight away. I was obsessed with it … through that era in the early '30s … But I was obsessed with it and if there hadn't been a war there's no way in the world that I could have flown. That helped my ambition – to join the Air Force.[143]

In the discussion of broad rationales for Indigenous voluntary service, it is worth keeping in mind the individual. Finally, there are of course the

---

[139] Leonard Clarkson, LOC AFC/2001/001/61307.
[140] Boxer, "Citizen Soldiers," 20.
[141] Bill Edwards, in Jackomos and Fowell, *Forgotten Heroes*, 53.
[142] Oodgeroo Noonuccal, in Hall, *Fighters from the Fringe*, 130–131.
[143] Leonard Waters, in Ibid., 157.

cases of those who never intended to join but were conscripted. Their stories are explained in more detail in chapter seven.

### Conclusion

Voluntary Indigenous military service marked the apogee of sacrifice and a highly visible offering to defend the settler nation in which they resided. Across the United States, New Zealand, Canada and Australia, Indigenous men and women volunteered in large numbers and served in an enormous variety of roles in settler military forces. Perhaps surprisingly, though, this macro lens reveals consistent patterns of Indigenous military service across all four countries, as well as the underlying factors that produced them. Firstly, the overwhelming majority of Indigenous volunteers joined the various settler armies, rather than the air and naval forces. This reflected the fact that each army was relatively much larger, had more demand for soldiers and had easier entrance requirements, particularly in education. It is also plausible that Indigenous preponderance in army service may have reflected preference in many cases, though any evidence for this is unsystematic and anecdotal. While Indigenous volunteers were able to access many settler military forces at the start of the war, some racial barriers remained, such as in the RCN, and any Australian force for a time, but there was a clear trend towards widening opportunities for voluntary Indigenous enlistment as the war progressed. This was the case everywhere except New Zealand where Māori recruits found their non-Army options narrowed and eventually eliminated by mid-war.

All of this means that in most cases, while there were varied policies and practices within each settler society, it was the very nature of those policies which necessitated Indigenous agency to enlist. The result made Indigenous military service a predominantly individual, rather than collective, experience. Segregated service was a highly unusual experience for Indigenous service personnel. Even in New Zealand, which had the highest profile segregated unit of the war in the form of the 28th (Maori) Battalion, more Māori served as integrated individuals in RNZAF, RNZN or other Army units overseas or in Territorial or Home Guard units back home. Other segregation experiments conducted in the United States and Australia were eclectic and always involved relatively tiny numbers. Thus, despite the profile that famous units like the US Marine Corps' Navajo Code Talkers have developed in the popular memory, Indigenous military service was first and foremost an individual and integrated experience in massive settler organisations.

This brings us to the most common question that arises when people are introduced to this subject matter: Why did Indigenous men and women volunteer to fight on behalf of countries that marginalised and oppressed their people? First, it is false to assume that Indigenous voluntarism was invariably an affirmation of the state system and political order that that had subordinated their population. For Indigenous people, there was no one rationale for volunteering, any more than for the millions of diverse citizenry that enlisted in these settler nations during the Second World War. Many motivations cut across ethnic and other social lines, such as the desire to join one's buddies or the economic rewards, which were prevalent for many at the late stages of the Great Depression. But the same could be said for patriotism, even if indigenous patriotisms were often articulated in distinct forms from those of non-Indigenous recruits. Many Indigenous people thus responded, as did others to the developing sense of national crusade that marked the war effort.

At the same time, there were a number of motivations that were distinct amongst some Indigenous communities. In parts of North America and New Zealand, many Indigenous nations had long-standing traditions of fighting as allies of one or other Euro-American political entity. These traditions had been renewed in the Great War and the ground thus prepared by that precedent in 1939–45. Still other Indigenous peoples in New Zealand and North America sustained cultural imperatives of their own that venerated warriors and encouraged men to volunteer. While this has sometimes been overplayed in the popular memory and literature, it was a fundamental internal dynamic in those communities concerned. One other factor that marked Indigenous voluntarism as different, and sometimes provided motivation, was its unavoidably symbolic and potentially political nature. To marginalised peoples, often bereft of citizenship rights or genuine acceptance, volunteering to fight contained a powerful challenge to settler pretentions to democracy, equality and freedom.

In the end, much of the decision and the rationale(s) came down to the individual concerned. The idiosyncratic nature of the decision-making combined with impulsiveness make any effort at generalising across Indigenous populations in these four states problematic. Even within a single First Nations or Torres Strait Islander community, each person that made the decision to volunteer likely did so for a reason, or more likely a constellation of reasons, all their own.

# 4    Experiences of Military Life

Without doubt, the most challenging histories to reconstruct are the experiences of Indigenous men and women in settler military forces during the Second World War. There are only a few written accounts, and only in the United States is there a substantive body of oral testimonies about this dynamic part of their lives available from the Library of Congress American History and Folklife Collection. Consequently, there is a void in the historical record, with much of the secondary literature in all four countries focussed less on the service aspect of the war years. Instead, most studies concentrate on the administration of military recruitment, Indigenous policy changes and the home front, for which archival records provide a firmer research foundation.

Specific military records might help to fill in the edges of the picture, except that most Indigenous service personnel were integrated relatively seamlessly into vast corporate entities. Archival records of Indigenous war service are meagre because settler militaries rarely denoted race on recruitment documents (besides 'black' or 'white' in the United States), making it difficult to pinpoint or even gather statistics. Whilst projects are underway in institutions such as the Australian War Memorial to compile lists of Indigenous servicemen and women, historiographically there has been a reliance on estimates and little engagement with individual service records. Personnel files would also reveal training trajectories, disciplinary records, promotions, wounds and commendations.

Studies tend to lean heavily on anecdotal evidence, highlighting bravery and soldierly qualities or perceived 'natural' racial traits. We hear of the medals won and the remarkable exploits of superb soldiers from each settler nation, such as Sergeant Thomas Prince – the most decorated Status Indian soldier in Canadian history, or of Second Lieutenant Te Moana-Nui-a-Kiwa Ngarimu – the first Māori Victoria Cross recipient, or of Lieutenant Ernest Childers – a Creek soldier awarded the

Congressional Medal of Honour in 1943.[1] Indigenous personnel who achieved promotion during the war likewise garner mention: men such as the only Second World War Aboriginal Australian officer, Reg Saunders (who also commanded a company at the rank of captain in the Korean War) or Brigadier Oliver Martin, the most senior First Nations officer in Canada during the war.[2] Still, others gained fame they never sought, such as Ira Hayes, a Pima and a Marine who was photographed helping to raise the US flag over Mount Suribachi on Iwo Jima, who returned to the glare of the media spotlight and a tragic post-war demise.[3]

Such stories are important, but we hear less about the Indigenous servicemen and women outside of the spotlight, who served in anonymity with countless comrades in arms. Many were capable and inspiring members of their respective militaries, but others struggled in their roles. Certainly, adjusting to potential language demands, the authoritarian and hierarchical culture and the limited freedom of action in settler militaries must have presented real challenges – just as for non-Indigenous personnel. The Gender Perspectives on Civil-Military Relations in Changing Security Environment project at the University of Helsinki states that there is a 'gendered logic of the military, which celebrate male power, particularly the male warrior, and devalue all things feminine, produce the kind of masculinities and femininities that are asserted in national gender hierarchies. The logic of the armed forces affirms a "right" kind of nationhood, gendered citizenship and gendered division of labour.'[4] This martial masculinity shaped how Indigenous servicemen and women alike interacted with their peers and chain of command.

One reason stories that counter dominant narratives of martial masculinity have received little attention is the underlying political need for recognition and commemoration of Indigenous service across the four

---

[1] P. Whitney Lackenbauer, "'A Hell of a Warrior': Remembering Sergeant Thomas George Prince," *Journal of Historical Biography* 1, no. 1 (Spring 2007): 27–78; Gardiner, *Te Mura O Te Ahi*, 115–116; NARA, RG 75, Box 1, Entry 998A.

[2] Hall, *Fighters from the Fringe*, 61–89; Harry Gordon, *The Embarrassing Australian: The Story of an Aboriginal Warrior* (Melbourne: Cheshire-Lansdowne, 1962); John Ramsland and Christopher Mooney, *Remembering Aboriginal Heroes: Struggle, Identity and the Media* (Melbourne: Brolga Publishing Pty Ltd, 2006), 182–201; Fred Gaffen, *Forgotten Soldiers* (Penticton, BC: Theytus Books, 1985), 24; Summerby, *Native Soldiers, Foreign Battlefields*, 26–28.

[3] Albert Hemingway, *Ira Hayes: Pima Indian* (New York: University Press of America, 1988).

[4] "Objectives and Methods," *GENCIMIL – Gender Perspectives on Civil-Military Relations in Changing Security Environment*, available from http://blogs.helsinki.fi/civmil/objectives-and-methods/, accessed 30 June 2015. See also Teemu Tallberg and Johanna Valenius, "Men, Militaries and Civilian Societies in Interaction," *norma: Nordic Journal for Masculinity Studies* 3, no. 2 (2008): 85–98.

countries. As indicated in the introduction, the initial wave of literature on the subject, from the 1980s through the early 2000s, contained
within it a passionate desire to salvage the often forgotten war service
of Indigenous veterans from oblivion. Seeking recognition with(in) the
settler nation has meant that Indigenous histories of service have tended
to align with the dominant-masculine narratives of war service, whether
that be the Anzac mythology in Australia and New Zealand or the Greatest
Generation trope in the United States.[5] Such salvage history, often
writing into a void of public and scholarly awareness, emphasises high
Indigenous enlistment rates and success in military service to strengthen
the case for recognition and inclusion within the national consciousness.
The emphasis on skill, courage and sacrifice – as well as masculinity –
produces powerful political and moral capital in the contested contemporary settler-Indigenous relationships. Historiographically, there has been
less room to explore mediocrity or the potentially nondescript nature
and relative anonymity of Indigenous service, as well as the non-combat
roles of Indigenous servicewomen and men.

This chapter looks beyond the well-known heroes and exploits to
understand Indigenous recruits' transition into settler military service.
From the initial culture shock of basic training, Indigenous servicemen and women worked hard to learn their new roles and to meet the
expectations of their comrades and superiors. The majority managed
this transition successfully and found, through their time in the military,
acceptance and respect that they had never experienced in peacetime. In
many ways, Indigenous experiences of military life, and even of combat,
were largely a parallel of the broader Australian, Canadian, New Zealand
and American experiences. In this chapter, we seek to understand the
complexity of this human experience, balancing potentially important
cultural distinctiveness with the broader context of life in military service.

## Expanded Interaction and Acculturation

First and foremost, enlistment or conscription for a Cherokee, Wet'suwet'en,
Wiradjuri or Ngāti Tūwharetoa young person meant immersion in a massive settler organisation. These alien military entities each had their own
distinct corporate identity, rigidly hierarchical structure, totalising sociocultural uniformity and crusade-like sense of purpose. The implications for
Indigenous servicemen and women were profoundly acculturative, particularly for the bulk serving in integrated units. Many had not encountered
this degree of personal interaction and involvement with settler society

---

[5] Tom Brokaw, *The Greatest Generation* (New York: Random House, 2004).

prior to the war. Rates of integration and engagement between Indigenous populations and settler society varied tremendously within, and between, the four countries prior to the war. The overall colonial pattern of the early twentieth century had seen Indigenous populations largely segregated into increasingly smaller pieces of territory, usually located away from centres of European settlement. Bernstein argues that in the United States, the war and military service was the first time men left the reservations en masse.[6] To this, we could add Indigenous women as well, even if not in the same large numbers. Such isolation was relatively easy to come by in the transcontinental countries, but even in New Zealand, the majority of Māori were rural and many Pākehā rarely interacted with them.[7]

This is not to suggest that Aboriginal people, Torres Strait Islanders, First Nations, Māori and Native Americans were free from the colonial touch of settler society and government. Far from it – Indigenous populations were amongst the most heavily administered social groups, and the hand of the state was intrusive and often oppressive. Indeed, in the United States, Canada, New Zealand and Australia, assimilation and protection regimes set up between the 1880s and 1920s consistently reduced Indigenous people's abilities to live as equals alongside or within settler society.[8] Even still, for those who volunteered or were conscripted into military service, the full force of state and settler mechanisms and culture was felt in every waking moment, and in ways most could not have formerly imagined.

Acculturative influence was pervasive both from within and without. Each individual Indigenous serviceman and woman undoubtedly faced intense internal desire to fit in with the other members of their unit, from basic training right through the end of their service. Indigenous personnel, given their pre-war marginalised status, sometimes felt they needed to prove themselves to their fellows and to their superiors. In the case of Royal Australian Air Force pilot Leonard Waters, this meant achieving selection for pilot training:

I was terribly keen to prove myself in the elite, which it is. There is no doubt about that. The flying part of the Air Force is the elite. Well, I was the coloured boy in it and I might add that there was 169 of us I think there was, started, on the course, and there were 44 or 46 finished up as pilots that graduated and got our wings ... there were only three blokes in front of me on my average. So, from my humble beginning I was pretty proud of what I am ... accomplished like.[9]

[6]  Bernstein, *American Indians and World War II*, 40.
[7]  Belich, *Paradise Reforged*, 191.
[8]  Evans et al., *Equal Subjects, Unequal Rights*; Ellinghaus, *Taking Assimilation to Heart*.
[9]  Leonard Waters, in Hall, *Fighters from the Fringe*, 160.

*Figure 4.1*    Three Native American women reservists in the Marine Corps at Camp Lejeune, North Carolina in October 1943. An estimated 800 Native American women enlisted in the US forces. (l to r) Minnie Spotted Wolf (Blackfoot), Celia Mix (Potawatomi) and Viola Eastman (Chippewa). National Archives and Records Administration, identifier 535876.

Fitting in, gaining acceptance and earning respect required Indigenous individuals to adapt to the routine and behaviour expected of all military personnel; standing out, even if due to their Indigenous heritage, potentially threatened the integration into their unit. Bernstein argues that Native Americans mostly did not discuss their race and quotes a Cherokee pilot who claimed: 'We are only doing our job' and 'did not feel different from his fellow officers because he flew alongside whites'.[10] Aboriginal soldier Reg Saunders similarly states: 'So I wasn't aware that there was anything extraordinary about me, but I thought I was a pretty good soldier.'[11] As military sociologist Ben Wadham explains, modern militaries are fratriarchal institutions where soldiers are socialised into seeing themselves as bands of brothers (intentionally gendered). Any visible site of difference, whether with sexuality, gender or race, has the potential to attract ostracism as an 'other'.[12] Failure to adapt may have led to unofficial social sanction from fellow soldiers, which may have been especially painful for an individual Indigenous person already isolated from the support of their community, friends and family.

Beyond the individual, military organisations across the Western world had, over centuries of practice, developed highly effective, purpose-built mechanisms to transform diverse individuals into members of a sociocultural-homogenous group. Military law and regulation, hierarchy, training programs and culture all embodied the capacity to coerce and police adherence to prescribed (masculine) behavioural patterns. It is important to distinguish the particular form, direction and purpose of the militaries' assimilative programs from that developed by settler states and Indigenous administration. Military officials in Canada or the United States, for instance, cared little about the broader raison d'être of Indian Affairs departments. The military assimilation was not targeting any particular race or creed but was universal and applied equally to non-Indigenous personnel. The risk from commanders' perspectives was that substandard individuals who had not fully assimilated could get themselves killed and that such weak links potentially threatened group cohesion and others' lives. Of course, there was a positive side of this for Indigenous peoples: the assimilative, conformist nature of the military represented equality as well.[13] Jeré Bishop Franco argues that Indigenous people had, after 300 years of colonialism, grown adept at adapting to European systems and structures (the logic of survival).[14]

Contrary to white observations, for Indigenous people, a desire to acculturate to military standards did not necessarily signify acquiescence to assimilation or abandonment of their Indigenous identity. Indeed,

[10] Bernstein, *American Indians and World War II*, 54.
[11] Reg Saunders, in Hall, *Fighters from the Fringe*, 80.
[12] Ben Wadham, "Brotherhood: Homosociality, Totality and Military Subjectivity," *Australian Feminist Studies* 28, no. 76 (2013): 212–235.
[13] See Riseman, "Aboriginal Military Service and Assimilation," 155–178.
[14] Franco, *Crossing the Pond*, 156.

a gendered reading of Indigenous service reveals the ways that participation in settler militaries both reinforced *and* challenged traditional
practices. As discussed in the previous chapter, for many First Nations,
Native Americans and Māori especially, men's participation in settler
militaries was an adaptation of longstanding warrior traditions. In this
sense, there was an overlap between Indigenous and settler hegemonic,
martial masculinities. For Indigenous women, though, military service
represented the opportunity to challenge the gendered nature of the warrior within their own cultures. For instance, the *New York Times* quoted
Princess Silver Star as saying: 'We have rifles, we have some ammunition,
and we know how to shoot. We are looking for a firing range to practice. We are disappointed because our fighting women cannot go to the
front.'[15] Given that combat roles remained closed to women – a way to
preserve masculine superiority and to legitimise their dominant power
in society – women could not overturn such longstanding masculine
Indigenous traditions.[16] Just the opening of participation in the women's
services represented the first crack; as opportunities for women in settler
militaries opened over the rest of the twentieth century, the next generations of Indigenous women would carve a space for women warriors.

Of course, women's participation in the war effort represented a
remarkable acculturative opportunity, as for men, to leave reserves,
acquire new skills and more economic independence. The women's services were a distinct sphere in all four countries, originally designed to
employ female labour to undertake tasks compatible with ideas of white,
middle-class women's work: typists, drivers, telephonists, wireless operators, orderlies and cooks. Women represented a source of cheap labour,
as they had lower pay rates as men, and they also freed more men for
combat roles.[17] Labour shortages in some places such as Australia and
the United States led to women's expansion into non-combat roles traditionally viewed as men's work. For instance, Betty Pike served in the
Women's Auxiliary Australian Air Force as a mechanic repairing aircraft
engines. She remembers:

When you were in a group that worked on an aircraft you have to go up on test
flights. That was for security to make sure you'd done a good job and that you
hadn't sabotaged the aircraft. And I was sick. Oh every time I went up and that
was ear trouble... And then they used to skim over the water and they used to,

---

[15] "Indian Women Await Foe," *New York Times*, 13 December 1941, 36.
[16] Corinna Peniston-Bird and Emma Vickers, "Introduction," in *Gender and the Second
World War*, ed. Corinna Peniston-Bird and Emma Vickers (London: Palgrave, 2017), 6.
[17] Riseman, "Escaping Assimilation's Grasp," 760–761; Grace Mary Gouveia, "'We Also
Serve': American Indian Women's Role in World War II," *Michigan Historical Review* 20,
no. 2 (1994): 153–182; Poulin, *Invisible Women*.

wave hopping. You'd just be that, so low you would just sort of skimming. And tree tops, you'd be just – it was horrendous. Those flights were horrendous for me.[18]

Among the four nations, the United States was unique for setting up the Women Airforce Service Pilots (WASPs), who worked at 120 bases across the US flying aircraft as transport, instructing male pilots and even test piloting (a small number of Canadian women served with Britain's Air Transport auxiliary as well).[19] Among the 1,074 WASPs was one Native American pilot: Oglala Sioux woman Ola Mildred Rexroat. She was previously working for the BIA on the Navajo Reservation, then moved to Washington around 1940–1 and worked for the US military. While working for the Army Corps of Engineers, Rexroat learned about the WASPs:

I thought if I could learn how to fly or do something like that that I might not end up behind a typewriter. So, I called and asked what – what was necessary for me to take flight lessons and how much did it cost? And they told me, 'You can't take – unless you have your own airplane or you are in the civil air patrol or you're going to be a WASP.' So, I said, 'Well, what is WASP?' And they said, 'That's the Women Airforce Service Pilots.' And I said, 'That's what I'm going to do.' So, I was able to take flight lessons.

Rexroat graduated as a WASP in 1944 and was posted at the Eagle Pass Army Air Base near the Mexican border. Her main job was towing targets behind her aircraft for male pilots to practice their guns. After the war, when the WASP was decommissioned, Rexroat worked for the Federal Aviation Authority for almost thirty years. She had one significant hiatus from that job: during the Korean War, she was briefly recalled in a reserve unit as a fighter interceptor controller. Reflecting on the acculturative influence war service had on her life, Rexroat states: 'Well, for me it was very significant and it changed my life. It gave me a lot of confidence in myself, my decisions and my ability to learn and use my learning afterwards, because I had been very unsure of myself. And [I] was more or less afraid to make decisions on my own, but I knew that I had to earn a living because nobody else was able to support me.'[20]

As Rexroat's tale alludes, acculturation to military norms provided Indigenous servicewomen and men alike with greater familiarity with settler society, enhanced linguistic and cultural fluency and the confidence that came with being respected and accepted as an equal. Aboriginal

[18] Betty Pike, interview with Noah Riseman.
[19] Sarah Myers, "Battling Contested Airspaces: The American Women Airforce Service Pilots of World War II," in *Gender and the Second World War*, 11–24.
[20] Ola Mildred Rexroat, interviewed by Patricia Jernigan, Women Airforce Service Pilots Oral History Project, 8 September 2006, The Woman's Collection, Texas Woman's University.

servicewoman Oodgeroo Noonuccal once wrote to Ann Howard: 'I joined the AWAS [Australian Women's Army Service] principally because I did not accept Fascism as a way of life. It was also a good opportunity for an Aboriginal to further their education. In fact there were only two places where an Aboriginal could get an education, in jail or the Army and I didn't fancy jail!'[21] Navajo man Peter MacDonald remembers the moment when he realised that he, as a Native American, was not inferior to white men. A white soldier asked him to read a letter from home and then write his reply. At first, MacDonald thought it was a test, but he later learned that the white man was illiterate. MacDonald recalls: 'I was both shocked and excited. White people *weren't* better than I was. White people had to go to school just like the Navajo … Once I realized that white people didn't have any more skills than I did unless they got an education, I no longer thought of them as a super race.'[22]

The sense of immersion could be muted if service occurred in a segregated Indigenous unit. The fellowship, linguistic comfort and cultural affirmation of their compatriots, in units like the 28th (Maori) Battalion or the Torres Strait Light Infantry Battalion (TSLI), provided a buffer of sorts for it members. In the latter case, virtually every adult male in the community was enlisted in the TSLI, enabling its members to draw on the support not only of fellow Torres Strait Islanders but of their friends, brothers, fathers and cousins. Saulo Waia recalls of the TSLI: 'I have six brothers. In the Army, all of us, everyone. Well, we, you know … what I say that number … that's ah … six … six altogether. Remember that! Yes, my father was in the Army too … yeah.'[23] The ability to converse in one's own language contributed to individual psychological well-being and the effectiveness of segregated units. For instance, while English was the main operative language for the Maori Battalion, Te Reo Māori was the majority of soldiers' first language. For convenience's sake, some instructors used Te Reo Māori at times and observed that this produced better outcomes from the soldiers.[24]

The case of the Navajo Code Talkers was somewhat distinct from Māori and Torres Strait Islander segregated service. Though they were trained together and required to speak their own language in the conduct of their duties, in operational theatres they were distributed widely into

[21] Ann Howard, *You'll be Sorry!* (Sydney and Melbourne: TARKA Publishing, 1990), 154. See also Ann Howard *Where Do We Go From Here?* (Sydney: TARKA Publishing, 1994), 161.
[22] Peter MacDonald with Ted Schwarz, *The Last Warrior: Peter MacDonald and the Navajo Nation* (New York: Orion Books, 1993), 63.
[23] Saulo Waia, in Hall, *Fighters from the Fringe*, 148.
[24] Soutar, *Nga Tama Toa*, 60.

Marine units. By virtue of working in communications with each other, they always came across other Navajos – sometimes in unexpected ways. Roy Hawthorne remembers one particular example:

I met one of my cousins on Okinawa. We were talking, doing field training with the Navajo code and I was talking to this person and asked him about himself and he told me and, it was my cousin. And so I visited him there, he was in a different division, and we visited. But the thing is that while we were here, in our land, it was practically impossible to go these distances and visit one another. So we had to wait for the war to come along and take us a long ways from home and bring us together in that way.[25]

Indigenous servicemen and women did not need to be in segregated units to find the company of fellow Indigenous personnel. The enthusiasm with which Indigenous soldiers speak of such encounters and friendships indicates how important the occasional chance meeting was to them.[26] In one instance, Colville Indian member Roscoe Owhi wrote in a letter home:

The other day I went on a pass and was walking down a street; a sailor passed me and I recognized him right away and chased him across the street, stopping him. It was Walt Williams, and while talking with him and recalling of our past at Nespelem, along came another sailor, looking right at us and smiling too. It was Albert Andrews, my cousin. For awhile [sic] I thought I was dreaming, all standing there just as if we were at some of our street corners in Nespelem.[27]

Hollis Stabler, an Omaha soldier, later recalled his encounter with a Sioux sailor prior to the invasion of southern France: 'We talked about home ... I wish I could remember that Indian's name. He was an Indian and so was I. We recognized that "brotherhood". If he's not dead, I sure wish I could find him.'[28]

In this context, the ethnic make-up of an individual's primary unit (platoon, ship or squadron) could have a significant effect on an Indigenous service member's sense of acculturative immersion. If they were the lone individual of Indigenous background, the experience may have differed from those who enjoyed the companionship of another or several Indigenous comrades. Franco makes this point, drawing on numerous examples of Native American servicemen from the Southwest who lamented in letters home that they were still the only Indian in their unit or who missed speaking their own language.[29] How broadly applicable

[25] Roy O. Hawthorne, LOC AFC/2001/001/52528.
[26] Hall, *Fighters from the Fringe*, 100–101.
[27] "Indians meet across ocean," *Spokesman-Review* (Spokane, WA), 4 January 1944, NARA, RG 75, Box 1, Entry 998A.
[28] Hollis Stabler, *No One Ever Asked Me: The World War II Memoirs of an Omaha Soldier* (Lincoln & London: University of Nebraska Press, 2005), 111.
[29] Franco, *Crossing the Pond*, 164–168.

*Figure 4.2*  Māori soldier reading letters in the Western Desert at Christmas time, World War II. War History Collection, Alexander Turnbull Library.

this phenomenon was remains a matter of speculation. Sebastian Junger argues that unit cohesion – 'strong emotional bonds within the company or the platoon' – is a natural consequence of the intensive training and sometimes combat danger within an armed force.[30] Echoing this sentiment, Euclide Boyer, a Métis soldier in the Canadian Army, remembered that there 'were a few Indians and Métis, but in those days every fellow soldier was like a brother to you, so it didn't make much difference'.[31]

---

[30] Sebastian Junger, *Tribe: On Homecoming and Belonging* (London: HarperCollins Publishers, 2016), 85.
[31] Euclide Boyer, in *Remembrances*, 18.

### Adjusting to Military life

Regardless of their degree of isolation in a massive settler military organ-isation, Indigenous servicemen and women faced the challenge of adjust-ment to a strange, even bizarre world with its own arcane rituals, language, values and demands. Much would be asked of them and the transition was rarely an easy one, with the culture shock beginning with basic train-ing. Despite the doubts some settler militaries held about Indigenous recruits, most would manage the journey from civilian to soldier relatively successfully. Not all avoided the pitfalls, with some suffering punishments and sometimes discharge, but these were seemingly a small minority.

It was not just Indigenous recruits who experienced the novelty and unfamiliarity of military life. The vast majority of settler forces mobi-lised during the Second World War were drawn from a broad spectrum of civilian society, most of whom had no prior military experience. Whether volunteers or conscripts, few found the discipline, obedience and regimentation of military training and service anything but utterly foreign to the freedoms and individualism of their former daily lives.[32] Though Indigenous recruits were not alone in struggling to adjust, it is also evident that many had a greater cultural and social distance to cover. For instance, the gendered divisions of labour, economy, spirit-uality and leadership in Indigenous societies fit well with the gender-defined roles within settler militaries. Yet within their gendered spheres, most Indigenous societies had traditionally been fairly egalitarian, with social hierarchies built primarily around Elders and cultural knowledge, significant personal choice exercised within clear sociocultural bounda-ries and consensual decision-making and leadership. One Navajo Code Talker recalled, 'When we got to camp we thought we were in a peniten-tiary, after the free life on the reservation.'[33]

Other more specific cultural values and practices could complicate the adjustment process. Navajo sailor Dan S. Benally recalls:

We met some Pueblos that had long hair. They were mad when the officers cut their long hair off. Next, military clothes were issued to us to wear. Some of us had long hair and some Navajos had queues. Our queues were cut off and sent back to our wives, parents and relatives. I sent my clothes, shoes and hat to my mother in Crownpoint. Afterward, the officers asked questions which made us a little big frightened. That was the way we went about getting started on our training at that place.[34]

[32] Richard Holmes, *Acts of War: The Behavior of Men in Battle* (New York: The Free Press, 1985), 79–92.
[33] Paul, *The Navajo Code Talkers*, 15.
[34] Dan Benally, "Ex-Prisoner of War, European Theater, World War II," in *Navajos and World War II*, 66.

Navajo Code Talker Chester Nez also recalls:

Soon we learned the real challenges in the military were cultural, not physical. Marine officers looked us in the eye and expected us to look back. To a Navajo, doing this was very bad manners. The drill instructor confronted us recruits, his face inches from ours, and yelled at the top of his lungs. We had always been taught to keep our voices modulated. The unaccustomed shouting rattled us, making it difficult to respond. There were times we men, accustomed to reservation life, felt like we'd arrived on a different planet.[35]

People coming from more remote locations like the Torres Strait were more likely to experience the shock. Charles Mene described his adjustment this way:

... being new, it was a bit difficult at first and then, when I got to know the boys and the training, I enjoyed it. This was my first time away from Thursday Island. Yes, it was a great change for me. It was difficult because, Islanders, you see, we got our own language. I had to mix with the boys and sometimes I found it a bit difficult to understand the English, but anyway, I learned my way. But I had no difficulty making friends and getting on with the white soldiers. We were all in it [together].[36]

East Coast Māori likewise felt the weight of the occasion upon the arrival of their train at Palmerston North where they underwent their initial training. The Pākehā commanding officer, Lieutenant-Colonel Dittmer, greeted them and the Company Sergeant-Major, Henry Ngata, remembered the 'railcar was filled with Ngati Porou recruits ... the train was something new then, especially here in Gisborne ... They were quite noisy during the transfer from the station to the camp. But when they reached the camp, most of them went quiet: it was as though this was a new world.'[37]

The initial impact could be overwhelming, only amplified by the shock value that drill sergeants seem to revel in the world over when breaking in new recruits. Some of the first Māori soldiers took to calling their Pākehā instructor, a Major McCulloch, by the evocative nickname the 'Screaming Skull'.[38] Navajo Code Talker Chester Nez recalls:

The constant shouting and hassling took a toll on us. Several men feared they had made a mistake in joining the Marines. Some talked with me about how out of place they felt in this new 'white man's' environment. And many had begun to wonder whether they'd make it out of the war alive. I listened to their fears, knowing that they were voicing the same doubts I felt. But we encouraged each other, together conquering any misgivings. We had not made a mistake.[39]

---

[35] Chester Nez and Judith Schiess Avila, *Code Talker: The First and Only Memoir by One of the Original Navajo Code Talkers of WWII* (New York: Berkley Caliber, 2011), chapter 9.

[36] Charles Mene, in Hall, *Fighters from the Fringe*, 93.

[37] Soutar, *Nga Tama Toa*, 56.

[38] Ibid., 48.

[39] Nez and Avila, *Code Talker*, chapter 9.

Notwithstanding the separate roles and living arrangements, basic train-ing could be just as harsh for Indigenous (and non-Indigenous) women as for the men. Natalie Coates, who entered training for the Royal Canadian Air Force Women's Division, found herself:

very frightened in Basic, where they take your life and turn it upside down, because I didn't know what they [the Air Force] would do if I didn't do it right ... Take this girl from a little town and send her to Rockcliffe. I did nothing but cry for two months, asking myself 'what have I done? What HAVE I done?' It was a real culture shock ... There was no coddling. There were male officers on the Parade Square because they could yell louder, otherwise there were female officers.[40]

Women, of course, had a double minority status and could be targets not just of racism but also sexism. Historians have written about ways that authorities faced a dilemma about the women's services; on one hand they needed women workers in the defence forces, but on the other hand, they wanted to uphold contemporary gender norms about femi-ninity. Anxieties about the fear of lesbianism (which was prevalent in the women's services) and masculinisation of the sex led authorities to draft regulations designed to police servicewomen's bodies.[41] Notwithstanding these discriminatory institutional frameworks – as well as the unequal pay and restrictions on work within the forces – most Indigenous ex-servicewomen do not recall individual encounters with sexism. Ola Rexroat says of her experience: 'the commander – he liked WASPs and thought they did a good job of flying and he even requested more'.[42] WAAAF Betty Pike says of the men: 'They used to call me Sunshine. My name was, my single name was Ray, R-A-Y, and they connected that with a ray of sunshine ... I don't think they took too much notice of me ... I never had any conflict, except I didn't like their swearing.'[43]

This is not to say that sexism never occurred. Grace Poulin presents a few examples from the Canadian forces, including Anishnabe woman Mamie Wetelainen's statement: 'Gender discrimination did exist. Senior officers in the canteen would grab women wherever they [men] wanted,

---

[40] Grace Poulin, "Invisible Women: Aboriginal Servicewomen in Canada's Second World War Military," in *Aboriginal Peoples and the Canadian Military*, 142–143.

[41] Myers, "Battling Contested Airspaces," 11–24; Ruth Ford, "Lesbians and Loose Women: Female Sexuality and the Women's Services During World War II," in *Gender and War: Australians at War in the Twentieth Century*, ed. Joy Damousi and Marilyn Lake (Cambridge: Cambridge University Press, 1995), 81–104; John Moremon, "After 'the Girls' Came Home: Ex-Servicewomen of Australia's Wartime Women's Auxiliaries," in *When the Soldiers Return: November 2007 Conference Proceedings*, ed. Martin Crotty and Craig Barrett (Melbourne: RMIT Publishing in association with the School of History, Philosophy, Religion and Classics, University of Queensland, 2009), 203–211.

[42] Rexroat, Women Airforce Service Pilots Oral History Project.

[43] Betty Pike, interview with Noah Riseman.

including the genital area.'[44] Such examples demonstrate the continuing subjugation of women within the services, but they also reinforce the more common narratives of a relative decline of sexism in the wartime context. Ex-servicewomen clearly understand the meaning behind sexism and their statements that it did not happen should not be written off as blindness to something acceptable during that era.

One pre-war factor that does appear to have affected the initial transition to military life for Indigenous recruits regardless of gender was their education. The separate education systems established in settler states typically encouraged assimilation amongst the young pupils, preparing them to fill unskilled labour positions on the margins of the settler economy.[45] Poor literacy skills or not completing school did not necessarily hinder enlisting. Edith Merrifield recalls that she managed to get into the Canadian Women's Army Corps underage and short of the requirements when her Indian Agent fabricated a Grade 8 certificate. She says: 'did I have it rough with no education – just Grade Four! I couldn't advance. I just stayed a private. All I was qualified for was waitress and general duties. I applied for and took a course in military policing. I got a lot of help from the girls.'[46] Alec Kruger tells a similar story from central Australia in 1942, where he knew the recruitment officer: 'He took me straight into the recruitment office and started filling in my forms. Where I couldn't answer he made something up. He even told me what age to say I was. So I became twenty years old and not needing any consent papers done. I was signed up straightaway and in the army.'[47] In other instances, as the war progressed and there were stronger man (and woman) power demands, lower entry requirements benefited Indigenous people. Navajo Teddy Draper, Sr. was still in high school when the war broke out, and he recalls the Marine Corps visiting in early 1942: 'So they pick up a few boys, not many, who are high school graduates and a few are from the high school graduate. And then, after they went back to the, I guess, to San Diego, and then they came back and they changed the age. They dropped the age from 21 years to 18 years old. And I'm in it. And the rest of the boys are in it then.'[48]

[44] Mamie Wetelainen, in Poulin, *Invisible Women*, 32–33.
[45] McClain, *Navajo Weapon*, 41; Barry, "Broken Promises"; Miller, *Shinguak's Vision*; David Wallace Adams, *Education for Extinction: American Indians and the Boarding School Experience, 1875–1928* (Lawrence: University Press of Kansas, 1995); Judith Simon, ed., *Nga Kura Maori: The Native Schools System 1867–1969* (Auckland: Auckland University Press, 1998).
[46] Poulin, *Invisible Women*, 58.
[47] Alec Kruger and Gerard Waterford, *Alone on the soaks: The life and times of Alec Kruger* (Alice Springs, NT: IAD Press, 2007), 123.
[48] Teddy Draper, Sr, LOC AFC/2001/001/52556.

The very nature of some state schools, particularly the residential and industrial schools developed in Canada and the United States, had already familiarised young people with a hierarchical and tightly controlled institutional system. As with basic military training, pupils in Canadian Indian Residential schools were expected to be completely obedient to the school staff and to divide their day in a rigidly regimented fashion. If they stepped out of line, students were punished severely, including corporal and group punishments for individual infractions.[49] Such a system was not greatly different from that encountered in basic training camps. Shirley Quentin Red Boy recalled feeling somewhat prepared: 'I already knew the nomenclatures of marching, drill stuff cause I went to boarding school.'[50] This is not a ringing endorsement for these much-maligned educational systems, but it could help Indigenous recruits during their transformation into soldiers. For example, Cowichan recruit, Russell Modeste, noted that in school, students:

lined up every morning for whatever, breakfast, lunch, supper, church ... So when I entered the military, this was nothing new to me, I just blended right in with it and little easier than some of the white boys who came out of cities who had no inkling of any discipline in the military.[51]

In addition, several Canadian residential schools established army cadet programs, which provided a more explicit taste of military life for young men like Tommy Prince. 'I liked being in the Cadets at Elkhorn [Residential School]', he later told a reporter: 'As soon as I put on my uniform I felt like a better man. I even tried to wear it to class.'[52] The Canadian Army recognised the link between Indian schools and success as soldiers, as evidenced by a special note on the 'Enlistment of Indians and Half Breeds' in the 1944 recruiters' manual:

Care should be taken when accepting applications from or approaching Indians as prospective recruits. Here education standards are strictly adhered to. Experience has shown that they cannot stand long periods of confinement, discipline and the strenuous physical and nervous demand incidental to modern army routine. On the other hand, some very fine Indians have been enlisted, but these are usually persons who have had their schooling and training in an Indian Residential School.[53]

---

[49] See Miller, *Shingwuak's Vision*; Adams, *Education for Extinction*.
[50] Elise Boxer, "Citizen Soldiers: Fort Peck Indian Reservation's Company B, 1940–1945" (MA Thesis, Utah State University, 2004), 23.
[51] Lackenbauer et al., *A Commemorative History of Aboriginal Peoples in the Canadian Military*, 136.
[52] Quoted in Lackenbauer, "'A Hell of a Warrior': Sergeant Thomas George Prince," in *Intrepid Warriors: Perspectives on Canadian Military Leaders*, ed. Colonel Bernd Horn (Kingston, ON: Canadian Defence Academy Press, 2007), 96.
[53] Shoulder to Shoulder: Information for Recruiting Personnel and Civilian Recruiting Advisors, 1944, DHIST, 113,3A2009/ D2.

In Australia as well, there is evidence especially from the post-Second World War era that Aboriginal members of the Stolen Generations, raised in institutions, adapted well to the regimentation of military life.[54]

## Segregation Proposals to Aid Transition

Government and military officials contemplated or undertook some efforts and initiatives to ease the rocky road for Indigenous recruits. These sometimes arose from Indigenous communities' concerns, as well as from settler state and military officials dubious about the prospects of deploying Indigenous service personnel. Prominent amongst these was a strong push originating with American anthropologist and Indian New Deal advocate, Oliver LaFarge, and subsequently led by prominent Navajo, J. C. Morgan, to create segregated Native units solely for training purposes. The intent was to enable a segment of the Native American population, labelled 'primitive Indians' by LaFarge, who supposedly lacked the social, educational and especially linguistic tools to gain acceptance to the US Army. Though John Collier, BIA Commissioner, was ambivalent about segregation of Indian soldiers, he agreed to this plan in early 1941 as an interim step so long as such men would transfer to regular units. The Assistant-Chief of Staff, General William E. Shedd, rejected the proposal as further segregation beyond African Americans was only going to add additional expenses and administrative confusion to the Army.[55]

Enthusiastic Māori communities in some rural regions of New Zealand, especially the east coast of the North Island, adopted a scheme proposed by Apirana Ngata. The plan was to develop voluntary preliminary training, with Great War veterans as instructors, to maintain the interest of men already registered but not yet taken on strength.[56] On Canada's Pacific coast, racial barriers had scuppered early efforts to enrol First Nations crews and vessels in the Fisherman's Reserve, but Indian Affairs officials renewed attempts in early 1942 following Japan's entry into the war.[57] Part of the sales pitch to military officials was that the segregated service in the Fisherman's Reserve 'would stimulate a more general interest among the Indians for the more advanced training to be secured in the active units'.[58]

---

[54] Noah Riseman, "The Stolen Veteran: Institutionalisation, Military Service and the Stolen Generations," *Aboriginal History* 35 (2011): 57–77.

[55] Townsend, *World War II and the American Indian*, 68–72.

[56] Soutar, *Nga Tama Toa*, 41.

[57] See Maclachlan to Camsell, 18 March 1941, DHist 112.3H1.009/D293 and LAC, RG 10 Vol. 11289 File 214-5.b.

[58] Coleman to Goodman, 26 January 1942, LAC, RG 10 Vol. 11289, file 214-5.

In Australia, as regulations barred men and women 'not substantially of European origin or descent', there was no plan to transition Aboriginal or Torres Strait Islander service personnel. There was, however, a short-lived group of Lake Tyers Aboriginal men who served together in 1940. As early as 1939, several men from this Victorian Aboriginal reserve petitioned to join the 2nd AIF, but due to legislation deeming them wards of the state, they had to apply through the station manager.[59] By June 1940, they received approval; a group of seventeen men enlisted together in June 1940, and a further fifteen signed up in July. Press reports described these men as receiving heroes' welcomes as they journeyed through towns from Gippsland to Melbourne. The reports also emphasised the men's physical capabilities, pointing to sporting achievements in boxing and football.[60] Most of these men served together, though the records about this group are sparse. Reg Saunders speculates that they were meant to be a special reconnaissance unit drawing on Aboriginal bush skills.[61] This never came to fruition, and in the group's short existence, they were primarily a form of propaganda to garner wider support for the war effort. The men formed a gumleaf band, which played at Army recruitment drives and outside the Melbourne Town Hall every Friday.[62] A Cinesound Newsreel from 7 March 1941, entitled 'Aborigines are True Soldiers of the King', depicts the troop in training. The narrator remarks:

Original Aboriginal Anzacs. They're not in the Army as a curiosity; they are volunteers in the service of the country they love. They come from Australia's oldest family. They've got a fighting tradition thousands of years old. In the battle dress of the soldier of 1941, hunting through the Australian bush, where, once like black shadows their ancestors stalked the fold. Here, surely, is one of the strangest sidelights of the greatest war the world has known. With thick bayonets instead of the spears their forefathers carried, with bullets instead of boomerangs, the dark-heeled diggers go into action.[63]

The Army had little interest in this group, though. As Saunders recalls, 'they didn't know the first thing about soldiering and I don't think the sergeants and officers were interested enough to train them, they would have probably have made a very fine unit, but I don't think that was the way to do it at all'.[64] Aboriginal veteran George Birkett states that

59  "Blacks Want to Serve," *The Argus* (Melbourne), 25 September 1939, 2.
60  See photos AWM P01066.001; P02522.016; "Aborigines in AIF," *The Argus*, 16 July 1940, 5; "17 Aborigines in Sale AIF Draft," *The Argus*, 27 June 1940, 5.
61  Reg Saunders, in Hall, *Fighters from the Fringe*, 84.
62  Jackomos and Fowell, *Forgotten Heroes: Aborigines at War from the Somme to Vietnam*, 14.
63  Charles Lawrence, narrator, *Aborigines are True Soldiers of the King* (Cinesound news No. 488), March 1941, AWM, F00519.
64  Reg Saunders, in Hall, *Fighters from the Fringe*, 83.

when there was a battalion restructure, the majority of the Lake Tyers Aboriginal men were discharged. He comments, 'The army could have given them jobs in base ordnance depots or as cooks or something and released fit men, but they didn't. They were used up as a promotion ... I think they were only brought in as a publicity stunt.'[65]

While most suggestions of segregation aimed at political impacts or raising Indigenous enlistment numbers, part of segregation's attraction was to soften the culture shock of military service and to increase the likelihood of successful transition. One way in which segregation could smooth the transition was through the pivotal role of Indigenous officers as interlocutors: explaining the challenges faced by Indigenous personnel to settler military officers and interpreting the peculiarities and imperatives of settler military service, discipline and justice to Indigenous personnel. For example, when a spike in disciplinary issues occurred in England in November 1940 amongst C Company of the Maori Battalion, Henry Ngata wrote:

> We've been having a spot of bother with the chaps lately, for they have been inclined to play up a little more than usual. Capt. Scott had spoken to them, but it wasn't till Arnold spoke to them in Maori, that we had the response we wanted. It wasn't merely that Arnold spoke to them in Maori, it was mainly because he expressed conceptions like 'discipline' in a Maori way and quoted old Maori ideas on the subject.[66]

Indigenous soldiers serving in integrated units did not have the luxury of having foreign settler military culture and structure reconceptualised into a more comprehensible and meaningful format for their consumption.

Another way segregation could aid Indigenous soldiers' transition was by presenting a larger umbrella under which their transgressions might be hidden or, at least, receive a more sympathetic response. The collective offered the chance to blend in, blurred the distinctiveness of the individual and offered protection against external threats. The larger group identity enabled the development of behavioural norms more amenable to Indigenous understanding and culture. The prime example here is the Maori Battalion, which developed a reputation for looser discipline than was the norm within 2nd NZ Division. Monty Soutar explains that this cultural distinction arose from the 'different sense of justice among the Maori soldiers', whose hero, the deity Maui, 'was admired for his mischievous personality, willingness to take risks, and general disobedience of rules in pursuit of his goals'.[67] The unit was infamous for its penchant for battlefield scrounging and making use of captured enemy weapons,

[65] George Birkett, in Jackomos and Fowell, *Forgotten Heroes*, 25.
[66] Quoted in Soutar, *Nga Tama Toa*, 98.
[67] Ibid., 368.

up to and including artillery. One 24th Battalion member recalled Māori soldiers at Cassino, 'Armed to the teeth, festooned with Spandaus, Schmeissers, Brens, tommy-guns, carbines, and the odd rifle. I had never seen such a body of men so completely armed with automatic weapons.'[68] Such unorthodoxy was understood and, within limits, indulged by the Battalion's officers. Even Pākehā senior officers at brigade and divisional level were willing to turn a blind eye because of their respect for the unit's performance. In one instance, Brigadier W. G. Stevens suggested that some of the battalion's offences were 'better forgotten, especially in view of the wonderful showing put up by the Battalion'.[69]

Importantly, even service in a segregated unit did not wholly buffer Indigenous servicemen from the cultural onslaught. Navajo or Comanche Code Talkers may have trained together, but were dispersed for operational service to perform their communication duties. The TSLI did train and serve together throughout the war. No Torres Strait Islander member rose above the rank of sergeant, and while the TSLI's white Australian officers were often sympathetic and supportive, they were regular Army and could not fulfil the cultural interpreter and liaison roles. Not even the 28th (Maori) Battalion could completely shield individual soldiers in its ranks from the acculturative impact of military service – nor was it ever intended to.

## Transitions to Service Life

The sheer numbers of Indigenous men and women who managed the transition and became functional members of the armed forces suggest that the culture shock was fairly brief and surmountable. The accounts left by Indigenous service people reveal the sense of accomplishment and pride that they derived from having adapted to military life. The physical components of the training were usually manageable and, for some individuals, even easy. Private Augustino Lavato found the obstacle course in his US Army Basic Training entertaining: 'You should have seen the boys fall from the swings into ditches that were filled with water ... I laughed at them until I was exhausted. I came thru [sic] without a scratch, and it was my first time.'[70] Similarly, when eighteen-year-old Marion Hill joined the Canadian Women's Army Corps, she found that 'basic was not so hard. I was used to hard work on a farm. I looked after cattle, and cut wood on the reserve, and had to do the chores. Marching wasn't

---

[68] Quoted in Ibid., 369.
[69] Quoted in Ibid.
[70] Quoted in Franco, *Crossing the Pond*, 156.

difficult.'[71] Yorta Yorta Aboriginal man Doug Nicholls had been a famous runner and played Australian Rules football with the Fitzroy Lions. When Nicholls showed up to boot camp, his sergeant-major and other officers recognised him and even shook his hand.[72] Indigenous people from rural areas were more accustomed to hardship, to the elements and to doing without than their more urban settler fellows.[73] Indeed, Navajo man Dan Akee says: 'They're [Marines boot camp] strict, but I've seen a lot of white people living out of cities, they do have a hard time, but not Navajos. You know, being a reservation, only mostly on foot, to run, everything I did, you know, so we didn't have no problem with the exercise or already knowing what to do, even with our rifle, because the way we raised – that's it, you know.'[74]

It was not simply the physical exercise that many Indigenous recruits grasped quickly. The first groups of Māori that entered training had to quickly master the intricacies of military parade ground drill. The national celebrations of the hundredth anniversary of the Treaty of Waitangi (1840) opened with a centennial exhibition in Wellington, and a request came through for a company of Māori soldiers to provide an honour guard to help open the Māori Court there on 14 December 1939.[75] As Soutar points out, it was extraordinary that the recruits with little drill experience managed to master such complex movements so quickly – just two weeks into training.[76] Navajo man Teddy Draper, Sr. says that he had been a member of the Boy Scouts, so he was already familiar with some of the regimentation of military life. He also had been an athlete, even running a track state championship, so he found the running aspect of boot camp to be manageable.[77] When a general visited the TSLI in July 1944, a Torres Strait publication entitled *Zero Post* reported: 'Most of us accepted the invitation [to the feast] partly out of curiosity. We did not expect to witness a military display of such excellent standard.'[78]

Importantly though, not all servicemen or women found the transition straightforward, and some were unable to become soldiers, sailors or aircrew. The bewildering range of new regulations to follow and behavioural expectations sometimes left Indigenous recruits on the wrong side of their sergeants or the broader military establishment. Several Navajo

[71] Poulin, "Invisible Women," 143.
[72] Mavis Thrope Clark, *The Boy from Cumeroogunga: The Story of Sir Douglas Ralph Nicholls, Aboriginal Leader* (Sydney: Hodder and Stoughton, 1979), 118–119.
[73] Holmes, *Acts of War*, 133–134.
[74] Dan Akee, LOC AFC/2001/001/52555.
[75] Māori Participation in the Exhibition, 1939–40, ANZ, MA 1 19-1-411.
[76] Soutar, *Nga Tama Toa*, 48.
[77] Teddy Draper, Sr, LOC AFC/2001/001/52556.
[78] "Our Appreciation by The Editor," *Zero Post*, 29 July 1944.

Code Talkers recalled running afoul of the system, to their chagrin. One veteran remarks:

'I was always working off demerits for some offense: not standing up straight, not giving a proper salute, my eyes were crooked, or something!' [Wilsie] Bitsie recalled. 'I had to work them off by either digging a 6 foot by 6 foot foxhole, do extra KP [kitchen patrol] duty, and once by standing on the parade ground with a metal bucket on my head.' The last was because he had forgotten his weapon when called to a surprise drill one morning. He had run to get it saying 'Sarge, I forgot my gun!' After the drill he was marched to the parade ground and, with a bucket on his head, made to repeat 50 times, 'Ten thousand Marines have a rifle, but I'm the only shithead with a "gun"!'[79]

Another Code Talker decided that he 'could not stand the stress [of boot camp] any longer and finally "went over the hill". He started back to the reservation and had been absent from camp for three days when he decided he had made a grave mistake.'[80] He sneaked back into camp but was eventually brought before officers for discipline.

An incomplete nominal role of seventy-seven Aboriginal men enlisted in Western Australia during the war, prepared in the Office of Native Affairs, included: five discharged as U.B.E.S. or 'unlikely to become an efficient soldier', four discharged with a disciplinary charge, one listed as discharged because he was 'unfit for further military service' and a final individual whose services were 'no longer required'.[81] The first two categories indicate a number of men who appear to have struggled in military service, and the final two dishonourable discharges could have been for a variety of reasons. This discharge rate does not seem especially high, suggesting that far more Aboriginal men succeeded in adapting to military service than failed.

### Acceptance and Respect

For those men and women who did manage the transition, military service opened up a novel, memorable and vibrantly alive experience. The same might have been said of any veteran of the Second World War, but there was a distinct and consistent additional theme for Indigenous servicemen and women: the unprecedented sense of respect and acceptance they received from their comrades and superiors. As Russell McGregor argues, acceptance 'is a rather amorphous achievement, and it is impossible to precisely calibrate the degree of acceptance at a particular point

[79] McClain, *Navajo Weapon*, 42–43.
[80] Paul, *The Navajo Code Talkers*, 17–18.
[81] Nominal Role, Natives Enlisted in the Army, no date, SRO WA, Acc 993 529-40.

in time'.[82] Nevertheless, for Indigenous servicemen and women, the contrast from their former civilian lives was so profoundly striking that almost all veterans make note of the difference in their written memoirs or interviews. It is impossible to pinpoint a single explanation for this decline in racial prejudice while in the armed forces, but there are a number of plausible contributing factors.

The crusade-like mission of the Second World War combined with the nature of military service to drive this process. The crisis atmosphere of wartime and the sense of purpose seem to have ranked high in the minds of Indigenous service personnel as a causal factor in the change. Oodgeroo Noonuccal, a wireless operator in the Australian Women's Army Service, claimed that there:

was a difference between the way we were being treated in the Army and before the war. Oh yes! A complete difference, because in the Army they didn't give a stuff what colour you were. There was a job to be done, just to get it done, and all of a sudden the colour line disappeared, it just completely disappeared.[83]

Augmenting the mission was military training designed to break down pre-existing civilian social and cultural norms and identities and to replace them with a new set of sociocultural values. In their subsequent military service, new identifiers would be privileged, particularly membership in a particular cohort, unit or military branch, largely supplanting pre-war versions where race had been a crucial indicator. What mattered in this context were rank, ability and courage. An Australian infantry section commander spoke of the power of that bond in relation to an Aboriginal soldier in his unit:

We came to love one another in that section. We depended on each other, and through some fairly stiff actions we got to know just about everything about each other ... we lived with Harry Saunders as a brother ... Our love for him was such that there could be no place for any colour barriers ... we were forced together by events, and our comradeship was completely necessary.[84]

This phenomenon was most pronounced on the front lines but was not just reserved for combat roles. Aboriginal soldier Arthur Baumgarten was posted in Darwin throughout the war, and he recalls: 'In the Army, we were treated like white people, got everything we wanted and done what we wanted to do ... night leave, or week or a fortnight leave home, all that sort of thing ... things you couldn't get, lollies and things for your kids to take home. Smoke they badly wanted up here because it was all

---

[82] McGregor, *Indifferent Inclusion*, xi.
[83] Oodgeroo Noonuccal, in Hall, *Fighters from the Fringe*, 118–19.
[84] Hall, *The Black Diggers*, 69.

*Figure 4.3*    Informal group portrait of members of the 2/18th Australian
Field Workshop. All except two of the men are Aboriginal, reflecting the
interracial friendships formed among service members during the war.
Courtesy Australian War Memorial, accession number P00898.001.

rations. I used to try to get as much as I could.'[85] The words of Dorothy
Askwith, a Métis veteran of the women's auxiliary RCAF, also reinforce
this point:

Discrimination? Everybody was so involved in what was happening with the war
that nobody was involved in such pettiness. I don't think you bothered to look at
the colour of your buddy's skin, especially the guys who were involved in warfare.

[85] Arthur Baumgarten, in Stuart Rintoul, *The Wailing: A National Black Oral History* (Port
Melbourne, VIC: William Heinemann Australia, 1993), 361.

A couple cousins of mine said, 'Who the hell ever stopped to look at colour?' We were so gall darn glad that you could get a place to duck into; who gave a damn who's with you? We were there together, two lives.[86]

Nevertheless, even amongst their closest comrades, a degree of awareness of their Indigeneity lingered, as Reg Saunders acknowledged: 'Being black, everybody sees a black man.'[87] Dorothy Askwith recalled what she wrote off as 'a couple gestures of discrimination' from a senior officer, who was inclined to return her salute by raising his hand and saying 'How'. When this occurred she was stunned: 'it just floored me, but what do you do?' A friend advised her to ignore it, and she subsequently avoided the individual whenever possible.[88] Indigenous identifiers such as the nickname 'chief' were common for Native American men, but Bernstein suggests that the 'word [Chief] was not the equivalent of a racial slur ... "Chief" signified something other than condescension; it signified respect. Indians may have preferred to be addressed by their own names, but they did not perceive "chief" as a term of derision.'[89] Ira Hayes did not share this sentiment; a member of his platoon recalled how that term made Hayes angry. Though Hayes never provoked a confrontation, 'He would just glower at them something terrible.'[90]

A different set of tropes affected Indigenous women, most notably the notion of the Indigenous princess in the United States and Canada. The Native American princess featured in numerous articles about women enlisting, such as a 1944 article titled 'Princess of Yakima Indian Tribe to Enlist in Service'. The article states, 'Nancy [Wac-Wac], 22, is the great-grand-daughter of "the last hero of the Yakimas", famous Chief Ka-Mi-Akin, who signed the treaty with Gov Isaac Stevens which brought peace between the Indians and the whites in Washington.'[91] The coverage of these women's enlistments represents what Rayna Green and Angela Ross describe as the princess representation or the Pocahontas Perplex, constituting the 'good' Indian woman who symbolises civilisation and works to save the white man (as opposed to the squaw 'bad' Indian woman).[92] The princess trope also followed women while they

---

[86] Dorothy Askwith, in *Remembrances*, 6.

[87] Reg Saunders, in Hall, *Fighters from the Fringe*, 69.

[88] Askwith, in *Remembrances*, 6–7.

[89] Bernstein, *American Indians and World War II*, 56. Doris Paul also mentions the frequency of 'Geronimo' or 'Chief' nicknames, *The Navajo Code Talkers*, 91–94.

[90] Carroll, *Medicine Bags and Dog Tags*, 131.

[91] Beatrice Bliss, "Princess of Yakima Indian Tribe to Enlist in Service," 1 March 1944 (unknown newspaper), in NARA, RG 75, Box 1, Entry 998A. See also "Wac-Wac Wac," *Lawrence Journal-World*, 18 March 1944, 5.

[92] Angela M Ross, "The Princess Production: Locating Pocahontas in Time and Place" (PhD thesis, University of Arizona, 2008), 29–32; Rayna Green, "The Pocahontas

served; Marcella Ryan Le Beau, a member of the Two Kettle Band of the Cheyenne River Sioux, definitively states: 'No, I never experienced any relation or any racism. In fact, because some of them knew that my great-great-grandfather was a chief, they thought I was a princess.'[93]

Leonard Waters' experience in the RAAF suggests that many Indigenous people may have viewed monikers benignly: 'They used to, you know, just refer to us as "boongs", but there was no discrimination, none at all, you know.'[94] While the cavalier use of such terms seems shockingly racist to a contemporary audience, it is significant that so many Indigenous service personnel viewed this more neutrally. Their Indigeneity had not disappeared, but the overt, hateful nature of the racism they had faced in civilian life prior to the war receded. What was left appears to have been balanced in their minds by the positive recognition, affirmation and fellowship they received from most other soldiers, sailors and aircrew with whom they served.

While some Indigenous servicemen and women endeavoured to entwine themselves seamlessly in settler military organisations, others advertised their Indigenous identity, wearing it almost like a second uniform. Canadian soldier Tommy Prince claimed that his military prowess was innate, and he always reminded his comrades that he was First Nations. For instance, when he received mail, Prince would make statements like 'I've got a smoke signal from the chief.' Biographers actually found it intriguing that Prince constantly reaffirmed his Indian identity, ensuring that the other soldiers always remembered his race.[95] Reg Saunders articulated a similar perspective in an interview:

Well, I've always used my colour as a flag. I'd say, 'Look, it's me, I'm black.' And I don't think I've let the side down. I tried not to anyway and it's always worked ... And it can be used to an advantage. Due to that sort of thing and [the fact that] I did genuinely like people ... So I got ... yes, rapid promotion I suppose. I was a Sergeant when I sailed overseas at 20 ... I got a lot of respect from people as well.[96]

It is difficult to say how many Indigenous men and women shared this need to represent their communities, to prove their capacity through their own example or the lengths to which they might have gone to achieve

---

Perplex: The Image of Indian Women in American Culture," *The Massachusetts Review* 16, no. 4 (1975): 698–714.

[93] Marcella Ryan Le Beau, LOC AFC/2001/001/24202.

[94] Leonard Waters, in Hall, *Fighters from the Fringe*, 167–168.

[95] Lackenbauer, "'A Hell of a Warrior': Remembering Sergeant Thomas George Prince," 30–31.

[96] Reg Saunders, in Hall, *Fighters from the Fringe*, 69.

*Figure 4.4* Native American mechanics in the US Army Air Corps dance during training at Sheppard Field, TX: Pvt. Abraham Little Beaver, Winnebago of Nebraska; Corp. Adam Bearcup, Sioux of Montana; Sgt. Delray B. Echo-Hawk, Pawnee of Oklahoma; Corp. David Box, Sioux of Colorado. Photo by © CORBIS/Corbis via Getty Images.

such a result. Even so, what is clear is that across the four settler societies, there was a general sense that non-Indigenous personnel welcomed and embraced Indigenous members based on their skills and abilities, rather than their skin colour or culture.

## Combat Experiences

While assessing the experience of life in a military organisation is feasible with the voices of Indigenous servicemen and women, entering the hazy world of combat is more problematic. The sheer complexity, chaos, physical intensity and emotional trauma of battle make piecing together the experience and articulating it notoriously difficult for soldiers.[97] In any event, the ordeal was intensely personal and internal to each individual, and, as John Newton argues, 'few clues were given to observers ... any observers always remained outside the true experience of combat'.[98] Part of the challenge, John Ellis suggests, is that for various reasons, the memories that combat troops share tend to be 'those of rear echelon life, mainly featuring male boisterousness and relatively minor discomforts and ennui ... it becomes much more difficult to try and describe trench-foot, battle exhaustion, soiled trousers and eviscerated mates'.[99] There is also the extra challenge that memory and national narratives pose for veterans recollecting a war. Alistair Thomson's oral history research with Australian First World War veterans found that many composed their own memories of trauma to fit within the dominant national discourses about the ANZACs and Gallipoli, diverging significantly from the first-hand written accounts.[100]

Veterans are often loath to let outsiders into this part of their wartime experience. Canadian Métis veteran, Euclide Boyer, never liked to talk about the war, 'especially with people who don't know anything about it. I find it much easier talking to a man who's been there; then we both know what the other guy is talking about.'[101] For historians seeking to get inside the heads of servicemen and gain understanding of what combat actually felt like, what motivated soldiers in combat can seem an impossible task. Much of what we know of Indigenous experiences in combat has been

---

[97] Holmes, *Acts of War*, 10.

[98] John Ellis, *At the Sharp End: The Fighting Man in World War II* (Newton Abbot, UK: David & Charles, 1980), 97–98.

[99] John Ellis, "Reflections on the 'Sharp End' of War," in *Time to Kill: The Soldier's Experience of War in the West*, ed. Paul Addison and Angus Calder (London: Pimlico, 1997), 14.

[100] Alistair Thomson, *Anzac Memories: Living with the Legend*, 2nd edn. (Clayton, VIC: Monash University Publishing, 2013), 1–29; "Anzac Memories Revisited: Trauma, Memory and Oral History," *Oral History Review* 42, no. 1 (2015): 1–29.

[101] Euclide Boyer, in *Remembrances*, 21–22.

reconstructed from anecdotal snippets about particularly noteworthy actions. It is often by extrapolating from tales of high drama and brave actions that scholars in all four states have concluded that Indigenous soldiers achieved a remarkable Second World War combat record. Such fragments are hardly representative, and some amount to little more than apocryphal tales highlighting perceived racial fighting abilities, bravery or sacrifice. Less commonly publicised are memories of survival, which lack heroic elements, such as Maori Battalion member Patira Edwards' description of surviving a German attack in Greece in 1941: 'On our way back they were machine-gunning the area where we were walking. They were spraying the area with machine-gun fire. You could hear them zinging all around you. They make a peculiar noise. They zing … That was the first time that I'd been shot at. Well, if your number's on it, that's it. You just duck and dive around, hoping you're ducking the right way.'[102] Too often, the archetypal great Indigenous soldiers were essentialised to represent the broader Indigenous combat record. Such material provides a problematic foundation for understanding Indigenous combat experiences writ large.

The problem with Indigenous exceptionalism is that it creates at best a partial and unrealistic image of the war experience of these men. Surely not every single Indigenous soldier, sailor or airmen was a superlative fighter. As Lloyd Jones argues:

Maori soldiers, like their Pakeha colleagues, could be brave, fearsome, efficient, skilled, obedient, humorous, uncomplaining and clever. Like Pakeha, they could also be afraid, shell-shocked, incompetent, disobedient, whinging and transgressors of the prevailing codes of conduct in war. The latter attributes of New Zealand soldiers were seldom or never reported on in the press. The former were constantly paraded before New Zealand readers as standard characteristics of the 'brave Kiwi fighting man', Maori and Pakeha.[103]

Indeed, in one recollection of a battle, Tini Glover succinctly states of the Maori Battalion: 'But we were all frightened.'[104] Treating Indigenous soldiers as inherently exceptional is a dehumanising stereotype like any other, and it denies these men the frailties, foibles and diversity of experience that was their reality of combat. Moreover, the stereotype of the

[102] Ngāpuhi Patira Edwards, Alexander Turnbull Library Oral History Centre, OHInt-0729-08, available from www.28maoribattalion.org.nz/audio/patira-edwards-first-encounter-with-germans.
[103] Lloyd Jones, "Images of Maori in the Pakeha Press: Pakeha Representations of Maori in the Popular Press, 1935–1965" (Master's Thesis, University of Auckland, 1998), 56.
[104] Tautini (Tini) Glover, Te Aitanga a Hauiti, Alexander Turnbull Library Oral History Centre, OHInt-0748-02, available from www.28maoribattalion.org.nz/audio/tini-glover-describes-going-battle.

strong Indigenous soldier could have the adverse effect of disempowering, shaming and silencing those Indigenous men whose memories and war record did not conform to the dominant narrative.

Examining Indigenous servicemen's recollections of their war experience certainly suggests much in common with non-Indigenous soldiers. Their reactions speak to what were often shared human physiological and psychological reactions to the fear, exhaustion, intense stress, boredom, brutality and camaraderie of soldiers in combat.[105] In line with Ellis' observations, Indigenous veterans' oral history narratives, too, emphasise the non-combat experiences even while on the front lines. For instance, Tommy Lyon, an Aboriginal member of the famed Rats of Tobruk, does not discuss the combat actions of the unit. Instead, he tells tales about coping:

Tobruk, it was a good place, mate (laughing). Plenty of fleas and sand and, Jesus, bugs by the thousands. Oh, it was good, mate. You had plenty of company. At times I thought if I could only grow wings I could fly home. A mate said to me, 'It's a long way to fly, bud, you'd have to take more than a couple of dog biscuits with you and a tin of bully beef. Forget about that. You'd only get up and someone would mistake you for a crow and shoot you down again.' So that settled that argument ... Little things like that were how we got by, laughing and cracking jokes.[106]

Humorous anecdotes permeate all ex-servicemen and women's stories, and for combat veterans focusing on humour was likely a coping mechanism to deal with the trauma of war. Fear is an interesting emotion that does not arise in many testimonies, and Navajo veteran Roy Hawthorne's reflection about the Battle of Okinawa provides some insights as to why: 'Actually I wasn't [scared]. I didn't know enough about what was going on to really assess the situation. I suppose that's the way it was. But I don't remember having been afraid or scared or frightened, but I probably was because the brain has a way of blocking out some things that are unpleasant to remember, and so, I think probably I was.'[107]

Veterans who talk about combat experiences tend to do so very matter-of-factly, withholding the sense of fear or other emotions. Victorian Aboriginal veteran Bill Egan describes a Japanese ambush in Bougainville:

I spotted Japanese trip wires and land mines and I sensed danger. I said, 'I'm not going any further', so I stopped. And that was when they opened up on us with machine guns. They never shot any gunners. All they done was the officers.

---

[105] See Nigel de Lee, "Oral History and British Soldiers' Experience of Battle in the Second World War," in *Time to Kill: The Soldier's Experience of War in the West,* ed. Paul Addison and Angus Calder (London: Pimlico, 1997), 359–368.

[106] Tommy Lyons, in Rintoul, *The Wailing,* 302–303.

[107] Roy O. Hawthorne, LOC AFC/2001/001/52528.

The Japanese they just whipped the officers. We raced for cover, and as we did we tripped booby traps and mines. They were blowing up all around us ... We were lucky to get out of that ambush.[108]

Egan mentions the loss of specific mates, and that is a common trope: stories of combat often relate to other soldiers' suffering or deaths. John Palmer describes encountering another member of the Maori Battalion while trying to escape the doomed defence of Greece:

So we stopped and in the fern, this grass, we'd found one of our boys, Maori chap, soldier, he'd been shot through the mouth. And the bullet was still in the mouth, and he'd gone all yellow, you know. So we took him down to Battalion Headquarters where there was still a tent and we fed him on all the juice out of the tins, but it wasn't any good. Luckily across the road and across the river on the other side maybe half a mile away was a sanatorium, see. So we told him he may as well go down to the road and be captured by the Germans and they'd fix him. We heard later on, three months later that he was cured.[109]

Maiki Parkinson describes the Maori Battalion withstanding a German attack at El Alamein:

We could see which way the shells were coming and we headed for that, going like the hammers of hell. We were stumbling along, dragging other fellas, carrying other fellas. A German shell landed amongst us and hit one of our boys and took his thigh off. It was the first time I'd seen blood spurting out. We tried putting on a tourniquet, but we had no stretcher so we used the straps from our rifles and carried him out. The shells were landing around us.[110]

Following a lengthy recitation of several courageous Native American soldiers whose exploits captured media headlines, Townsend argues that:

Quinton, Bremner, Stevens and Webber were typical of American soldiers in both theatres of war – not American Indian soldiers, but soldiers. Race commanded no role in displays of courage. Situations arose in battle; individuals responded as best they could to immediate circumstances. A warrior spirit did not propel these men into action; patriotism and thoughts of family did not influence their behaviour. Anyone who experienced the sheer terror of combat understood. Quinton, Bremner, and Stevens fought as they did to preserve their own lives and the lives of men who stood with them. Webber had a job to do. He knew he could not go home until the enemy was defeated. These men were no 'warriors' possessed with inherent skills and natural talents, but soldiers who found themselves in situations they would have preferred not to experience.[111]

[108] Jack Kennedy, in Jackomos and Fowell, *Forgotten Heroes*, 33.
[109] John Palmer, Ngāti Raukawa, Ngāti Toa Rangatira, Ngāti Tūwharetoa, available from www.28maoribattalion.org.nz/audio/john-palmer-discusses-trying-find-m%C4%81ori-battalion-greece.
[110] Jerome (Maiki or Jules) Parkinson, Alexander Turnbull Library Oral History Centre, OHInt-0798-12, available from www.28maoribattalion.org.nz/audio/maiki-parkinson-describes-being-attacked-el-alamein.
[111] Townsend, *World War II and the American Indian*, 143.

We are largely in agreement with Townsend in his description of the shared nature of such events. We should set aside the assumptions of exceptionalism and acknowledge the humanity of these men – a humanity they shared with their comrades in arms. These men had endured much the same basic training: a re-socialisation program developed over centuries by Western armies to break down the civilian cultural and social norms of individual recruits and reconstruct them as members of a collective organism, with a new settler-army masculine code of behaviour. This process combined with the shared experiences of combat to weld soldiers into cohesive, intensely intimate, groups that were closer than brothers. That deep bond undoubtedly influenced soldiers' motivation to stand, fight or charge into the face of a blazing machine gun.

We are also hesitant about such a categorical and dogmatic rejection of any potential differences. Acknowledging a shared human experience between Indigenous and non-Indigenous combatants should not require us to see only sameness. Military re-socialisation does not utterly erase a person's identity. For example, during the Maori Battalion's campaign in Crete, after a hard battle and long demoralising retreat across the island to disembarkation points, they turned and counterattacked their pursuers. This action, known as the Battle of 42nd Street, was to begin when a commander signalled the advance. When he did so, according to Rangitepuru Waretini:

> ... no bugger moved. It wasn't until he blew it again and he jumped up himself and Sam O'Brien from Te Puke got up with him and started to 'mea' his rifle [demonstrates use of the rifle like a taiaha]. You wouldn't think he was a soldier at all ... He had two left feet ... But oh, something must have stirred inside him, I suppose, when he got up and did this.[112]

Some seventy men stood up and joined in performing the traditional haka, 'Ka mate' – one of the only known performances of a Māori haka on the field of battle during the war. The remainder of the inspired Maori Battalion charged the German paratroopers, overran them and inflicted heavy losses. As any exhausted and demoralised soldiers might, the Māori did not instantly leap to the attack; what inspired them arose from a distinct cultural military ethos that would not have elicited the same response from their Pākehā comrades.

In this instance, the segregated nature of the Maori Battalion amplified the cultural expression of that Māori masculine code to the collective response. Nevertheless, it seems logical that individuals serving

---

[112] Soutar, *Nga Tama Toa*, 148–149. A taiaha was a traditional Māori melee weapon, with a point at one end and flattened to a broad heavy blade at the other, used like a quarter staff, and warriors practiced spinning it in intricate series of manoeuvres and footwork ('mea').

in integrated units might have functioned within their own cultural frame of reference in combat or, perhaps, some syncretic combination of Indigenous and settler military codes (there was likely much overlap). While some may, indeed, have consciously undertaken military service for such an end, others would have found themselves in circumstances where their Indigenous values and cultural frames of reference would have come to the fore. Carroll suggests:

accounts of personal medicine are easy to find. Navajo elders gave Navajo servicemen sacred corn pollen and holy water. Zunis carried sacred prayer meals and fetishes (carved amulets of small animals). Chippewa servicemen asked for protection from their guardian spirits and had totemic spirit marks tattooed on their right forearm. Apache servicemen carried peyote buttons. Sometimes Native ceremonies reconciled servicemen to their fates.[113]

One example is Potawatomi soldier Leroy 'Mickey' Mzhickteno, who kept Indian tobacco with him throughout the war. He remarks, 'It's good medicine even though you can't pinpoint what it does for you. It's not like medicine you take to get well or something like that. It's just something ... [I kept it in] a pill bottle. I don't remember when I ran out. I guess I had too many close calls!'[114] Such visible cultural expressions are relatively easy to see and may well have provided Indigenous soldiers with unique and important coping mechanisms different from their non-Indigenous fellows.

Yet, this is only one aspect from the spectrum of the combat experience. Though less visible perhaps, other fundamental concepts such as courage, leadership, mercy, death, fear, rage, vengeance and brotherhood, or 'mateship' in 'down under' parlance, had meaning only within a specific cultural frame of reference. These complex concepts may well have had different meanings for many Indigenous personnel than their settler comrades or at least manifested in distinct ways. For example, Arapeta Awatere's response, when he discovered his brother had been killed by an enemy anti-tank gun during the Maori Battalion's participation in Operation Crusader in North Africa in November 1941, is illustrative:

So with my pistol I shot the fellow who fired the gun. I then ordered my lot to shoot. Those [prisoners] were mowed down like ninepins ... I went over, saw my brother's body and swore that until the end of the war I will kill every man of the enemy that opposed me anywhere at anytime as 'utu' or 'ngaki mate' for my brother mainly and then the rest ... I turned cold and ruthless till the end of the war, till the old 'pure' was performed at Rotorua.[115]

---

[113] Carroll, *Medicine Bags and Dog Tags*, 121–122.
[114] Leroy "Mickey" Mzhickteno, LOC AFC/2001/001/38223.
[115] Soutar, *Nga Tama Toa*, 185.

Awatere conceptualised his hatred of the enemy, his desire for vengeance, and his spiritual and psychological healing post-war in a distinctly Māori manner.

Similarly, Navajo beliefs about death and the dead proved deeply troubling for them in a battlefield where death and corpses were ubiquitous. Nathan Aaseng writes:

> Traditional Navajos believed that only the evil part of a dead creature or person lingered on Earth. The *chindi*, as these spirits were called, returned to the place of their dying to terrorize the living. *Chindi* were to be avoided at all costs ... In the Pacific war, the Navajo code talkers were surrounded by *chindi*, more *chindi* than they could have imagined in their worst fears ... As much as they feared the *chindi*, there was no escape from the dead. Death was a fact of life in the Pacific war. Survival instincts were stronger even than the fear of all traditional taboos, and so the Navajo simply learned to live with the situation.[116]

All service personnel had to make peace with the dead, but each would have processed the experience through their own cultural and spiritual lens. Such examples are but the tip of the iceberg, illustrating how relatively shallow is our understanding of Indigenous combat experiences in settler militaries. These examples also suggest the potential value of a more culturally attuned approach to understanding Indigenous experiences of combat.

## Conclusion

What emerges from this transnational exploration of Indigenous experiences in the military forces is a remarkably similar pattern. Generally, young Indigenous men and women coped with the culture shock of entering military training and successfully negotiated the transition into soldiers, sailors, marines and aircrew. Like non-Indigenous service personnel, there were varying responses among Indigenous recruits to the new regimentation of military life. Documents and testimonies suggest, though, that most men and women did adapt to the military and thrived in what was a genuinely equal environment. The martial masculinity of the military often suited Indigenous men, particularly those who came from cultures with warrior traditions, while Indigenous women fitted well within a structure that provided new opportunities previously unavailable. In all four countries, Indigenous service personnel experienced a degree of acceptance and respect they had never encountered before; they were judged on their ability and character rather than their Indigeneity.

[116] Nathan Aaseng, *Navajo Code Talkers: America's Secret Weapon in World War II* (New York: Walker and Co., 1992), 55–56.

This did not mean that their Indigenous identity vanished, either in the minds of Indigenous soldiers or in the eyes of their comrades and superiors. Yet, being Indigenous did not seem to prescribe how settler soldiers perceived and valued these servicemen and women. Moreover, this pattern held for segregated Indigenous units like the 28th (Maori) Battalion and the Torres Strait Light Infantry Battalion just as much as for Indigenous individuals integrated into settler units. For many, the experience in settler militaries was powerfully (re)affirming of their Indigenous identity and cultural vitality and bred a confidence in their ability to deal with settler society and seek an integrated future.

Addressing questions of the distinctiveness or the effectiveness of Indigenous service personnel in combat is a more problematic undertaking. There is always a tension: highlighting their difference runs the risk of overplaying exceptional Indigenous service personnel or reaffirming martial race stereotypes of 'natural' warriors; highlighting similarities runs the risk of subsuming Indigenous military history into the wider Second World War canon which has, mostly, overlooked Indigenous contributions. We have sought a balance in this uncomfortable binary, arguing for caution against unduly segregating Indigenous experiences from those of the men and women who served and sacrificed alongside them. There is, potentially, fruitful cross-fertilisation in assessing Indigenous experiences in the context of the citizen soldiers, sailors and aircrew of these four settler states. While we can learn much from seeing Indigenous service personnel as part of their unit, we also need to be sensitive to the nuances and diversity of cultural meaning and how that may have shaped Indigenous experiences and understandings of the conflict. Each individual Indigenous serviceman and woman brought with them into their war experience a worldview and core values fostered by their Haudenosaunee, Ngati Kahungunu, Mi'kmaq or Noongar upbringing. Some came from communities that honoured the avocation and exploits of the warrior, others from communities who saw warriors and violent acts as troubling or repugnant. While such profound differences obviously shaped an individual's understanding and experience in military service, subtler cultural distinctions, too, would have made their presence felt in myriad ways across the breadth of wartime interactions, decisions and events.

# 5    Mobilising Indigeneity

## Indigenous Knowledge, Language and Culture in the War Effort

Colonisers and colonial authorities had complex relationships with Indigenous knowledge since the moments of first contact. On one hand colonisers generally denigrated Indigenous people's beliefs, practices, skills, languages and technology as inferior to Europeans'. On the other hand, especially on the frontiers, colonists relied on Indigenous knowledge and sometimes technologies to traverse, adapt to and survive on the land. This bipolar relationship of dependence and denigration applied in all colonial contexts, and policing and military engagements were a prominent site of this duality. Across temporal and geographical contexts, colonising armies or police forces relied on Indigenous skills to track and even do battle with other Indigenous peoples. As discussed in the introduction, often the settler governments used martial race epithets to justify the employment of Indigenous scouts, auxiliaries, trackers or soldiers, claiming that they were racially suited to such roles. Recognising their supposed militaristic prowess did not necessarily associate with supporting equality or rights to land or sovereignty. Whether it be through assimilation, protection or segregation, a common theme across the four settler states was the desire to eliminate Indigenous people's culture and, in the process, their knowledge and knowledge systems. That is why it is seems remarkable that, in the Second World War, settler governments turned to Indigenous knowledge to fight the war.

The mobilisation of Indigenous knowledge could be formal or informal, deployed by individuals or Indigenous communities. Indigenous identity sometimes led to differentiated service: where military authorities explicitly sought the cultural 'otherness' of a target group, and where that otherness subsequently defined Indigenous roles in the war. Some of the more prominent collective examples of differentiated Indigenous service include the Maori Battalion, code talkers, the Torres Strait Light Infantry Battalion (TSLI) and the Northern Territory Special Reconnaissance Unit (NTSRU). Other servicemen or women who served in integrated units, accepted as equals, could still be subjected to episodic and individualised differentiated service. For instance, officers might look to Indigenous servicemen with an expectation that they were especially skilled for dangerous patrolling or sniper roles.

An extra layer of complexity is that in some instances, Indigenous people themselves were initiating their own differentiation, most prominently in the case of the Maori Battalion. There were also informal examples of Indigenous people deploying their knowledge for the war effort on their own initiative. These examples, such as patrols of remote territories such as Arnhem Land or the Canadian Arctic, were informal in the sense that the Indigenous people were not enlisted in the armed forces or militia. There were also examples of Indigenous people within formal groups, such as the Canadian Pacific Coast Militia Rangers, who voluntarily applied their knowledge to advance the objectives of the force. Even in most cases that were settler initiatives, Indigenous service members were active, willing agents who accepted and even embraced their differentiated status, taking pride in their ability to use their Indigenous knowledge to advance the war effort and/or protect their homelands.

Indigeneity was mobilised for both military service abroad and also for home defence. In home defence, there were two aligning, overarching objectives: one Indigenous and one non-Indigenous. Intimate, ancestral ties to the land invested Indigenous locals with a sense of purpose to resist (another) invasion. Key settler figures recognised this, and often served as intermediaries or even initiators of Indigenous defence networks. From settler government perspectives, in remote regions that were now potential or even active front lines, Indigenous people were cheap, lightly equipped, irregular forces already in situ that obviated the need to move in permanent garrisons. When these agendas aligned, some distinct and even clever initiatives emerged to defend against the Japanese through traditional bush warfare. There were constantly shifting power relationships at play in these forces, where Indigenous people controlled the knowledge and skills, but military officials controlled the pay and official command/oversight. These forces in many ways constituted sites of constant negotiations, with multiple agencies and relationships constantly in tension.

This chapter looks at the various examples of Indigenous knowledge being mobilised for the war effort, first within general integrated units, and then turning, in particular, to the specialised or heavily Indigenous units that operated during the war. As this Table 5.1 shows, the different Indigenous units fit into either home or overseas defence and Indigenous or non-Indigenous initiatives. The chapter focuses on themes such as who proposed these units and why, how military authorities and government officials reacted to the proposals, the ways Indigenous people conceived of and took ownership

Table 5.1. *Indigenous-specific military units*

|  | Home defence | Overseas defence |
|---|---|---|
| Indigenous-initiated | Coastal patrols (Australia) | Maori Battalion (NZ) |
| Non-indigenous organised | NTSRU (Australia) TSLI (Australia) Alaska Territorial Guard (USA) *Pacific Coast Militia Rangers (Canada) *not exclusively Indigenous, but a significant proportion in particular regions | Navajo, Comanche and other Code Talkers (USA) |

of these forces, and the implementation of Indigenous knowledge in the field. For Indigenous people, these units or individual feats became an opportunity to showcase the value of their skills and knowledge, challenging settler assumptions about the value of assimilation and inferiority of Indigenous cultures. Yet, with the notable exception of the Maori Battalion, the Indigenous units received minimal, if any, attention during and after the war. As such, most settler societies were not aware of the ways that Indigenous knowledge contributed to the war effort, again marginalising Indigenous people from military traditions and national narratives, and in the process, depriving them of the very aims they hoped to achieve through their war service.

## Real and Perceived Fighting Spirit/Ability

The common perception of Indigenous people as warriors, with all the ferocity and fighting spirit that the popular imagination could conjure, inevitably influenced their treatment even within the most egalitarian of units. Martial race ideas could manifest both positively and negatively at the same time, and even Indigenous service members themselves often subscribed to them. Of course, in any unit there would be a variety of service personnel with different backgrounds and skill sets. What made the Indigenous differentiations distinct, though, were that they were often based on racialist assumptions about inherent abilities that made them more suited to particular dangerous tasks. This is best summarised by what Tom Holm refers to as the Indian scout syndrome: 'This mentality attributes to Indian warriors the ability to detect the presence of an enemy from a bent blade of grass or to hide themselves in an open field. Not only that, but some whites seem to think that these attributes are genetically acquired rather than learned.'[1] Such stereotypes were applicable not only to Native Americans but to Indigenous people in all four settler states.

Why this is complicated is because, in truth, many Indigenous people's cultural upbringings meant that they *did* have skill sets that suited them to scouting or sniping roles. These were not racially or genetically inherent but rather tied to the knowledge and skills they had acquired through their life experiences. An excellent example comes from recollections of Maori Battalion member Tautini (Tini) Glover about surviving an attack in Italy:

Nepia Mahuika was our officer. We went into a grove of trees for the night, and in the morning he told us to go across this slope. We were halfway across and he said, 'Get back! Get back into the copse of trees.' As soon as we got back, down came the screaming meemees, six-barrel mortars, and peppered the whole area. We would have all died except for Nepia. I said to him, 'Nep, why did you send us back?' He said, 'Well, I thought about getting the cows in, in Ruatoria. When I go to get the cows, early in the morning, the birds are singing, and they've got their wings down, drying themselves on the top of the trees in the sun. I didn't hear a bird.' Now, that's from the old people. That's an inheritance, in my opinion. Bushcraft is there. He was a good man.[2]

This is a great example because neither Tini nor Mahuika subscribed to some racial prowess attributable to all Māori. During the war, though, problematically there were general presumptions that *all* Indigenous members should be, because of their race, excellent shooters, hand-to-hand fighters or trackers at one with nature.

In some instances, more commonly in Canada and the United States, commanders chose Indigenous men, or pressured them to volunteer, for patrolling and reconnaissance roles due to perceived racial abilities. Raymond Anderson, from Sandy Hook, Manitoba, went overseas in 1943 with the 1st Canadian Parachute Battalion. He parachuted into France just before midnight on 5 June 1944 to set up the drop zone for the remainder of his battalion. He later remarked, 'I was picked for this job and leading patrols because I was a Métis and they thought my skills as a Métis, with an aboriginal background, should be come [sic] very valuable.'[3] Earl Ervin McClung from the Colville Indian Reservation served in the US 82nd Airborne and did his first combat jump in Normandy as well.

---

[1] Tom Holm, *Strong Hearts, Wounded Souls: Native American Veterans of the Vietnam War* (Austin: University of Texas Press, 1996), 88–89.

[2] Tautini (Tini) Glover, Te Aitanga a Hauiti, OHInt-0748-02, available from www.28maoribattalion.org.nz/audio/tini-glover-describes-being-attacked-italy.

[3] Lackenbauer et al., *A Commemorative History of Aboriginal Peoples in the Canadian Military*, 146.

He nonchalantly addressed how the Indian scout syndrome affected his tasks:

EM:              I was a first scout. Being an Indian and from a reservation you were automatically a first scout.

INTERVIEWER:  That's kind of scary – you're going out in front?

EM:              They had been trying to kill us for two hundred years so why change it?

McClung was not suggesting that the commanders were actively using him as cannon fodder per se but rather that the long history of colonialism and racialist ideas were clearly affecting assignments for Native American troops. Yet, as McClung commented later in the interview, there was also agency on his part when he would regularly volunteer for scouting roles: 'I was the one always selected to go on patrol through no one's fault of their own. You get to the point where you don't want to see your buddies shot, wounded or killed, so you think you can do the job better than they can, and you go out and do it. That was the reason really.'[4] These examples demonstrate how many First Nations and Native American servicemen embraced the martial race construct; what is less clear is if they had always believed it, became convinced of it through their own valiant efforts, or if they became resigned to accepting the belief to retain the esteem of their squad mates.

In Australia, the notion of differentiated Indigenous service is less common in Indigenous memories of their war service. Of course, differentiated service did happen occasionally; Merve Bundle from Wallaga Lake Mission recalls: 'I am Aboriginal and they reckoned I had good eyesight – that is how I became a spotter.'[5] Yet, in Australia, the Indian scout syndrome was less commonly imposed from above but rather emerged occasionally from below. Aboriginal soldier Reg Saunders remembered his success as a patrol leader in extensive combat against the Japanese in New Guinea, attributing both his cultural upbringing around the bush and perceived 'racial' abilities:

I used to patrol a lot ... I liked fighting patrols and I liked passive patrols and, don't forget I am an Aborigine so I had good eyes and good senses. My perception of a situation and appreciation of a situation and the change of colour of camouflage and that the Japanese used was pretty good ... And I used to do a lot of forward scouting, and if it was a really dangerous situation, I used to say, 'Well, I'm not going to ask another man to go there. I'll go there myself', because I thought I had better eyes and I had a better chance of getting away.[6]

---

[4] Earl Ervin McClung, LOC AFC/2001/001/34734.
[5] Merve Bundle, in Jackomos and Fowell, *Forgotten Heroes*, 62.
[6] Reg Saunders, in Hall, *Fighters from the Fringe*, 78–79.

## The 28th (Maori) Battalion

Only in New Zealand did Indigenous people have sufficient clout and wherewithal to influence the formation of a discrete unit within the wider 2nd New Zealand Expeditionary Force. Just the notion of a unit that was concurrently segregated and integrated represents a microcosm for how New Zealanders, and particularly Māori, saw their relationship as being both a part of, and distinct within, the nation. Unlike the settler-initiated Indigenous units of the other countries, the Maori Battalion was as old as the war itself. With Apirana Ngata leading the charge, the Māori MPs, numerous iwis and Māori organisations petitioned the government to form a distinctly Māori battalion. There were disagreements among iwi over whether this force should, like in the First World War, be a pioneer battalion, be for home defence or be an infantry unit. Cabinet approved the creation of a Māori infantry battalion in mid-September 1939, and the Defence Minister announced its formation on 4 October 1939.[7]

Based on the numbers in initial recruiting, and the suggestions of senior Māori political leaders, the Battalion's four infantry companies were divided up along iwi lines thus: A Company, Ngapuhi and others from Auckland and northern iwi; B Company, Arawa and other Bay of Plenty and Taupo iwi; C Company, Ngati Porou and other northeast iwi; and D Company, composed of all other North Island and South Island iwi.[8] Sir Charles Bennett, commanding officer of the Maori Battalion, recalls the positive effect of this organisational structure:

These Companies were more or less family groups, whānau groups, so that every NCO belonged to the tribe and where possible the Officer himself was a member of the tribe. So that, both when they were out of war and when they went into war they fought as a group. ... I think that kind of tribal setup ... whānau composition of the Companies and platoons of the Battalion had a lot to do with its achievement.9

Having to locate a sufficient complement of able and experienced officers from within each company region proved a serious challenge during the early stages of forming the Battalion because the most suitable men were not evenly distributed.[10]

---

[7] Soutar, *Nga Tama Toa*, 35–37.
[8] Confidential Report Re Appointment: Officers & NCO's, No. 28 (Maori) BN, 24 January 1940, ANZ AD1, 319-1-21.
[9] Sir Charles Bennett, Alexander Turnbull Library Oral History Centre, OHColl-0217-1, available from www.28maoribattalion.org.nz/audio/charles-bennett-discusses-tribal-formation-battalions-companies.
[10] Confidential Report Re Appointment: Officers & NCO's, No. 28 (Maori) BN, 24 January 1940, ANZ, AD1, 319-1-21.

The first 681 men of the Maori Battalion set sail for Europe in May 1940. Their first active engagement was in the doomed defence of Greece and Crete from March until May 1941. Along with other New Zealand, Australian and British forces, the Maori Battalion was forced into retreat, and those not killed or captured were evacuated to North Africa. From late 1941 until May 1943, the Maori Battalion participated in fighting against German and Italian forces in Egypt, Libya and Tunisia. From October 1943 until the end of the war, the Maori Battalion battled through Italy, ending the war occupying the city of Trieste. The dominant narrative of the Maori Battalion, and, indeed, the entire 2nd New Zealand Expeditionary Force, focuses on these sites and has over time

*Figure 5.1* Members of the Maori Battalion performing the haka for the King of Greece, at Helwan, Egypt. War History Collection, Alexander Turnbull Library.

absorbed the Anzac mythology of the valiant antipodean soldier (the martial masculine Kiwi), fighting against the odds in tough climatic conditions on foreign soil. Greece and Crete were debacles for the Allied forces, so the stories about Māori and Pākehā soldiers alike focus on their survival and escape against the odds. The Libyan and Italian campaigns focus on the hard-fought victories against a strong Afrika Korps.

Much to the disappointment of Māori – and in line with the practices reflected in other countries' later Indigenous units – the initial officers appointed to command the Maori Battalion were mostly Pākehā. How these commanders related to the Māori soldiers varied, with some seen as brotherly figures and others rejected. For instance, Wharetini Rangi described a commanding officer in a 1943 letter to Sir Apirana Ngata thus: 'Great are my complements [sic] for Ormond, he has a Maori heart, he takes care with the boys.'[11] On the opposite end of the spectrum, Rangi Logan described an officer in a 1944 letter as 'a pakeha colonel who is typically pakeha, and doesn't understand us, telling me, whom the men refer to as "the old man" or "the chief" that he had no room for me.'[12] It is interesting how both of these letters racialise the Pākehā, with the positive assessment portraying the Pākehā officer as having 'a Maori heart' while the negative colonel was described as 'typically pakeha'. Such language shows how Indigenous people, too, could apply their own racialist ideologies; even when (or perhaps because) there was a power imbalance, Indigenous people, too, could exercise judgments that positioned whites as an inferior other.

The Maori Battalion earned a reputation for aggressive and unorthodox tactics. Its achievements and victories, especially those involving a bayonet assault, invariably captured the imagination of Pākehā media because they embodied and reinforced the warrior image. Māori soldiers were active agents in these media portrayals, including participating in radio broadcasts in English and Te Reo Māori. In this way, they were able to shape the martial race construct as a projection of their own Māori warrior traditions. In one December 1941 radio broadcast, Padre Harawira stated: 'The order given by the CO of the Battalion [3 December 1941 in Libya] was, "Allow them to come close." This is a difficult thing to do in modern warfare. However, because all the officers are Maori at this time,

[11] Wharetini Rangi, letter to Sir Apirana Ngata, 19 February 1943, Alexander Turnbull Library, MS-Papers-6919-0788, available from www.28maoribattalion.org.nz/node/15640.
[12] Rangi Logan, letter to parents, 18 March 1944, Alexander Turnbull Library, MS-0196-275, available from www.28maoribattalion.org.nz/memory/rangi-logan-writes-home.

*well this was an opportunity* to adopt the way their ancestors fought... *We did well again because our ancestors/officers were in control.*'[13] It was during the Libya campaign in May 1942 that the first Māori commander, Lieutenant-Colonel Eruera (Tiwi) Love, joined the Battalion.

For the most part, the Maori Battalion operated in a similar manner and performed similar tasks as other New Zealand battalions, but there were some distinctions in the use of language and respect of cultural traditions. In the field, communications were generally in English, but letters home, songs, radio broadcasts and invariably casual conversation amongst soldiers were in Te Reo Māori. Even the parcels soldiers received drew on traditional food. Ben Rata wrote to his mother in 1942: 'I received your most welcome parcel of Kutai [traditional mussels], and you cannot imagine how glad I was in receiving it, and it was still in perfect order and condition. (What I liked best was the puha [staple green vegetable] by gee it lasted alright.) I hope you will send some more of that Toroi [mussel] over.'[14] Members of the Battalion performed the haka off the battlefield; there are mixed reports of whether this was done on or before battles. Tautini (Tini) Glover recalls:

I tell you what, I never heard a haka. Somebody asked me, 'Did you haka when you went into action?' I said, 'Not haka really.' But we screamed. We screamed like devils and I think that was our inheritance coming out. The old people ... 'Ka mate, ka mate', we had no time for that; but that scream, it seemed to help us.[15]

Even as they embraced the warrior trope, members of the Maori Battalion experienced the same war-weariness as so many other servicemen. For some, the discontent came from a cultural perspective, unhappy with Pākehā leadership of the Battalion. Rangi Logan wrote in 1944:

It seems to me that we are just employed without any consideration of the unique nature of our Bn. We don't want to get any different treatment; we don't ask or expect favours, but we would like, in fact we expect, to be consulted on matters that are of interest to the people and which it is our duty as leaders of our Bn., the men and youth of our people to uphold. I am sorry to say that we are losing our identity.[16]

Logan's sentiments reflect the internal tensions all members of the Maori Battalion had to confront: seeking input into decisions, respect for culture

---

[13] Padre Harawira, December 1941 broadcast, available from www.28maoribattalion.org.nz/audio/libyan-campaign-part-4-padre-harawira. Original emphasis.
[14] Ben Rata, to his mother, 30 May 1942, Alexander Turnbull Library, MS-0196-275, available from www.28maoribattalion.org.nz/memory/ben-rata-writes-home.
[15] Tautini (Tini) Glover, Te Aitanga a Hauiti, Alexander Turnbull Library Oral History Centre, OHInt-0748-02, available from www.28maoribattalion.org.nz/audio/tini-glover-describes-going-battle.
[16] Rangi Logan, letter to parents, 18 March 1944, Alexander Turnbull Library, MS-0196-275, available from www.28maoribattalion.org.nz/memory/rangi-logan-writes-home.

and wishing to prioritise the Māori nature of the Battalion rather than seeing it as another battalion that just happened to be staffed with Māori. In other cases, it was simply the horrors of war and the general malaise of fighting on foreign fields that left Māori soldiers melancholy. Ben Rata wrote to his parents from the Middle East: 'This is an awful place. We are all wishing to get home. We are very sick and tired of this land. However one does not know when this War will end.'[17] As Chapter 7 describes, there were arrangements made in 1943 to accommodate Māori fatigue through longer furloughs in New Zealand.

Out of the 16,000 Māori who served in the war, 3,600 – 22.5 per cent – served in the Maori Battalion. As nearly one-quarter of all Māori service personnel, this is a significant proportion, yet what is intriguing is how public memory of the war tends to overlook the other 77.5 per cent who served in integrated units and other branches of the military. Essentially, the discourse around the Maori Battalion is so strong that popular discourse implies that *all* Māori served in the Battalion. The most likely explanation for this phenomenon is because Māori themselves have asserted ownership over the Battalion's memory and mythology. They have claimed the warrior status and the honour reflected in the Battalion's accomplishment and high profile, asserting it as a mark of Indigenous knowledge and tradition mobilised for the greater war effort and defence of Aotearoa/New Zealand.

## Indigenous Language: Code Talkers

Centuries of colonialism in each settler state led to the end of hundreds of spoken Indigenous languages (though some Indigenous people say the languages are still alive in the land and spirits). Given assimilation practices in all nations meant to discourage or in many instances forbid Indigenous people from speaking their languages, it is remarkable that settler military forces, in some cases, looked to fluent speakers of Indigenous languages as a solution to the problem of providing rapid, accurate and secure communications in a combat zone.

While the Maori Battalion was distinctive as an Indigenous-initiated overseas force, code talkers were distinct for the way their language became a weapon in the war. Code talkers were Native Americans who communicated in their own languages so that Japanese, Germans and Italians intercepting Allied communications could not understand the messages. Whereas code talking had been a spontaneous improvisation

---

[17] Ben Rata of D Company to his parents, no date, Alexander Turnbull Library, MS-0196-275, available from www.28maoribattalion.org.nz/node/4969.

using Choctaw soldiers in the First World War, in the Second World War it had a much more pronounced presence. Historian and anthropologist, William Meadows, distinguishes between two categories of code talkers: Type 1, in which there were specific vocabularies developed as a code to encompass military and strategic terminology, and Type 2, when Native Americans communicated in their languages but without a specific code or military vocabulary. The four known cases of Type 1 code talkers were the Comanche, Meskwaki, Chippewa-Oneida and Hopi while Meadows has identified twelve other groups of Type 2 code talkers.[18]

Usually, a commanding officer set up Type 2 talkers after stumbling across two members of the same Native American nation in his unit. For example, Seminole man Edmund Harjo from Oklahoma overheard another man singing a Christian hymn in Creek a few days after D-Day. He went up to the man, and as they were conversing in the Creek language, a captain overheard them and decided to use them on the same radio line for communications. In other cases, men who knew each other would speak in their traditional languages and come to officers' attention.[19] Such small-scale innovations on the battlefield were useful and represented both the agency of the Native American code talkers as well as commanding officers recognising the value of their language in war. This did not necessarily represent a wider valuation of Native American culture, but at the same time, the code talking innovation was not informed by, nor did it perpetuate, martial race ideology.

The only Canadian example of code talkers actually served with the US Army Air Force, which was unable to locate sufficient fluent speakers of Indigenous languages. An initial experiment was held on 22 August 1942, involving eight First Nations men from 'A' Group, Canadian Reinforcement Unit, working in pairs in Cree, Ojibwa and Shawnee to pass messages that were tested for accuracy. The enthusiastic report of the test recommended proceeding with an expanded group:

As the Indian dialects and language are almost never written, and in most cases cannot be transcribed, enemy interception, even 'in clear' would be practically impossible. A series of vowel sounds would be the net result, and in some cases not even vowel sounds but merely grunts with inflections in the desired places constitute the message.[20]

---

[18] William Meadows, "'They Had a Chance to Talk to One Another ...': The Role of Incidence in Native American Code Talking," *Ethnohistory* 56, no. 2 (2009): 269; *Comanche Code Talkers of World War II* (Austin: University of Texas Press, 2002), 242.

[19] Meadows, "'They Had a Chance to Talk to One Another ...'," 272–276.

[20] Memorandum, Lieutenant J.K. Starnes, Canadian Military Headquarters, 22 August 1942, LAC, RG 24, Vol. 9801 2/IND RTcomm/1.

By October, Canadian Military Headquarters in the United Kingdom had located fifty-four Cree speakers and thirty-two Ojibwa who met the other standards required (including an IQ test) but noted that no more than seven or eight speakers of any other language could be located.[21] A number of Cree veterans serving in England recalled being ordered to London where a US Army Air Force officer explained an interest in their language for communications to a hall of nearly 100 other First Nations servicemen from various Canadian units.[22] Meadows has identified at least six of these Cree men who were seconded to the US 8th Air Force where they served as code talkers for six months before returning to their Canadian units for the remainder of the war.[23] It is not clear why the US Army Air Force discontinued their code talkers project.

The first more formalised Type 1 code talkers began when the US Army started recruiting Oneida and Chippewa speakers in the fall of 1940, more than a year before the US actually entered the war. Authorities extended the project to include Meskwaki and Comanche recruits.[24] The eight Meskwaki (then known as the Sac and Fox) even received a minor mention in the *New York Times* in a February 1941 article: 'They will speak their own dialect so that an enemy would be unable to understand their reports even if their messages were coded.'[25] The Meskwaki were deployed to North Africa in 1942 where some were captured and others continued to serve through the September 1943 invasion of Italy.[26]

Of the Army code talker units, the Comanche were the largest with seventeen participants. The recruitment of Comanche Code Talkers occurred in December 1940 and January 1941, as military authorities worked with Indian Agents to travel around rural Oklahoma Comanche communities in search of single young men.[27] Most of the code development occurred in September and October 1941 when the Comanche devised nearly 250 code words for weapons and geographic formations that had no extant words in Comanche, such as 'pregnant bird' for a bomber aircraft.[28] When the United States formally entered the war, the Comanches

---

[21] A.G.2, re: Indian Speaking Personnel, from I.J. Stone, Capt., 21 October 1942, LAC RG 24, Vol. 9801, 2/IND RTcomm/1.

[22] William Meadows, "North American Indian Code Talkers: Current Developments and Research," in *Aboriginal Peoples and Military Participation: Canadian and International Perspectives*, eds. P. Whitney Lackenbauer, R. Scott Sheffield and Craig Leslie Mantle (Kingston, ON: Canadian Defence Academy Press, 2007), 161–213.

[23] Meadows, "'They Had a Chance to Talk to One Another …'," 271.

[24] Meadows, *Comanche Code Talkers of World War II*, 69.

[25] "To Speak Another Dialect," *New York Times* (16 February 1941), 32.

[26] Mary Bennett, "Meskwaki Code Talkers," *Iowa Heritage Illustrated* 84, no. 4 (Winter 2003): 154–156.

[27] Meadows, *Comanche Code Talkers of World War II*, 78–82.

[28] Ibid., 100–103.

served in the European theatre, primarily in headquarters or battalion commands with only occasional deployment on front lines. They only sent messages in Comanche when absolute secrecy was vital.[29] Given the shifting nature of the war, the combat experiences of the Comanche Code Talkers varied, with some seeing significant front line action and others spending more time in the relative safety of headquarters.[30]

Despite early interest and the ongoing operation of the Comanches and other code talkers, many Army officials were sceptical about the utility of code talkers. The Army did initiate another small-scale program in 1943 to train eight Hopi code talkers, who were subsequently deployed in the Pacific at the Marshall Islands and then as part of General MacArthur's campaign to retake the Philippines.[31] A trial use of two Creek as code talkers in the Solomon Islands campaign in September 1943 also found: 'results appear sufficiently good to warrant further exploitation use of Indian language for this purpose'.[32] Yet, internal correspondence within the Army in 1943–4 revealed a clear disinterest in expanding any code talker programs, citing the difficulty of locating sufficient numbers of fluent speakers for any single Native American language group. There were also racial presumptions, which denigrated the abilities of Native Americans, with one background paper asserting that Native Americans from the Southwest 'are not able to follow orders, since they either do not understand English, or their command of the language is limited, with very few exceptions'.[33]

The Marine Corps, too, was sceptical of code talkers, but it was the persistence of white intermediary Philip Johnston and the Navajos' exceptional work that led to the most famous code talkers. Johnston was the son of a missionary who had grown up on the Navajo Reservation where he learned to speak Navajo proficiently. When he read about the Comanche Code Talkers in a newspaper, he came up with the idea of Navajo Code Talkers and pitched the idea to the Marine Corps. Johnston set up a demonstration of two Navajo communicating perfectly across a football field in March 1942, impressing General Clayton Vogel, the commanding officer of the Marine Corps' Pacific Fleet. The next month the Marine Corps recruited twenty-nine Navajos to develop their language into a code. Chester Nez recalls when the

[29] Ibid., 123–134.
[30] Ibid., 161–166.
[31] Ibid., 68.
[32] Telegram from COMGENSOPAC to AGWAR, 6 September 1943, NARA, RG 457, SRH-120, Box 34, folder 020.
[33] "Background Material Regarding the American Indians who Have Lived Much or all of their Lives Upon the Reservations and Not in Direct Contact with White People," no date, 1943, NARA, RG 457, SRH-120, Box 34, folder 042.

*Figure 5.2* Navajo Code Talkers of the 3rd Marine Division in Bougainville, December 1943. Front row from left to right: Pvt. Early Johnny, Pvt. Kee Etsicitty, Pvt. John V. Goodluck and Pfc. David Jordan; Second row: Pvt. Jack C. Morgan, Pvt. George H. Kirk, Pvt. Tom H. Jones and Cpl Henry Bahe, Jr. Courtesy of National Archives and Records Administration, 127-MN-069896.

Marine officer 'told us we were to use our native language to devise an unbreakable code. I read expressions of shock on every face. A code based on the Navajo language? After we'd been so severely punished at boarding school for speaking it?'[34] The final code was 413 words, as well as an alphabet of twenty-six words for each letter (later increased to forty-four words to provide alternates).[35] By war's end, 420 Navajo Code Talkers served across the Pacific theatre.

The first Navajo Code Talkers served at Guadalcanal in the fall of 1942 and proved an eminent success. Subsequently, the Marine Corps

---

[34] Nez and Avila, *Code Talker*, Chapter 10.
[35] Philip Johnston, "Indian Jargon Won Our Battles," *The Masterkey for Indian Lore and History* 38, no. 4 (1964): 134; Adam Jevec, "Semper Fidelis, Code Talkers," *Prologue: Quarterly of the National Archives and Records Administration* 33, no. 4 (2001): 270–277.

assigned teams of code talkers to each of its six Pacific divisions. Several code talkers tell stories about being mistaken for Japanese because of their racial appearance, in some cases almost leading to them being shot. Merril Sandoval remembers one example succinctly:

On Iwo Jima, maybe first or second week, one of my buddies, another Code Talker, we decided to walk away from our command post just to stride, just to relax a little bit, when two marines, our own men, came up with their rifles and their guns. They thought we were Japanese. But then we told them we were Navajo Code Talkers, but they wouldn't believe us; they were ready to kill us. And then my buddy said, 'Well, take us to your command post so we can give identification there.' So we walked – they marched us over there with guns in our back – and before we got there they recognized us, and two sergeants jumped up with their rifles and yelled at those guys all kinds of cussing words. 'You leave our code talkers alone or we're gonna kill you two.' That was the end of it, they took off.[36]

Mistaken identity became such a problem that bodyguards were assigned to protect the code talkers, dramatised as a protection of the code in the 2002 film *Windtalkers*. In other instances, their racial appearance worked in the Navajos' favour; Tom White tells a story of stripping to his waist at Cape Gloucester, walking up to two Japanese pillboxes and machine-gunning them.[37] Navajo Code Talkers were also able to practice other cultural traditions on the battlefield in unique ways. Chester Nez remembers innovative methods for cooking fry bread in their helmets with a stick; he recalls, 'We men swore we could smell that fry bread turning golden in its oil from two or three miles away.'[38]

The Navajo code became quite central in the Pacific campaign as summarised in a famous quote by Major Howard Connor, 5th Marine Division signal officer: 'Were it not for the Navajos, the Marines would never have taken Iwo Jima.' Navajos did not necessarily recognise this during the war, but they certainly realised it afterward. Sam Billison states, 'The more I studied, the more I realized the importance of this thing [code], the value of it, that it came from Navajo and that this was our weapon, so to speak. I didn't realize that it would be really significant in these island hopping campaigns throughout the Pacific war.'[39] Thomas Begay similarly remarks, 'But our language was a weapon. We used it to kill the enemy. That's how I saw it. We have all kinds of battle scars, but I don't think we got enough recognition.'[40]

[36] Merril Sandoval, LOC AFC/2001/001/14223.
[37] Margaret Bixler, *Winds of Freedom: The Story of the Navajo Code Talkers of World War II* (Darien, CT: Two Bytes Publishing Company, 1992), 88.
[38] Nez and Avila, *Code Talker*, Chapter 15.
[39] Sam Billison, interview by Sally McClain, 31 May 1993.
[40] Thomas Begay, interview by Sally McClain, August 1992.

Begay's comment about recognition is important because they demonstrate how the code talkers' story became forgotten, but, since his 1992 interview, that has changed dramatically. When the war ended, the Navajo and other code talkers had to remain silent about their wartime activities because the code was still classified, and code talkers even served on a smaller scale in Korea and Vietnam. In 1968 the government declassified the Navajo and Comanche codes, and since the 1970s, with the activism of the Navajo Code Talkers' Association, the group gradually gained recognition. By the late 1990s, the story of the Navajo Code Talkers had become part of the Second World War popular mythology. The Honoring the Navajo Code Talkers Act awarded the Navajo Code Talkers the Congressional Gold and Silver Medals in 2001, and extensive lobbying led to the Code Talkers Recognition Act of 2008 to award medals to the other code talkers and their tribes at a ceremony in 2013.[41]

The Navajo Code Talkers, and to a lesser extent the other nations' code talkers as well, have thus come to form the dominant narrative of the Native American war effort. In a similar process as the Maori Battalion, there has been some willingness among Native Americans to embrace this mythology, but there is a significant difference from the Māori case. Whereas the Maori Battalion drew from across numerous iwis, the code talkers were from particular Native American nations and quite small in number; meaning, that the majority, which did not provide code talkers, must measure their participation against this narrative. As such, there has been more interest and willingness on the part of Native Americans to expand (not so much challenge) the dominant war narrative; whereas, Māori have been in concert with Pākehā in using the Maori Battalion as the iconic, representative story of their Second World War service. Why both sets of stories are so powerful, though, is that they centre Indigenous knowledge as a vital aspect of the Allied war effort.

### Home Defence and Soldier-Bodies: Torres Strait Light Infantry Battalion and Pacific Coast Militia Rangers

As authorities in Australia, Canada and the United States became aware of the growing Japanese threat, they were quick to recognise the vulnerability of sparsely populated coastal regions in the path of any Japanese advance. Northern Australia and Torres Strait were a case in point.

---

[41] William Meadows, "An Honor Long Overdue: The 2013 Congressional Gold and Silver Medal Ceremonies in Honor of Native American Code Talkers," *American Indian Culture and Research Journal* 40, no. 2 (2016): 91–121. See also Riseman, *Defending Whose Country?* 213–219.

Largely the realm of the missionary, the lugger, the cattle-station manager and the occasional police patrol, there was but a tiny government presence and little interest in directly supporting Indigenous inhabitants. Japanese aggression at the end of 1941 and the escalation of the Pacific War changed the strategic and security equation. Scenarios of Japanese invasion catapulted remote coastal regions onto the mental map of defence planners, and raids, on Darwin, Broome and Katherine and invasion of the Aleutian chain in 1942, brought the war directly to Indigenous homelands in Australia and Alaska. All three nations would turn to local Indigenous populations in these remote and threatened regions, with multiple motives and objectives. First, most pronounced in Australia, was the need to ensure that Indigenous populations did not willingly or unwittingly assist potential Japanese invaders. Second, in these regions, there were few white settlers, often limited to a handful of missionaries, miners, fur traders, farmers or pastoralists and police. Finally, white intermediaries would convince military authorities of the Indigenous knowledge of the geography and their capacity to traverse it and survive.

The worries about Aboriginal or Torres Strait Islander collaboration derived from the decades of contact between Indigenous Australians and Japanese pearlers and fishermen. These relationships varied from friendly and intimate through to hostile, with a famous case of Yolngu killing Japanese fishing for trepang (sea cucumbers) in 1932 in Caledon Bay.[42] Concerns tended to come from local white residents of remote regions. For instance, at Onslow in Western Australia, there were reports that Aboriginal station workers 'have spoken of the benefits which will be theirs when the Japanese occupy the territory, which will include the right to take white wives'.[43] In the Cooktown district of north Queensland, a letter from A. Stanfield Sampson to Mrs Bennet read: 'these aboriginals have openly stated that the Japs told them that the country belonged to the blacks, had been stolen from them by the whites and that "bye and bye" they (the Japs) would give it back to them (the blacks)'.[44] None of these worries ever came to fruition, with Yolngu man Gerry Blitner best summarising Aboriginal perspectives:

The Japs used to tell the [Torres Strait] Islanders, and the Aboriginals, that we are not coming back to fight Aboriginals, Torres Strait Islanders; we are coming back to fight the white man. I don't know whether they were trying to gain favour

---

[42] See Ted Egan, *Justice All Their Own: The Caledon Bay and Woodah Island Killings 1932–1933* (Carlton, VIC: Melbourne University Press, 1996).
[43] Department of the Navy Minute Paper, NAA, MP729/6, 29/401/618.
[44] Extract from letter from A. Stanfield Sampson to Mrs. Bennet, in memo to Director-General of Security, 16 July 1942, NAA, MP729/6, 29/401/626.

with them or not. But not one Aboriginal or Islander took their side. Everybody was ready to fight the Japs, and we knew that they were our enemies.[45]

The worries about Indigenous collaboration tended to be localised and did not stir significant attention from Canberra. Instead, military authorities saw Indigenous men (and occasionally women) as vital to fill Army labour needs in areas of particular strategic value. In Australia, the first such region was the Torres Strait because of its importance as a shipping passage, connecting southeastern Australia to both Darwin and the British base at Singapore. In Canada, it was northern British Columbia's coast, seen as unprotected and a possible northern flank for attack. Although British Columbia did not face the same direct threat as Alaska or northern Australia, a Japanese submarine did shell the lighthouse at Estevan Point, and a few balloon bombs fell later in the war.

To help garrison the Torres Strait, the War Cabinet approved the enlistment of a company of Torres Strait Islanders in March 1941. Eventually, this troop would reach a total strength of 488 personnel, 440 of whom were Torres Strait Islanders. Other Torres Strait units raised during the war – including artillery and transport companies – brought the total number of Torres Strait Islanders in the Australian Army to approximately 850.[46] These men were formally enlisted, so they received combat training with standard weaponry. The majority of their work was manual labour such as loading and unloading ships and embarking on patrols. Yet, as Elizabeth Osborne has documented, Torres Strait Islander men performed a variety of tasks and learned new skills including working as wireless operators, air compressor operators, carpenters, transport drivers, plumbers, signallers, tractor drivers, tinsmiths and bootmakers.[47]

In Canada, the Army stood up the Pacific Coast Militia Rangers (PCMR) in March 1942 as a way for men who were usually exempt or unfit for overseas military service to patrol their local area, to report any findings of a suspicious nature and to fight as guerrilla bands if an enemy invaded. A year later, nearly 15,000 British Columbia and Yukon trappers, loggers and fishermen had organised in 126 companies along the coast and well into the interior. Though the PCMR was not an Indigenous unit per se, it was inevitable that First Nations people, being a significant population in rural British Columbia and the Yukon Territory, would

[45] Gerry Blitner, in *No Bugles, No Drums*, produced by Debra Beattie-Burnett, directed by John Burnett, Seven Emus Productions in association with Australian Television Network, 1990.

[46] "Minutes of Conference AAG First Aust Army and Mr McCracken," Public Service Commissioner, Q'Land State Government, no date, AWM, series 54, item 628/1/1B.

[47] Elizabeth Osborne, *Torres Strait Islander Women and the Pacific War* (Canberra: Aboriginal Studies Press, 1997), 118–119.

become part of this force. The Nisga'a of the Nass Valley, for instance, enthusiastically organised a PCMR company in 1943. The community was patriotic and engaged, with 'Indian chiefs of their respective districts' serving as the Ranger officers. 'All the Indians of these parts are strongly and enthusiastically (almost too much) for the Ranger organization', the Army officer sent to organise the company observed. 'They see in it their opportunity to do their bit & to be prepared to help in home defence in country (and this was emphasised) and in terrain & surroundings with which they were familiar and in which they would be most useful.' As Lackenbauer notes, the Rangers in the Nass River communities elected their own officers and non-commissioned officers by secret ballot, with their respective Indian councils and Indian Agents approving their choices.[48]

Motivations to enlist in the TSLI similarly centred on the importance of defending their own country against Japanese invasion, but their enlistments were not so simple and voluntary. Army authorities recruited Torres Strait Islanders by sending a vessel around Torres Strait and advising Torres Strait Islander men to report to their nearest Army recruitment post. The testimonies of Torres Strait Islanders include phrases like 'we were caught by the Australian Army and ordered to go to Cairns', 'They called everyone' and 'they grabbed those boys off the boats and what's left on the islands they went around recruiting', describing themselves as forced to join the TSLI, sometimes even at gunpoint.[49] Notwithstanding such aggressive recruitment, veterans of the TSLI and their families speak fondly of their work in the unit and recognise its importance to their homeland's defence. Saulo Waia summarises: 'Because during the war, in the middle of the war, we joined in … 1941 … we joined in: War in New Guinea already. Japanese in there already. So, we only last chance. Only last chance, we are. Not very far from New Guinea. Thursday Island group of Torres Strait.'[50] Elizabeth Osborne reconciles the many testimonies of coercion with statements about wanting to join the Army by arguing that the men were happy to join, but the Army's coercive recruitment methods frightened them and triggered associations to longstanding encounters with colonial violence and intimidation.[51]

---

[48] P. Whitney Lackenbauer, *The Canadian Rangers: A Living History* (Vancouver: University of British Columbia Press, 2013), 50–51; P. Whitney Lackenbauer, "Guerrillas in Our Midst: The Pacific Coast Militia Rangers, 1942–45," *BC Studies* 155 (December 2007): 95–131.

[49] Osborne, *Torres Strait Islander Women and the Pacific War*, 108–115. See also Tom Lowah, in Hall, *Fighters from the Fringe*, 173–174.

[50] Saulo Waia, in Hall, *Fighters from the Fringe*, 142.

[51] Osborne, *Torres Strait Islander Women and the Pacific War*, 113–115.

As Lackenbauer observed in his studies of the PCMR, newspapers described British Columbian First Nations as 'natural' Rangers and their patriotism as a model for all Canadians to emulate. A *Victoria Colonist* editorial proclaimed on 3 April 1943:

Up and down the length of British Columbia's Coast, both on the main reservations and at many an isolated inlet and forest hamlet besides, the Indians have taken a very keen interest in the war. Where they could serve, they have joined the colors. Where they could not, they have left no stone unturned to assist those who are engaged in the war effort.

Reporter Marion Angus held up the story of a '102-year-old Dog Creek Indian who offered his services as a guide or marksmen and pointed back to a long, successful career as suitable qualifications' as 'indicative of the way the Indians are backing the war effort'. He was made an Honorary Ranger for his sincere offer.[52]

In Australia, too, racialist ideas came to the foray when planning the TSLI because commanders were adamant that no Aboriginal people were to be enlisted. Racial hierarchical ideas had traditionally positioned Torres Strait Islanders as racially superior to Aboriginal people, with one major writing: 'These Aboriginals, I feel certain, would be nothing but an embarrassment to me in the event of any action, as they are not in the same fighting class as the Torres Strait Islanders.'[53] The TSLI retained white commanders and served alongside Malay soldiers, yet Torres Strait Islanders were subjected to different rules. They were not permitted to drink or gamble, and most importantly, their pay was set at one-third the pay of regular soldiers of the same rank. Moreover, because of the protection legislation in place in Queensland, a portion of their pay went to the Chief Protector of Aborigines as an allotment.[54] Members of the TSLI expressed dissatisfaction with this arrangement on multiple occasions, culminating in a formal strike in January 1944, discussed in more detail in Chapter 7.[55] In February 1944 the wages increased retrospectively to July 1943 but still only at two-thirds of the white soldiers' wages. Additionally, there were no changes to the Chief Protector receiving a portion of wages. It would not be until 1983 that the Commonwealth

[52] Lackenbauer, *The Canadian Rangers*, 49.
[53] Major, for Lieutenant-General, Comd First Aust Army, AOD, to ADV LHQ, HQ QLD L of C Area, 10 October 1942, AWM, series 54, item 628/1/1B.
[54] Lieutenant Colonel, District Finance Officer, 1st M.D., to Deputy Director of Native Affairs, 15 September 1941, AWM, series 54, item 628/1/1B.
[55] Captain Foley, "Strikes by Torres Strait Lt Inf Bn," 22 January 1944, in AWM, series 54, item 628/1/1B.

Cabinet agreed to award back-pay for TSLI members' underpayment during the war.[56]

While both the TSLI and PCMR were small in the larger war effort, they demonstrate the significance of Indigenous soldier-bodies for home defence. For example, when six Nisga'a attended the Ranger training school at Sardis, reports of their exceptional performance so impressed the commander of the Army's Mountain and Jungle Warfare School that he requested that they serve as instructors for soldiers who came through to train.[57] In the Torres Strait, as well, the TSLI's performance impressed commanding officers. Tom Lowah remembers the August 1944 visit of General Thomas Blamey, commander of the 2nd AIF: 'You know, Blamey said, "I haven't see an army on parade such as this". He gave us credit. Oh, goodness me. I don't blame him because I know myself. People the white people among the soldiers, the white soldiers in Thursday Island couldn't get over, you know, [how professional the Islander soldiers were].'[58] Lackenbauer explains: 'In the Rangers, Indigenous skills were valued and their dispersed reserves, dotting the province's periphery, placed them at key strategic points. In wartime, their intimate, ancestral ties to the land invested them with a sense of purpose', shared with Queensland and British Columbia's white communities: a desire to defend their homeland.[59]

## Home Defence through Tradition: Alaska and Australia

Two other regions vulnerable to Japanese attack also turned to Indigenous knowledge, but in innovative, unconventional ways that would forefront traditional Indigenous skills, rather than employing them just as local soldier-bodies: the Northern Territory and Alaska. The decision to look to Indigenous defence networks was neither immediate nor obvious to military authorities. Instead, like the case of the Navajo Code Talkers, white intermediaries who had some knowledge of the local Indigenous communities were the ones who usually proposed the formation of Indigenous units. In Alaska, it was Major Marvin 'Muktuk' Marston, an air officer in Anchorage, who came up with the idea of an Inuit

---

[56] See NAA, A13977, 326, Item barcode 31405912; NAA, E791, D357/1/11, 5387420; NAA, A13977, 431, 31406010.

[57] Quoted in Kerry Ragnar Steeves, "Pacific Coast Militia Rangers, 1942–1954," (Masters Thesis: University of British Columbia, 1990), 57, and Lackenbauer, *The Canadian Rangers*, 496 f93.

[58] Tom Lowah, in Hall, *Fighters from the Fringe*, 183–84.

[59] P. Whitney Lackenbauer, "Indigenous Peoples and the Defence of Remote Regions in Canada, Alaska, and Australia," paper delivered at the Native American and Indigenous Studies Association conference, University of Saskatchewan, 15 June 2013.

defence network. After a visit to St Lawrence Island, Marston realised that the land was unguarded, the locals had longstanding historical ties to Russian and Japanese visitors and no awareness of the global events transpiring. He pitched the idea of forming an Alaskan Territorial Guard to a major in the Intelligence Division of the Alaskan Department, whom Marston convinced that organising local Inuit defence was a smart idea. As the proposal worked its way through the bureaucracy, though, there were doubts, delays and rejections. Only after the Japanese attack on Dutch Harbor in June 1942, and with the support of Governor Ernest Gruening, did the military support the formation of a territorial guard made up of Inuit.[60]

In Australia, it was anthropologist Dr Donald Thomson who proposed organising a group of Yolngu men in east Arnhem Land as a guerrilla force. Thomson had befriended the Yolngu people during two expeditions between 1935 and 1937. Thomson, now serving as a RAAF squadron leader, delivered a speech in June 1941 that caught the attention of the Army director of special operations. The lieutenant-colonel approached Thomson with the idea of training Yolngu men as a guerrilla force and, from then, Thomson ran with the idea. By February 1942, the plan was in place: Thomson would travel along the Arnhem Land coast with a crew of two other white men, six Solomon Islanders, a Torres Strait Islander and his Aboriginal friend and guide Raiwalla. Their mission was to recruit Yolngu men and train them to patrol the region, monitor for any Japanese landings and use their traditional bush warfare and weaponry to fight a guerrilla war. The military would issue them with knives, fishing lines and hooks to improve their efficiency in gathering food on the land. Although these Yolngu soldiers were given regimental numbers, the Army never formally enlisted them, and their 'pay' consisted of three sticks of trade tobacco per week. The payment in trade goods made them particularly attractive to military planners because they were so cost-effective (or cheap). This force was to be known as the Northern Territory Special Reconnaissance Unit (NTSRU).[61]

Thomson utilised the connections he had made with influential Elders in his earlier expeditions, and by March 1942, Thomson had recruited the nucleus of fifty men, with the aim being for them to recruit others if a Japanese attack did come to fruition. Although Thomson taught the Yolngu men how to evade machine-gun fire and the use of Molotov cocktails, he emphasised the importance of them using traditional weaponry

---

[60] Muktuk Marston, *Men of the Tundra: Eskimos at War* (New York: October House Inc, 1969), 37–48.
[61] See Riseman, *Defending Whose Country?* 38–48.

such as spears. He wrote: 'It was not intended to attempt, in training these nomadic people ... to turn them into orthodox soldiers or train them in parade ground tactics ... but merely to instil into them the elements of discipline, so that they would be capable of carrying out scouting work in conjunction with regular formations.'[62] There was significant Yolngu agency in the recruitment and operation of the NTSRU; the final surviving member, Mowarra Gamanbarr, recollected in 2000: 'Thomson said, "If they win, this will be Japanese country, and our children won't have the chance to learn our culture." Thomson said we had to combine with the white people. This was never done before. We all went to war, fighting for this country of ours.'[63] More telling in 2005, Elder Phyllis Batumbil described the Yolngu war effort thus: 'And they knew that they'll help the Army – Balanda [white persons] army, Australian, and Americans, and New Zealand because they knew that Japanese were the enemy.'[64] Essentially, Batumbil was positioning the Yolngu people as allies, rather than merely as subjects obliged to render service.

In Alaska, too, the trusted intermediary, in this case Marston, was vital for recruitment efforts. Marston travelled with the governor to small villages via light plane, and on another excursion, he hired an Inuit guide to travel by dogsled to remote communities. In their appeals to assembled communities, the governor addressed them as 'fellow citizens of the United States'. Marston appealed: 'They [Japanese] want to drive you out of your villages so they can take the fish, the whale, and the seal for their people. Uncle Sam does not have enough soldiers to watch all your coastline. Will you help keep the Japanese out? Will you keep a lookout along your shores? ... You men who will help your country against the Jap, come forward now and sign your names here on this paper.'[65] Describing the purpose of the Inuits in the Alaska Territorial Guard, Marston writes: 'The Eskimo is very receptive and enthusiastic about such drill. The purpose of this work was not to perfect the Eskimos in its technique so much as to build up their own morale by making them feel they were a real part of the regular Army.'[66]

Marston did confront opposition to this Tundra Army, both from local whites and sceptical military commanders. He wrote, 'In the Arctic as

---

[62] "Report on Northern Territory Special Reconnaissance Unit, by Squadron Leader D F Thomson, R.A.A.F.," AWM, series 54, item 741/5/9, Part I, p. 48.

[63] Mowarra Gamanbarr, in *Thomson of Arnhem Land*, produced by Michael Cummins and John Moore, directed by John Moore, Film Australia, in association with John Moore Productions, 2000.

[64] Phyllis Batumbil, interview with Noah Riseman, Australian Institute for Aboriginal and Torres Strait Islander Studies, RISEMAN_N01.

[65] Marston, *Men of the Tundra*, 58.

[66] Ibid., 89.

in the United States we have those who still cling to the outmoded and antiquated delusion of white superiority. In Alaska as in Georgia the discriminatory laws and customs are breaking down, and there is even now dawning a new era of truer equality and justice for all races.'[67] During winter 1943, Marston encountered a major at a small Army air base 100 miles inland from the Bering Sea. When Marston asked what the major was doing about the Alaska Territorial Guard companies in the region, his response was: 'They're just Eskimos and of no concern to my command.' The major was surprised to hear that the 750 men had guns and ammunition and queried, 'How do you know they won't turn those guns on us?'[68] Marston then showed on a map how inadequate the major's defence network was, shaming him into realising the importance of making contact with the 750 members of the Alaska Territorial Guard.

Local white men caused significant troubles for Thomson and the NTSRU as well. The owner of a local pastoral station reported a theft to the local police depot in May 1942 and accused members of the NTSRU. The police investigator, describing their clan as 'a very tricky and murderous tribe to have dealings with', visited the NTSRU when Thomson was not around, scaring those men into fleeing to their home territory. Eventually, the true culprits were revealed to be workers at the station, but the critical point of this story is that even in the wartime climate, the colonial attitudes denigrating Yolngu people endured among the local white population.[69]

Both Marston and Thomson wrote of the significant pride the Indigenous members of these forces felt in their work. Marston commented: 'Everywhere I went in the Arctic I found the Eskimos eager and anxious to be permitted to serve in the Guard units. Now, for the first time, they realized their importance to Uncle Sam and felt themselves to be citizens of a great democracy.'[70] Thomson's praise of the NTSRU stated: 'Not one of the men obtained, or asked for, any leave or relief, there being no grumbling or discontent, but every man in this unit carried out willingly and cheerfully what should have been the work of two men.'[71] Also of importance, both Marston and Thomson understood the importance of working closely with local Elders to facilitate support and recruitment for these units.

---

[67] Ibid., 102.
[68] Ibid., 153–154.
[69] Riseman, *Defending Whose Country?* 57–59.
[70] Marston, *Men of the Tundra*, 127.
[71] "Report on Northern Territory Special Reconnaissance Unit, by Squadron Leader D F Thomson, R.A.A.F.," AWM, series 54, item 741/5/9, Part I, p. 29.

As the tide of the war turned and the Japanese threat eased, military officials on both sides of the Pacific lost interest in these Indigenous defence networks. By the end of 1944, there were about 2,700 armed members of the Alaska Territorial Guard – including auxiliary services such as quartermaster and food provisions provided by women and children. Marston estimated about 20,000 Inuits were involved in the Guard. In summer 1944, Marston wrote: 'Now that the Jap had been driven from the Aleutians, and the threat of enemy submarines in the coastal waters or attack by air was no more, the whites thought it safe to disband the natives. Indeed, it was high time they were put back in their places.'[72] Investigations into the Alaska Territorial Guard's finances were ongoing throughout 1945, and there was even an order issued for Marston to repossess all of the equipment issued to the Guard members. According to Marston, what made the colonel change his mind was when Marston wrote, 'There just might be some Eskimo germs on this equipment that the Eskimo has become immune to, which might spread throughout the entire United States Army, upon reissuing this equipment.'[73]

In Australia, two factors led to the demise of the NTSRU. The first was Thomson's own exhaustion. On 20 September 1942, Thomson departed Arnhem Land, leaving one of the other white soldiers in charge of the NTSRU. Tensions between that sergeant and the NTSRU members forced Thomson to return in October both to replace the sergeant and to reprimand the NTSRU members. Thomson continued to patrol with the NTSRU from January to April 1943, but strained from this work, he requested to be relieved and was never replaced.[74] Instead, what replaced the NTSRU was another scouting unit that operated across northern Australia known as the North Australia Observer Unit. It was similar to the NTSRU in that it was to patrol and watch for Japanese invasions, but it was different in two senses: first, its members were not trained for guerrilla warfare against Japanese but rather were just to report movements. More importantly, it was a group of regularly enlisted white men. Yet, even these white men grew to rely on Aboriginal trackers and locals to complete their patrols and survive in the bush.[75]

Notwithstanding the short-term demise of the NTSRU and Alaska Territorial Guard, the forces did highlight the importance of continuing defence of remote regions and inspired new, more modern incarnations in the post-war era. The formal disbandment of the Alaska

72 Marston, *Men of the Tundra*, 159.
73 Ibid., 171–172.
74 Riseman, *Defending Whose Country?* 62–65.
75 Richard Walker and Helen Walker, *Curtin's Cowboys: Australia's Secret Bush Commandos* (Sydney: Allen & Unwin, 1986).

Territorial Guard was on 31 March 1947. Governor Gruening urged the War Department to re-establish it, and the National Guard Bureau authorised the formation of two scout battalions in the far north and west. The legislature then re-established the Alaska National Guard in 1949.[76] The Australian Army in 1981 formed the North-West Mobile Force (NORFORCE) as an Aboriginal reserve unit to patrol northern Australia along the Northern Territory coast and parts of the Kimberley in Western Australia. In January 1982, the Army established the Pilbara Company (renamed Pilbara Regiment in 1985) and in 1985 the 51st Battalion, Far North Queensland Regiment. While these units are not exclusively Indigenous, they draw the majority of their membership from local Aboriginal and Torres Strait Islander communities and maintain close connections with them.[77] Canada, too, reincarnated the PCMR as an expanded Canadian Rangers group across the Arctic.[78] It would not be until 1991 that the Australian government, building on the precedent set in 1983 with the TSLI, agreed to award proper back-pay to surviving members of the NTSRU and their families.[79]

### Informal Home Defence

Working through the layers of Indigenous knowledge deployed by the settler militaries: there were the overseas forces, the home defence units regularly enlisted, the home defence units that were distinctly Indigenous in their operation, and what remains were the informal, non-enlisted Indigenous defence networks. While there were isolated examples of Indigenous individuals contributing to the war effort in remote regions discussed in Chapter 6, the examples discussed here were organised groups never formally sanctioned by the respective settler militaries. Such groups were especially pronounced in northern Australia but also with some smaller examples in Canada. The most common example was the RAAF employment of Aboriginal men to build airstrips in the Northern Territory. The RAAF tended to hire labourers from local missions to undertake these tasks, and most oral histories and RAAF reports favourably describe the relationships between airmen and Aboriginal people. The Air Officer Commanding North-West Area said that when times were desperate, the obvious place to put an outlying post was near

---

[76] Major General C.F. Necrason, epilogue to Marston, 176–177.
[77] Noah Riseman and Richard Trembath, *Defending Country: Aboriginal and Torres Strait Islander Military Service since 1945* (St Lucia: University of Queensland Press, 2016), 144–157; Allison Cadzow, "North West Mobile Force," in *Serving Our Country*, 282–303.
[78] Lackenbauer, *The Canadian Rangers*.
[79] See NAA, A11116, CA693 PART 1, 31172567; NAA, A14039, 7866, 31750481.

*Figure 5.3* A group of men from Melville Island working with the Royal Australian Navy for special duties such as locating crashed airmen and Japanese mines. Courtesy Australian War Memorial, accession number 062344.

a mission: 'If a plane crashed, if wreckage came ashore, if a mine was washed up, or a belly tank found, the natives had the news, and often the evidence to the missions in a few hours. The benefit of such institutions in aiding the protection of this part of Australia can scarcely be over-estimated.'[80]

This statement proved prophetic, for Aboriginal coastwatching patrols, usually at the behest of missionaries, proved vital at locating crashed aircraft and rescuing surviving Australian or American pilots. There are several stories from the Northern Territory. One is of American pilot Clarence Sanford, whose plane went down in Caledon Bay, and he washed ashore unconscious. Two Aboriginal men came across Sanford and were at first unsure whether he were friend or foe. When they saw a crucifix around his neck, they realised he was an ally and brought him to

[80] Quoted in Hall, *The Black Diggers*, 177.

safety at the Yirrkala Mission.[81] In another tale, George Booth and two other airmen survived a crash in Caledon Bay. When they were on Elcho Island, a Yolngu man named Paddy/Matui came to their rescue, canoeing through a wild storm to bring them to safety at Milingimbi.[82] Lazarus Lamilami recalls the rescue of several Americans who survived a crash near Croker Island. The Aboriginal men watched as six men parachuted out of the plane; a group of Aboriginal men dispatched from the local mission found all of them as well as four dead and another survivor at the crash site.[83] The Yanyuwa people at Borroloola choreographed the *Aeroplane Dance* to tell the story of how they rescued a crashed American pilot who was near death after twenty weeks in the wilderness.[84]

## Conclusion

Indigenous knowledge became indispensable to certain parts of the war effort, even in ways that settler states were unaware. Because most of the Indigenous home defence forces were small or never actually had to engage in combat, they did not receive significant attention during or after the war. The NTSRU, TSLI, PCMR and Alaska Territorial Guard were in remote locations which, while potential front lines in 1942, became peripheral sites in the wider Second World War historical narrative. Instead, more glorious tales like the Maori Battalion and, decades later, the Navajo Code Talkers would enter the national consciousness because of their direct implications for the war effort. They were not hypothetical Indigenous defence networks; they really were fighting the enemy and proving the value of their Indigenous traditions in a wartime environment.

The dynamics of all of these examples of differentiated Indigenous service reflect the complexities of settler-Indigenous relations and constantly shifting power relationships. These forces relied on Indigenous agency and knowledge, yet they also relied on settler support and often command. They represented settler control over materiel, orders and even the very existence of such forces, yet the forces could not function

---

[81] Harold Thornell, as told to Estelle Thompson, *A Bridge Over Time: Living in Arnhemland with the Aborigines 1938–1944* (Melbourne: J.M. Dent Pty Limited, 1986), 129–133; *No Bugles, No Drums*; Wandjuk Marika, as told to Jennifer Isaacs, *Wandjuk Marika: Life Story* (St Lucia: University of Queensland Press, 1995), 65–67.

[82] George Booth, *33 Days* (Elwood, VIC: Greenhouse Publications, 1988); *No Bugles, No Drums*.

[83] Lazarus Lamilami, *Lamilami Speaks: The Cry Went Up: A Story of the People of Goulburn Islands, Northern Australia* (Sydney: Ure Smith, 1974), 188–193.

[84] *Ka-wayawayama: Aeroplane Dance*, produced and directed by Trevor Graham, Film Australia, 1994.

without Indigenous bodies and knowledge. There was tremendous irony that the very communities and their cultural and social characteristics that settler governments had been working to erase through the colonial process were so widely and specifically targeted for the cause. They demonstrated the value of Indigenous knowledge and peoples as distinct cultural entities, and of their capacity to contribute to settler society in innovative ways. Of course, in the process settler martial race notions were reinforced – and in the post-war years, the value of Indigenous knowledge and culture was less recognised; its value was situational in a militarised setting.

# 6    Home Front Experiences

The term 'total war' refers to a conflict in which the participant states mobilise all of their human and material resources for the war effort. For the majority of Second World War combatants, including the four settler societies in this book, the conflict was a classic total war, which necessitated the involvement of not just servicemen and women in uniform but also of civilians on the home front. The dominant narratives of the four nations entail much of the 'standard' home front experience in modern war: increasing industrial work, shifting gender roles, raising funds, rationing, censorship, sacrifice and loss. This 'standard' story of the war has an Indigenous variant through much of the literature, which also includes urbanisation, decreasing prejudice, increasing acculturative pressure and diverse reaffirmations of cultural and community identity.

Historical treatments of the home front tend to be eclectic and wide-ranging, and this chapter reflects this broader pattern. The totalising impact of the war generated a range of important macro-influences felt broadly, if unevenly, across all four countries. Pressure to expand wartime production and industrial output both opened up unprecedented economic opportunities and encouraged Indigenous people to relocate to urban centres. Indigenous people also noticed a general reduction in overt prejudice, a breaking down of boundaries and more inclusivity as people pulled together in a common war effort. In growing urban Indigenous populations, new forms of community developed to support individuals and families suddenly isolated from their cultural heritage.

A second important theme was the war's impact on those regions across the remote north of Australia, Canada and Alaska that had previously been relatively sheltered from the full impact of settler society and state. This effect was twofold: indirectly as settler military and civilian agencies 'invaded' traditional Indigenous territories in response to the Japanese threat, and sometimes directly when these home fronts became military front lines under attack. The consequences were far reaching for the inhabitants.

*Figure 6.1* An Aboriginal woman receiving her ration book at Brunswick Town Hall in June 1943. Indigenous people on the urban home front shared measures and participated in the wartime economy alongside non-Indigenous citizens. Courtesy Australian War Memorial, accession number 139015.

Finally, at a more finite level, the war's tremendous impact can be seen in the myriad ways it penetrated the daily lived experiences of Indigenous communities, families and individuals whether urban, rural or remote. For Indigenous and non-Indigenous people alike, the climate was emotionally charged when men and women left their shores to risk their lives. Indigenous men and especially women on the home front had a variety of motivations to join the war effort: patriotism, loyalty, support for their kin in the forces, economic opportunity, hope for greater civil rights and acceptance after the war.

Indigenous people, especially new urban dwellers, became exposed to new ideas, fashion trends, pop culture and sexual relationships; in Australia, New Zealand and northwest Canada this included relations with American servicemen passing through. At the personal level, the war expanded interaction and assimilation into settler society. Even so, throughout these narratives there were still elements of continuing discriminatory policies being enforced piecemeal, suggesting that the

*Figure 6.2*   Picture released on 28 February 1940 of Hopi artist Fred Kabotie (L) and Apache Miguel Flores (R), along with other Indian tribes of Arizona, signing the parchment document banning the use of the swastika from all designs in their basket weaving and blanket making and other hand-crafted objects, against Nazi 'act of oppression'. Photo AFP/Getty Images.

structures of colonial domination lingered beneath the façade of wartime solidarity. This chapter examines all of these points to reveal the multifaceted ways that the home front experience mirrored the service experience of change and continuity for Indigenous peoples.

## Continuity and Discontinuity of Discrimination

The rapidly shifting conditions during the early years of the war would lead to growing contact between Indigenous and non-Indigenous people. At times this could be a boon, as non-Indigenous people, especially urban-dwellers, who often had little or no previous experience meeting an Indigenous person, could now be neighbours or workmates. Yet, positive relationships were not always the result, as discrimination could rear its ugly head unexpectedly, reminding Indigenous men and women that they were still living under the yoke of settler colonialism. Mihi Edwards

describes discrimination in Wellington: 'It is very hard, very embarrassing, trying to get a place to stay. Because I am a Māori, they just look
at me and shut the door. ... There weren't even a lot of Māori people in
Wellington. I pretend I am a Pākehā, try and make myself white. I didn't
know how to use make-up. With this white powder all over my face I look
like a clown – but I forget about my neck.'[1] Numerous memos in New
Zealand's National Service Department recorded prejudices against Māori
women, such as not being welcome at hostels, not wanted in particular
munitions factories or being seen as more suited to substandard work.[2]
Robert Gideon sought the aid of the Indian Affairs Branch, wondering 'as
an Indian am I entitled to a job in any of the munitions plants here in the
city [of Montreal]. I have tried But [sic] it seems that I did not yet [have]
any satisfaction.' He hoped that with a written statement from the department, 'it would not be so hard to seek employment'.[3] Testimonies about
racial discrimination during the war are especially prominent from rural
areas where segregation practices were long-entrenched. Alec Kruger
joined the Army in Alice Springs, and he recollects:

Despite being in the army we were still looked down on and treated with suspicion by most in the white civilian population. You had to be careful not to be seen
outsmarting even the dumbest of them, or else you risked a hiding. You had to
be careful not to beat them in a fight or else they might seek you out later on. So
you kept your eyes low, said 'yes boss' to even the most unlikely crap, and tried to
keep moving in a group wherever possible.[4]

Notwithstanding some continuity of prejudice, the wartime conditions
and enhanced interactions also provided venues and mechanisms to challenge such views. Kristyn Harman writes about the Aborigines Uplift
Society's national comforts auxiliary, which recruited white woman volunteers to 'adopt' Aboriginal soldiers, writing them letters and sending
parcels containing goods such as knitted clothes, toiletries and choco-
lates.[5] Oodgeroo Noonuccal recalls how the war broke down barriers
between white and Aboriginal women on Stradbroke Island:

... it was the women who broke down this silly barrier of racial discrimination
because it was the white women who went to the black women here on the island,

---

[1] Mihi Edwards, *Mihipeka: Time of Turmoil; Ngā Wā Raruraru* (Auckland: Penguin Books,
  1992), 125.
[2] Deborah Montgomerie, *The Women's War: New Zealand Women 1939-1945* (Auckland:
  Auckland University Press, 2001), 68; 98–99.
[3] Robert Gideon to the Department of Indian Affairs, 1 June 1941, LAC, RG 10, Vol.6765,
  file 452-6-17.
[4] Kruger and Waterford, *Alone on the Soaks*, 130.
[5] Kristyn Harman, "'The Families Were ... Too Poor to Send Them Parcels': The Provision
  of Comforts to Aboriginal Soldiers in the Aif in the Second World War," *Aboriginal
  History* 39 (2015): 223–232.

and said, 'Look, you make socks better than us, you are better at all these things', and they came together in the Australian Comforts Fund. Because the white women had sons across there too, as well as my mother.[6]

What also comes across in Indigenous testimonies, though, are cases where either they or bystanders challenged individual instances of discrimination. In one case from Alaska, a mixed-descent woman named Alberta Skenk was fired from her job at the cinema in Nome when she questioned the manager's policy of segregated seating. About a week later, a white Army sergeant invited Skenk to accompany him to a movie and escorted her to the whites section. The manager angrily demanded that Skenk move, even as the sergeant stood up for her. Police arrived, pulled Skenk from her seat and threw her into the street. A few days later, a crowd of Inuit purchased movie tickets and sat wherever they wanted in the theatre. As the protests escalated, the white Major 'Muktuk' Marston drafted a letter on Skenk's behalf and sent it to the governor of Alaska. The governor wrote to the mayor of Nome, who responded 'A mistake has been made. It won't happen again.' A few weeks later, the soldiers stationed at Nome voted in a popular ballot to elect the annual Queen of Nome: Alberta Skenk. Furthermore, with the support of Governor Ernest Gruening, anti-discrimination legislation passed through the territorial legislature in 1945.[7]

In Australia, as well, there could be white support when Indigenous people challenged blatant cases of discrimination. Banjo Clarke recalls attending a dance hall in Queensland, and a white American soldier pushed him in the back, kicking him out. Afterward, two girls hit the white soldier, attracting attention. Clarke writes, 'And I heard one of the young girls say, "This dirty Yank threw our Aboriginal friend out down the stairs, and he could have been hurt. He might get away with doing that in America, but he can't in Australia." Immediately, all the men left the walls, and they took the young soldier by the back of his trousers and threw him outside' where Clarke fought the American.[8] The tormenter's outsider identity as an American undoubtedly facilitated the locals' strong response.

In New Zealand, Mihi Edwards suggests that Wellington's famous Battle of Manners Street began when American servicemen tried to discriminate against Māori servicemen. She writes:

A brawl breaks out in Manners Street. It was started, so I believe, by soldiers from the southern states of America who couldn't understand why the Pākehā

[6] Oodgeroo Noonuccal, in Hall, *Fighters from the Fringe*, 119.
[7] Marston, *Men of the Tundra*, 134–140.
[8] Banjo Clarke, *Wisdom Man* (Camberwell, VIC: Penguin Books, 2003), 112–113.

would allow Māori soldiers to drink in the same Allied Services Club as the white man. During the time the Yanks are here, I hardly see any black sailors or marines on the streets of Wellington so I suppose it was quite a shock to them when the Pākehā defended the Māori.[9]

Taken in conjunction with the Clarke example, it seems as though the notions of 'us' and 'them' could transform during the war, drawing Indigenous people within the boundaries of 'us' to be defended from external challenge. This does not mean that Indigenous people were now seen as equals or even that racism disappeared. Indeed, Mihi Edwards suggests that the new wartime situation merely transferred racism to other targets: 'The Pākehā seem to stop calling us "black niggers". But they are now calling the Italian people "dagos".'[10]

The wartime transformation of the home front was therefore complex and uneven, creating a new paradigm that had the potential to support Indigenous people against longstanding discriminatory practices. Yet it was not clear that this rupture would persist without a common external enemy. Oodgeroo's testimony perhaps best summarises how the war temporarily changed white mindsets: 'All of a sudden they forgot about us being second-class citizens because they needed our help ... They were too busy worrying about their lives to worry about what colour you were.'[11]

## For Those Left Behind

Perhaps one of the most significant dimensions of the home front was the emotional toll on families of those men (mostly) and women who went off to war. For many, departures were a moment of mixed emotions, as families both took pride in their relatives' service while at the same time feared what awaited them overseas. Indigenous families also relished the status that military service bestowed upon their relatives, whether because of their own warrior traditions or because it promised an elevated position vis-à-vis settler society. Métis woman Maria Campbell was a small child during the war, and she encompasses the fearful sentiments of many families: 'The idea of travelling across Canada was unbelievable enough, but the sea was frightening for those who had to let loved ones go. Many of our men never returned, and those who did were never

---

[9] Edwards, *Mihipeka: Time of Turmoil*, 133.
[10] Ibid., 114. See also Margaret Tucker, *If Everyone Cared: Autobiography of Margaret Tucker M.B.E.* (Sydney: Ure Smith, 1977), 159.
[11] Oodgeroo Noonuccal, in Hall, *Fighters from the Fringe*, 120–121.

the same again.'[12] Some men who went off to war had young families, placing extra financial and emotional strains on the mothers left behind. Tepara Mabel Waititi married just before the war broke out in 1939. Two years later she had a son, and her husband was heading overseas with the Maori Battalion; she recollects:

I didn't like the idea but he was determined he was going to go. I had my fears they might get bombed from the air or torpedoed in the sea and they may not reach their destination. And the other fears I had – he might come back minus one arm, one eye or leg or even both. And then there'd be a lifetime looking after him.[13]

Mixed emotions underscored every farewell, and this could be even more the case where Indigenous men left without the blessing of their families. Russell Modeste of the Cowichan First Nation wanted to 'do his bit' and enlisted, but when he did so, his father was upset. 'He said I know what you've done and it's none of your business,' Modest explained. 'If the War was on in Canada I would expect you to do what you've done and help the country. But the War's in Europe, it's a European War, it has nothing to do with you, it's none of your business and I don't appreciate what you've done. I said dad it's too late I've given my oath I have to go through with it.'[14] One Mi'Kmaq woman wrote to the Indian Affairs Branch (IAB) seeking the return of her husband who had enlisted: 'last summer without my consent and now I am asking the Department of Indian Affairs to discharge him off from war service, or otherwise I will go direct to Ottawa and get a lawyer to desist him from going overseas'.[15]

In the wake of the departures, some Indigenous families struggled to cope with the absence of young men and women who had been important supports to their families. Gunditjmara woman Iris Lovett-Gardiner recalls that when both her father and an uncle went to war, her mother and aunty struggled to manage the household, including tough 'men's work' like carting water and chopping wood. But with the help of the children, the families persevered.[16] Mrs William Martin from Burnt Church, New Brunswick, wrote to the IAB on 10 December 1941 asking for the release of one son from war service, '... on account of my poor

[12] Maria Campbell, *Halfbreed* (Lincoln and London: University of Nebraska Press, 1973), 24.
[13] Tepara Mabel Waititi, in *War Stories Our Mothers Never Told Us*, ed. Judith Fyfe (Auckland: Penguin Books, 1995), 130–131.
[14] Lackenbauer et al., *A Commemorative History of Aboriginal Peoples in the Canadian Military*, 136.
[15] Mrs Soloman Francis to Department of Indian Affairs, 16 December 1941, LAC, RG 10, Vol. 6767, file 452-15, pt.2.
[16] Aunty Iris Lovett-Gardiner, *Lady of the Lake: Aunty Iris's Story* (Melbourne: Koorie Heritage Trust, Inc, 1997), 33.

helth [sic], since my both boys away I start to work to [sic] hard, and since then my helth [sic] getting fail and I am still getting worse. I know I never get along when the cold winter weather has come, and no body who will help me. My husband died a year and a half ago, I mind 3 small Children [sic].'[17]

Families would wait anxiously for news, whether through letters, newspapers, or the dreaded official cables. One letter from the Maria Reserve in Quebec conveys that depth of worry; a grandmother wrote the IAB requesting information of her grandson: 'Please be kind enough as to write + inquire if he is dead or not? I am very uneasy about him.'[18] Navajo woman Agnes Begay's brother was captured as a Japanese POW early in the war. She recalls:

When I learned he had been captured by the Japanese I tried to send him letters and some materials which I thought he might need. I did that through the American Red Cross. In return they allowed him to write 10 lines of whatever he wanted to say, and that was all for three whole years. I kept inquiring about him every two months and I never lost track of him after he was captured until he returned home to us.[19]

In other instances, Indigenous families received news of confirmed fatalities, which were devastating. Common among numerous testimonies across the four states is a sense that the Indigenous community would rally to support the family, emotionally and financially. Iris Lovett-Gardiner recalls one example:

When Aunty Fanny got word about her son, Wally, we were all at the Heywood Show. All the Aboriginal people walked off the showgrounds because of the sorrow they felt. Everybody's heart was with everybody else. That's the way we were, if there was a sorrow in one family, there was a sorrow in all of them.[20]

Tepara Mabel Waititi explains similar communal grieving among Māori:

When the word is received that a soldier had died, we all go to that particular marae, if they got a marae, or to their home, and help the ones that lost a soldier. But the thing is ... they're crying over just the photo, and they know the body will never be returned. Aue, that really saddened us. That saddened me most – see them crying just over a photo. At the marae, at the homes, not long after they put memorial stones up with the names of the soldiers that were killed.[21]

[17] Mrs. William Martin to Indian Affairs Branch, 10 December 1941, LAC, RG 10, Vol. 6767, file 452-15, pt. 2.
[18] Mrs. John Martin to the Department of Indian Affairs, 1 August 1941, LAC, RG 10, Vol. 6765, file 452-6-17.
[19] Agnes Begay, "History – Munitions Plant Work During World War II," in *Navajos and World War II*, 49.
[20] Lovett-Gardiner, *Lady of the Lake: Aunty Iris's Story*, 53.
[21] Tepara Mabel Waititi, in *War Stories Our Mothers Never Told Us*, 137–138.

Common words within testimonies of servicemen's family members – whether they be sisters, children or wives – are terms like 'trauma', 'hardship' or 'sad'. Just as they were coping emotionally with the departure and sometimes loss of loved ones, they also went out of their way to support those who had gone to fight. Part of the coping process often involved engaging in the war effort, which increasingly drew Indigenous women and men away from their communities.

### Urbanisation

Urbanisation of Indigenous communities began in the respective settler states in varying, but generally limited, degrees from the earliest moments of colonisation.[22] The Second World War massively accelerated this process, drawing Indigenous people into cities such as Melbourne, Sydney, Wellington, Auckland, San Francisco, San Diego, Toronto and Vancouver. They joined non-Indigenous men and women who were participating in the booming wartime economies, particularly working in factories. They also partook in rationing regimes, including sharing with Indigenous and non-Indigenous friends and neighbours to support one another.[23] Some Indigenous people have recollections of ongoing employment discrimination early in the war, but as the demands for man and womanpower increased, the factory doors opened.[24] In rural areas as well, Indigenous people were now being offered jobs previously closed to them. Western Australian Aboriginal man Jack McPhee recalls being encouraged to apply for a job at the Comet mine in Marble Bar that had twice before refused to employ him. A mate said to him, 'It's wartime mate, not enough blokes to go around, why don't you give it another go, I'm going to.' This time the employer hired McPhee. [25]

Aboriginal woman Marg Tucker's wartime experience aligns with many of the common tropes of women entering the workforce in droves in all four settler societies: conducting heavy industrial work traditionally associated with men, attaining more economic and therefore social independence, patriotically contributing to the war effort, and leaving work at war's end.[26] For Indigenous women, whose voices within this narrative

---

[22] See, for example, Edmonds, *Urbanizing Frontiers*.
[23] Lovett-Gardiner, *Lady of the Lake*, 33–34.
[24] Clarke, *Wisdom Man*, 126–130.
[25] Sally Morgan, *Wanamurraganya: The Story of Jack McPhee* (Fremantle, WA: Fremantle Arts Centre Press, 1989), 143.
[26] Ruth Roach Pierson, *They're Still Women After All: The Second World War and Canadian Womanhood* (Toronto: McClelland & Stewart, 1986); Montgomerie, *The Women's War*;

*Figure 6.3*   Munitions workers at a factory in Hamilton having a meal break. John Pascoe Collection, Alexander Turnbull Library.

have been mostly hidden, war work offered employment opportunities often previously denied them because of racial discrimination and/or education levels. In most countries there are no exact statistics about the types of work that Indigenous women did during the war, but New Zealand is a notable exception. In 1943 about 700 Māori women resided in Auckland, and by 1945 there were 1,700 working in essential industries in the region.[27] Census data shows a threefold increase in Māori women working in the Public Administration and Professional category

Kate Darian-Smith, *On the Home Front: Melbourne in Wartime 1939–1945*, 2nd edn. (Carlton, VIC: Melbourne University Press, 2009).

[27] Angela Wanhalla and Kate Stevens, "'I Don't Like Maori Girls Going out with Yanks': Māori-American Encounters in New Zealand," in *Mothers' Darlings of the South Pacific:*

between 1936 and 1945; by 1951, 20.7 per cent of Māori women were recorded as paid members of the workforce, up from 12.2 per cent in 1936.[28] In the United States, Bertha Eckert of the YWCA estimated that 12,000 Native American women had joined the workforce by 1943, many of whom had left their reservations for the first time in their lives.[29]

Most testimonies report war work happening in industrial jobs. For women like Marg Tucker, who had previously worked as a domestic servant, a factory job meant being treated as an equal with white, mostly working-class, women. Aboriginal woman Connie Albert remembers: 'There was always a big load of women going to the [ammunition] factory. We would all come to work together, hundreds of us, all getting off the buses together.'[30] First Nations women also migrated to urban centres for work in domestic service and war industries where, according to the 1943 Annual Report of Indian Affairs, 'reports indicate that the service tendered has been uniformly satisfactory ... the demand for these girls far exceeded the supply'.[31] The multiracial nature of employment was, just as in the services, an unprecedented opportunity for intercultural exchange between Indigenous and white workers. Nellie Sarracino recalls when she and other Native American workers at the Santa Fe Railway Yard in Richmond, California staged a Thanksgiving performance in tribal regalia for visitors. The local Richmond newspaper ran a feature about the event, commenting: 'Just like the WACs, the WAVES, and the Women Marines, our women workers on the Santa Fe have taken the places of men who have gone off to war.'[32]

Not all the new employment required leaving reservation communities, as sometimes military bases and establishments on or near Indigenous lands provided opportunities. One example was the Navajo Ordnance Depot, opened in 1942 as an ammunition storage site. It employed and housed Navajo and other Native American workers such as Agnes Begay, who remembers: 'I was selected to work in the personnel office and help the people get jobs, especially Navajos who had no formal education. I did some interpreting, and I helped them fill out applications, etc. My late husband, Seth, took a job as a truck driver. He worked with 15 men

---

The Children of Indigenous Women and US Servicemen, World War II, ed. Judith A. Bennett and Angela Wanhalla (Dunedin, New Zealand: Otago University Press, 2016), 207.

[28] Barbara Brookes, A History of New Zealand Women (Wellington: Bridget Williams Books, 2016), 267.

[29] Franco, Crossing the Pond, 141–142; "Indian Girls Now at War Jobs; Others Serving as Army Nurses," New York Times, 6 February 1943, 16.

[30] Connie Alberts, in Jackomos and Fowell, Forgotten Heroes, 43.

[31] Department of Mines and Resources, Annual Report (Ottawa: 1943), 151.

[32] Nellie Sarracino, The Bancroft Library, Regional Oral History Office, Rosie the Riveter World War II American Home front Oral History Project.

hauling ammunition in big semi-trailer trucks.' The Depot also provided
services for its resident-workers, transforming it into a community. Agnes
Begay recalls: 'At the camp we were assigned to nice two-bedroom quar-
ters, and education was provided for our children. A child care center
was provided, where lots of women were given jobs. Some that had more
qualifications worked in offices, and some worked as checkers.'[33]

More generally, Tom Holm notes that, 'On the reservations, which by
1944 were critically short of a male workforce, Indian women accounted
for much of the production of food. They drove heavy equipment,
repaired tractors and herded cattle.'[34] It was not only women who took
advantage of the new industrial jobs, especially in the cities. New Zealand
Department of National Service statistics show that as of 1 April 1945,
15,000 Māori were employed in essential industry and 10,000 directions
had been issued to Māori for industrial conscription.[35] Statistics from
British Columbia's Department of Labour show First Nations employment in enumerated industries doubled from 1940 to 1941 and almost
doubled again by 1942. Logging, road maintenance, railways and agriculture drew many men away from their traditional fishing work.[36] At the
same time, thousands of First Nations men and women found work in the
Pacific salmon fishing fleet and canneries respectively, filling the spaces
left vacant by the internment of the Japanese-Canadian population who
had formerly been a major component of that industry.[37] Papago man
James McCarthy had served in the First World War and was too old to
enlist again. He had numerous jobs during the war including a special
appointment on the Ajo Reservation as a police deputy, patrolling to stop
alcohol being smuggled across the Mexican border. From 1944 to 1945,
McCarthy worked in a rubber plant loading and unloading boxcars, at a
factory making artillery shell casings, then a small aircraft factory. Of the
artillery factory job, he remembers: 'The machine was making shell casings for the Army. After I was trained, I ran the machine while the men
poured the hot copper in it. It was a hot job in a hot place. This job did
not last long. The Army contract for making shell casings ended, so the
foundry closed in 1945 and laid off all the men.'[38] The tenuous nature

[33] Agnes Begay, "History – Munitions Plant Work During World War II," 48.
[34] Tom Holm, "Fighting a White Man's War: The Extent and Legacy of American Indian Participation in World War II," *Journal of Ethnic Studies* 9, no. 2 (1981): 73.
[35] Montgomerie, *The Women's War*, 97.
[36] John Sutton Lutz, *Makúk: A New History of Aboriginal-White Relations* (Vancouver: University of British Columbia Press, 2008), 227.
[37] Roy Toomey, "Canadian Indians in World War II" (MA Thesis, University of Northern British Columbia, 2006), 54.
[38] James McCarthy, *A Papago Traveler: The Memories of James McCarthy* (Tucson: Sun Tracks and the University of Arizona Press, 1985), 162.

of employment could affect anyone; although, as McCarthy's experience demonstrates, there were often ample job opportunities for men during the war.

The war's impacts could affect even industries seemingly removed from any clear military context. For instance, the Tsilqot'in people in coastal British Columbia found traditional work now could turn a significant profit. The price of furs skyrocketed, with even squirrel pelts earning high returns. Logging and sawmilling became new industries, with significant demand for timber driving economic growth into the 1950s. Even chopping down Christmas trees became profitable because there was such a shortage of available men to do this work during the holiday season.[39] In New Zealand, Jean Matekitewhawhai Andrews recalls traditional and new work in Paikakariki: 'we were also doing preserving puha and tahu-ing pauas and mussels and that to send to our Battalion boys over there, as well as the usual family chores ... I used to have to clean the Liberty trains, hop on the last one, finish that at 3 in the morning and start this laundry business straight away'.[40]

For Indigenous men and women who moved to the cities, new forms of community sprung up to unite people otherwise from disparate tribal or cultural backgrounds. In Melbourne, Fitzroy had been the Aboriginal hub since the Great Depression, and Connie Alberts remembers: 'All us Aboriginal people used to meet there. People used to live in little apartments around Fitzroy and we'd all meet at the Exhibition Gardens on Sundays. It was nice, especially in the summer.'[41] Yankton Sioux woman Faith Traversie worked as a welder in a naval repair yard in the San Francisco Bay Area. She remembers being treated as an equal and also remembers Indian organisations emerging all over the West Coast:

There were big Indian Centers where Indians go to in the cities and meet each other, and there was nothing – they really – oh, because they shipped a lot of Indian people in to work because they came in experienced, you know. They had had schooling. A lot of them, they had schooling in different trades.[42]

Urban communities even developed unique ways to assert self-determination. Laguna Pueblo woman Nellie Sarracino moved to Richmond, California and worked for the Santa Fe Railroad as an engine wiper. Her family was one of about thirty Laguna and Acoma Pueblo

[39] Lutz, *Makúk*, 152.
[40] Jean Matekitewhawhai Andrews, in *War Stories Our Mothers Never Told Us*, 82.
[41] Connie Alberts, in Jackomos and Fowell, *Forgotten Heroes*, 45.
[42] Faith Traversie, The Bancroft Library, Regional Oral History Office, Rosie the Riveter World War II American Home front Oral History Project.

families living in boxcars converted into makeshift housing known as the Santa Fe Indian Village. This Indian community within the San Francisco Bay Area elected its own (male) officers, voted on decisions relating to the reservation in New Mexico and held weekly meetings to run the village. The Santa Fe Indian Village had its own baseball team, and Nellie recalls Laguna and Acoma people holding their own traditional 'Indian dances' as well as going out to 'American dances'. Residents of the village spoke both English and Pueblo languages, and they also participated in events hosted by the burgeoning Bay Area Indian community.[43] In Wellington, Māori groups like the Ngati Poneke Young Maori Club presented themselves as a social and cultural space for Māori women recently moved to the city. The Maori War Effort Organisation (MWEO), with its 315 local committees, set up a system of welfare officers in the cities to work with the authorities to support women, especially those who were new to the environments.[44] The Te Hokowhitu Maori Club in Wellington had culture clubs, Māori acts and other entertainment, including dances.[45] Women's organisations and church groups set up hostels, recreational facilities and social activities to cater to women without family support. It was not just Pākehā anxious about Māori women moving to the cities – many Māori leaders from rural areas had similar worries.[46] The post-war continuity of urbanisation was common across the four countries, and after a brief return to traditional territories and a hiatus, the phenomenon was renewed by the 1950s.

## Participation in Voluntarism

Many of those on the home front also poured their anxieties for their departed loved ones and their shared desire to contribute into voluntary work. Often voluntarism and giving were orchestrated through tribal revenues and decision-making. In 1944, Secretary of the Interior, Harold Ickes, reported that Native Americans had purchased at least $2 million worth of war bonds from tribal funds, and Collier estimated that the total Native American commitment in 1944 alone reached $50 million.[47] Tribes also found innovative ways of raising money; the Zuni bartered and traded foodstuffs such as corn, beans, wheat and oats to raise $62.31

---

[43] Nellie Sarracino, Rosie the Riveter World War II American Home front Oral History Project.
[44] Wanhalla and Stevens, "I Don't Like Maori Girls Going out with Yanks," 207.
[45] Jean Matekitewhawhai Andrews, in *War Stories Our Mothers Never Told Us*, 84.
[46] Wanhalla and Stevens, "I Don't Like Maori Girls Going out with Yanks," 108.
[47] Holm, "Fighting a White Man's War," 73.

for the Red Cross War Fund.[48] North of the border, First Nations also gave generously and purchased Victory Bonds in patriotic campaigns, something appreciated by Canadians. In 1941, local dignitaries in Cardston, Alberta, feted Kanai chiefs from the neighbouring reserve after their $200 contribution helped the region meet its Victory Bond quota.[49] First Nations bands officially purchased $26,493 of Victory Bonds through Indian Affairs channels, before Indian Affairs officials halted the drain on finite resources.[50] As a result, most First Nations' voluntary giving took place outside official channels, making it difficult to quantify accurately: but officials estimated contributions of all types in 1943 exceeded $400,000.[51]

In addition to tribal donations, individuals participated alongside non-Indigenous people in fundraising and other war-support activities. Marg Tucker accompanied a group that would sing at Melbourne's military hospital. She also recalls the emotional rollercoaster that this volunteer work could affect: 'We loved doing that, and would shed tears when we would go the next time only to find a bed empty, where a friendly lad had passed on.'[52] Men who had not signed up, too, would pitch in. Jack McPhee from Western Australia did not enlist because he only had one good eye, so, as he puts it, 'I tried to support the fund-raising as much as I could. Susie and I went along to all the picnics and dances and tried to help out in any way we could.'[53]

One interesting dimension to war-support services was the mobilisation of entire communities, resulting in the breakdown of interracial divisions. For example, Stó:lō children from the Colqualeetza Residential School in Chilliwack, British Columbia, sewed and knit goods suitable for the wartime cause.[54] Blackfoot Elders in southern Alberta pointed out ancient buffalo-jump sites so that community members might unearth old bones wanted by the government for the war effort.[55] Even in remote northern reaches of the Yukon, the Old Crow Band (Vuntut Gwitchin) cobbled together through fundraising a huge donation of $432.30 for

---

[48] "Zunis Aid Red Cross," *Albuquerque Tribune*, 29 March 1944, NARA, RG 75, Box 1, Entry 998A.

[49] "Blood Indians Generous To War Service Fund," *Cardston News*, 29 April 1941, 1, 2.

[50] Janet Davison, "We Shall Remember Them: Canadian Indians and World War II" (Masters Thesis, Trent University, 1992) 83; Toomey, "Canadian Indians and the Second World War," 65.

[51] Gaffen, *Forgotten Soldiers*; Toomey, "Canadian Indians and the Second World War," 66; Department of Mines and Resources, *Annual Report* (Ottawa: 1943), 157.

[52] Tucker, *If Everyone Cared*, 160.

[53] Morgan, *Wanamurraganya*, 136.

[54] "Indian Children Assist Red Cross," *Vancouver Sun*, 6 July 1940, 16.

[55] "Canada's Indians Are Helping With Tons of Old Buffalo Bones," *Saturday Night*, 10 June 1944.

the London Orphans Fund.[56] The *Regina Leader-Post* newspaper recognised Indigenous enlistments, noting also that, 'Generous donations to the Red Cross; purchase of war savings stamps; money for the purchase of an ambulance; band funds diverted to the war cause; sports days and bazaars; socials and teas; donations even of cows; knitting of socks and sweaters. All war work.'[57]

Harman has written about particular settlements where Aboriginal women organised fundraising dances, purchased wool and other material to knit socks and winter clothing, and they worked with organisations such as the Country Women's Association to facilitate these tasks. Cummeragunja Aboriginal mission on the Murray River in New South Wales was especially prolific in its production of socks, mittens and gloves, even earning a photo in the widely read magazine *Pix*.[58] Similarly, a Tsimshian church circle from Hartley Bay on the Canadian Pacific coast, 'hand-knitted thirty-two articles of clothing to be sent overseas to British children displaced by German bombing raids. The hamper included "beautifully made dresses and underclothing for little girls, knitted garments and socks made by an 11-year old member of the Junior Red Cross and babies wooly clothing".' Reporting on this example, an Ontario newspaper indicated that a note accompanied the Hartley Bay hamper of clothes, which read: 'Usually people are helping us; now we can help others not so fortunate as we are.'[59] The *Arizona Republic* reported in January 1944 about the Navajo service chapter of the American Red Cross preparing ninety-one kit bags for the US forces as well as dozens of socks, gloves, sweaters and other knitted items for the home front.[60]

Māori organisations that formed during the war increasingly performed similar fundraising, support and even entertainment tasks. One reason that Māori organised their own groups was to assert their own control and to ensure that their relatives would receive the goods they personally arranged. Tepara Mabel Waititi recalls that in Whangarei:

They said a lot of the things went astray, the soldiers did not get them. So myself and a cousin of mine Ada Walker, we looked after the money for the Maori Patriotic Committee in our area, and were responsible for sending the parcels over for the soldiers.[61]

---

[56] Letter to the Commissioner, RCMP, 25 September 1942, LAC, RG 10, Vol. 6763, 452-5 NWT.

[57] "Saskatchewan Indians Respond Well," *Regina Leader-Post*, 24 July 1940.

[58] Harman, "'The Families Were ... Too Poor to Send Them Parcels'," 232–244. See also Jackomos and Fowell, *Forgotten Heroes*, 47.

[59] "Indian Women Aid Evacuees," Unknown Newspaper, Vancouver, 14 March 1941, LAC, RG-I0, v. 6763, f. 452-5, pt. 2.

[60] "Articles made by Navajo unit," *Arizona Republic*, 14 January 1944, NARA, RG 75, Box 1, Entry 998A.

[61] Tepara Mabel Waititi, in *War Stories Our Mothers Never Told Us*, 137.

Maree Millar recalls of the Māori Women's League: 'We enjoyed going around various areas putting on concerts, organising basket socials or whatever was in line for fund-raising. Everyone was involved.'[62] Waikato groups led by Princess Te Puea Herangi organised dances, garden parties and fruit and vegetable sales to raise money, an estimated £30,000 to £40,000.[63] An October 1941 letter from Te Puea states: 'We sent £100 for our Maori prisoners of war camp in Germany, £100 for a marquee tent for the Maori Battalion overseas ... and £200 towards comforts for the battalion, also £100 for the general purposes fund of the Waikato Red Cross.'[64] The most famous Māori wartime organisation was the Wellington-based Ngāti Pōneke Club, which was particularly effective at providing entertainment on ships, at the Majestic Cabaret Opera House, Town Hall, in army camps and when visitors came or when Māori boys went away.[65]

Indigenous peoples also often asserted a distinct Indigenous identity and sovereignty through their war support activities. In June 1940, at a Blackfoot council meeting in southern Alberta, Ted Yellowfly stated that:

we the Blackfoot Tribe of Indians, desire to show out [sic] loyalty to Canada and the Empire, by doing our humble bit to help in the struggle for freedom from tyranny. Canada has, and always shall be, our home; the outlook of the Indian is purely Canadian in its nature and character, and therefore we ask that a sum of $850.00 representing $1.00 from each Blackfoot soul, be donated to the Red Cross of Southern Alberta from the Blackfoot Band Funds.[66]

The voluntarism in this instance was couched in a declarative statement of belonging and the right to participate.

Other voluntary efforts were also articulations of Indigenous autonomy and control over their engagement in the war effort. For example, the Squamish people in Vancouver organised their own campaign, in the face of Indian Affairs opposition, to raise the $25,000 needed to purchase a Spitfire fighter, rather than contributing to similar settler campaigns. Other First Nations throughout British Columbia contributed to the Squamish Spitfire Fund by staging concerts, craft bazaars and

62 Maree Millar, interviewed in Whāngārei, 1990, in *Early Stories from Te Tīmatanga Tātau Tātau: Founding Members of the Māori Women's Welfare League; Te Rōpū Wāhine Māori Toko I Te Ora*, ed. Anna Rogers and Mīria Simpson (Wellington: Māori Women's Welfare League – Bridget Williams Books Limited, 1993), 94.
63 Brookes, *A History of New Zealand Women*, 272; Michael King, *Te Puea: A Biography* (Auckland: Hodder and Stoughton, 1977), 210.
64 Quoted in King, *Te Puea*, 209.
65 Edwards, *Mihipeka: Time of Turmoil*, 137–138.
66 Blackfoot Minutes of Council Meeting, 19 June 1940, LAC, RG 10, Vol. 6763, file 452-5 Alta.

other activities to achieve the common goal.[67] One fascinating example of this behaviour occurred when the Peigan in Alberta invited the public to attend a Sun Dance if they brought a donation for the Red Cross in 1940. According to the *Lethbridge Herald*, they had already raised $150 and hoped to reach $1,000. What was striking here was that the Sun Dance was illegal, yet the Peigan defiantly and openly advertised and hosted the event because they knew the Indian Agent would not dare interfere in something supporting the war.[68]

Women found their own ways to assert their sense of self. They continued to host ceremonies in their men's absence, such as the Inter-Tribal Indian Ceremonial of Gallup, New Mexico. A Navajo man serving in New Guinea wrote home requesting: 'How about a pin-up gal selected at the Inter-Tribal Indian Ceremonial?' The Ceremonial held a competition for Native American pin-up girls – selecting a winner and two runners-up. Newspaper captions indicate that two of them were working in war industries.[69] Women also invoked distinct Indian modernities through their cultural and spiritual relationships to servicemen. The *Oklahoman* reported in 1944: 'The women have organized Victory clubs and War Mothers clubs. Members proudly wear new shawls, with the names of their sons or husbands embroidered on them. The shawls tell of men who have fought at Tulagi, at Salerno, in the Aleutians and the southwest Pacific – anywhere around the world where American fighting men are to be found.'[70] Marie Maker was the president of this group, and she remembers that it had an Osage name: Me-Tho-Ta-Maci American War Mothers Club. Marie describes them performing the Soldier Dance, which the Omaha Indians had composed during the First World War, and the Ponca-written Veteran Song. She describes part of the ceremony: 'Start dancing and they used to have special songs. These different – they'd [veterans] even have a song they own. Some of them did, which we have special songs sung in the afternoon until they were all sung.'[71]

[67] "Indians Help to Raise Funds For Purchase of Spitfires," *Vancouver Province*, 18 December 1941; "Seek $25,000 Indians Help to Raise Funds for Purchase of Spitfires," *Vancouver Province*, 19 December 1940, LAC, RG-10, Vol. 6763, file 452-5, BC. See also F.J.C. Ball to the Secretary, 24 October 1940, LAC, RG 10, Vol. 6763, 452-5 BC.
[68] "Indians Assist Red Cross Fund," *Lethbridge Herald*, 18 July 1940, LAC, RG-I 0, v. 6763, f. 452-5, pt. 2.
[69] "Navajo Suggests Pin-Up Girl Be Named At Reunion," *Gallup Independent*, 25 July 1944; "Indian Beauties Selected as Pin Up Girls," unknown newspaper, 21 August 1944, NARA, RG 75, Box 1, Entry 998A.
[70] "Tribal Dances Honor Indian Hero's Return," *Oklahoman* (Oklahoma City, OK), 9 April 1944, NARA, RG 75, Box 1, Entry 998A. See also "Indian Women 'Honoring the Returning Warrior'," *New York Times*, 10 April 1944, 13.
[71] Marie Maker, interviewed by Leonard Maker, 20 June 1969, University of Oklahoma, Norman, OK, Western History Collections, T-407.

Marie Maker thus reveals a ritual that co-opted and shaped a white organisation to fit with traditional Native American practices. Moreover, her story shows the ways that the group drew on other Indigenous traditions, formulating a modern, almost pan-Indian practice for returning veterans.

The war also presented new leadership opportunities for Native American women in certain reservations. Grace Gouveia notes that at least fifteen tribal councils had female members during the war, with Josephine Kelly chairing the Standing Rock Reservation Council and Nell Scott beginning a thirty-year tenure as chair of an Arapaho council. Women also began to take up positions on tribal judiciaries. James Frechette, a member of the Menominee Advisory Council, stated in 1942: 'the time has come when women on the Reservation will take an active interest in the affairs of the tribe'.[72] The changing political status for women on reservations began with pre-war reforms under the Indian New Deal, but it was the wartime climate and women's newfound economic clout on the reservations which accelerated their entry into tribal leadership positions.

What these many forms of the war effort demonstrate are the ways that Indigenous people on the home front asserted a distinct but vital positionality within the nations' war effort. They were contributing to a common cause, but were doing so on their own terms and in their own self-determined capacities, with a particular interest in supporting their own kin who were overseas. Such demonstrations of support for the war effort exemplified the ways that Indigenous people could articulate themselves as distinct, allied and/or a part of the settler nation.

### Women, Gender and Sexuality

There was another significant reason for the support systems set up for women moving to the cities: anxieties about morality, idleness and sexuality. In the United States, there was an interesting dichotomy between support for Native American women moving to the cities as a positive sign of assimilation, while expressing paternalistic anxieties about the threat to their moral virtue and capacity to survive on their own. A March 1944 article, entitled 'Indians on Warpath: More than 50,000 Redskins under Arms', briefly mentioned women using assimilationist and patriarchal language: 'Women have given up tribal handicrafts for war plant jobs. A touch of rouge, a fashionable hair do, and modern clothes ease their

---

[72] Quoted in Gouveia, "We also serve," 178.

assimilation into the community of workers.'[73] The flip side to the assimilationist story was worry that Native American women may not be adequately prepared for such a life. A 1943 *New York Times* article reported:

Their problems are similar to those of other rural girls now surging into munitions towns, Miss Eckert [secretary for Indian Work at the National YWCA] reports. There is danger of handling money for the first time, without any idea of how to budget wisely – of being attracted by that which is 'flashy' rather than practical, and the hazard of making the wrong type of friends.[74]

The moral anxieties about single Indigenous women moving to the cities were more commonly about women's sexuality. In New Zealand, for instance, public health campaigns about venereal disease specifically targeted Māori women, whom authorities stereotyped as being too loose and prone to corruption. Indeed, several Māori women were arrested and charged with being idle and disorderly, particularly in Auckland.[75] In the New Zealand parliament in 1943, Apirana Ngata declared, 'Ever since the beginning of the war we have been endeavouring to dissuade our young women, despite the attractions of uniforms, from going into the cities, pointing out that the cities were vile ...'[76] Female liaison officers were appointed in major urban centres in August 1943 to look after the welfare of Māori women in paid employment. Their job was 'to inspire young women with pride of race, to help build their characters so that they could stand against the difficulties of life, which would be accelerated by wartime conditions, and to prevent their exploitation by those who employed them and those who provided them with accommodation'.[77]

In Australia and New Zealand, and to a lesser extent in Canada, part of what fuelled these anxieties was the influx of American servicemen – black and white – whose presence provided an exciting wartime diversion for young women. Even in Hawai'i, the massive military presence brought Kanaka Maoli into contact with service personnel from the mainland. One issue of the magazine *Paradise of the Pacific* noted a stark increase in local women visiting beauty parlours to impress 'malihinis' (American servicemen) while another published a list of Hawai'ian vocabulary to assist servicemen.[78] It has been well documented how the arrival of large

[73] "Indians on Warpath: More than 50,000 Redskins under Arms," *Alabama Journal* (Montgomery, AL), 9 March 1944, NARA, RG 75, Box 1, Entry 998A.

[74] "Indian Girls Now at War Jobs; Others Serving as Army Nurses," *New York Times*, 6 February 1943, 16; Franco, *Crossing the Pond*, 141–142.

[75] Wanhalla and Stevens, "I Don't Like Maori Girls Going out with Yanks," 205–207; Montgomerie, *The Women's War*, 153.

[76] Quoted in Montgomerie, *The Women's War*, 97.

[77] Ibid., 98.

[78] Eileen O'Brien, "Ke Kauwa Nei O Kauai (Kauai at War)," January 1943, reproduced in Bob Dye, ed. *Hawai'i Chronicles III: World War Two in Hawai'i, from the Pages of Paradise*

numbers of American servicemen in Australia and New Zealand from 1942 whipped up frenzies of excitement in the population, with women (and sometimes men) being romanced by those American servicemen who were oversexed, overpaid and over here. In both New Zealand and Australia, the local servicemen grew jealous of the Americans, even culminating in riots in Wellington and Brisbane.[79] What has received less attention, though, is the ways in which Aboriginal and Māori women experienced this friendly invasion of the American GIs. Anxieties about gender, sexuality and race came into play in how American, Australian and New Zealand authorities discussed this potential 'problem', both in terms of Indigenous-white and Indigenous-black relationships.

While there is evidence of some tensions between Māori and US troops, usually over Māori women, Māori generally welcomed the Americans. For example, the Marine Commanding Officer at American headquarters made an appointment to visit Princess Te Puea at Waikato, at her insistence, as a marker both of her sovereignty in the region as well as to establish an appropriate respectful relationship. They agreed that controlled socialisation would help dispel any tension, and thus, on 19 November 1942, sixty American officers came for a day's entertainment and to enjoy the Waikato people's hospitality. This was followed in March 1943 by a visit of over 400 American Marines for the annual regatta.[80] Lasting connections with American servicemen permeate testimonies as well. Jean Matekitewhawhai Andrews' family resided at Paikakariki which at its height was the base for about 20,000 American servicemen. She remembers a rainy night when two Americans knocked on her family's door asking to rent a room. Her family said they did not rent rooms and instead invited them in, showing Māori hospitality. With the two men came another thirty who all proved to be generous guests, sharing chocolate with the kids, telling stories and playing music. After their stay, Jean offered to write letters to the men's families. Ever since, Auntie Jean has welcomed visiting Marines who made pilgrimages to revisit their wartime stomping ground. In 1968, she was made a Life Member of the

---

of the Pacific (Honolulu: University of Hawai'i Press, 2000), 109; Milly Lou Donnelly, "'G.I.' Hawaiian," Paradise of the Pacific, April 1943, reproduced in Ibid., 117–123.

[79] See Kate Darian-Smith; "Pacific Partners: Gendered Memories of the US Marines in Melbourne, 1943," in Gender and the Second World War, 135–150; Sean Brawley and Chris Dixon, "Jim Crow Downunder? African American Encounters with White Australia, 1942–1945," Pacific Historical Review 71, no. 4 (2002): 607–632; Yorick Smaal, Sex, Soldiers and the South Pacific, 1939–45 (Basingstoke: Palgrave Macmillan, 2015); Eli Daniel Potts and Annette Potts, Yanks Down Under, 1941–45: The American Impact on Australia (Melbourne: Oxford University Press, 1985); Harry Bioletti, The Yanks Are Coming: The American Invasion of New Zealand, 1942–1945 (Auckland: Century Hutchison, 1989).

[80] Wanhalla and Stevens, "I Don't Like Maori Girls Going out with Yanks," 204–205.

National Second Marine Division and was awarded the Golden Brooch, a special award normally only presented to Marines' wives.[81]

In Australia, the majority of American troops passed through Brisbane, but sizeable numbers also passed through Sydney, Melbourne, Townsville and Perth. Most Aboriginal people's memories of interactions between Indigenous Australians and the Americans centre on black Americans. Oodgeroo Noonuccal states:

We used to meet lots of US servicemen, particularly black servicemen. Oh yes, all the time. My mother, who lived on Stradbroke, she is dead now, while I was away she and Dad would write to me and say, 'We are doing our bit too, girl. We are entertaining United States personnel'. And they would throw their home open for them to come in because they had the Australian and United States Army personnel guarding the outside beach at Stradbroke.[82]

While Indigenous families were generally welcoming of the Americans, it was the relationships with women which receive the most attention in Indigenous memories. Jean Matekitewhawhai Andrews recalls, 'We used to chase the Negros in particular – oh, we used to chase after them because they could dance, *really dance*. They were really good.'[83] Testimonies show significant agency on the part of the Indigenous women; they were not just chased and taken advantage by the Americans, as some anxieties of the era would suggest. Rather, they were actively pursuing the American men themselves. Mihipeka Edwards, who was in an unhappy marriage with an overseas soldier, eventually fell in love with an American Marine. He said she reminded him of his 'mother's people' in the United States: 'My mother is part Cherokee, they look very much like the Māori people. My mother's people do not have a very good time from the system back home, but they are very good proud people.'[84] Mihipeka and the Marine saw each other about three times a week, experiencing an intense whirlwind romance; yet, according to Mihipeka, they never had sexual relations, 'for fear I will become pregnant.'[85] This example also shows the ways that Mihipeka positioned herself as maintaining respectability and avoiding the social stigma of infidelity. This awareness was another form of Indigenous women's agency, contrary to assumptions about Indigenous women's promiscuity.

Of course, there were other cases when Indigenous women did have sexual relations and fell pregnant. In 1945, approximately 25 per cent of

[81] Jean Matekitewhawhai Andrews, in *War Stories Our Mothers Never Told Us*, 74–77; 90.
[82] Oodgeroo Noonuccal, in Hall, *Fighters from the Fringe*, 122.
[83] Jean Matekitewhawhai Andrews, in *War Stories Our Mothers Never Told Us*, 85. Original emphasis.
[84] Edwards, *Mihipeka: Time of Turmoil*, 140.
[85] Ibid., 141.

children born to Kanaka Maoli women of full descent and 10 per cent born to women of mixed descent were illegitimate.[86] As Angela Wanhalla and Kate Stevens have written, it is difficult to track American servicemen's offspring because the fathers are usually not on birth certificates. The women may have tried to conceal their relationships with American men for fear of being labelled as pleasure-seeking, or in some cases, the offspring may have been the result of rape.[87] Mabel Quakawoot, a Baialai and South Sea Islander woman born in 1937, remembers being a small child of about five when a group of white American servicemen tried to break into her home to rape her mother.[88] There were some cases of abortion or adoptions, but, more often than not, children of mixed-race families who were not adopted out would be raised by the wider kin of the family – sometimes even the circumstances of their birth kept secret for decades.[89] Quakawoot remembers growing up with some Aboriginal and South Sea Islander children born to white Americans in Mackay, Queensland. She comments, 'They [the children] were accepted. But if, if they did something wrong they'd say "Oh that half American", you know, that. But wouldn't let the mother hear you saying that.'[90] Sexual relations and illegitimate births occurred anywhere servicemen, of any nation, came close to Indigenous communities, even remote areas. For instance, the Tyendinaga aerodrome in Canada was leased on Mohawk land and brought numerous British and Canadian airmen into the region as part of the British Commonwealth Air Training Program. Chief Maracle recalls generally positive relations between the communities, but he similarly remembers 'A lot of illegitimate children were left behind after the war.'[91]

Intersectional racial anxieties played out in remote parts of both Canada and Australia over the presence of black American troops. As P. Whitney Lackenbauer argues, Canadian authorities expressed anxieties in 1942 about black troops coming into contact with Inuit women. Canadian authorities subscribed to stereotypes of black men spreading venereal disease and, as Lackenbauer effectively summarises,

[86] Gwenfread Allen, *Hawaii's War Years 1941–1945* (Honolulu: University of Hawaii Press, 1950), 353.
[87] Wanhalla and Stevens, "I Don't Like Maori Girls Going out with Yanks," 214–215.
[88] Mabel Quakawoot, interview with Noah Riseman, 5 June 2011. See also Noah Riseman, *In Defence of Country: Life Stories of Aboriginal and Torres Strait Islander Servicemen and Women* (Acton: Australian National University Press, 2016), 13.
[89] Wanhalla and Stevens, "I Don't Like Maori Girls Going out with Yanks," 215–216.
[90] Mabel Quakawoot, interview with Noah Riseman, 5 June 2011. See also Riseman, *In Defence of Country*, 13.
[91] Chief Maracle, quoted in P. Whitney Lackenbauer, *Battle Grounds: The Canadian Military and Aboriginal Lands* (Vancouver: University of British Columbia Press, 2007), 109.

(re)constructed an intersectional racial discourse: 'Inuit women were not dirty but pure, needing paternal protection by their Great White Father. Thus, by racializing masculinity using African Americans, men could be held responsible for the spread of diseases usually blamed on women.'[92] In Australia, there were reports in late 1942 and early 1943 from outback northern Queensland, near the mission at Aurukun, of widespread venereal disease among the Aboriginal women. Rather than search for a cause, the Army proposed that the women be removed from the area. This drew protests from both missionaries and the Queensland government and instead of removing the women, the alleged culprits were removed: black American soldiers stationed nearby. One report declared that 'Negro personnel were highly sexed and a menace near aboriginal camps' while another document concluded that after their departure, 'it has been ascertained that the white troops are having nothing to do whatsoever with the natives'.[93] While the veracity of these racial claims is questionable, it is clear that American troops (white or black) were engaged in sexual relations with local Aboriginal women.

Even though these were often whirlwind flings, many were genuinely loving and enduring relationships. In Hawai'i there was a marked increase in interracial marriages, including among white men marrying Kanaka Maoli women.[94] Most overseas interracial engagements came to nought, though. The US War Department issued Circular No. 179 in June 1942, requiring servicemen to obtain permission from commanding officers two months before any potential wedding. The commanding officer was then required to investigate the woman and her family, taking into account several factors including American immigration laws that restricted entry to non-white people from outside the western hemisphere. Wanhalla and Stevens report that 1,588 New Zealand women married US servicemen, and only fourteen were 'believed to be racially excluded', according to the US Consulate.[95]

In Australia a January 1944 memo specifically about marriage between Aboriginal women and American servicemen stated:

Advice has now been received that where such [marriage] occurs, the Australian will not, under the law of the United States of America, be permitted to enter the

[92] P. Whitney Lackenbauer, "Race, Gender, and International 'Relations': African Americans and Aboriginal People on the Margins in Canada's North, 1942–48," in *Dominion of Race: Rethinking Canada's International History*, ed. Laura Madokoro, Francine McKenzie, and David Meren (Vancouver: University of British Columbia Press, 2017), 114.
[93] NAA, MP 729/6, 16/402/111.
[94] "Inter-racial Marriage in Hawaii," *Paradise of the Pacific*, October 1944, reproduced in *Hawai'i Chronicles III*, 212–13.
[95] Wanhalla and Stevens, "I Don't Like Maori Girls Going out with Yanks," 209–10; 213.

country if she has a strain of Aboriginal blood of 50% or more. Consequently in view of future hardship, it is inadvisable for such unions to be allowed. If any case of intended marriage comes under notice, it should be reported to the Director immediately with full details of the female party's breed. Unless there are particularly extenuating circumstances, the parties can be given to understand permission will be refused.[96]

Indigenous women who were aware of these regulations protested or searched for ways around them.[97] In most cases, the answer was that the Indigenous women could not get past racially discriminatory regulations, but there were occasions when Indigenous women did manage to marry American servicemen and some even immigrated to the United States as war brides.[98] How and why these Māori and Aboriginal women circumvented US immigration laws is unknown. It is possible that they were of mixed descent and therefore did not classify as non-white when their immigration applications were processed. It is also possible that authorities for whatever reason did not realise they were Indigenous or simply turned a blind eye. Regardless, aside from a few exceptions, for most Indigenous women who had a wartime romance with American servicemen, the men's departure marked the end of that relationship.

There is one extra twist on the Indigenous war brides issue – Indigenous men who returned with their own war brides. Métis woman, Maria Campbell, remembers: 'Many of our men brought home Scottish and English wives, which of course didn't go over very well with our people. They marry either their own kind or Indians. (It is more common among Indians to marry a white.) However, these women came and everyone did their best to make them welcome and comfortable.'[99] In the cases that Campbell describes, it was actually a shock for the British women to move to a poor Métis community; Campbell speculates that the women presumed they would be moving to a productive farm or ranch. Not all of these women received a welcome from the local community. Campbell remembers one Englishwoman who came as a bride to a poor Métis man from northern Saskatchewan; the war bride thought he was French. Campbell states: 'he owned nothing, not even the shack where a woman and two children were waiting for him. When they arrived, his woman

---

[96] Queensland Aboriginal Dept – General Circulars, 20 January 1944, Re Marriage of Aboriginals to American Soldiers, NAA, A659, 1945/1/1563.

[97] Quoted in Angela Wanhalla and Erica Buxton, "Pacific Brides: US Forces and Interracial Marriage During the Pacific War," *Journal of New Zealand Studies* 14 (2013): 143.

[98] Karen Hughes, "Mobilising across colour lines: Intimate encounters between Aboriginal women and African American and other allied servicemen on the World War II Australian home front," *Aboriginal History* 41 (2017): 47–70; Angela Wanhalla and Erica Buxton, "Pacific Brides," 138–139; Oodgeroo Noonuccal, in Hall, *Fighters from the Fringe*, 125.

[99] Campbell, *Halfbreed*, 24.

promptly beat the English lady up and gave her five minutes to get out of her sight, and told the man she'd do what the Germans didn't do (shoot him) if he didn't get his ass in the house immediately.' Campbell's mother invited the woman home, arranged a collection of money to send the woman to Regina and eventually she returned to England.[100] These cases that Campbell briefly mentions are intriguing because they suggest that Indigenous men sometimes positioned themselves in dishonest or misleading ways to attract women from overseas. When the war brides discovered the false pretences of their relationships, they may have been trapped in the marriage, searching for ways out. It seems that Indigenous men could just as easily prey on non-Indigenous women – the very gendered anxieties that authorities feared.

### War and Development Invade Remote Regions

The Second World War's impacts reached Indigenous people even living in the most remote parts of North America and Australasia, (re)shaping social discourses and the economic, physical and cultural geographies of interaction. The early war years attracted limited attention to remote regions' defence. The United States had begun plans to build military bases at Sitka, Kodiak and Dutch Harbor in 1938 as part of bolstering its Pacific defences, more generally, and specifically to guard against a possible Japanese attack via the Aleutian Islands. In Australia in 1940, the RAAF, realising that the sea approaches to Darwin were vital to the defence of the town, constructed airstrips on Darwin's flanks, extending air cover over the shipping lanes across the country's northern coast. The build-up of Darwin necessitated labour and Aboriginal and Torres Strait Islander people were a proportion of the workforce as early as 1933.[101]

Indigenous labourers were still under the control of the Chief Protector and Native Ordinances, which restricted their movement, segregated living facilities and ensured unequal pay. Joe McGinness, an Aboriginal man working for the Public Works Department building roads in Darwin early in the war, recollects one of the challenges to retaining labour: most of his friends, including Aboriginal ones, joined the Army even before the city was bombed on 19 February 1942.[102]

The second largest township in Australia's Northern Territory was Alice Springs, one of the major stops between southern Australia and

---

[100] Ibid.

[101] A/Secretary to the Military Board, to Officer Commanding Troops, Darwin, 26 September 1933, NAA, MP508/1, 82/710/2.

[102] Joe McGinness, *Son of Alyandabu: My Fight for Aboriginal Rights* (St. Lucia: University of Queensland Press, 1991), 30.

*Figure 6.4* Aboriginal men employed by the Department of the Interior in Alice Springs, assisting in construction work in December 1942. Courtesy Australian War Memorial, accession number 028353.

Darwin, which elevated its significance and military presence after Pearl Harbor. There as well, Aboriginal civilians remained under the control of Native Affairs and worked in sanitation and cleaning jobs but still resided segregated from white settlements at the Bungalow – an institution for Aboriginal children of mixed descent north of town. Even with their restricted lives, Aboriginal workers who moved into Alice Springs could earn more money than they had previously made on cattle stations.[103]

The other Australian region to feel the war's build-up was the Torres Strait. In August 1939, the Australian Air Board recommended the construction of an air base on Nurupai (Horn Island), just north of Cape York Peninsula and adjacent to Torres Strait's administrative hub, Thursday Island. This airstrip was completed in late 1941, both strengthening Australia's defence capabilities in the region while simultaneously making it a target for Japanese attack.[104] Building this airstrip and the other

---

[103] Kruger and Waterford, *Alone on the Soaks*, 135.
[104] Osborne, *Torres Strait Islander Women and the Pacific War*, 128–129.

infrastructure on Thursday Island and Nurupai meant employment for
Torres Strait Islanders outside the traditional pearling industry. Tales of
Indigenous men from remote communities working with Air Force personnel to construct such remote airstrips are prevalent across northern
Australia. This was unpaid labour, Indigenous participants sometimes
received trade goods from the local military officials. Local missionaries
often expressed dissatisfaction because the military presence was challenging their authority and disrupting their assimilationist agendas.[105]

Across the northern regions of Australia, cattle stations had employed
Aboriginal Australians since the early twentieth century under generally
deplorable conditions. Aboriginal workers and their families were forced
to endure ramshackle housing, poor diet, low or sometimes no pay, inadequate medical attention and poor hygiene facilities.[106] These conditions
changed when the military began large-scale employment of Aboriginal
people, sometimes in special labour camps in 1942. By the war's end,
the Army ran five labour camps in the Northern Territory, housing about
1,000 Aboriginal people, often from different language groups.[107] Most
men were taken each morning by trucks to work at various job sites while
others worked in the camps on sanitation, gardening or collecting fire-
wood; women also worked on domestic duties such as cooking, washing,
ironing, cleaning and gardening. Camp members worked an 8.5 hour
day, 5.5 days a week, and all residents received three meals a day, pay
and rationed goods and clothing.[108] The camps were so successful that
the Northern Territory's Deputy Director of Native Affairs wrote to the
Chief Administrator that 'the native population of the Northern Territory
has made a valuable contribution to the war effort, and at present may be
regarded as indispensable towards its furtherance.'[109]

Aboriginal work on military projects represented a direct challenge to
the pre-war order. Alec Kruger recalls:

The idea of getting equal pay was a shock for us all. The local station owners and
bosses were not happy about it. The stations had already lost a lot of their staff
since the war started. Now they were losing us. The bosses talked of it being the
ruin of us, without having them as bosses telling us what to do and protecting us

[105] Riseman, *Defending Whose Country?* 70–77.
[106] See Ann McGrath, *Born in the Cattle: Aborigines in Cattle Country* (Sydney: Allen & Unwin, 1987); Deborah Bird Rose, *Hidden Histories: Black Stories from Victoria River Downs, Humbert River and Wave Hill Stations* (Canberra: Aboriginal Studies Press, 1991).
[107] Ronald Berndt and Catherine Berndt, *End of an Era: Aboriginal Labour in the Northern Territory* (Canberra: Australian Institute of Aboriginal Studies, 1987), 155–156; 177.
[108] Ibid., 159–167.
[109] V.J. White, Deputy Director of Native Affairs, to the Administrator, 23 December 1942, NAA, MP742/1, 94/1/915.

from our lazy and evil inclinations. What they really meant was that they might have to start paying us properly and looking after us better if they needed us to stay.[110]

The Secretary of the Department of Native Affairs wrote to the Minister of the Interior regarding pastoral owners' misgivings, claiming they felt 'that the native is being treated vt [sic] the Army in a way in which it will be impossible for station owners to treat them after the war is over. In other words, they feel that the natives will return to the station somewhat pampered in an arrogant and insolent mood.'[111] Military officials largely dismissed such criticisms. In a letter responding to strident critiques from Archie Cameron MP, Major General A.S. Allen wrote, 'The Army's objective is to make the Australian aboriginal a happy, healthy and eventually useful member of the community, in his proper sphere. I gather that your views would appear to be opposed to ours on this objective.'[112]

Although Australia's north was the most significant remote site of activity and Indigenous employment during the war, development projects on a major scale also affected Alaska and northern Canada. The Japanese invasion of the Aleutians in June 1942 confirmed fears of Alaska's vulnerability and prompted one of the most rapid military build-ups in modern military history. Georgeanne Reynolds summarises, 'During the course of the war, the U.S. War Department spent nearly three billion dollars on military construction and operations in Alaska. It also sent some 300,000 military personnel to a territory that in 1940 had harbored barely more than 73,000 residents, 500 of whom were military.'[113] Pre-war plans for a highway connecting the southern forty-eight states to Alaska would finally be realised in response to the Japanese threat.

Canada agreed to construct the Alcan (Alaska) Highway, Northwest Staging Route airfields across British Columbia to Fairbanks and the Canol oil pipeline. Athapaskan people were still relatively isolated from settler society but had witnessed small-scale incursions from whalers, miners, traders, police and occasional bureaucrats. The Second World War influx of outsiders was on a new, unprecedented scale.[114] Dene and Métis guides led land surveyors over traditional hunting trails to select routes through

---

[110] Kruger and Waterford, *Alone on the Soaks*, 121–122.
[111] Secretary, Department of Native Affairs, to Minister of the Interior, 26 January 1944, NAA, AA1978/215, item 24.
[112] Major General A.S. Allen, 26 September 1944, NAA, AA1978/215, item 33.
[113] Georgeanne Reynolds, "Introduction," in *Alaska at War 1941–1945: The Forgotten War Remembered*, ed. Fern Chandonnet (Fairbanks: University of Alaska Press, 2008), ix.
[114] Lackenbauer, "Race, Gender, and International 'Relations'," 116.

*Figure 6.5*   RCAF Officer talks to a First Nations man employed on a construction site of one of the bases as part of operations concerning the Northwest Staging Route, September 1944.

mountains. Sahtú Dene man George Blondin found consistent work with American surveyor crews along the Canol pipeline in 1942–3. Then in early 1944 he and a friend made about $1,000 each in just three months selling caribou meat to the Canadian government's Eldorado Uranium Mine.[115] Outside the regions directly affected by the development projects, however, there were still parts of the Canadian north 'where relief costs remain practically as high as similar costs during the worst years of the depression'.[116]

Despite the economic possibilities, for the majority of Indigenous residents, the arrival of so many southerners was unexpected and disruptive, as authorities did not consult with or inform the local Inuit communities

---

[115] George Blondin, "When the world was new: Stories of the Sahtú Dene," in *Out of the Background: Readings in Canadian Native History*, ed. Kenneth Coates and Robin Fisher, 2nd edn. (Toronto: Irwin Publishing 1998), 261–265.
[116] Department of Mines and Resources, *Annual Report* (Ottawa: 1944), 156.

about the impending construction projects. By the end of 1942, nearly 4,000 black Americans had arrived into the region, constituting approximately 28 per cent of the American soldiers.[117] George Blondin recalled that his aunt woke him one morning: '"There are coloured people outside", she said excitedly. The Dene in the tiny community of Tulít'a had never seen a black person before. Some of the old women screamed and locked their doors. Other people hid and watched the strangers from a distance. Some ran away and hid in the bush.'[118]

The flood of Americans into the region incited a sovereignty panic in Ottawa. Wartime developments did not erode Canadian sovereignty, but they did 'more harm than good to the Native people of the Northwest', according to Kenneth Coates and William Morrison in their extensive work on the Northwest Defence Projects. Despite the labour opportunities or the briefly strong market for traditional crafts, full-time, long-term employment was seldom open to Indigenous residents along the new transportation network. Worse, soldiers and construction crews brought diseases for which Indigenous residents had no natural immunity, and epidemics swept through communities, leading to soaring death rates during the war years.[119] The Alaska Highway improved access to fish and game in southern Yukon for Indigenous people's subsistence, but it also increased non-Indigenous competition for these resources. The highway also meant more government scrutiny and control, including a stronger police presence and more pressure for children to attend school.[120] The impacts of the military 'invasion' thus extended beyond the exigencies of war itself.

As Lackenbauer's work makes clear, the effects of the war in the eastern North American Arctic were more localised than in the northwest. Frobisher Bay (Iqaluit) was a temporary fishing spot for the Inuit of southern Baffin Island but had never hosted a settlement or trading post. Its first permanent incarnation was Crystal Two, an airbase and weather station at the head of the bay. Tomassie Naglingniq encountered the Americans in 1941 when they first arrived in Frobisher Bay. He remembers:

On a Saturday or a Sunday, when the Americans were not working, they took us to the ship and we watched a movie. We had never seen anything like that ... When the movie started, everybody started yelling 'ajait ajait' [meaning I'm scared] because we never saw anything like that before. It was like the people in the movie were coming and shooting at us, and we were crying, us children

[117] Lackenbauer, "Race, Gender, and International 'Relations'," 117.
[118] Blondin, "When the World Was New," 260.
[119] William Morrison and Kenneth Coates, *Working the North: Labor and the Northwest Defense Projects 1942–1946* (Fairbanks: University of Alaska Press, 1994), 119–123.
[120] Ken Coates and William Morrison, *Land of the Midnight Sun: A History of the Yukon* (Montreal and Kingston: McGill-Queen's University Press, 2005), 249.

anyway ... The Inuit were ducking and taking cover, because they thought they were being shot at.

Food, cigarettes and movies (usually westerns) are common elements in Inuit narratives of their encounters with armed service personnel. Before the war, Naglingniq's family had never seen mechanised vehicles like bulldozers. Naglingniq recounts, 'When they started unloading the ship, their vehicles just started moving on the ground even though they were made of metal. Looking back, we must have thought they were from the moon.'[121]

The Canadian government's paternalistic predilections meant that it sought to protect Inuit in and around American airbases, initially prohibiting socialising with military personnel.[122] At northern bases, the Royal Canadian Mounted Police arranged for an officer to patrol day and night, ensuring that only Inuit working at the base entered the military camps and that no soldiers ventured into Inuit camps.[123]

## Home-Front, Bombings and Evacuations

As Chapter 5 described, Indigenous-specific or Indigenous-dominated units such as the NTSRU, PCMR and Alaska Territorial Guard became part of the defence of these remote regions that doubled as front lines. Japanese assaults, though, did not distinguish military from civilian, and in Alaska, Hawai'i and northern Australia, Indigenous residents became victims of Japanese bombs. While fear of Japanese invasion was real in all four settler states, only in Alaska did it genuinely come to fruition. In some of the most remote northern and interior regions, local Inuit life continued almost unaffected by the war.[124] On the other extreme, the Japanese invaded Attu and bombed American military forces at Dutch Harbor in June 1942.[125] US Navy plans to evacuate Attuans were too

[121] Melanie Gagnon and Iqaluit Elders, *Inuit Recollections on the Military Presence in Iqaluit* (Iqaluit: Nunavut Arctic College, 2002), 10–12, quoted in P. Whitney Lackenbauer, "At the Crossroads of Militarism and Modernization: Inuit-Military Relations in the Cold War Arctic," in *Roots of Entanglement: Essays in Native-Newcomer Relations*, ed. Myra Rutherdale, P. Whitney Lackenbauer, and Kerry Abel (Toronto: University of Toronto Press, 2018), 120–121.
[122] Gagnon and Iqaluit Elders, *Inuit Recollections*, 72; P. Whitney Lackenbauer and Ryan Shackleton, "Inuit-Air Force Relations in the Qikiqtani Region during the Early Cold War," in *De-Icing Required: The Canadian Air Force's Experience in the Arctic*, ed. P.W. Lackenbauer and W.A. March (Trenton: Canadian Forces Air Warfare Centre, 2012), 73–94.
[123] US Military Activities in Canada 1943–1946, LAC, RG 85, 1005-2-3 vol. 1; Gagnon and Iqaluit Elders, *Inuit Recollections*, 74.
[124] See Waldo Bodfish Sr., *Kusiq: An Eskimo Life History from the Arctic Coast of Alaska* (Fairbanks: University of Alaska Press, 1991), 125.
[125] See Brian Garfield, *The Thousand-Mile War: World War II in Alaska and the Aleutians* (Anchorage: University of Alaska Press, 1969); Fern Chandonnet, ed. *Alaska at War 1941–1945: The Forgotten War Remembered* (Fairbanks: University of Alaska Press, 2008).

late and many were in church when Japanese troops attacked on 7 June 1942.[126] Nick Golodoff remembers the Japanese opening fire on Attu, only just missing him.[127] Massively outnumbered, Elders counselled against resisting and the Japanese quickly occupied the island. Three months later, the forty-five Aleut captives on the island were shipped to Hokkaido, Japan, where they spent the remainder of the war as unpaid labourers in terrible conditions.[128] Some twenty-one would die as a result of starvation, malnutrition and disease.[129] After the war, the Attuans were not able to return because their village had been destroyed in raids and the Battle of Attu.[130]

While not invaded, northern Australia was the site of almost 100 Japanese bombing raids from Torres Strait across to Broome in Western Australia. The most powerful and destructive was the first raid on Darwin on 19 February 1942, killing at least 243 and wounding almost 400, including some Aboriginal people.[131]

Sometimes the intrusion of the war into these home fronts transformed Indigenous civilians into temporary combatants. One Japanese pilot from the Pearl Harbor attack actually crashed on the island of Nihau. Local Kanaka Maoli apprehended the pilot, but he tried to escape by taking hostages with the collaboration of three Japanese residents. Nihauans Benjamin and Emily Kanahele killed the Japanese pilot; *Paradise of the Pacific* reported Benjamin saying: 'I picked up that flier and threw him against the stone wall. I knocked him cold … All this time my wife was going into action. She was plenty *huhu*, that woman. She picked up a big rock and beat that flier's brains out. She did a pretty good job.'[132] The first Japanese prisoner-of-war captured on Australian soil was a downed Japanese flier captured by a Tiwi Islander after the Darwin raid. Tiwi Islander, Richard Miller, recalls the story:

After this crash, that Japanese fella out the plane and start wandering around in the bush [Bathurst Island]. He didn't know there were Aborigines people just

[126] Mike Lokanin, interviewed in 1947, reproduced in Nick Golodoff, *Attu Boy: A Young Alaskan's WWII Memoir* (Fairbanks: University of Alaska Press, 2015), 52; Innokenty Golodoff, interviewed in 1966, reproduced in Ibid., 55.
[127] Ibid., 13–14.
[128] Alex Prossoff, interviewed in 1947, reproduced in Ibid., 73.
[129] Rachel Mason, Introduction to Ibid., 1; Olean Prokopeuff (Golodoff), interview in 1981 and Alex Prossoff, interviewed in 1947, reproduced in Ibid., 70–71.
[130] Ibid., 63–65.
[131] See Alan Powell, *The Shadow's Edge: Australia's Northern War*, Rev. ed. (Darwin: Charles Darwin University Press, 2007); Peter Stanley, *Invading Australia: Japan and the Battle for Australia, 1942* (Camberwell, VIC: Viking, 2008).
[132] "There Always Will Be Heroes," *Paradise of the Pacific*, February 1942, reproduced in *Hawai'i Chronicles III*, 46.

camping there, nearby. So, wandering around and walked through bushes, he finally came out of the camp ... and this fella, his name is Matthias Ulungura, he had the little tomahawk. So he went and hide behind the tree. So, the Japanese fella came by and then passed him and Matthias then came behind him with the little tomahawk; he pointed at his back and say 'Stick 'em up!'[133]

There are unsubstantiated claims in other oral histories that suggest Australian forces may have taken some captured Japanese prisoners to Darwin and killed them, using Aboriginal labour to burn the bodies.[134] There is no documentary evidence to support the claims, but the story itself, even if untrue, shows how Aboriginal memories of the war recognise the blurred lines between good and bad; war versus war crime; and the many shades of grey clouding wartime behaviour.

Residents on and near northern Australia's missions and other settlements were generally aware of the danger and learned how to spot Japanese planes. Clare Henty-Gebert resided at Croker Island, a mission for 'half-caste' Aboriginal children off the coast of Arnhem Land. She remembers:

The missionaries warned us that if we saw a plane with the rising sun on the side of the plane and its wings it would be the enemy, the Japanese. Each time we saw a plane someone would shout 'Japes' [sic] and we'd run for cover. If we were close to the jungle or thick bushes we'd hide in the foliage. If not, we lay flat on our tummies and kept still.[135]

Though in most cases these were false alarms, there were other occasions when Japanese bombings did indeed strike Aboriginal and Torres Strait Islander military personnel and civilians, such as the bombing of Nurupai in March 1942:

The Japanese come over. When they come close, right up to Nurupai and we were looking after the post, they dropped a bomb – boom, boom. We were frightened, we cried, we never saw a bomb in our life. They fired that machine gun on top of us. They fired one way and came back ... The white soldiers ran away, went outside the trench and leave us. We black boys left.[136]

Japanese planes bombed not only military installations but also the coastal towns of Broome, Derby, Townsville and Wyndham and targeted Aboriginal missions such as Goulburn Island and Milingimbi, killing at least two and injuring more. On 27 September 1943, Japanese planes

[133] James Miller, in *No Bugles, No Drums*.
[134] Paul Toohey, "Were Japanese soldiers slaughtered on our soil?" *The Australian*, 2 March 2002, 6.
[135] Claire Henty-Gebert, *Paint Me Black: Memories of Croker Island and Other Journeys* (Canberra: Aboriginal Studies Press, 2011), 18.
[136] Osborne, *Torres Strait Islander Women and the Pacific War*, 129–130.

virtually wiped out the Drysdale Mission at Kalumburu in the Kimberley of Western Australia, killing six people including four children.[137]

The Japanese attacks on places like Attu and Darwin prompted settler officials to initiate evacuations of exposed civilian populations, including a number of Indigenous communities in Alaska and northern Australia. Several histories have relayed the experiences of 881 Aleuts evacuated from their homes in 1942 and relocated to camps on the southern Alaskan coast. In Australia, some evacuations of Indigenous people were for similar purposes while others were because of security concerns. In some of the most remote locations, like Mornington Island, these were voluntary departures.[138] More commonly, the evacuations were mandated by government or military officials. In Broome, however, the Aboriginal residents essentially demanded an evacuation after only white women and children were evacuated on 27 February 1942. Luckily, the majority of Aboriginal women and children were out of Broome before the Japanese raid on 3 March 1942.[139]

In most cases, such evacuations sent children and women on long journeys away from Australia's coastal north, to southern destinations. The order to evacuate all women and children from Thursday Island came on 24 January 1942. Torres Strait Islander families relocated to various sites in North Queensland, from Cape York through to Cairns and Townsville. In the larger settlements, like Cairns and Townsville, there were sometimes family members already living there to support evacuees, but in other instances, they were housed in segregated accommodations to preserve the towns' racist divisions. The longest journeys were undertaken by an additional wave of evacuations focussed on Aboriginal children from Northern Territory missions. The children were gathered at Alice Springs and then shipped south to Adelaide, then on to Sydney before being divided again, based on age, gender and religion and sent to their final destinations. John Moriarty, evacuated to Mulgoa in Sydney, remembers:

The Aboriginal women who came down with us from Borroloola took on very strong mother/aunt roles, just as they would have in a normal Aboriginal community in the bush. We looked to them for sustenance and strength. Things like love and affection carried over, I'm sure, from the Aboriginal life we had been living up in the north.[140]

---

[137] "Mary", in *No Bugles, No Drums*.
[138] Elsie Roughsey Labumore *n Aboriginal Mother Tells of the Old and the New* (Fitzroy, VIC: McPhee Gribble Publishers Pty Ltd, 1984), 49.
[139] Inspector O'Neill to Commissioner of Native Affairs F. Bray, 7 March 1942, SRO WA, Acc 933 Item 619/42.
[140] John Moriarty, *Saltwater Fella* (Ringwood, VIC: Viking, 2000), 35. See also Gordon Briscoe, *Racial Folly: A Twentieth Century Aboriginal Family* (Canberra: ANU E Press and Aboriginal History Incorporated, 2010), 17–29.

*Figure 6.6*    Three Aboriginal children evacuated from central Australia, pictured in Melbourne in June 1942 en route to a Church Missionary Society evacuation camp in the Blue Mountains west of Sydney. Courtesy Australian War Memorial, accession number 136302.

Sadly, a number of evacuations in Alaska and Australia proved tragic for many of those moved due to gross mismanagement and indifference on the part of the officials responsible. For example, the camps in southern Alaska to which the US Navy sent Aleut evacuees were often described as unfit for habitation. The appalling conditions at Ward Camp, near Ketchikan, were described bleakly in a local editorial during the war:

Then crawled the serpent ... in the form of bootleggers and others with whiskey, demoralizing and spreading venereal disease, and also aggravating incipient germs of tuberculosis so that 20 of their loved ones died, others being taken away, with more now stricken, and being classed as a menace and undesirable.[141]

Even after the military threat to Alaska diminished, many Aleuts remained in camps until 1944 or even spring 1945. Sadly, 10 per cent of the Aleuts

---

[141] Editorial, *Alaska Fishing News*, 24 May 1943, in *The Relocation and Internment of Aleuts during World War II*, vol. 3, ed. John C. Kirtland and David F. Coffin Jr. (Anchorage: Aleutian-Pribilof Islands Association, 1981), 89.

evacuated died away from home, and many others were left debilitated by disease.[142] In their absence, military personnel occupied Aleut houses not razed, leaving them dirty and vandalised. Even more painfully, irreplaceable eighteenth- and nineteenth-century church icons, central to their Russian Orthodox faith, were destroyed or desecrated. The United States Commission on Wartime Relocation and Internment of Civilians later found that the Aleuts should be compensated for losses and trauma associated with their evacuation, relocation and internment. In 1990, the Aleuts received $12,000 each.[143]

The evacuation of Cape Bedford Mission, from Cape York, was dramatic and similarly dreadful for those removed. Military officials arrested the missionary, a German Lutheran, suggesting that the forced evacuation had more to do with internal security fears than safety of residents. Of the 285 Aboriginal residents, fifty elderly or ill were sent to Palm Island, and the remainder were sent to the Woorabinda Aboriginal Reserve, about 160 kilometres west of Rockhampton. Within months, almost one-quarter of the evacuees were dead from disease, malnutrition or exposure. The survivors were forced into Manpower Directorate programs in the region, with men working mostly in agricultural production and women as domestic servants. They remained at Woorabinda until 1950 when Cape Bedford reopened. The Cape Bedford Mission evacuation was the only case where a state government collaborated with the military to remove Indigenous people ostensibly for security purposes. All other evacuations were either for health or residents' protection and while there were clearly elements of compulsion, were technically voluntary (at least for the adults).[144] Because evacuations targeted townships and missions, Aboriginal and Torres Strait Islander people in more remote locations were essentially left behind.

---

[142] See Kirtland and Coffin, eds., *The Relocation and Internment of Aleuts during World War II*, 8 vols.; United States Commission on Wartime Relocation and Internment of Civilians, Personal Justice Denied: Report of the Commission on Wartime Relocation and Internment of Civilians (Washington: Government Printing Office, 1983), 317–359.

[143] Ryan Madden, "The Forgotten People: The Relocation and Internment of Aleuts during World War II," *American Indian Culture and Research Journal* 16, no.4 (1992), 70–71; Lackenbauer, "Indigenous Peoples and the Defence of Remote Regions in Canada, Alaska, and Australia."

[144] Kirstie Close, "Invisible Labourers: Cape Bedford (Hopevale) Mission and the 'Paradox' of Aboriginal Labour in the Second World War" (MA thesis, University of Melbourne, 2009); Jonathan Richards, "'What a Howl There Would Be If Some of Our Folk Were So Treated by an Enemy': The Evacuation of Aboriginal People from Cape Bedford Mission, 1942," *Aboriginal History* 36 (2012): 67–98.

## Conclusion

As this chapter has shown, the home front experiences of Indigenous people were as diverse as the Indigenous communities themselves. Urbanisation brought costs and benefits in the forms of economic opportunities, intercultural relations and adaptations to Indigenous traditions and practices. Indigenous employment opportunities, usually in heavy industry, exposed Indigenous and non-Indigenous people to each other as equals. Women, in particular, benefited from the newfound independence and the economic opportunities afforded them in urban environments. In remote areas, the influx of service personnel also transformed the economic and physical landscape, challenging the status quo of discrimination and exclusion. Local white figures, who previously held a monopoly on Indigenous employment, now had to confront competition from a better-resourced and more generous (even if not entirely equal) group of white men. This exposure caused resentment among local non-Indigenous populations because, as was feared, it opened Indigenous people's eyes to new possibilities beyond what white settlers had previously offered.

Women played such a significant role in the home front that they, as such, are quite prominent in this chapter. Not only were women working to fill vacant jobs when their brothers, sons and fathers went off to war, but they also were working to maintain traditions. Whether through raising funds through performances or preparing care packages of traditional food or performing dances to protect their kin on the front lines, women were again proving their vital role, protecting their communities. Anxieties over gender and sexuality were heightened in the war for all women, particularly in the wake of the friendly GI invasions of Australia, New Zealand and northwest Canada. Indigenous women had the extra burden of being seen as loose, easy targets and in need of control to protect them from vice – especially from supposedly oversexed black Americans. Yet, Indigenous women exercised significant agency, choosing those whom they loved and, when faced with American immigration rules separating them from their new lovers, developed strategies to protect their own and their children's virtue.

The logic of survival and longstanding Indigenous ability to adapt their traditions persisted on the home front. In cities, new forms of pan-Indigenous community and organisations formed, providing new platforms for Indigenous people to learn, share and practice their culture. The precedents and organisations established in the Second World War often laid the foundations for post-war urban Indigenous communities, which would prove vital to resist the post-war tidal wave of assimilation pressures in all four states. Even in remote communities, it was not a binary question of either to live traditionally or to join the war effort; rather, the war showed Indigenous people's continuing capacity to adapt longstanding traditions to new environments. At times these were merely ephemeral or cosmetic changes, but others had long-term consequences across the urban-rural divide. One such was the culturally affirming and individually empowering legacy that the war left on Indigenous civilians just as much as the service personnel. Empowerment on the home front would also prove vital for Indigenous people to organise politically and to outline their own visions of the war and the extent of their communities' contributions. Though they usually were supportive of the war effort, as the next chapter reveals, even support sometimes had its limits.

# 7    Contesting Engagement

## Conscription and the Limits of Indigenous Collaboration

Previous chapters have explored aspects of the contested wartime negotiations between settler states and Indigenous populations. In many respects, whether political, economic, social or cultural, those negotiations – within Indigenous communities, families and for individuals – were marked by varying degrees of collaboration and cooperation. Indeed, if Indigenous people ran into challenges, often the obstacles were about securing the right to participate in the war effort. Yet, the story of Indigenous participation in all four countries was never a straightforward tale of Indigenous efforts to get in the door. Periodically, Indigenous leaders, communities, and individuals found themselves at odds with the demands of the wartime settler state, sparking forthright discussion, vocal protest, civil disobedience and, very rarely, violence. In a sense, such points of negotiation functioned like borders between Indigenous populations and the state. Historian Lynette Russell describes metaphorical cross-cultural boundaries as 'spaces, both physical and intellectual, which are never neutrally positioned, but are assertive, contested, and dialogic. Boundaries and frontiers are sometimes negotiated, sometimes violent and often are structured by convention and protocol that are not immediately obvious to those standing on either one side or the other.'[1] This chapter explores the boundaries where Indigenous people contested their engagement in the settler war effort, asserted their own vision of the lengths to which they were prepared to go and/or sought control over the extent of their participation.

Episodes of Indigenous resistance, activism and protest garnered significant attention from scholars of the latter twentieth and early twenty-first centuries who have been steeped in the histories of confrontational and contested Indigenous-state relations. Historians and Indigenous activists have often juxtaposed periods of protest and opposition against Indigenous loyalty and sacrifice during the war. The resulting binary portrayal of the

---

[1] Lynette Russell, "Introduction," in *Colonial Frontiers: Indigenous-European encounters in settler societies*, ed. Lynette Russell (Manchester: Manchester University Press, 2001), 1.

Indigenous war experience has oversimplified the story. While guarding against overstating the salience of confrontation, the moments where Indigenous views on their war service differed from settler states and militaries were important, especially for Indigenous peoples, and provide crucial insights into the Second World War experiences. A variety of common factors underlay ambivalence and indifference to the settler war effort in many Indigenous communities across the four settler states. Often long-standing grievances and chronic issues pre-dating the war became entangled in Indigenous-state relations; sometimes the war exacerbated the fraught relations, and in other situations the war facilitated negotiations. The war also indirectly produced a range of new issues for both settler administrators and Indigenous leadership to address, such as wartime employment, increased taxation, identity/citizenship and state acquisition or use of Indigenous lands for war purposes. Military service, whether voluntary or compulsory, proved a common lightning rod for disagreement and contention between Indigenous individuals and communities on the one hand, and settler governments and militaries on the other. Having won the right to participate, or been included without Indigenous consultation or consent, it sometimes proved difficult to put brakes on the enthusiasm and/or indifference of settler states and militaries.

This chapter seeks to understand episodes of contested engagement as part of the larger tableaux of enormously complex settler-Indigenous relationships in wartime and as nuanced, situational and interrelated phenomena rather than either/or dualities. Each Indigenous community did not decide on either loyalty, massive enlistment and support for the war effort, or a vigorous and categorical opposition to the increasingly intrusive and diverse state demands for the war. Instead, individual communities acted and reacted in more diverse and complex ways, tailored to the specifics of the situation, which could include cooperative or confrontational strategies or both. Within communities, individuals similarly exercised their own agency, whether in their decisions to participate in, resist or conditionally support the war effort. This chapter, therefore, is not just focusing on examples of resistance or reacting to settler governments and militaries. Rather, it is about how Indigenous communities asserted their own ideas of how they wanted to participate in the war effort, and defined the shape of their contributions. Indigenous responses to the war, and the actions that flowed from them, were usually the result of consideration and calculation by Indigenous leadership, based on varying degrees of principle and pragmatism depending on the situation. In the end, many, though certainly not all, Indigenous leaders and communities achieved some degree of success by contesting aspects of their engagement with(in) settler war efforts.

## Common Factors Underlying Wartime
## Resistance or Indifference

Indigenous communities entered the Second World War with widely divergent degrees of awareness, interest and engagement – both within and between each country. Some Indigenous communities were negatively disposed even before war broke out, and others were moved to indifference or opposition by wartime events. Only rarely did communities opt to distance themselves completely or oppose any role in the Second World War. Much more common were varying levels of interest depending on the community as well as the circumstances and issues at play. Across the four settler states, a number of shared factors were important in shaping particular Indigenous peoples' predisposition towards the war and the settler state.

The first major factor underlying Indigenous stances to the Second World War was the historical relationship between themselves and the settler state, society and military. While all Indigenous societies had struggled with the heavy weight of colonialism over the preceding centuries, certain aspects of that process had left some communities more embittered towards, or, at best, deeply suspicious of the settler state. Many British Columbia First Nations still walked in the shadow of the acrimonious Indian land struggle that they had waged for more than half a century until all avenues were finally shut down by government in 1927.[2] In Australia, grievances tended to be directed at state governments, rather than the Commonwealth. For instance, the Cummeragunja Reserve had suffered decades of neglect at the hands of the New South Wales Aborigines Protection Board. Petitions from the mostly Yorta Yorta residents about poor housing, lack of sanitation and the station superintendent's harsh rule continuously fell on deaf ears. Even a 1937–8 Select Committee of Inquiry into the administration of the Aborigines Protection Board ignored Aboriginal submissions, instead blaming residents for their own disadvantage. This all culminated in February 1939 when approximately 150 residents walked off the reserve in protest, crossing the Murray River into Victoria.[3]

Another prime example was the various Māori communities in the *raupatu* regions that had seen massive land confiscations following the New Zealand Wars of the 1860s. Despite the Sims Commission in 1928 that had recommended the government compensate some Taranaki and Waikato iwi, many Māori in these areas remained angry or at best

---

[2] Tennant, *Aboriginal People and Politics.*
[3] Fiona Davis, *Australian Settler Colonialism and the Cummeragunja Aboriginal Station: Redrawing Boundaries* (Brighton, UK: Sussex Academic Press, 2014).

ambivalent towards the settler state. Princess Te Puea, for example, was not enthusiastic when war broke out in 1939, as she was aware that the land issue was still open. Te Rata quoted her as saying: 'The blood is not yet dry.'[4] The fact that the Pākehā state had singled out Kingite Māori for persecution over their resistance to military service during the First World War only entrenched anxiety and distrust of the settler war effort. Chief Te Kanawa stated at Turangawaewae:

Why should the Maori people guard this island? ... It is no longer ours. The British evidently do not wish to keep their word as Rangatiras ... What difference does it make if the Tiamana [Germans] come here? The British have taken our land. They have killed our wives and children. The Treaty of Waitangi is only a delusion to make the Maori people believe that the British people will keep their word of honour.[5]

Colonialism's lingering baggage thus figured prominently for many Indigenous peoples when the war broke out.

Linked with the history of colonialism, though also distinct, was the effect of isolation. This was primarily apparent in the three continental-scale settler states of Australia, Canada and the United States where many Indigenous settlements and traditional territories were located well-removed from centres of settler society. Across the northern reaches of Australia and Canada as well as Alaska and several Hawai'ian islands, Indigenous communities' interaction with settler society was often meagre and intermittent. Settler educational institutions were still thin on the ground and other state machinery rudimentary in the mid-twentieth century, leaving missionaries, police and the thin edge of the settler economic wedge (fur trade posts or pastoral stations depending on hemisphere) as the main sources of information about the international tensions and conflict. Even in New Zealand, most Māori and Pākehā 'lived discreet lives', and the 'points of contact between Maori and Pakeha were superficial', leaving isolation a continuing factor.[6] Often illiteracy and linguistic barriers augmented isolation and complicated access to settler media. Indigenous communities removed from the war fervour of settler society may have felt little interest or collective engagement in the Second World War. This is not to suggest simply that ignorance was bliss but rather that communities without direct threat to their own lands had little reason for concern over what was a distant and intangible phenomenon.

[4] King, Te Puea: A Biography, 206.
[5] Quoted in ibid., 206–207.
[6] Ranginui Walker, Ka Whawhai Tonu Matou: Struggle Without End (Auckland: Penguin, 2004), 186.

Isolation was not completely deterministic in this regard, as there are examples of Indigenous engagement from very remote communities or individuals.[7] In the United States, given the war was going on in Europe for two years before Pearl Harbor, news had time to filter to even quite isolated communities. For instance, as late as 1947 there was only one radio available among the Rimrock Navajos, and no one from that community subscribed to any newspaper or magazine besides *The Farm Journal*.[8] Even so, anthropologists John Adair and Evan Vogt observed: 'Navahos who lived many miles from the railroad, read no and spoke no English would constantly ask: "What is happening in the war?" "Who is winning, the Germans or the English?"'[9] For those in northern Australia and northwestern North America, as the last two chapters revealed, isolation changed after Japan's entry brought both the war and massive settler military presence to their doorsteps. While it is easy to assume the war mattered to all Indigenous peoples, in the living histories of remote Indigenous peoples, the Second World War may have registered as little more than a ripple in their oral traditions.

Physical or linguistic isolation was not the only divider; Indigenous peoples' legal and social marginalisation often left them feeling disassociated from the settler society. Without a sense of belonging, or even the basic citizenship rights in Australia or Canada, Indigenous individuals were less personally vested in the well-being of the settler society and state than non-Indigenous residents. Mihipeka Edwards recalls her attitude at the outbreak of the war: 'It is your [Pākehā] war. It does not belong to the Māori.'[10] Métis man, Herb Belacourt, recalled when he and a cousin tried to enlist in the Canadian forces underage:

They gave me some papers for our parents to sign, so I went home with these papers in my pocket. My mother went through my clothes and found them, and she became very upset because she thought I had actually joined up. Dad looked at these papers. He didn't say a word. He crumpled them up in his hand, walked over to the wood stove, and threw them in the fire. 'That's the end of your army career', he said.[11]

---

[7] See "Cree Indians Given Thanks of Canada," *Brantford Expositor*, 27 January 1940, 7; Bernstein, *American Indians and World War II*, 43.

[8] Evon Vogt, *Navaho Veterans; a Study of Changing Values*, Papers of the Peabody Museum of American Archaeology and Ethnology, Harvard University (Cambridge, MA: The Museum, 1951), 27.

[9] John Adair and Evon Vogt, "Navaho and Zuni Veterans: A Study of Contrasting Modes of Culture Change," *American Anthropologist* 51, no. 4 (1949): 552.

[10] Edwards, *Mihipeka: Time of Turmoil*, 101.

[11] Herb Belacourt, *Walking in the Woods: A Métis Journey* (Nanoose Bay, BC: Brindle & Glass, 2006), 75–76.

His parents' response suggests that not all Métis saw this as their war, or at least they were not prepared to sacrifice their children on its altar. Maria Campbell recalled, 'Daddy signed up but was rejected, much to his disappointment and everyone's relief, especially Cheechum's. She was violently opposed to the whole thing and said we had no business going anywhere to shoot people, especially in another country. The war was white business, not ours, and was just between rich and greedy people who wanted power.'[12] Simply put, the Second World War was not their war.

Cultural factors also motivated communities that chose not to engage, either broadly or in a particular instance. For example, traditional spiritual and cultural values motivated both the Hopi and Zuni peoples of the American southwest, who diligently remained aloof from the United States war effort and military service. The defence of the community against an external aggressor was acceptable – and even this required spiritual intervention and vindication – but offensive warfare was almost always anathema. Both Hopi and Zuni had sought to buffer themselves from the cultural onslaught of colonialism, taking on only those Anglo-American attributes that aided defence of traditional beliefs and social structures. While both communities had acquiesced to draft registration initially, neither community was inclined to engage with the settler state as it moved towards a state of war through 1941. Perceiving the coming American war effort as an offensive one, both communities sought deferment from military service as conscientious objectors. Oddly, while American Selective Service officials accepted the Zunis' claims and granted exemptions to spiritual leaders (though not the blanket exemption requested for the whole tribe), authorities denied the Hopi conscientious objector status and prosecuted them for draft evasion. In spite of Zuni efforts, 213 men (roughly 10 per cent of their population) were drafted and served during the war.[13]

## Settler-Indigenous Relations in Wartime

On matters related to Indigenous autonomy/self-government, land rights, citizenship/identity, social welfare and assimilation, the war complicated relationships, sometimes amplifying tensions, sometimes deflecting or subverting them. The result could cut both ways for Indigenous leaders and communities, sometimes opening up opportunities to make

---

[12] Campbell, *Halfbreed*, 24.
[13] Adair and Vogt, "Navaho and Zuni Veterans," 547–561; Carroll, *Medicine Bags and Dog Tags*, 117; Franco, *Crossing the Pond*, 53–55.

headway in otherwise intractable disputes, other times making it tough even to be heard or hardening settler agencies' willingness to compromise. Indigenous efforts required varying levels of negotiation, protest and opposition as well as diverse techniques to reach their goals.

For example, a number of Australian Aboriginal leaders and organisations had been advocating for greater citizenship rights and inclusion of Aboriginal people in national life through the 1930s. William Cooper, Secretary and spokesman for the Australian Aborigines' League, wrote to Prime Minister Joseph Lyons in March 1938 in one of his many communications championing a better deal for Aboriginal Australians:

> We have no right to vote. We are not even counted. We are not recognised as British subjects and have therefore no rights, and are unable to defend ourselves ... The time is long overdue when the Aborigines should be considered as much and as fully under the protection of the law as any other citizen of the Empire, and equally entitled to the privileges of British citizenship.[14]

Cooper and other Aboriginal rights advocates' campaign for greater rights did not end with the outbreak of hostilities; instead, these organisations seized upon the additional leverage the war and military service provided to strengthen their hand. Just prior to the war, Cooper argued that 'the enlistment of natives should be preceded by the removal of all disabilities.'[15] After war broke out, Bill Ferguson of the Aborigines' Progressive Association wrote to the Premier of New South Wales in 1940 suggesting that the 'young men of our race are fighting with the armies of the British Empire for democracy, therefore we suggest that your government must grant our people full democratic rights.'[16]

While across the board grants of citizenship were not forthcoming, the efforts of activists did bear some fruit, especially when they limited their demand for the franchise only for those Aboriginal Australians serving in the military. A letter from the Aborigines Uplift Society in June 1940 demanded citizenship rights for soldiers; it generated significant traction and a flurry of correspondence between the Department of the Interior and the Chief Electoral Officer.[17] This became a matter for parliamentary consideration and was submitted to the cabinet in late 1940, where an amendment to the Commonwealth Electoral Act was accepted that made 'provision for the enrolment on the Federal Roll of any aboriginal native "who has enlisted and done honourable service in

---

[14] William Cooper to Joseph Lyons, 31 March 1938, reproduced in Attwood and Markus, *Thinking Black*, 90–97.

[15] William Cooper to Jack McEwan, 3 January 1939, NAA, A659, 40/1/858.

[16] Bill Ferguson, quoted in McGregor, *Indifferent Inclusion*, 51.

[17] Correspondence in, NAA, A431, 1949/822.

the Australian Imperial Forces abroad"'.[18] In March 1941, prior to the actual amendment making its way into law, it was realised that under the terms of the Electoral (War Time) Act, any serving member was actually entitled to vote in federal elections for the duration of the conflict and for six months after. This was regardless of whether they were under the twenty-one years of age normally required to vote, or, as it turned out, regardless of their race. While government officials consistently deferred consideration of a wider franchise until after war's end, perhaps Aboriginal activists hoped that soldiers' franchise would serve as the thin edge of the wedge.[19] In a 1940 letter protesting against the NSW Aborigines' Protection Board, Aboriginal activist Pearl Gibbs invoked both First and Second World War service: 'Our men fought for democracy and Christianity in 1914–1918, and are doing the same today.'[20] At the very least, the persistent protest achieved some success via the leverage of Aboriginal military service but could not completely overcome the degree of government resistance to major policy development in wartime.

Another long-standing dispute that became enmeshed in wartime issues was the campaign by traditionalist elements of the Six Nations Iroquois to assert their sovereignty. Based on historical treaties signed between the Six Nations and the British Crown or the US government, Six Nations nationalists denied they were either British subjects or US citizens under the Citizenship Act (1924).[21] As such, they believed neither government had jurisdiction over them. This ongoing confrontation ran headlong into efforts by both governments to register Six Nations members for compulsory military service in 1940–1. On both sides of the United States–Canada border, the effort to register Six Nations people provoked sharp reactions, opening another front for Six Nations nationalists to challenge Canada and the United States in the long battle for sovereignty. Chief Wilfred Crause in New York and Arthur Anderson in Ohsweken, Ontario, circulated communications to

---

[18] T. H. Garrett to the Secretary, Prime Minister's Department, 4 February 1941, NAA, A431, 1949/822.

[19] Chief Electoral Officer to the Secretary, Department of the Interior, 5 March 1941 and T.M. Garrett to the Commonwealth Electoral Officer, 8 April 1941, NAA, A431, 1949/822.

[20] Pearl Gibbs, "Case for the Aborigine", to Mr Norman Paul, Aborigine Station, Brewarrina, *Nowra Leader*, 21 June 1940, in Rachel Standfield, Ray Peckham, and John Nolan, "Aunty Pearl Gibbs: Leading for Aboriginal Rights," in *Diversity in Leadership: Australian Women, Past and Present*, ed. Joy Damousi, Kim Rubenstein, and Mary Tomsic (Canberra: Australian National University Press, 2014), 60.

[21] Bernstein, *American Indians and World War II*, 29–30; Lawrence Hauptman, *The Iroquois Struggle for Survival: From World War II to Red Power* (Syracuse: Syracuse University Press, 1986), 5.

different authorities to block the application of the law and encouraged members of the Six Nations communities not to register.[22]

In September 1940, Anderson went so far as to post notices around the Six Nations reserve in Ontario assuring residents that they were not liable to register just as the authorities were attempting to register the whole population; the registration effort failed. One official reacted furiously to the interference:

this incident at the Six Nations Reserve at Brantford presents an opportunity of declaring the whole Long House Group, the Mohawk Workers' Organization, and all other organizations harbouring the theory that they are not British subjects illegal organizations, and definitely and finally putting them out of business. This in the judgement of the writer should be followed by a seizure of all their books and records on all reserves, and particularly in the case at Brantford the arrest of Anderson and possibly all members of the hereditary council on charges to be preferred under The Defence of Canada Regulations.[23]

Even by March 1941, roughly a thousand men and women still refused to register under the National Resources Mobilisation Act (1940), but cooler heads prevailed, and officials did not undertake such actions. In New York, Lawrence Hauptman writes, although 'not against participation in war on moral or patriotic grounds, the Iroquois clung to traditional beliefs about their sovereignty. Consequently, many were arrested, and some were prosecuted as draft evaders, even after the United States gave them warnings.'[24] The issue in both countries was what nationality to list on their registration, with traditionalists refusing to put anything that compromised claims to sovereign independence.

The resulting deadlocks looked incapable of solution save through large-scale incarceration. Canadian officials were daunted by the potential outcome. T. C. Davis, the Deputy Minister of National War Services, wrote, 'If we move in to compel registration on the Reserve, then if the Indians refuse to register, it will mean their prosecution and wholesale conviction and incarceration. I doubt if the Ontario Government has the gaol facilities to deal with the ensuing problem.'[25] Interestingly, both Canadian and American authorities resorted to legal sleight of hand to defuse the crisis; Canadians deemed this approach 'preferable to trying to enforce registration through the imposition of penalties provided

---

[22] In Canada, see correspondence in LAC, RG 10, Vol. 6770, file 452-26, pt. 2. On Six Nations resistance in New York, see Franco, *Crossing the Pond*, 48, and Bernstein, *American Indians and World War II*, 29–32.

[23] D. J. Allen to the Director, 25 September 1940, LAC, RG 10, Vol. 6770, file 452-26, pt. 2.

[24] Hauptman, *The Iroquois Struggle for Survival*, 6.

[25] T. C. Davis to Dr. H. W. McGill, 2 May 1941, LAC, RG 10, Vol. 6770, file 452-26, pt. 2.

under the National Registration regulations and thereby antagonizing a group of Indians for the duration of the war.'[26] In the United States, BIA Director John Collier encouraged the Six Nations to register because even 'if they could establish separate nation status, they would still have to register [as aliens]', assuring them that after registering, the Six Nations could 'seek a court decision to support their views'.[27] North of the border, Canadian officials conceded that recalcitrant members at Oshweken could list their nationality as 'Canadian-born members of the Six Nations Indians', believing that 'this description could not mean anything else but a British subject'.[28] In the end, the bulk of the population on Six Nations reserves on both sides of the border was eventually registered, though resistance never completely disappeared.

While the war seemed more inclined to exacerbate problems, in certain instances, wartime conditions actually proved catalytic in Indigenous-settler disputes that had proved intractable in peacetime. A case in point was the complex and difficult dealings in New Zealand over compensation for nineteenth-century confiscations of Māori land. Although the government and relevant iwis negotiated some settlements during the interwar years, these had been monetary only and insufficient to satisfy those iwi concerned. The election of a more sympathetic Labour Government after 1935, far from advancing an agreement, saw tensions between Māori and the Labour Party leadership amplified. The criticisms eased when the war broke out and both sides agreed to postpone the negotiations until after the 'national emergency' finished.[29] Nevertheless, throughout the war, Māori leaders reminded the Labour Government that this was only a hiatus, and the government for its part reiterated its commitment to concluding a settlement. Favourable reactions to Māori wartime contributions emboldened Māori MPs, who in the lead-up to the 1943 election pressed cabinet on reparations in the context of post-war reconstruction. Labour pledged a quick and full settlement, won all four Māori parliamentary seats and reopened negotiations in 1944. Māori remained divided and unhappy about aspects of the process and settlements, but most opted to seize what might prove an ephemeral climate of governmental willingness to make a deal. Taranaki iwi and Ngai Tahu accepted settlements before 1944 ended, and others followed for Tainui-Waikato iwi in the immediate wake of the war.[30]

[26] C. W. Jackson to Dr. McGill, 14 February 1941, LAC, RG 10, Vol. 6770, file 452-26, pt. 2.
[27] Bernstein, *American Indians and World War II*, 31.
[28] Davis to Jackson, 12 February 1941. LAC, RG 10, Vol. 6770, file 452-26, pt. 2.
[29] Hill, *State Authority, Indigenous Autonomy*, 180.
[30] Ibid., 216–219.

In many ways, the Maori War Effort Organisation (MWEO) epitomises wartime cooperation and achievement for an Indigenous people, yet even seemingly collaborative relationships required persistent vigilance and vigorous negotiation. Formed in June 1942, initially for a six month trial period, the MWEO had to argue for its renewal with a lengthy recitation of its many achievements.[31] This process recurred numerous times, against the increasing resistance of the Native Affairs Department, which seized on any rationale to oppose the organisation's continuing existence. For instance, the department argued there was no need for further recruitment efforts targeting Māori. The Treasury warned that an organisation which the government could not control may pose a danger to the fabric of the state.[32] Native Affairs' officials even tried to resuscitate an old departmentally controlled scheme of local Māori Komiti to replace the MWEO, presenting this to a meeting in 1943 of senior MWEO leaders and Māori parliamentarians without any prior consultation.[33] Māori opposition to the scheme was so vociferous because it would destroy the autonomy that made the MWEO successful, that the Prime Minister and Native Affairs Department backed down.[34] Subsequently, Prime Minister Fraser was sufficiently persuaded of the organisation's importance and the threat of Māori backlash if the government terminated the MWEO that he helped defend it. Nevertheless, the Prime Minister remained nervous about the MWEO's significant autonomy. Perhaps, ironically then, the very breadth and intensity of Māori involvement in the MWEO, and its undeniable success, was itself an act of resistance to Pākehā state control.

Wartime issues of taxation and conscription sparked persistent Indigenous opposition and protest in Canada through the first half of the war. For example, prominent First Nations leaders gathered in Ottawa in October 1943 to raise new as well as other old grievances with government officials and to discuss forming a national Indigenous political organisation. The Indian Affairs Branch had historically reacted aggressively to such initiatives by blocking gatherings, suppressing First Nations political organisation and de-legitimising vocal Indigenous spokespeople. Yet, this time the Branch's response was relatively muted beyond refusing to meet with the delegation for two days. Even more remarkably, the extensive press coverage of the meetings was even-handed and accepting

[31] Memorandum for the Honorable Minister of Defence, 19 January 1943, ANZ, EA 1 Box 394, 81-1-11.

[32] Hill, *State Authority, Indigenous Autonomy*, 202.

[33] Claudia Orange, "An Exercise in Maori Autonomy: The Rise and Demise of the Maori War Effort Organization," in *Aboriginal Peoples and Military Participation*, 248–249.

[34] Hill, *State Authority, Indigenous Autonomy*, 200–201.

of Indigenous grievances.[35] Instead of focusing on the spectacle of the leaders' traditional dress, newspapers portrayed Native grievances as reasonable. The First Nations' visible support of the war effort opened the minds of the Canadian public to the legitimacy of their protests against Indian Affairs policies.[36] From this point in the war onwards, a political climate more open to Indigenous criticisms and policy reform emerged, which would underlie the post-war processes across these four states.

## Indigenous Lands and War Purposes

One commonality across all four settler states was the general increase in state involvement in the lives of Indigenous populations. Of course, state intervention encroached on the lives of all residents in all combatant nations. Though the war could divert state attentions and resources from Indigenous populations generally, it also potentially multiplied the states' interests in, and agencies involved with, Aboriginal and Torres Strait Islander Australians, First Nations, Māori and Native Americans. Between those signing up for military service and those moving to the cities, Indigenous rural lands lost a significant proportion of their populations during the war. The war affected these communities in other ways, as government officials in the four settler states sought to use Indigenous lands for war related purposes, including enhanced agricultural productivity, military training, weapons testing or even internment of enemy POWs or aliens (especially Japanese). Indigenous lands were targeted because they tended to be away from the major urban populations, perceived as underdeveloped and sometimes inexpensive compared to settler lands. How the settler governments approached the Indigenous communities differed across and within the nations, and how Indigenous residents responded varied from complete support to hostile opposition and combinations of both.

The US government compulsorily acquired 500,000 acres of Native American land during the war for gun ranges, bombing practice and air bases, including high-profile cases where Papago and Sioux communities opposed land sales for an air base and gunnery range respectively.[37] According to Franco, the mineral and oil wealth in remote western American lands, combined with the sparse populations, generally dry climate and lack of agricultural or industrial production, made them ideal sites for airfields, bombing and artillery ranges. In addition, the US

---

[35] See, "Indians Ask Tax Exemptions," *Vancouver Sun*, 21 October 1943, 25; "Indians Press Gov't to Grant Exemptions," *Calgary Herald*, 23 October 1943, 7; "Indians ask for Army, Tax Exemptions," *Globe and Mail*, 22 October 1943, 7.

[36] Sheffield, *The Red Man's on the War path*, 89–90.

[37] Bernstein, *American Indians and World War II*, 81–82; 141–142.

government also purchased or leased approximately 375,000 acres.[38] One of the more controversial aspects of Indian land use during the war was for Japanese internment. In March 1942, BIA Commissioner Collier advocated the lease of reservation land to house Japanese-American internees who had been removed from the west coast. Collier thought the internment camp infrastructure would benefit the local Native American nations after the war. Eventually, Collier offered land from two Native American reservations: the Colorado River Reservation and the Pima people's Gila Reservation. Collier never consulted with the local residents, though, who strongly opposed leasing their lands for Japanese internment. The Colorado River Reservation was vocal in their opposition, and the Pima Tribal Council only reluctantly set aside a remote part of the reservation for Japanese internees. From 1942, approximately 20,000 Japanese-Americans arrived at Colorado River Reservation and 5,000 on the Gila Reservation. Although the Native American nations made some money from the leases, generally there was little interaction between the residents and the Japanese-American internees, and after the war, even the barracks were dismantled.[39]

In Canada as well, the federal government acquisitioned First Nations land for military purposes. As Lackenbauer has written, this practice had been occurring since the early twentieth century and would continue during the Cold War.[40] One of the more prominent Second World War examples was the attempt to build aerodromes, landing strips and bombing ranges for the British Commonwealth Air Training Plan. Given the flat and vast expanses of sparsely settled land, the plains and southern Ontario were prime locations for pilot training, and the Six Nations Indian Reserve near Brantford, Ontario became one of the proposed sites. Military officials never consulted with the residents or even the Reserve Superintendent, but the presence of surveyors in early 1940 tipped off the locals to government interest in the land.[41] The local council then deliberated over a reserve position, and on 4 April 1940 they voted against negotiating leases with the Crown. Discussions, disagreements, media reports, protests and divisions within the Six Nations community continued but so too did council opposition to leasing land for an airfield. The resistance was ultimately successful as the RCAF instead purchased private property not far from the reserve in May 1940.[42]

---

[38] Franco, *Crossing the Pond*, 103.
[39] Bernstein, *American Indians and World War II*, 82–85.
[40] Lackenbauer, *Battle Grounds*.
[41] P. Whitney Lackenbauer, "The Irony and the Tragedy of Negotiated Space: A Case Study of Narrative Form and Aboriginal Government Relations during the Second World War," *Journal of the Canadian Historical Society* 1, no. 15 (2004): 182.
[42] Lackenbauer, *Battle Grounds*, 84–99.

Yet, only weeks later, France fell, and the British Empire stood alone against the Axis powers; the impact of this was profound across Canada, and the Six Nations council that had stood resolutely against leasing land for an airfield now reversed its decision in the face of the critical war situation. The Six Nations council would go on to lease a different portion of its reserve known as the Glebe property for an Army training camp that summer. Even more striking was that they patriotically offered this property to the government for a nominal rent, forgoing the hundreds of dollars per annum for market value rent. In October, the same council offered little resistance to leasing a 700-acre site for a practice bombing range. Indigenous opposition then was not a constant but rather situational, subject to broader contextual considerations.[43]

In other instances, First Nations negotiated constructively from the outset with the Canadian government to allow use of their lands. The Mohawks of the Bay of Quinte had allowed the air force to use some of their lands until 1 May 1940. After that date, the base continued to operate even though there was no agreed extension. The air force negotiated back-pay and continued use of the land for the duration of the war, even as the base steadily expanded. Earlier agreements to retain the base as a grass airfield needed to be renegotiated to allow a paved runway. Again the government and Mohawks came to an agreement, and it even provided employment for thirty Mohawk men on the base's construction. There were other reserves across the prairies as well that negotiated fair leases to use their lands for bombing and gunnery ranges.[44] Thus government-Indigenous dealings over land in wartime Canada were complex and did not follow any single narrative.[45]

In the most controversial case, though, on 1 February 1942, the Kettle and Stony Point Band Council voted 59-13 against a proposal to sell reserve land to make way for an infantry training centre in southwestern Ontario. Angry with the outcome, Canadian military officials turned to the War Measures Act to acquire land forcibly for security purposes. On 8 April 1942, order-in-council PC 2652 expropriated the reserve land at the price that the Band had rejected two months earlier. First Nations members of the Kettle and Stony Point Band wrote letters protesting the land seizure, citing treaty rights and their longstanding loyalty to the Crown. Such protests were in vain because authorities prepared to pay Band members $50,000 for the land and to relocate their homes. Oral histories talk about the stress of severing the spiritual and physical connections to the land and the emotional toll of giving up treasured

[43] Ibid., 200–202.
[44] Ibid., 99–111.
[45] Ibid., 203–206.

possessions and access to sacred burial grounds. In late November 1942, what had previously been First Nations land now reopened as Camp Ipperwash. The camp was still close to many residents who had not been forced to leave, and they had to endure the noise of the rifle range and interactions with the influx of infantrymen, many of whom regularly trespassed onto the remaining Kettle Point Reserve. When the war was over, notwithstanding vague references in PC 2652 about returning the land, Camp Ipperwash continued to operate.[46] This exemplifies continuing dispossession of Indigenous peoples when their interests clashed with the settler state, especially when wartime urgency overrode Indigenous opposition.

Even in New Zealand, the government acquired Māori lands for defence purposes without Indigenous consent, in this case at Paekakariki for American servicemen's camps. In that space alone, the village of approximately 530 coped with an influx of 26,000 troops. Remembering the Americans' arrival, Jean Matekitewhawhai Andrews recalls: 'We were overrun by contractors building and carting coal … Camps just popped up everywhere, and the contractors all moving in – it was just a hive of activity … the village grew milk bars and things that we never even knew about.'[47] Unlike the Canadian examples, after the war the departure of the Americans meant that most of the community returned to normal. Yet the land at Paekakariki continued to be in government control, and decades later the New Zealand government was still in negotiations with local iwi over return of the land.[48] In Australia, the situation was similar in that the war brought an influx of military forces to lands inhabited predominantly by Indigenous people. Where there was a difference, though, was that the Australian government did not recognise Aboriginal or Torres Strait Islander land rights and, therefore, under Commonwealth law there was no need to expropriate the land.

### Voluntary Military Service

The negotiation of engagement at the community level was perhaps the most evident in the tricky, but crucial, realm of military service. Some communities never wished to participate, but those that did often had clear ideas about how much they were prepared to contribute, the grounds on which that contribution was offered and sometimes the nature or form that they wished their contribution to take.

---

[46] Ibid., 115–143.
[47] Jean Matekitewhawhai Andrews, in *War Stories Our Mothers Never Told Us*, 72–73.
[48] Ibid., 71.

An interesting starting place to examine this is with Māori participation. One look at the huge numbers enlisted during the war or the very public exploits of the Maori Battalion might suggest an unambiguous example of an Indigenous society throwing itself 'all-in' to the war effort. Yet, the story of Māori enlistment and military service is more complex. Enthusiasm for military service did exist in a number of Māori communities, but the levels of engagement varied significantly between and even within them. For instance, a conference of northland Māori in Whangarei shortly after war was declared unanimously resolved and approved 'eligible members of the Maori race enlisting for military service for home defence alone'.[49] This sentiment reflected the large number of Māori unwilling to volunteer for the Pākehā's war overseas with the 2nd NZ Expeditionary Force but still willing to serve in defence of New Zealand/Aotearoa with the Territorial Force. By February 1943, 2,969 North Island Māori were registered for the Territorial Force, with 1,272 posted to units – a very large number relative to the 3,600 Māori who served in the Maori Battalion throughout the war. While it might be overreaching to portray home defence service as an act of resistance, it was very clearly expressing a particular vision of participation for some Māori men that did not include service overseas.[50]

Another important example of Māori seeking to shape the demands on their military service came in the form of the 1943 furlough crisis, following a government decision to return long-service personnel home for extended leave. Part of what helped the New Zealand cabinet implement the furlough was a February 1943 letter from eight senior officers of C Company, 28th Maori Battalion, to Apirana Ngata, explaining the war weariness of the men after hard fighting across North Africa in 1942: 'We have been in three major campaigns; there is no man here with a sound body to take our places that we may rest. There is only one place in this case and that is home.'[51] Ngata wrote to the prime minister, forwarding the original officers' letter, and he requested that the Maori Battalion be transferred to the Middle East. Ngata wrote, 'The argument that Maori and Pakeha should be treated alike stands, but it should be remembered that the 28th Maori Battalion is attached and non-divisional.'[52] Ngata debunked the mythology that Māori soldiers sought either to die

[49] "Maori Suggestion," *Northern Advocate*, 15 September 1939, ANZ, AD1 226-19-7, vol. 1, 1935–1941.
[50] Territorial Force correspondence regarding Māori in ANZ, AD1 226/19/7, vol. 4.
[51] Letter to Sir Apirana Ngata, 18 February 1943, Alexander Turnbull Library, Ngata Family Papers, MS-Papers-6919-0788, available from http://www.28maoribattalion .org.nz/node/15335.
[52] Sir Apirana Ngata, to PM Fraser, 30 March 1943, available from http://www .28maoribattalion.org.nz/node/15348.

in battle or continue fighting indefinitely and emphasised the Maori Battalion's simultaneous distinctiveness and equality.

In response to Ngata's letter, the government in May 1943 agreed to three-month furloughs for Maori Battalion members. On 12 July 1943, the Ruapehu furlough draft of 5,300, including 184 officers and men of the Maori Battalion, landed in Wellington. As the Māori soldiers made their way through various marae on a welcome home tour, everywhere they encountered sympathetic sentiments from Māori communities. According to Ngata, 'the talk [was], no more, they had done enough. They looked tired, thin and sickly.'[53] This feeling proved common amongst Pākehā as well. The government delayed and exempted married men with children or those over forty-one years of age from having to return to war, in what proved a politically fraught crisis.[54] Many still refused to return to the Middle East, resulting in several mutinies in various camps into early 1944.[55] The apparent unanimity of Māori community support ensured that all of the Māori soldiers on furlough were permitted to remain and re-enter civilian life, without the sanction or court martial some Pākehā resisters faced.[56] Thus Māori, both those in the service and those at home, sought to shape the nature and sometimes the extent of the service they provided and encouraged government acceptance of those decisions.

Māori were not the only people who sought to constrain their service to home defence only. The Burns Lake First Nations in British Columbia clearly linked their own status at home to the military service of their soldiers:

we are following the law of our King, yet they [the local settler community] never even let us allowed in the hotel or in the beer and so forth. If you are not going to give us the same privileges as the white people. Then we want you to bring the Indian boys back to Canada who is overseas ... They separate us from the white people here at home and mix our Indian boys with the white in the army. If you are not going to give us the same privileges as the white, then bring our boys back to guard Canada only. If the boys are going to stay overseas. Then we want to be mix with white people like one ...[57]

In the United States and Australia, there is no evidence of Indigenous communities or organisations arguing for their men to participate solely in home defence. One reason is because all four settler militaries

---

[53] Soutar, *Nga Tama Toa* 278.
[54] Gardiner, *Te Mura o Te Ahi*, 137.
[55] Belich, *Paradise Reforged*, 285.
[56] See McGibbon, ed., "Furlough Affair," *The Oxford Companion to New Zealand Military History*, 189.
[57] Petition to Indian Affairs from Burns Lake Band, 7 February 1944, LAC, RG 10, Vol. 6769, file #452-20-3.

developed home defence forces of diverse types: the United States had its National Guard and Alaska Territorial Guard; New Zealand developed the Territorial Force and the Home Guard; Australia developed the Citizen Military Forces and Indigenous-specific Torres Strait Light Infantry Battalion and NTSRU; and Canada conscripted people into the Militia and set up the volunteer PCMR. Indigenous personnel served in most, if not all of these, and it is not always clear whether this was because such service met their desires to contribute or provided a means of constraining their service from overseas.

Seeking to shape their military service was common amongst Indigenous communities in all four countries. Often the particulars of the service created points of contention that could sour Indigenous responses to the war or even foster resistance. For instance, the very basis on which their young men might enlist, and with whom they would serve, mattered. This was very much evident in Virginia where several small Native American communities were denied recognition as Native Americans and classified as 'coloured' in a state draft system that recognised only two categories: 'white' and 'coloured'.[58] This broader issue of identity intertwined with military service because of the segregated service streams for whites and blacks in the US military. Recruits classed as 'coloured' were inducted into all-black units, something to which Native recruits and their communities were hostile. The development of the draft exacerbated the classification issue, sparking a spirited resistance: in 1942, two groups of Chickahominy inductees refused to leave their barracks after being sent to a black training camp instead of a white one. Virginian Native leaders sustained the resistance with court challenges and communications that flew to state and federal authorities, including the governor, the secretary of the interior, and at one point even the president, in the search for a satisfactory resolution.[59] Logistically, the result was muddled, with local boards making decisions on individual applicants' 'racial' status, though in practice increasingly delineating them as 'white'.[60] In the end, the resolute stand of Virginia Native Americans succeeded in winning the distinct Indian Status for which they had fought and ensured integrated service alongside whites for their young men and women.

Along Canada's Pacific coast, First Nations communities were moved by millennia-old seafaring traditions to seek service in the RCN but

---

[58] Townsend, *World War II and the American Indian*, 87–89.
[59] Paul Murray, "Who is an Indian? Who is a Negro? Virginia Indians in the World War II Draft," *Virginia Magazine of History and Biography* 95, no. 2 (1987): 215–231.
[60] Townsend, *World War II and the American Indian*, 87–102.

were repeatedly rejected due to racial restrictions in recruitment policy. Both the mainstream RCN and the volunteer reserve forces remained stubbornly inaccessible, though consistent pressure through bureaucratic channels did eventually lever open the Fisherman's Reserve to an experiment with a single Indigenous vessel.[61] In the end, even this never came to fruition, it being determined 'preferable if Indians are allowed to remain in the fishing industry where their services are most needed'.[62] The frustration and anger at their rejection led to a broad withdrawal of many coastal communities from military service for the duration of the war. Thus the Indian agent for the large Kwawkewlth Agency reported in March 1944 that from a population of 1,269, only one man was serving overseas, four were in general service in Canada, two were conscripts serving in Canada and 106 had requested and gained deferment from compulsory training due to essential service in the Pacific fishing fleet. According to the Agent:

Indians are very loyal. At the outbreak of the war many Indians tried to enlist in the Naval Service, as they felt that ... they were best suited to serve in this Branch of the Service ... to this date no Registered [Status] Indian has ever been allowed to enter the Canadian Navy ... It is this discrimination against the B.C. Indian that has made them oppose being called up and put in the army.

Interestingly, the Kwakwaka'wakw people did not fully withdraw from the war effort, purchasing thousands of dollars of Victory Bonds, donating to the Red Cross and joining the PCMR.[63] In this case, they found ways to continue their support for the war effort that suited their cultural traditions, financial means and geographical location but outside mainstream military service.

Even within the services, despite the relative degree of equality and acceptance that Indigenous service personnel encountered, unequal conditions and pay could provoke anger and opposition both on the home front and in the services. One example of this was in the separate administrative system established for managing the assigned pay and dependent's allowance provided to dependants of Canadian Status Indian service personnel. Here Indian Affairs' officials sought and gained authority to control the monthly cheques, which otherwise would go

---

[61] Ian Mackenzie to T. A. Crerar, 16 May 1939 and D. M. MacKay to F. E. Anfield, 11 February 1942, LAC, RG 10, Vol. 11289, file #214-5; Maclachlan to Camsell, 18 March 1941, DHIST, 112.3H1.009/D293.

[62] Commanding Officer Pacific Coast to The Indian Commissioner, 27 April 1942, LAC, RG 10, Vol. 11289, file #214-5.

[63] Report of Kwawkewlth Agency for Month of March 1944, NAC, RG 10, vol. 6769, file #452-20-3.

directly to their recipients.[64] Many women whose cheques were redirected to their Indian Agent wrote to the Dependants' Allowance Board (DAB) protesting this and succeeded in regaining control over the money due them.[65] Indian Agents' complaints about waste of this money when not controlled encouraged the DAB arbitrarily to reduce the amounts paid to Status Indians living on reserves in 1942. Once again many First Nations dependants made vocal complaints to their Indian Agents, this time with the support of Indian Affairs. They argued that such reductions were in effect discriminatory and 'contrary to the principles for which this war is being fought', and they encouraged the DAB to restore the full amounts.[66]

The most striking example of military pay inequities fostering protest and resistance took place in Australia in December 1943. Three companies of the Torres Strait Light Infantry Battalion staged a sit-down strike to protest their low pay and deteriorating community conditions. Torres Strait Islander soldiers' pay was set at one-third of standard AIF rates, with a substantial portion assigned to a spouse or dependant and no dependants' allowance provided. Officials initially set these rates and conditions in consultation with Queensland authorities based on pre-war standards of living, but almost two years before this strike, the Premier of Queensland was already writing to the Prime Minister requesting dependants' allowances be paid due to rising costs of living.[67] The standard of living of Torres Strait Islander populations steadily deteriorated, and Torres Strait Islander servicemen actually witnessed their families' suffering because they were stationed in their home islands. Seeing white and Malay service personnel serving alongside them with much higher pay and benefits only amplified their frustration and anger.

By late December 1943, these grievances culminated in the Torres Strait Islander soldiers going on strike to demand equal pay with white soldiers, removal of Army regulations ('island laws') that imposed special restrictions on Torres Strait Islander personnel, equal application of discipline between Islander and white soldiers and more frequent leave.[68] This action proved partially successful, forcing the Army and cabinet to

---

[64] See R. Scott Sheffield, *A Search for Equity: A Study of the Treatment Accorded to First Nations Veterans and Dependents of the Second World War and the Korean Conflict. The Final Report of the National Round Table on First Nations Veterans' Issues* (Ottawa: Assembly of First Nations, May 2001), 21–29.
[65] R. O. C. Bennett, Chairman of the DAB to J. P. Ostrander, 4 March 1942, LAC, RG10, Vol. 6772, file# 452-42.
[66] J.P Ostrander to unknown, 25 March 1942, LAC, RG10, Vol. 6772, file# 452-42.
[67] Premier to the Prime Minster, 5 December 1941, NAA, A1608 AG45/1/12.
[68] Hall, *The Black Diggers*, 52; Osborne, *Torres Strait Islander Women and the Pacific War*, 120–122.

review their pay and allowance rates, which were revised upward to two-thirds of standard rates, with a small dependents' allowance provided.[69] The dependents' allowance was to be paid through the Queensland State Director of Native Affairs, which in practice meant that the money usually did not reach the families and became part of withheld government payments collectively known as the Stolen Wages.[70] The manner in which the Torres Strait Islander soldiers implemented their strike was measured. B and C Companies returned to work within hours, while A Company held out slightly longer. The short strike did not represent a rejection of Torres Strait Islander support for the broader conflict, nor an end to their specific military contributions, but rather a targeted protest against unequal working conditions.

The most successful and far-reaching control exerted over their military contribution was undoubtedly the 28th Maori Battalion. Ensuring that Māori held senior positions in command of the battalion and its four infantry companies remained an enduring preoccupation throughout the war. For instance, the initial decision to assign many of the senior positions in the 28th Battalion to Pākehā officers due to a dearth of qualified Māori provoked a surge of protests, including one petition from Ruatoria, which argued, 'Ngatiporou people strongly resent the attitude of the Authorities as published in the press in delegating the position of Officers of the Maori Battalion to Europeans. Our Loyalty and earnestness were greatly gratified by your Government's permission to form a Special Maori Battalion, but we feel that the PURITY of that Battalion is not kept if not officered by men of our race.'[71] The usual fervent loyalty of the Te Awara Maori Returned Soldiers' League conveyed the 'emphatic resentment' of their community as a whole, and they threatened that if the situation were not addressed, they could not 'guarantee Arawa Recruits presenting themselves, either for Medical Examination or Attestation'.[72] Even as Māori personnel gradually filled the senior positions in the Battalion overseas, Māori in New Zealand maintained their surveillance from afar. In early 1944, after a series of Māori commanding officers had become casualties, a Pākehā was placed in command. Once again a wave of protest pressed the Army Headquarters to telegraph General Freyberg, commanding officer of 2nd NZ Division, informing him of the pressure and asking to be advised how soon a suitable Māori replace-

[69] War Cabinet Agenda, 14 March 1944, NAA, A2671, 145/1944.
[70] Rosalind Kidd, *Trustees on Trial: Recovering the Stolen Wages* (Canberra: Aboriginal Studies Press, 2006).
[71] Petition to Minister of Defence, 3 November 1939, ANZ, AD1 319-1-9 vol. 1.
[72] President, Te Arawa Maori Returned Soldiers' League to F. Jones, 3 November 1939, ANZ, AD1 319-1-9 vol. 1.

ment might be available. In this case, Freyberg replied that there was no candidate presently available but that he was determined to appoint one as soon as possible.[73]

Māori involvement extended well beyond the purity of Māori command to police the tribal structure of the unit. Particularly problematic for the battalion commanding officer was the doubtful status of Lieutenant Harding Leaf, a First World War veteran who was, at forty-nine years old, believed to be too old to proceed overseas.[74] A unanimous vote of members of the Ngapuhi community in January determined Lieutenant Leaf should command 'the Ngapuhi boys', placing the NZ Army in a difficult position: leave Leaf home and 'many of the Ngapuhi would have returned with him', yet the only other option was to assign an officer deemed more suitable from another tribal group.[75] In this case, Leaf went along as one of the senior officers in A Company and led effectively, until his death in action in Crete in May 1941. Māori iwi continued to recommend their chosen officers to replace casualties throughout the war and forthrightly informed the Army of their desires.[76] One reverend from Waikato-Maniopoto warned military officials 'that officers for our portion of the Battalion should be selected out of our own crowd and not from other tribes. Feeling between certain tribes is not the best, and your move in this matter will be watched, and future enlistments, especially from the Waikato will depend on it.'[77] Despite occasional frustration at the levels of Māori involvement, New Zealand Army officials proved remarkably considerate and responsive, balanced against ensuring capable leadership within the Battalion.

## Conscription

Without doubt, efforts to compel Indigenous men into military training and/or service proved, potentially, the most problematic and produced the greatest opposition, in scope, duration and intensity. All four settler states would institute a draft system in 1940. Australia had compulsory military training early in the century, which was suspended in 1929, but revived at the beginning of 1940. The Citizen Military Forces

---

[73] Cable, Army HQ, Wellington to H.Q. 2N.Z.E.F., 19 April 1944 and Cable, H.W. 2nd NZ Division to Army Headquarters Wellington, 23 April 1944, AD1, 319-1-21.

[74] Memorandum for: Army Headquarters, 22 December 1939, AD1, 319-1-21.

[75] The first quote is from, Renata Kaiere and six others representing whole of Ngapuhi to the Hon. Minister for Defence, 26 January 1940, AD1, 319-1-21. The second is from Lieutenant-Colonel H. G. Dyer, quoted in Gardiner, *Te Mura O Te Ahi*, 26.

[76] Many such communiqués are visible in ANZ, AD1 1265, 300-1-2, pt. 5.

[77] Reverend N. K. Kakitahi to the Director, Overseas Forces, 2 October 1941, ANZ, AD1-1265 300-1-2, pt. 5.

(CMF) was, theoretically, only for home defence and not connected to the raising of the 2nd AIF; however, it did see active combat. Papua and the Mandated Territory of New Guinea were both Australian colonies, and therefore the CMF was dispatched to defend against Japanese in 1942. In February 1943, Prime Minister John Curtin pushed through an amendment expanding the CMF's remit to include all of New Guinea (including what is now West Papua) and adjacent islands, known as the South-West Pacific Zone.[78] Canada and New Zealand were both pushed to conscription by the fall of France in June 1940. New Zealanders felt the measure the fairest means of 'ensuring equality of sacrifice'.[79] Conscription was politically divisive in Canada and, initially, only brought in for home defence, though it moved incrementally towards a more complete system of conscription for overseas combat service by the winter of 1944–5. While the majority of Indigenous populations in Australia, Canada, New Zealand and the United States supported voluntary service, the same cannot be said for compelling their young men into military uniforms. Draft systems provoked the sharpest reactions of any wartime measure, or at least threatened to do so. Influential in both Indigenous and settler state decision-making was the legacy of conscription policies during the Great War.

Compulsory military training proved the least contentious in Australia for two reasons. First, despite the presence of approximately 1,000 Aboriginal men with the First AIF, no collective memory of their service survived in white Australian society by 1939, shutting these men out of the developing digger mythology. Few other societies invested so much energy and self-identity in their Great War experience as did Australians in the Anzac ethos and their iconic diggers. No black diggers disturbed this identity, so tightly connected to whiteness, masculinity and imperial defence. This amnesia in officialdom meant only profound military urgency unofficially opened the door to Aboriginal enlistments in 1942, but it would likewise leave Aboriginal men 'not substantially of European origin or descent' outside compulsory training eligibility from 1940 onwards. A January 1940 clipping from the *West Australian* newspaper noted:

The Commissioner of Native Affairs (Mr. A. O. Neville) said yesterday that the question had been raised whether natives were liable to compulsory military training. Persons who were more European than native were liable. Persons in

[78] Jeffrey Grey, *A Military History of Australia*, 3rd edn. (Cambridge and Port Melbourne: Cambridge University Press, 2008), 183.
[79] Ian McGibbon, *New Zealand and the Second World War: The People, the Battles and the Legacy* (Auckland: Hodder Moa Beckett, 2004), 49.

this category included quarter-castes and those who had less native blood than a half-caste. This ruling he said would affect a number of people.[80]

The underlying rationale was articulated in a post-war assessment of wartime recruitment and conscription policies: 'Australian aboriginals continue to be deprived of full citizenship, it seems more just they should be free of compulsion from all military service.'[81]

Even so, as Chapter 5 discussed, there are some suggestions that the military deployed tactics amounting to conscription in remote regions of Australia's north. There is no evidence of Aboriginal or Torres Strait Islander protests over their lack of liability for the national compulsory training system. Indeed, even when the Commonwealth introduced national service in 1951–9, the legislation exempted Aboriginal men and there was no protest. It would not be until the national service scheme from 1964 to 1972, in the context of the Vietnam War, that Aboriginal people and other organisations protested discriminatory provisions in national service legislation.[82]

The American draft legislation and process met a more diverse response from Native Americans, with episodic, localised but often vigorous resistance. For many Native Americans, their liability for the draft was a potent symbol of inclusion and of citizenship, and they responded by registering, reporting when called and serving proudly alongside other Americans. Indeed, the US Congress passed the Nationality Act in October 1940, explicitly granting citizenship to all Native Americans, to resolve any lingering confusion regarding their citizenship status.[83] Not all viewed the draft as benign, let alone positive. The National American Indian Defense Association opposed Indian liability for the draft, arguing that the poverty on reservations effectively deprived Native Americans of all constitutional rights and thus rendered them wards, regardless of legislation purporting to grant citizenship.[84] More typically, the Native American voices against the draft tended to be centred in specific communities such as the Zuni and Hopi, mentioned earlier.

Other cases of resistance occurred amongst particularly remote communities who had little interaction with settler society. One example was the Hickiwan Papagos who, under the leadership of eighty-year-old

---

[80] "Liability of Natives," West Australian, 13 January 1940, SRO WA, Acc993-39-1940.

[81] Notes for Australian Military Recruiting 1939-45, AWM, 834/1/1, 7.

[82] Noah Riseman, "The Curious Case of Mervyn Eades: National Service, Discrimination and Aboriginal People," Australian Journal of Politics & History 59, no. 1 (2013): 63–79.

[83] Townsend, World War II and the American Indian, 81.

[84] Franco, Crossing the Pond, 47.

Chief Pia Machita, retained a powerful sense of their own independence in their remote piece of Arizona and rejected the jurisdiction of
Congressional laws. Despite efforts by government officials to explain
both the legislation and the penalties for non-compliance, Machita and
his community refused. In October 1940, after an ultimatum had passed,
a deputy marshall and six deputised men from other Papago communities arrived to arrest Machita for incitement and twenty men for draft
evasion. The community rallied to defend their chief and young men
from the authority of a government they rejected, assaulting, disarm-
ing and driving the police from their village.[85] After months of evasion,
negotiation and posturing, Machita and another chief were captured,
convicted and imprisoned, overwhelming the community's resistance.[86]

Seminole peoples in Florida had similarly long traditions of resistance
to the US government. The Seminoles were the only Native American
nation east of the Mississippi River that US authorities never succeeded
at forcibly removing to Indian Territory in the 1830s–50s. Many did not
see themselves as American citizens and lived in the Everglades largely
separate from settler society even into the 1940s. Some acquiesced to
draft registration rather than face prosecution in the fall of 1940, but
a significant segment refused and escaped into the deeper reaches of
the swamp, as in the 1850s, to avoid federal authorities. The problem
festered through 1943, with federal authorities of the Bureau of Indian
Affairs, the War Department and the Selective Service System unable
to apprehend the resisters, suppressing news of the ongoing issues and
sceptical whether any of the seventy-five men still holding out would even
qualify for service.[87] At that point, the government quietly dropped their
pursuit of Seminole draft dodgers. Carroll suggests that some Navajo
who objected to the draft similarly disappeared into remote regions of
their territory.[88] By contrast, the Yakima Nation in the Pacific Northwest
challenged their liability under the Selective Service Act (1940) based on
an 1859 treaty with US government and launched an immediate court
challenge. The judgement, handed down in May 1941, went against the
Yakima, and fearing an appeal would achieve only the same result, they
acquiesced to the draft.[89] Six Nations would also challenge conscription
in the courts, in both the United States and Canada, based largely on
their claims to sovereign nationhood.

[85] Townsend, *World War II and the American Indian*, 104–105.
[86] Carroll, *Medicine Bags and Dog Tags*, 117.
[87] Townsend, *World War II and the American Indian*, 106–110.
[88] Carroll, *Medicine Bags and Dog Tags*, 117.
[89] Townsend, *World War II and the American Indian*, 110–112.

*Figure 7.1* Canadian born members of the Iroquois staged a war dance in a Buffalo public square on 28 December 1940 as a protest against being compelled to register for the draft. After the dance, they went quietly to the post office and complied with the law. BPA 2 #2593.

In *Ex Parte Green* and *Le Roi v. Smallfence*, American and Canadian judges respectively rejected the case of Warren Green and Harris Smallfence, marking the death of efforts for legal avenues to exemption based on sovereignty arguments.[90] In both countries, Six Nations leaders continued to protest the application of conscription to their young men but without any eventual success. As young men began receiving calls for military service, opposition would reignite. In Canada, this would lead to sustained protests lasting throughout the war. These episodes, and the Iroquois and Hopi/Zuni cases, mentioned earlier, revealed resistance

---

[90] See R. Scott Sheffield and Hamar Foster, "Fighting the King's War: Harris Smallfence, Verbal Treaty Promises and the Conscription of Indian Men, 1944," *University of British Columbia Law Review* 33, no. 1 (1999): 53–74; Bernstein, *American Indians and World War II*, 31–33.

in all four corners of the continental United States, arising from treaty issues, sovereignty claims, isolation and spiritual values. Native American capacity to resist the draft was circumscribed, though, in the face of a government and BIA determination to quash any opposition, lest it grow or damage the impression of a united nation.

New Zealand's experience was unusual in that conscription was instituted in 1940, but the prospect of significant Māori resistance, subtly employed by Māori leadership, persuaded the Labour Government to exempt Māori men from compulsory service. Hanging over the decision-making was the highly divisive experience of conscription of Māori in the Great War, when large communities in the King Country and elsewhere had refused to volunteer and had conscription imposed on them. The civil disobedience and mass arrests of Waikato men left bitter memories that were certain to reawaken if conscription were again imposed on Māori. Apirana Ngata was clearly cognisant of this concern when he informed special Māori recruitment officers in October 1939 that their 'role does not include canvassing the young people. The decision to enlist rests with each individual and their parents.'[91]

Government sensitivity was also apparent once the process of instituting conscription began when on 12 July 1940, Prime Minister Fraser wrote a memo to the Minister of National Service indicating the War Council had decided to establish a separate Māori register to potentially ensure reinforcements for the 28th (Maori) Battalion. He ordered that 'no publicity is to be given to the existence of this register'.[92] This register never came to fruition; the Māori Labour MPs informed the Minister of National Service that while the Māori people would support and maintain reinforcements to the Maori Battalion, 'under the voluntary system the members were afraid that if compulsion were resorted to, many would fail to register and take to the bush in which case it would be next to impossible to administer the scheme'.[93] The prospect of widespread Māori withdrawal from the war effort and the serious political implications of that proved sufficiently daunting to Fraser's Labour Government that voluntary enlistment was reinstated and conscription for Māori withheld indefinitely. The question would be revisited as the war went on, but Māori enlistment under the MWEO proved capable of sustaining the reinforcement needs of the 28th Battalion, even with its high casualties.[94]

---

[91]  Quoted in Soutar, *Nga Tama Toa*, 37.
[92]  Quoted in Ibid., 116–117.
[93]  Quoted in Ibid., 117.
[94]  Orange, "An Exercise in Maori Autonomy," 245–247.

In Canada, more than any of the other three countries, conscription provoked strident, longstanding and nationwide protest amongst First Nations people, as well as civil disobedience, service evasion and disengagement. Here, too, the memory of the Great War powerfully shaped Indigenous reactions to conscription. In 1918, an Order-in-Council exempted Status Indians under the Military Service Act 1917, at least from combat service overseas for the duration of the Great War.[95] When the federal government passed the National Resources Mobilisation Act (NRMA) in July 1940 to bring in conscription for home defence only, most First Nations expected again to be exempted. The fact that they were legal wards of the Crown who lacked voting or other citizenship rights, and the fact that many had been promised exemption during nineteenth-century treaty negotiations, only strengthened this assumption. Nevertheless, Indian Affairs officials viewed military service as a positive assimilative experience for Status Indian men and, until December 1944, largely withdrew from policy formation regarding First Nations liability under the NRMA regulations.[96] The Department of Justice determined Status Indians were British subjects, who 'must hold themselves in readiness for call for military service', and the Department of National War Services, without any legal impediment, included Status Indians in conscription.[97] That remained the policy through the bulk of the war as compulsory training became progressively more onerous and dangerous.

The First Nations' reaction to the imposition of conscription was surprise and outrage across the breadth of the country. From the arrival of the first notices to report for medical assessment in September 1940, First Nations communities in virtually every province sent petitions, band council resolutions and letters to Indian Affairs in Ottawa protesting their liability to compulsory service.[98] Initial outrage somewhat dissipated because the early federal draft called for only thirty days of training before returning to civilian life. This was not especially onerous, and most First Nations were willing to support the defence of Canada itself. Gradual escalation of compulsory service, first to four months of training and permanent militia service, then to the national plebiscite supporting conscription for overseas service in 1942 and finally to the crisis in

[95] P.C. 111, 17 January 1918, LAC, RG 10, Vol. 6770, file 452-26, pt. 2. See also Winegard, *For King and Kanata*, 88–109.
[96] Sheffield, "… in the same manner as other people", especially Chapter 4.
[97] W. M. Cory to the Director of Indian Affairs, Dr. H McGill, 26 September 1940, LAC, RG-10, Vol. 6768, file 452-20, pt. 4. See also Stevenson, "The Mobilisation of Native Canadians," 210–211.
[98] There are scores of these communiqués in LAC, RG 10 Vol. 6768, file 452-20, pt. 4.

November 1944 when NRMA conscripts were sent overseas, provoked a fresh round of angry communications.[99] While this stream of correspondence put pressure on federal officials, First Nations leaders gained little immediate traction from writing to an Indian Affairs Branch, which abdicated any jurisdiction on the issue. A number of individuals from different First Nations also challenged the application of conscription in the courts during 1940, though to little avail.[100] Increasingly, frustrated communities began to send delegations, beginning in October 1940, to Ottawa in hopes of presenting their grievances directly to relevant government officials.[101] The Six Nations sent two delegations in 1943, another in 1944 and the last in March 1945.[102] Alternatively, Indigenous leaders sometimes went 'over the heads' of the Indian Affairs Branch to contact the Prime Minister, the British High Commissioner in Ottawa, the British government and even the King.[103] Opposition and vocal protests to conscription remained a ubiquitous element in Indigenous relations with the Canadian government from 1940 through the end of the war.

At an individual, family and community level, many First Nations resisted conscription by ignoring their notices and evading medical examinations or reporting for duty.[104] For those living in wilderness regions it proved simple to disappear into the remote areas of their traditional territories. In some cases, remotely located First Nations only came into contact with a fur trade station or treaty payment ceremony once per year, which was the only time they could receive mail. This meant some accidentally became delinquent when they failed to report for a medical exam and military call-up. Evasion of NRMA service notices, whether intentional or not, became endemic by the mid-point in the war, prompting the head of Indian Affairs, Dr. Harold McGill, to send a circular exhorting all Indian Agents to 'do everything within

---

[99]  Sheffield, ". . . in the same manner as other people," 91–93.

[100]  Stevenson, "The Mobilisation of Native Canadians," 209–210.

[101]  T. R. L. MacInnis to D. P. McNaughton, 30 October 1940, LAC RG 10, Vol. 6768, file #452-20, pt. 4. See also Sheffield, "... in the same manner as other people," 93–94.

[102]  Charles Camsell to E. P. Varcoe, 15 May 1943; T. Crerar to Louis St. Laurent, 26 February 1944; and R. A. Hoey to Gamble, 17 March 1945, all in LAC, RG 10, vol. 6769, file #452-20, pt. 6.

[103]  R. Scott Sheffield, "Canadian First Nations and the British Connection during the Second World War," in *Fighting with the Empire: Canada, Britain and Global Conflict, 1867–1947*, ed. Steven Marti and Tyler Turek (Vancouver: University of British Columbia Press, in press). See also Report of the Fourteenth Annual Convention of the Native Brotherhood of British Columbia, 1–7 December 1943, 7–8, LAC, RG 10, Vol. 6769, file #452-20, pt. 6; Hugh Shewell, "Jules Sioui and Indian Political Radicalism in Canada, 1943–44," *Journal of Canadian Studies* 34, no. 3 (1999): 211–242; Jules Sioui to His Majesty the King and the Queen, 27 March 1943, LAC, RG 10, Vol. 6770, file #452-26, pt. 3.

[104]  Sheffield, "... in the same manner as other people," 95–96.

your power to see that the Indians comply with the regulations' in light of the 'difficulty ... being experienced in the call up of Indians under the Mobilization Regulations'.[105]

These regulations were enforced somewhat unevenly across the country, depending on the mobilisation officials, police or Indian Affairs personnel in each jurisdiction, creating an administrative 'patchwork quilt'.[106] National War Services decided not to bother registering remote First Nations who did not speak English or French, doubting they could make 'any real contribution to the war effort'.[107] Some jurisdictions quietly dropped prosecution of First Nations delinquency cases, but others, especially in more settled and urban districts, diligently apprehended and prosecuted delinquent individuals.[108] One such effort in November 1943, on the Caughnawaga Reserve outside Montreal, sparked a violent confrontation when Mohawk community members rallied to prevent the Royal Canadian Mounted Police from removing three draft dodgers. The eight officers were assaulted with bricks and bottles, had their tires slashed, and they were forced to retreat without their captives, though not before one officer shot three Mohawks in his effort to escape.[109] While such violence was a rarity, it is indicative of the powerful emotions conscription stirred amongst many First Nations communities. A survey of Indian Affairs files covering conscription during the war years suggests an environment of roiling discontent that lasted for the duration.

As in the United States, First Nations' capacity to resist the state's imposition of conscription was very circumscribed. The decision of the IAB to step away from policymaking and deflect Indigenous protests to other departments only amplified the limitations. No formal alteration in policy or legislation occurred regarding Indigenous liability to compulsory service from 1940 until December 1944. Nevertheless, officials in Ottawa certainly noticed the persistent cacophony of correspondence, delegations and widespread, mostly passive resistance. When combined with military officials' ambivalent attitude to Indian soldiers generally, and the practical challenges of enrolling First Nations people living in remote regions, the groundswell of opposition encouraged officials to acquiesce to an informal system of granting deferment from military service to most Status Indians called-up in many parts of the country.

---

[105] H. McGill to All Indian Agents, Inspectors and the Indian Commissioner for BC, 31 July 1943, LAC, RG 10, Vol. 6768, file #452-20, pt. 4.
[106] Stevenson, "The Mobilisation of Native Canadians," 213.
[107] T. C. Davis to S. T. Wood, 18 November 1940, LAC, RG 10, Vol. 6770, file #452-26, pt. 2.
[108] Stevenson, "The Mobilisation of Native Canadians," 221.
[109] Brisebois to McGill, 2 December 1943, LAC, RG 10, Vol. 6769, file #452-20-10, pt. 2.

When a national conscription crisis finally erupted in November 1944, and the government decided to send 16,000 NRMA conscripts to Europe, the Indian Affairs Branch finally intervened. The IAB leadership had been content to give mobilisation officials free reign when conscription was for home defence only. Once those conscripts could be sent overseas into combat, verbal promises made during some treaty negotiations presented grounds for potential legal challenge. On 22 December 1944, the War Cabinet exempted Status Indians covered by Treaties 3, 6, 8 and 11 because 'only in the case of treaty Indians aforementioned would the government be justified in differentiating between Indians and other of His Majesty's subjects in the matter of military service, and then only in fulfilment of a verbal commitment made by Commissioners representing the Crown at the time the treaties were negotiated'.[110] This exemption covered only these four Numbered Treaties because IAB records revealed written evidence of verbal promises by Crown negotiators, even though never written into the text. Roughly 20,000 of the 125,000 Status Indians in Canada in 1945 resided in these four treaty areas. As a result of this decision, few if any First Nations conscripts were included with those shipped to Europe while their treaty status was sorted out. Arguably, the strident and continuous Indigenous opposition had a hand in the IAB decision to press Cabinet for an exemption. The entire conscription issue thus again showed the considered and conditional Indigenous support for the war effort. In Canada, and indeed across the four settler states, Indigenous communities often saw a stark difference between volunteering for war, versus obligations imposed by the settler state.

## Conclusion

This chapter has demonstrated remarkably diverse Indigenous opposition and resistance all along the boundaries between themselves and settler states during the Second World War. Overall, this was about control and power in an often massively unequal negotiation where Indigenous peoples might be expected to achieve little success. Cynthia Enloe argues, 'few ethnic groups possess the political resources needed to modify or halt enactment of conscription'; yet, the patterns in Canada and New Zealand suggest otherwise.[111] It seems clear that Indigenous populations in all four countries worked in differing ways to exert as much control over

---

[110] R. A. Hoey - Circular to all Indian Agents, Inspectors of Indian Agencies and the Indian Commissioner of British Columbia, 12 February 1945, LAC, RG 10, vol. 6769, file #452-20, pt. 6.
[111] Enloe, *Ethnic Soldiers*, 63.

their war participation and engagement as they could achieve – whether to be included, or to constrain their participation. From First Nations in the north opting not to report for medical exams, to Māori demands of control for their recruitment, Aboriginal protests over military service without citizenship and Seminole rejection of the draft, Indigenous peoples engaged in disparate acts of opposition during the war. Such acts, articulated and enacted in widely varied contexts, were, nonetheless, part of a shared aspiration to exert maximum autonomy and control over the nature and extent of their war efforts. The extent of autonomy achieved ranged across the spectrum from virtually nil to the relatively complete autonomy of the Maori War Effort Organisation. While Aboriginal and Torres Strait Islander people, Native Americans and First Nations could only have dreamed about the degree of control Māori were able to achieve, their efforts were part of a parallel process.

Conscription became a particularly prominent and important point of negotiation on the boundaries between Indigenous peoples and settler states. Despite Indigenous efforts to affect conscription, generally speaking settler governments set the terms and liabilities of compulsory service. There were sometimes informal agreements or blind eyes turned, either because of the logistical difficulties of enforcing conscription rules, or to avoid visible signs of disunity within the state. Only in rare cases did political expediency or legal impediments get in the way of settler efforts to build their war machine. For Indigenous peoples, though, conscription and the grounds on which it was justified became a marker of their place and sociolegal status within each country. Australian Aboriginal people were excluded from home conscription, indicative of their alien 'other' status beyond the pale of mainstream Australian society. The US draft was initiated pre-war, but inclusion in this universal national program came to symbolise belonging and citizenship for many Native Americans, and as such, it was largely accepted and leveraged on these grounds. In Canada, as British subjects, Status Indians were liable, even though they lacked any rights of citizenship, leaving First Nations in a nebulous liminal state that was neither wardship nor citizenship. Māori fought for and won exclusion from conscription, which was otherwise employed nationwide. This significantly amplified separateness, autonomy and rangatiratanga for Māori, but it would also inspire a state backlash at war's end to reel them back into state control.

In the end, can we say that Indigenous resistance and protest was successful? This is a mixed story, unsurprisingly, given the conditional and varied nature of Indigenous efforts to contest and control their engagement with the war effort. There were many failures. Native Americans opposed to the draft made relatively little impression on a settler state eager to enforce the regulations consistently across the population. Much the same could be said for First Nations, who could not alter government regulations on conscription and wartime taxation. Six Nations nationalists in North America made no progress, either legally or politically, in furthering their unacknowledged claims of sovereignty or avoiding conscription. Australian Aboriginal rights advocates struggled both to open the door to military service and to gain the civil rights such participation might have helped them achieve. Even Māori could not always get their way on appropriate commanders and officers within the 28th Maori Battalion. Yet, despite the long odds there were a number of conditional and partial successes, such as the inclusion of Native Americans in the national war effort and draft, Torres Strait Islanders' efforts to raise their wages (albeit not to an equal level) and Canadian First Nations' efforts to obtain exemption from conscription. Most obviously successful were Māori that sought a segregated battalion of their own, exemption from conscription, control over their own recruitment and broader ownership of what became very much their own war effort. Fundamentally, the ability of each Indigenous community and population to influence the settler state was finite and situational, often even more so in wartime conditions than during peacetime.

*Part III*

Post-War Reform

# 8    Homecomings

## Transition to Peace, Veterans' Return and Access to Veterans' Benefits

On 8 May 1945, Nazi Germany officially capitulated to the Allied powers. The much-anticipated VE Day was an occasion for celebrations across the victorious combatant nations. Similar scenes erupted across Australia, New Zealand, Canada and the United States, marked by ticker tape, bunting, kisses, dancing, bands and spontaneous acts of joy and relief. For nations still heavily engaged in the Pacific theatre, VJ Day on 15 August finally brought peace and opened, after years of anxiety, discipline and sacrifice, a new era for these societies.[1]

This chapter and the next explore the complex and important transitional period at the end of the Second World War for Indigenous veterans and their communities as well as for state Indigenous policies. In the various national literatures about Indigenous-settler relations, 1945 is a much utilised, if underinvestigated, pivot point dividing an interwar period from a distinctly different post-war era. Typically, survey texts on settler-Indigenous relations include a couple of pages providing enlistment numbers, claims of high rates of participation, perhaps mention of the home front impact and some generalities about changing attitudes in settler societies and new international respect for human rights that explained post-war changes.[2] While generally accurate, such overviews do not capture the tremendous complexity of transitioning to peacetime realities for Indigenous peoples and returning service personnel. This chapter examines the home front transition at war's end, the process of homecoming for Indigenous service personnel and the impact of veterans' re-establishment programs on Indigenous returned service personnel.

Indigenous communities and veterans approached war's end with vastly different expectations. Indigenous communities shared the joy, relief and eagerness for the return of loved ones. Yet, the end of wartime

---

[1] Stuart Macintyre, *Australia's Boldest Experiment: War and Reconstruction in the 1940s* (Sydney: NewSouth Publishing, 2015), 314.
[2] See Dickason, *A Concise History of Canada's First Nations*, 230; Broome, *Aboriginal Australians*, 207–210; Belich, *Paradise Reforged*, 475–476.

conditions and the return of peace presented prospects ranging from ambivalent at best to downright bleak. Far from a widespread acceptance achieved through wartime contributions, the war's end mostly marked the end of relative prosperity and a return to the economic, social and political marginalisation of the pre-war years. Still, Indigenous service personnel had reasons to view the war's end in more positive terms. The relief at surviving the war and leaving its terrors behind combined with the prospect of reuniting with family and picking up the threads of a normal life. But more than that, most Indigenous service personnel had experienced acceptance in military service that they expected would continue. Many had learned skilled trades, developed linguistic aptitude and gained experience amongst settler comrades that gave them more confidence about their economic prospects. One Winnebago soldier was 'tired of being treated like museum pieces. I'm a mechanic. I want a real job. They're not going to send me back to live in a shack and loaf around in a blanket.'[3] The talk of extensive benefits programs, and of a new order that settler societies aspired to create out of the ashes of conflict, only amplified Indigenous service personnel's expectations.

The literature on Indigenous wartime participation only briefly addresses the divergent trajectories between Indigenous veterans and their communities. Most studies touch on the homecoming, with an anecdote or two and unsystematic extrapolations, before shifting to the long-term consequences of the war on Indigenous-settler relations. There have been a few works that examine First Nations, Native American, Aboriginal and Torres Strait Islander veterans in varying degrees but virtually nothing on Māori returned service personnel. Canada is somewhat anomalous because Indigenous veterans' grievances over post-war benefits were politicised by a prolonged and ultimately successful campaign from the 1970s to 2000s.[4] Overall, the returning veterans' experiences within their own communities and accessing state veterans' benefits remain opaque.

The issue of veterans' benefits was crucial and part of a gradual integration of Indigenous ex-service personnel into developing settler state social welfare systems. For Indigenous peoples, access to military service had been a yardstick of belonging. Access to benefits and quality support for Indigenous veterans – at the very intersection of their Indigeneity and their veteran-ness – remained an important measurement of acceptance.

---

[3] Townsend, *World War II and the American*, 221.

[4] See the Senate Standing Committee on Aboriginal Peoples, "The Aboriginal Soldier After the Wars," Senate Report (March 1995); Royal Commission on Aboriginal Peoples (RCAP), *Report of the RCAP, Vol. 1: Looking Forward, Looking Back* (Ottawa: Supply and Services, 1996); Sheffield, *A Search for Equity*.

This transnational examination of post-war Indigenous veterans' benefits reveals that the war had made a difference and that veterans' status mattered. The mechanics of administering the benefits likewise demonstrates the continuing limits of acceptance and the circumscribed inclusion of Indigenous peoples in national social citizenship. The lingering legislative and administrative structures for Indigenous populations captured, to some degree, the benefits and subsumed them within existing paternalistic colonial systems resistant to change. Thus, while the Second World War and resulting veterans' benefits had the possibility to provoke change in the socio-economic position of Indigenous veterans and populations, the overall impact was muted.

### Wartime to Peacetime for Indigenous Populations on the Home Front

The wartime combination of acceptance and opportunity fostered a broadly shared sense of hope for the future among many Indigenous communities, having received improved pay, been exposed to new ideas and technologies and grasped new educational and training opportunities.[5] Nevertheless, the future for Indigenous people in 1945 was uncertain, and the return of peace threatened to revoke or restrain wartime opportunities. Alison Bernstein captures this effectively, saying: '[in] 1945 when Japan surrendered, the more than 65,000 Indians who had migrated from the reservations during the war years suddenly faced an uncertain future. White society had accepted them into the military and the work force in a time of crisis, but peace brought different realities.'[6]

Hundreds of thousands of veterans, returning home in search of work, brought pressure to depart on those who had filled the wartime labour void, notably women and Indigenous and other ethnic minorities. For women, the returning men often meant unemployment, though many testimonies do not suggest resentment about this. Victorian Aboriginal woman Connie Alberts states:

Like a lot of women, I learned new skills. The women did well during this time. Our boss was a woman. A lot of girls became skilled mechanics, and they had to fix the machines ... I worked there for nearly two years. When I finished, the war was over, and all our jobs had to go to the returned soldiers. We went back to our kitchens then. We accepted that then – I mean, the men went to war, didn't they? – but it wouldn't be accepted today.[7]

---

[5] Townsend, *World War II and the American Indian*, 193; Toomey, "Canadian Indians in World War II," 116; Hall, *The Black Diggers*, 192–193.
[6] Bernstein, *American Indians and World War II*, 131.
[7] Connie Alberts, in Jackomos and Fowell, *Forgotten Heroes*, 45.

Wartime migration of Indigenous youth into the armed forces and into urban centres to work in war industries had seriously depopulated some Indigenous reserves and communities. Consequently, many Indigenous people would return to traditional lands and family at war's end, but without the elevated hopes or the expectations of economic opportunity. Some Indigenous urbanites lingered, and the trend towards urbanisation renewed in all four states by the 1950s.[8] In remote regions, outsiders had arrived in previously sheltered Indigenous communities, causing both problems and opportunities. Overall then, it mattered little whether Indigenous people lived integrated into urban settler society, in segregated reserve communities or in previously hard-to-reach wilderness areas; everyone hung on the precipice of an uncertain future.

Part of the problem was that the relative prosperity enjoyed by individual Indigenous families during the war years was not paralleled in the funding of state Indigenous administrations. The budgets of Australian state and territory Aboriginal agencies, the American Bureau of Indian Affairs and the Canadian Indian Affairs Branch had all withered during the war years, often from already Depression-reduced levels.[9] In the United States, many federal services including schools and medical clinics had closed. Agriculture had suffered and even those reservations that had been active during the early years of the war had experienced economic slowdowns by the war's end.[10] In Canada, veterans returned to reserves bearing the marks of significant neglect. Housing was inadequate and suffered overcrowding, and as in the United States, funds normally allocated for education, health and other services had been diverted to the war effort.[11] The wartime material and personnel shortages lingered

---

[8] See Evelyn Peters, "'Our City Indians': Negotiating Meaning of First Nations Urbanization in Canada," *Historical Geography* 30 (2002): 75–92; George Morgan, *Unsettled Places: Aboriginal People and Urbanisation in New South Wales* (Kent Town, SA: Wakefield Press, 2006); Donald Fixico, *Termination and Relocation: Federal Indian Policy, 1945–1960* (Albuquerque: University of New Mexico Press, 1986); Dan Morrow, "Tradition and modernity in discourses of Maori urbanization," *Journal of New Zealand Studies* 18 (2014): 85–105; Richard Hill, "Maori Urban Migration and the Assertion of Indigeneity in Aotearoa/New Zealand, 1945–1975," *Interventions* 14, no. 2 (2012): 256–278.

[9] Anna Haebich, *For their Own Good: Aborigines and Government in the South West of Western Australia, 1900–1940* (Nedlands: University of Western Australia Press, 1992), 287–288; Canada, *Special Joint Committee of the Senate and House of Commons to examine and consider the Indian Act* (hereafter *SJC*), Minutes and Proceedings, no. 38 (24 June 1947), 1941; Graham Taylor, "The Divided Heart: The Indian New Deal," in *'They Made Us Many Promises': The American Indian Experience, 1524 to the Present*, ed. Philip Weeks, 2nd edn. (Wheeling, IL: Wiley-Blackwell, 2014), 186; Walker, *He Tipua*, 277–280; 315–317.

[10] Townsend, *World War II and the American Indian*, 215; Franco, *Crossing the Pond*, 99; Hauptman, *The Iroquois Struggle for Survival*, 9–10.

[11] Toomey, "Canadian Indians in World War II," 80–81.

for years after peace returned, prolonging the difficult conditions. Thus, as people returned from military service or wartime employment to their home communities and reservations, withered government services and administration threatened the transition to peace.

In New Zealand by contrast, the spending shortfall on Māori had been less pronounced pre-war. Māori voluntarism and the progressive extension of more equitable social welfare access to Māori by 1945 ameliorated wartime shortages to some degree. Pre-war negotiations over Māori tribal land grievances, which had been put on hold in 1939 by mutual agreement, were renewed by 1943–4. More settlements followed in the immediate wake of the war, including a perpetuity settlement with Waikato iwi in 1946. Though the amounts were not always substantial, Richard Hill claims that this new settlement period of the 1940s was marked by a spirit of optimism and tangible improvements in the quality of life for the iwis receiving settlements.[12] Settlement resources only reached a finite number of Māori and not all experienced a smooth transition to peace. Even so, relative to the substantial downward trend in incomes and quality of life witnessed at the close of the war in Australia, Canada and the United States, Māori appear to have fared better.

Such shortcomings in support may have had less effect if Indigenous workers in the wartime economies had not faced the prospect of mass lay-offs. In the United States, BIA Commissioner Collier predicted as early as 1941 that 'Indians will be among the first to be affected by the shrinkage of employment opportunities subsequent to the war'.[13] His forecast proved prophetic, evident even before the war ended in the population exodus to Indian reservations; the Indian population, which in 1940 was just under 334,000, jumped significantly to 401,819 by the beginning of 1945.[14] Bernstein argues that in the face of declining socio-economic prospects, service personnel's dependency allotments ended and war work had dried up. Native Americans' average individual income had more than doubled between 1938 and 1944, but much of those gains had diminished by 1947.[15] Canadian First Nations had experienced prosperity not felt since at least the 1880s, but by war's end, the opportunities were shrinking. Gitga'at Elder, Helen Clifton, recalled that, amongst other changes, post-war immigrants 'displaced a lot of our workers, you know, they went back to being the second-class citizens

---

[12] Hill, *State Authority, Indigenous Autonomy*, 224.
[13] *Annual Report of the Secretary of the Interior*, 1941, 104, quoted in Bernstein, *American Indians and World War II*, 132, f4.
[14] Franco, *Crossing the Pond*, 94.
[15] Bernstein, *American Indians and World War II*, 141.

they were before the war'.[16] Similar patterns of post-war return to economic marginalisation can be found across all four settler states to varying degrees.

In some reservations in the United States, conditions became so bad that communities faced widespread hardship and desperate poverty. Nowhere was the post-war decline felt more painfully than in the largest reservation in the United States, the Navajo. By spring 1946, the New Mexico Association of Indian Affairs reported that two-thirds of the collective income of the Navajo had disappeared in the previous year, with average earnings of only $471.[17] This financial deficiency was then coupled with a severe drought in the summer of 1947 and hard winters, raising the threat of starvation amidst an ongoing tuberculosis epidemic.[18] The federal government was initially slow to address press reports of the suffering. In response, a number of civic-minded organisations, especially the American Legion, conducted substantial food and supply collection drives to bring aid to Navajo communities. This action, perceived as an embarrassing indictment of BIA administration, combined with sustained public criticism to force the government's hand. In December 1947, Congress responded to President Truman's call for action by passing an emergency appropriation of $2 million to alleviate the suffering.[19] Although occurrences on other reservations were not so grim, the Navajo experience was only the most visible example of the downward trajectory of Native Americans' post-war economic fortunes.

While the overall trend was loss of jobs and job sectors, in some places, wartime employment improvements were not entirely reversed and, in some cases, they even altered the foundations of future Indigenous employment. For instance, in Canada when people of Japanese ancestry were interned in 1942, thousands of Indigenous men and women filled their prominent place in the Pacific salmon fishery.[20] Though not all retained their positions in the face of new pressures from returning service people and renewed immigration, First Nations remained a prominent segment of that industry for decades. In northern Australia, wartime labour opportunities with the military introduced many Aboriginal people to relatively more equitable treatment, a cash wage and better food and housing than they had experienced in pre-war pastoral industries. This was contentious during the war, as many station owners opposed

---

[16] Lutz, *Makúk*, 228.
[17] Bernstein, *American Indians and World War II*, 152; Townsend, *World War II and the American Indian*, 217–218.
[18] Townsend, *World War II and the American Indian*, 218; Iverson, *Diné*, 197.
[19] Bernstein, *American Indians and World War II*, 155.
[20] Lutz, *Makúk*, 228.

Aboriginal labourers becoming accustomed to their improved situation, fearing they would demand it after the war. These predictions proved accurate, and dissatisfied Aboriginal workers subsequently proved more willing to strike or to move to other regions for better wages.[21] In Arnhem Land, missionaries complained that residents who had worked with the RAAF were disgruntled that they could not use their newly acquired skills or earn wages. There were fears of a 'brain drain' if more Aboriginal people moved to Darwin.[22] Torres Strait Islanders, who had protested unequal pay scales in the army, continued to contest unequal wages in the pearling industry.[23] In both the cattle and pearling industries, only in the 1960s did Indigenous labour strikes achieve equal wages, perversely just as increased mechanisation of labour led to mass lay-offs of Indigenous workers.

On the whole, the narrative of hopeful anticipation evident in so much of the literature needs to be tempered to reflect a more ambivalent postwar transition for Indigenous populations. Across Canada, New Zealand, the United States and Australia, Indigenous men and women returned en mass to traditional lands and communities, facing the erosion of opportunity. One bright spot on the horizon in many of these communities, though, was the prospect of their loved ones returning from battle, as settler militaries accelerated their demobilisation processes.

## Homecomings

'One day a notice came out of the first sergeant's office with my name on it', Hollis Stabler, an Omaha soldier, recalled. 'It was my pass to go back to the states! After thirty-four months, five campaigns, and many battles, I was going home! I had made it, but my brother had not.'[24] After months or years away, it is difficult to imagine the immense and complex feelings that Indigenous service personnel experienced in anticipation of their homecomings. For many, the warmth of welcome, the kinship of family and the familiarity of home were deeply comforting. 'I didn't believe that I was home until I got to see my folks', one Canadian veteran recalled. 'I said to myself, "I'm on home ground now. I'm safe."'[25] Most Aboriginal first-hand testimonies do not talk about their homecomings, but rather

[21] Berndt and Berndt, *End of an era*.
[22] Riseman, *Defending Whose Country?* 76.
[23] Hall, *The Black Diggers*, 58–59.
[24] Stabler, *No One Ever Asked Me*, 118.
[25] Anonymous interview in Robert Innes, "'I'm On Home Ground Now. I'm Safe': Saskatchewan Aboriginal Veterans in the Immediate Postwar Years, 1945–1946," *American Indian Quarterly* 28, no. 3–4 (2004): 695.

contain short statements such as, 'I was demobbed in 1946', or, '... they brought me back to Brisbane for some leave and that was the end of the war for me'.[26] For all the nostalgic desire to return home, and the high expectations and hopes for the future, as Stabler said, 'coming home to a post-war world was a confusing experience at best'.[27]

On the other side of this exchange, home communities, whatever their misgivings about the future, were eager to welcome their war heroes. For example, Kiowa woman Jeanette Berry Mopope composed a song for the homecoming celebration of her nephew, Gus Palmer, which spoke briefly of the dangers of war and of the family's joy at his return. 'The enemy bounces as they are hit, he came home for us again', she noted, 'And we were elated (or very happy), and we felt good, and we were elated.'[28] Expectations of homecoming for communities, as for veterans, were more ambiguous and complicated than popular mythology would suggest. Some anxiously wondered what changes they might see in these individuals who had suffered through so much overseas. For those who had lost relatives to fighting, the return of the living could refresh the pain and grieving. For soldiers, the prospect of returning home merely brought recollections of comrades who did not survive the war. Communities with high enlistment numbers and corresponding casualty rates struggled to move on, such as the isolated Māori communities of Tairawhiti, in northeastern New Zealand, which saw 10 per cent of their population enlist – of whom 70 per cent became casualties.[29]

In Indigenous communities across the four countries, young men and women returned home, some to public pomp and ceremony, others to a quiet, warm embrace from kin and some to indifference or even suspicion. The vast majority of Indigenous servicemen and women returned home as individuals, rather than in formed units, which amplified the tremendous diversity of experiences for veterans. All four settler militaries wrestled with the repatriation process, weighing the recognition and grand welcome that would ensue if personnel returned home in their units, against the fairness of simply getting those overseas longest home first. In all four countries, the decision leaned in favour of first over, first back.[30] Thus, the norm was a potentially lonely experience,

26 Lester Marks Harradine and Bill Edwards, in Jackomos and Fowell, *Forgotten Heroes*, 54–55.
27 Stabler, *No One Ever Asked Me*, 119.
28 Carroll, *Medicine Bags and Dog Tags*, 124.
29 Soutar, *Nga Tama Toa*, 365; 373.
30 Dean Oliver, "Awaiting Return: Life in the Canadian Army's Overseas Repatriation Depots, 1945–46," in *The Veterans Charter and Post-World War II Canada*, ed. Peter Neary and J. L. Granatstein (Montreal & Kingston: McGill-Queen's University Press, 1998), 36; Thomson, "The Rehabilitation of Servicemen of World War II in New Zealand,

trickling home after long, ocean and rail voyages, passing through busy and chaotic demobilisation centres, only to arrive at a station platform or roadside. There, family and friends greeted them, and, once home, some communities collectively welcomed returned soldiers. In Canada, many communities organised feasts and other receptions, especially keen to involve First World War veterans too. Finally, at these public events, returning personnel could discuss their war experiences, the challenges and exotic places travelled.[31] The challenge, though, is that only in New Zealand do we have sufficient first-hand accounts and secondary analysis upon which to reconstruct the patterns of these individual experiences.

Often war accounts and homecomings were articulated in culturally prescribed ceremonial and spiritual forms, long established to cele-brate the return of warriors from battle. Many Indigenous cultures felt it important to cleanse the spirit of warriors of any taint or lingering damage from their actions and experiences in combat. Peta Awatere, who rose to command of the 28th (Maori) Battalion, recalled that, after the death of his brother, he 'turned cold and ruthless till the end of the war, till the old "pure" was performed at Rotorua'.[32] Amongst Navajo, as well, returned servicemen and women turned to the healing power of traditional customs to help them move past ghosts that haunted them – although one returned code talker lamented 'how the rejection of the old ways became common amongst Navajo veterans. Many turned to alcohol to deal with their difficulties.'[33] In societies with still-vibrant war-rior traditions, returning servicemen qualified for enhanced rank and social status. Upon his return, Joseph Medicine Crow sang his war song, describing his achievements against the Germans to community Elders, establishing that he had performed the requisite four brave deeds to be a warrior and war chief amongst the Crow people.[34] Similarly, Hollis Stabler described how, after being out of the military about a year:

the *hethúshka* warrior society welcomed me home … My cousin's daughter painted my wounded leg. All I had on was a breech-cloth, a long piece of cloth that you had to wrap and twist between your legs and let it hang down, front and back. My cousin, Mary Lyn embarrassed me by yelling out, 'Watch your *sho$^n$de*, don't accidentally twist it!' Henry Blackbird and George Woodhull Jr., called

1940–1954" (PhD Thesis, Victoria University of Wellington, 1983), 147–152; Macintyre, *Australia's Boldest Experiment*, 317.

[31]  Davison, "We Shall Remember Them," 172.

[32]  Soutar, *Nga Tama Toa*, 185.

[33]  Carroll, *Medicine Bags and Dog Tags*, 120.

[34]  Medicine Crow described this process in a video production, "History of Native American Military Service," CSPAN 3, www.c-span.org/Events/History-of-Native-American-Military-Service/10737426478/.

Horse Chief, gave me a song. All the women *loo-looed* and the men blew whistles the first time they sang my song.[35]

Women often played a significant role facilitating these ceremonies, just as they had been performing ritual prayers while their husbands, brothers and sons were overseas.[36] Navajo woman Agnes Begay recalls:

our elder folks planned a special ceremony to receive a person who had been gone for so long and who had been captured by the Japanese ... Then, later, the same summer we planned a Squaw Dance for him because he was very nervous and sort of upset and sleepless. After the dance was performed, he became normal again like he was before he had gone to war and had been captured.[37]

Several Navajo veterans in the collection *Navajos and World War II* appreciated such ceremonies and found them effective at healing symptoms associated with what we now call post-traumatic stress disorder (PTSD). Such events could draw together the community and reaffirm cultural practices. John Adair and Evon Vogt similarly found amongst the Zuni people that many veterans were struggling with mental scars and acting out, but, by 1948, the intervention of the traditional curing changed veterans' behaviours: drinking had reduced, many veterans had wives and more were working in the fields or at other jobs.[38] Such culturally distinct approaches to healing and renewal, for many Indigenous returned service personnel, appear to have been important. Tom Holm's work on Native American veterans of the Vietnam War struggling with PTSD certainly suggests this to be the case.[39]

To this point, the discussion has focused on pervasive individual experiences of return. There was a striking exception to this rule in the homecoming of the 28th (Maori) Battalion, whose 780 members landed in Wellington, 24 January 1946. Returning as a formed unit was unique to the 28th, as every other New Zealand unit disbanded overseas with men returning in drafts based on individual priorities.[40] Members of the unit made this decision, even though for some it meant a delay of several weeks. Māori politicians, Māori communities (especially those close to the capital), and government, military and Maori War Effort Organisation officials made extensive preparations to give a heroes'

[35] Stabler, *No One Ever Asked Me*, 125.
[36] Carroll, *Medicine Bags and Dog Tags*, 129.
[37] Begay, "History – Munitions Plant Work During World War II," 49.
[38] Adair and Vogt, "Navaho and Zuni Veterans," 550.
[39] Holm, *Strong Hearts, Wounded Souls*, 183–197; Tom Holm, "Culture, Ceremonialism, and Stress: American Indian Veterans and the Vietnam War," *Armed Forces & Society* 12, no. 2 (Winter 1986): 237–251.
[40] Gardiner, *Te Mura O Te Ahi*, 177.

*Figure 8.1* Return of Maori Battalion. John Pascoe Collection, Alexander Turnbull Library.

welcome.[41] The reception, attended by thousands of Māori and Pākehā on Aotea Quay, received widespread national media coverage, including a newsreel showing Māori women and civilian men preparing a feast in Porirua before the ship arrived.[42] Mararea Tippins remembers attending the event: 'When the Māori Battalion came back on the *Dominion Monarch* in 1946, we were still there, working at the clothing firm. I will never forget the Māori Battalion marching onto the wharf. Everybody was there; our people had come down … the crowd was so heavy. The service welcoming them home and the hymns they sang. Then afterwards they were allowed to mix.'[43] Historian Monty Soutar describes the scene:

B Company's Sergeant Nan Amohau, composer of the Battalion marching song, went out to challenge the [welcome] party, accompanied by Tuhwaratoa Chiefs

[41] Lt. Colonel Ferris, Chief Liaison Officer, MWEO, to Mr. Tirikatene, 26 July 1945, ANZ, MA 1 19-1-452.
[42] *Weekly Review* newsreel 232, 23 January 1946.
[43] Maraea Tippins, in *Early Stories from Te Tīmatanga Tātau Tātau*, 284.

Tureiti Rauhina and Tueri Papanui. At the head of the haka party was the par-
amount chief of Tuwharatoa, Hepi Te Heuheu, while Ngati Ponenke sang out
the songs of greeting. There followed for some time the tangi for the dead, the
most solemn part of the ceremony. Kuia, clad in black and adorned in greenery,
stood wailing as they recalled those who had not returned. Elders recited a chant
to satisfy the ritual of 'tango tapu' (removing tapu) ... To the elders, a soldier's
discharge from the army was not sufficient to convert him to a peaceful citizen.
The ritual had to be performed before the distinction between the warrior and
the ordinary citizen was dissolved.[44]

There were whaikorero (welcome speeches) before families finally
greeted their loved ones, rushing to embrace overwhelmed and emotional soldiers. After lunch, the Battalion members paraded for a final
powerful address by Lt. Colonel Henare, who concluded in Māori: 'Go
back to our mountains, go back to our people, go back to our marae.
But this is my last command to you all – stand as Maori, stand as Maori,
stand as Maori.'[45]

   The men dispersed to return to their own communities where other
ceremonies awaited in regional tribal centres and marae, such as
Wanganui (Putiki Pa), Ngaruawahia Pa, Auckland (Orakei Pa), Kaikohe,
Rotorua, Ruatoria, Wairoa, Hastings (Omahu Pa), Otaki and Taranaki.[46]
Crowds at each event repeated this spirit of enthusiasm and the collective context of Māori homecoming at war's end made for a massive
and memorable experience for both veterans and communities. Not all
the returned soldiers enjoyed the repeated welcome ceremonies, though.
Wira Gardiner gives the example of Rock Maika, who found the prospect of the 'proposed pilgrimage from Wellington to Palmerston North,
Ngaruawahia and then to Gisborne was ... "too annoying for words".'[47]
Yet, the events were also sites of mixed emotions for those families that
lost loved ones. Tepara Mabel Waititi remembers the ceremonies at the
local maraes when the Maori Battalion returned in 1946:

we went from marae to marae down to this side of Opotiki, before we came
home. There were tangis at every marae. Oh it was sad – sad for the mothers,
and the wives, who had lost their sons over there. At one marae, seven went in
the original lot and not one came back. There were expressions of sorrow all
the time. I think we went on to about six maraes, and spent about a day at each
marae up to the last lot and it was sad to see, especially some of the mothers had

---

[44] Soutar, Nga Tama Toa, 361–362.
[45] Quoted in Ibid., 362.
[46] Letter from Rangi Royal, Chief Welfare Officer, to the Under-Secretary, 19 December
   1945, and letter from the President of the Maori Land Board Office to the Under
   Secretary, 7 May 1945, both in ANZ, MA 1 19-1-452.
[47] Gardiner, Te Mura O Te Ahi, 179.

got old and crying. Seeing the ones that lost their beloved ones but still happy to receive the others.[48]

This theme of grief permeates other Māori women's memories of the war homecomings, including Mihipeka Edwards: 'I now look at the sorrow, the tears, the pain of the many kuia, women, girls – wives, mothers, sweethearts – who tangi for sons, husbands and mokopuna who will never return to them. They tangi, broken and wracked with pain.'[49] This gendered reading reveals more nuance to the story of the glorious Maori Battalion, returning to celebrations. For those whose sons, brothers and fathers did not return, the end of the war was not a time of celebration.

Not all Indigenous returned service personnel would find the welcome lived up to their imaginings during the long wait and voyage from the theatre of war. Though evidence on this subject is thin, different communities and cultural contexts responded in distinct ways. Navajo veteran Peter Macdonald recalls:

the Navajo veterans felt unappreciated by the Navajo community at large. They had been to Normandy, to Iwo Jima, to Guadalcanal, to numerous other places that were once unknown and had become a part of history. Yet when they spoke of what they did, of what they had seen, no one seemed to care. Their immediate families were proud of them, but on their way back to the Navajo Nation from their cities of discharge, they had witnessed numerous parades and celebrations. That was not the Navajo way, yet they still sought recognition and respect, none of which came to them.[50]

In the Canadian prairies, Robert Innes noted the variability from one Cree community to the next, citing George Redwood, a Cree veteran who recalled the Peepeekisis Reserve 'welcomed us back with open arms. They were glad to have us back, and that sort of stuff.' Contrastingly, Grand Chief Howard Anderson recalled that on Gordon's Reserve, 'nothing was ever done ... we just come home, we done our thing and that was it'.[51]

In some communities, cultural perspectives regarding war/warriors, combined with the sometimes transformative cultural experience of veterans, marked them as problematic individuals or potential threats to the community. Post-war fieldwork amongst the Navajo and Zuni by anthropologists John Adair and Evon Vogt suggested divergent experiences. Navajos tended to view returning veterans as future agents of positive

[48] Tepara Mabel Waititi, in *War Stories Our Mothers Never Told Us*, 139–140.
[49] Edwards, *Mihipeka: Time of Turmoil*, 147.
[50] MacDonald, *The Last Warrior*, 74.
[51] George Redwood and Howard Anderson, in Innes, "I'm On Home Ground Now. I'm Safe," 702.

change while Zuni perceived repatriated soldiers to be harbingers of destruction who must re-adapt to traditional Zuni values or leave.[52] Navajo veteran Peter MacDonald indicates that, for him and some other Navajo veterans, 'the returning soldiers of World War II brought new ideas with them. The Navajo religion did not explain what they had seen and experienced. Scientific knowledge alone – even the fact that the earth is round – was contrary to our religious upbringing.' Macdonald recalls when he challenged an old medicine man with the notion that the world was round, the Elder responded: 'Young man, you should never, ever say that again. Don't ever say the earth is moving, because the day that the earth moves is the day that all of us are going to die. So don't ever say that, don't ever think it, don't ever wish it. That's bad.'[53] This suggests a more diverse range of attitudes existed amongst Navajo than Adair found in one particular community. Amongst Coast Salish peoples in the Pacific Northwest, one veteran recalled that the:

tragic part is, our own people, looked down on us. They said, 'why did you have to go and join – it wasn't your fight ...' After we came back from overseas many of us fell back into little cracks and holes in our own villages – into obscurity. And that hurt a lot of the old veterans. They never did come forward. They never did attend big gatherings. The people of authority among our own people didn't want them to be recognized that way. That's what hurt us as veterans – myself as a veteran.[54]

Such experiences highlight the challenges in understanding Indigenous veterans' homecoming across such a cultural kaleidoscope.

After the emotional highs and lows of military service, trauma and euphoria of combat, the travel to distant lands, comradeship and shared sense of purpose, Indigenous veterans had to confront the reality of mundane routines. As one young First Nations veteran noted, 'how do you regain the kind of excitement that you get when you're in a war? You can't. Your life is pretty much downhill after that.'[55] Robert Innes argues that many Indigenous veterans in the Canadian prairies 'returned not only to the same jobs they had prior to the war but also to the same living conditions ... Some found life at home slow and uneventful, some were unable to find work and saw better opportunities elsewhere.'[56]

Heightened expectations, which many veterans developed during the war to help give meaning to the pain they endured, were a contributing factor. Indigenous servicemen and women shared this general

[52] Adair and Vogt, "Navaho and Zuni Veterans," 547.
[53] MacDonald, The Last Warrior, 75.
[54] Carlson, "Stó:lō Soldiers, Stó:lō Veterans," 135.
[55] Innes, "I'm On Home Ground Now. I'm Safe," 695.
[56] Ibid., 691.

phenomenon but also faced the additional expectations raised by the respect and acceptance they had found in the military forces. Perhaps such high aspirations could not help but fall short; to returning veterans, it was immediately clear that wartime equality did not transition to civilian life. Hollis Stabler had yet to remove his uniform on his journey home to Omaha in 1945 when he disembarked a train and entered a bar:

> I wanted a beer and a hamburger, so I went in there. Unknown to me, somebody called the police. Here comes a policeman in there. He said, 'Are you drinking?' I said, 'Yeah,' you know. 'Indians aren't supposed to drink.' That's what he said to me. I just dropped the bottle and walked out. I still had my uniform on … It made me wonder what I'd been fighting for. I never went back to that place.[57]

The bitterness of similar experiences is etched in the memories of many Indigenous veterans. Former Maori Battalion soldier, John Rangihau, recalled:

> We came back into a situation which had not changed in any way, where we were still treated as second-class citizens, where we were still not allowed to purchase alcohol … Suddenly there was an annoying thing at the pit of our stomach about having gone away to free this beautiful land and yet still be treated as aliens in our own country.[58]

Norman Harris found a mixed legacy after his discharge from the RAAF in Perth. He and his cousin were picked up by a police sergeant after a few drinks at a city hotel. Under the Native Welfare Act in Western Australia, it was illegal for Aboriginal people to drink, but in this instance, a magistrate dismissed the charge, declaring, 'if it was good enough to fight for your country, it was good enough to be a citizen'.[59] One Canadian veteran recalled:

> as long as you're on the reserve the nearest town won't have anything to do with you. They just regard you as nothing. And that's how we were treated. We were just another Indian … When we were discharged they told us that we would get first choice of any job at all. But that was impossible, I mean you go out and I've been rejected so many times.[60]

For most veterans, the racial norms of their pre-war lives seemed little altered upon their return home.

Alcohol played a significant role for many returned veterans, both practically and symbolically. As Peter MacDonald recalls, many Native

[57] Stabler, *No One Ever Asked Me*, 122.
[58] John Rangihau, "Being Maori," in *Te Ao Hurihuri: Aspects of Maoritanga*, ed. Michael King (Auckland: Reed, 1992), 187.
[59] Brian Willis, "Aborigines and the Defence Forces in Western Australia in World War II" (MA Thesis, University of Western Australia, 1995), 19.
[60] Innes, "I'm On Home Ground Now. I'm Safe," 694.

Americans veterans turned to alcohol to help them cope with their trauma and troubles readjusting: 'The alcohol seemed to quiet the intense desire these men had to relive the excitement and stimulation they had known during the war'.[61] He further argues that in the Navajo Reservation, it was only after the Second World War that alcohol use became widespread, leading to significant problems such as foetal alcohol syndrome. Notwithstanding the significant social problems that alcohol could bring, having the right to drink was still an important symbol of equality denied to many Indigenous veterans, particularly in Australia, Canada and the United States. In Canada and several American states, it was illegal for liquor stores to sell alcohol to Status Indians or Native Americans, though bootleggers or non-Indians readily provided alcohol at a price. In Australia, all states and territories still barred Aboriginal and Torres Strait Islander people from drinking unless they had an exemption certificate, colloquially known as a dog tag. Alec Kruger states, '"Only dogs get registered" was a saying of a lot of us blokes. If we had the exemption we couldn't associate with or marry into the Aboriginal community. Who needed that in a world where no white people were ever going to let you in?'[62]

Given the restrictive requirements to obtain a dog tag, few Aboriginal people took up the opportunity, leaving it illegal for most veterans to drink alcohol. The regulations in Canada were similar, with Status Indians having the option to enfranchise and, if qualified, surrender their Indian Status and obtain citizenship rights and the right to alcohol. In practice, very few opted to do so, which likewise left most veterans barred from alcohol. In some states, Aboriginal veterans found an ally in the otherwise conservative Returned Services League (RSL). As the RSL in New South Wales explained it, Aboriginal veterans 'had the discipline to serve with the forces, so they should be able to drink with equal discipline'.[63] In 1957, Victoria was the first state (besides Tasmania, which claimed not to have any Aboriginal people) to repeal the ban on Indigenous people's access to alcohol. Most other states followed suit between 1963 and 1965, and Western Australia finally repealed its ban in 1971.[64] The Canadian government removed the ban on Status Indians' access to alcohol as part of a major revamp of the Indian Act in 1951, largely in response to First Nations protest and the uncomfortable symbolism of First Nations veterans being barred from the halls of the Royal Canadian Legion due to the alcohol served therein.

[61]  MacDonald, *The Last Warrior*, 74.
[62]  Kruger and Waterford, *Alone on the Soaks*, 148.
[63]  Quoted in Riseman and Trembath, *Defending Country*, 44.
[64]  John Chesterman, *Civil Rights: How Indigenous Australians Won Formal Equality* (St Lucia: University of Queensland Press, 2005), 110.

Even within veterans' communities, Indigenous servicemen and women sometimes faced discrimination. Peter MacDonald recalls that organisations such as the American Legion and Veterans of Foreign Wars would not welcome Native Americans, prompting many to establish their own veterans' groups from the late 1950s.[65] In Australia, it was a much more complicated situation. The most prominent veterans' group, the RSL, has always had a devolved structure with significant local autonomy. While some branches were strong advocates for Indigenous equality, most notably in Victoria, others had no qualms discriminating against Indigenous veterans. The most famous case, which is by no means an isolated example, was the Walgett RSL in rural New South Wales, which would not let Aboriginal people in except on Anzac Day.[66]

Veterans not only found the return to societal racism painful, but they also struggled with re-entering the control that characterised settler administration of Indigenous populations. Veterans were no longer willing to accept the subservience expected from state administrators and the oppressive systems in which Indigenous populations often lived. Alec Kruger remembers of his return to Alice Springs: 'Us Aboriginal soldiers had hoped to return to a place where we could live on an equal footing with the white population. We weren't happy to be forced back into the overcrowded shacks and humpies of Rainbow Town [near Alice Springs]. Most of us had been politicized by our time in the army.'[67] Governments recognised the dissatisfaction Indigenous veterans would face, admitted candidly by the Commissioner of Native Affairs in Western Australia in 1943:

it has been found that enlistment has unsettled the natives. This effect is much more apparent upon their discharge from the Services. As soldiers certain privileges are extended to them, but this is not possible after discharge, the net result being a disgruntled native with a definite grudge against authority which compels him to observe the law.[68]

In Canada, Status Indian veterans felt more tightly the constraints of the Indian Act and the discretionary powers of the Indian Agent, intensifying frustration with authority. One veteran recalled how 'especially at that age when I came back, I was bitter against the Indian agent, the Indian

---

[65] MacDonald, The Last Warrior, 74.
[66] See Riseman and Trembath, Defending Country, 35–55; Ann Curthoys, Freedom Ride: A Freedom Rider Remembers (St Leonards, NSW: Allen & Unwin, 2002); Charles Perkins, A Bastard Like Me (Sydney: Ure Smith, 1975), 76–78.
[67] Kruger and Waterford, Alone on the Soaks, 146.
[68] Letter from Commissioner to Officer-In-Charge, Native Hospital, Broome, 19 April 1943, SRO WA – Acc993 – 38-1940.

Act, the government ... it's almost you know funny how a freedom loving people ... we were closed in here, simply closed in'.[69]

Many veterans also faced internal struggles to let go of the war, experiencing symptoms that were still poorly understood and generally undertreated. After the First World War, the expression 'shell shock' referred to the numerous mental health problems faced by returning veterans. It would not be until 1980, in the wake of the Vietnam War, that the American Psychiatric Association introduced PTSD into the *Diagnostic and Statistical Manual of Mental Disorders*. Of course, psychologists know much more about PTSD now than after the Second World War, and some of that knowledge helps to explain the causes and symptoms manifested by returning soldiers. For instance, Sebastian Junger argues that one of the largest challenges for soldiers returning from war is the shift from the collectivist experience of a military unit to the individualistic life in peacetime.[70]

In North America, Ira Hayes and Tommy Prince became the icons for this phenomenon, as both men struggled after their return from war, which for Prince included two tours of duty in Korea. Both turned to alcohol to cope. Hayes famously died of exposure in a ditch in 1955 while Prince's marriage broke down, and he lived out his life in anonymous poverty on the streets of Winnipeg until rediscovered near his death in 1977.[71] Soutar has documented suicides (never spoken of), alcoholism and family violence among Māori in the Tairawhiti region.[72] Native American veteran Draven Delkittie recalled a fellow Indigenous ex-serviceman who failed to come to terms with having killed others who drank himself to death.[73] In Australia, Reg Saunders recalled how:

I had a hard time after the war. I used to wake up in the bloody ... and I'd have my wife by the throat and all sorts of bloody things, you know. It was really bad there for awhile ... and poor old Dotty, she, you know, she didn't know what to make of it ... I started sleeping on my own so as I couldn't ... I used to hit her for no reason ... In my sleep, oh yes, yeah. Oh no I wasn't awake, I was fighting the bloody Germans, the Japanese or someone, and I used to be really violent.[74]

One of the often unspoken issues among families was how to live with traumatised servicemen – a problem confronting non-Indigenous families as well. Aboriginal woman Marg Tucker recalls, 'The young men who

[69] Innes, "I'm On Home Ground Now. I'm Safe," 697.
[70] Junger, *Tribe*, 92–98.
[71] Hemingway, *Ira Hayes*; Lackenbauer, "'A Hell of a Warrior': Sergeant Thomas George Prince," 95–138; 27–78.
[72] Soutar, *Nga Tama Toa*, 373.
[73] Carroll, *Medicine Bags and Dog Tags*, 119.
[74] Reg Saunders, in Hall, *Fighters from the Fringe*, 86.

went away, those who came home again, all needed such love and care, only to find wives who didn't know how to respond to their many needs and moods. Many drifted apart like we did. I for one am sorry for my thoughtlessness and lack of understanding.'[75] Women's stories suggest that they were more attuned to the changes that mental scars the war could leave on returning servicemen. Mihipeka Edwards reflects:

I look at the returned [Māori] soldiers as they listen to whaikōrero from the kaumātua. These remaining men were often no more than teenagers when they first left these shores to go to war. Filled with adventure, hope, as well as a chance to see other countries; most of all, offered a job they would be paid for, even if it was to kill people. Now they have returned and I gaze at serious-looking men, no longer boys. I wonder to myself what terrible tragedies they have locked away in their minds.[76]

The broader effect of volatile and mentally wounded veterans, on families and communities, when mixed with wartime infidelity, is captured by Connie Katae, who was a teacher in the Māori community of Te Araroa (Sleepy Hollow):

The years away from home had left a gap and a lack of closeness in the family. Some wives were unfaithful, which caused a greater gap and the children suffered. Not only were there quarrels and violence in the home, a stranger had entered their lives to become part of the family, a stranger who was their father. There were many broken homes and divorce. Sleepy Hollow was no longer a village of contentment. The war had not brought peace but betrayal, anguish and regret, for past indiscretions.[77]

Though it is not often acknowledged because it does not fit the 'good war' image prevalent in popular culture, Indigenous and non-Indigenous families alike experienced these same issues when the soldiers came home.[78]

While often lauded and admired in both Indigenous and settler societies, veterans' status could set returned service personnel apart from their community and potentially undermine their civil re-establishment. According to Innes, First Nations veterans sometimes left their communities because:

tension that existed between some community members and the veterans. Veterans' benefits, for example, were a cause of resentment among non-veteran

[75] Tucker, *If Everyone Cared*, 161.
[76] Edwards, *Mihipeka: Time of Turmoil*, 147.
[77] Soutar, *Nga Tama Toa*, 374.
[78] Stephen Garton, *The Cost of War: Australians Return* (Melbourne: Oxford University Press, 1996); Kristy Muir, "The hidden cost of war: the psychological effects of the Second World War and Indonesian confrontation on Australian veterans and their families" (PhD thesis, University of Wollongong, 2003).

community members. Indian veterans were eligible to acquire lands on reserves through the Veterans' Lands Act (VLA) ... Lands the veterans had received through the VLA, property many subsequently abandoned because of community pressure, reverted back to the band without compensation given to the veteran.[79]

Given the bleak economic prospects in Indigenous communities postwar, it is unsurprising that higher pay rates during the war and access to benefits and opportunities in peacetime might have engendered such jealousies. The relative lack of evidence across Australia, New Zealand and the United States suggests such incidents were localised.

Generally, though, veterans' families tried to welcome soldiers home, but the challenges of settling down led varying numbers eventually to leave their communities.[80] While there is evidence of this phenomenon across all four countries, local and individual circumstances varied enormously and a wide range of possible motivations could spark a veteran's departure. A number of issues already addressed could play into this: community attitudes, boredom, frustration with a return to state paternalism, mental scars and domestic discontent.[81] An additional pull factor was the need to find work or economic opportunity, something often in short supply in veterans' own communities and reserve lands. A Canadian veteran described the experience that he and his brother encountered on their return after the war:

my wife's brother ... he was in Regina Rifles and he got wounded on D-Day on the 6th of June 1944. But when he came back, he was no good for nothing cause [of] his leg and he had no skills, eh. Same as me. Just worked out wherever he could get a job, part time roofing, you know, whatever, helping carpenters, working on farms and you name it. And that's the way we were. Wherever we went, we tried to get a job – it didn't matter what the hell type of job, we took it, you know, not much money but we had to make a living ... You used to get odd jobs; you couldn't get a damn job you know, we were not qualified for nothing. How to soldier that's all.[82]

There was more work to be had in urban centres; indeed, government rehabilitation schemes and trade courses may have lured many returned men to the cities.[83] Women, too, moved to cities to take up education and employment opportunities. A small number of Aboriginal ex-servicewomen were able to use their new skills and training to obtain secretarial and other administrative positions previously staffed primarily

[79] Innes, "I'm On Home Ground Now. I'm Safe," 696.
[80] Soutar, *Nga Tama Toa,* 373.
[81] Innes, "I'm On Home Ground Now. I'm Safe," 702.
[82] Ibid., 693.
[83] Soutar, *Nga Tama Toa,* 373–374.

by white, middle-class women.[84] Regardless of the root cause, an overall pattern of restlessness and mobility was common amongst Indigenous veterans, many of whom, as Cree veteran Isaiah Halkett summarised: 'needed to find something they could not find at home'. Halkett, incidentally, was the sole veteran to remain in his community of Little Red River, Saskatchewan.[85] The long-range consequence was that Indigenous veterans formed an important component of post-war Indigenous urbanisation.

Even among those who moved away from community lands, there was often an eventual return. Sometimes this happened when a job opportunity ended, and a veteran wanted to return home. This was the case for Cozy Stanley Brown, who stayed in the US Marines after the war, then worked in Los Angeles for three years and after being laid off returned to the Navajo Reservation.[86] Alec Kruger moved north from Alice Springs after the war to reconnect with family and worked in various industries including droving cattle and pearling. By 1953, though, after having lived in communities such as Katherine and Darwin, he found it difficult to earn a steady wage and decided to return to Alice Springs where he had a support network of mates with whom he had lived as a removed child at the Bungalow.[87] There were other veterans who returned home later in life and were able to apply their education skills for community empowerment. Several tertiary-educated Native American veterans became leaders in tribal governments in the United States. Oodgeroo Noonaccul returned to Stradbroke Island in 1971, where she founded Moongalba as a place for teaching Aboriginal cultural practices to both Indigenous and non-Indigenous students.[88] A commonality among many of these Indigenous leaders was that they had made use of available veterans' benefits.

## Veterans' Benefits

Central in the Indigenous veterans' transition to civilian life was the support available to returning servicemen and women from a thankful country and government. Regardless of the name or the legislative mechanics, each country crafted a similar blend of financial reward, transitional funds, training provisions, employment support/advantages, loans for land or business development, disability pensions and other

[84] Riseman, "Escaping assimilation's grasp," 757–775.
[85] Innes, "I'm On Home Ground Now. I'm Safe," 694.
[86] Brown, "Code Talker – Pacific Theater," 60.
[87] Kruger and Waterford, *Alone on the Soaks*, 224–227.
[88] Riseman, "Escaping Assimilation's Grasp," 763.

miscellaneous measures.[89] The support was intended to fulfil multiple purposes: First, it conveyed gratitude for the service and sacrifices made by veterans; second, it represented direct compensation for time lost to men and women who, had they remained home, would have been educating themselves, wooing and building a family or developing their careers; third, the huge funds provided a Keynesian benefit, pumping money into the economy during the tricky transition from war to peace; finally, the measures were designed to ensure veterans made a smooth shift to civilian life and did not become a large disenchanted social group. In each country, governments learned from the mistakes made after the Great War and built a more flexible, compassionate and comprehensive system the second time around.[90] In each country, veterans' programs were massive experiments in state social welfare development. The relative success of re-establishment measures for the bulk of ex-service personnel has contributed massively to the popular view of the Second World War as the 'good war'. For all its importance though, the intricacies of the process of Indigenous veterans' re-establishment remains virtually unexamined outside Canada where Indigenous politicisation of the issue generated both public and academic interest since the 1980s.

In the announcements and legislation establishing programs for veterans' post-war re-establishment, the rhetoric across the four settler societies spoke strongly to the equality of access for all veterans. For example, the rehabilitation guidebook used by administrators in New Zealand opened with a special note regarding Māori veterans:

> The aim of the Rehabilitation Board has been to regard Maoris and pakehas alike and to extend equal facilities for re-establishment. For example, the following facilities which are given below are exactly the same for Maoris as for pakehas ...
> Wages while training, whether on the land or in a trade.
> Financial assistance for business, housing, furniture, tools of trade, etc.
> Land settlement loans for land, stock, etc.
> Rehabilitation allowances, separation allowances, etc.[91]

[89] Glenn C. Altschuler and Stuart M Blumin, *The G.I. Bill: A New Deal for Veterans* (Oxford and New York: Oxford University Press, 2009); Neary and Granatstein (eds.), *The Veterans Charter and Post-World War II Canada*; Thomson, "The Rehabilitation of Servicemen of World War II in New Zealand, 1940–1954"; Macintyre, *Australia's Boldest Experiment*.

[90] Thomson, "The Rehabilitation of Servicemen of World War II in New Zealand, 1940–1954," Chapter 1; Jeff Keshen, "Getting it Right the Second Time Around: The Reintegration of Canadian Veterans of World War II," in *The Veterans' Charter and Post-War Canada*, 62–84; Altschuler and Blumin, *The G.I. Bill*, 24–33; Clem Lloyd and Jacqui Rees, *The Last Shilling: A History of Repatriation in Australia* (Melbourne: Melbourne University Press, 1994); Grey, *A Military History of Australia*, 198.

[91] The Serviceman's Guide to Demobilization and Rehabilitation, 23, ANZ, WAII 1 DA550.1.1.

In a similar vein, a 1947 report by A. O. Neville, retired Western Australia Commissioner for Native Affairs, at a conference on reconstruction and Aboriginal veterans, alleged that the 'coloured ex-serviceman has exactly the same rights under the Re-establishment Act as the white ex-serviceman and it is desired that he should be informed of this'.[92] Such was also the case for Indigenous veterans in North America, where the provisions of the 1944 Serviceman's Readjustment Act (the GI Bill) and Canada's Veterans Charter were theoretically applicable to all ex-service personnel without regard to race, religion or gender.[93] Usually, Indigenous veterans could apply through normal channels and agencies set up for returning servicemen and women.

The records, both archival and oral testimonies, suggest that there is some genuine substance to the rhetoric of equal access and lack of distinctions for Indigenous veterans. In New Zealand, the United States and, to a lesser extent, Australia, there were no high-profile Indigenous grievances against veterans' administrations until after the Vietnam War. Even then, the majority of grievances were not about Indigeneity or race but rather reflected grievances common to all returned servicemen (and more recently, women). The silence implies that many Indigenous veterans had some, perhaps sufficient, access to re-establishment programs and support. Yet, this should in no way be interpreted as saying Indigenous veterans' experiences with veterans' benefits and civil re-establishment were free of challenges or disadvantage. Rather, given the era, it suggests that at least a remnant of the acceptance and equality Indigenous service personnel experienced in wartime lingered, at least in connection to *official* discourse about their veteran status. It was easy to adopt veterans' benefits, which appeared colour-blind. Delivering equal access to veterans' programs in practice proved much more difficult, especially as other legislation and practices in the four settler states disenfranchised and constrained Indigenous peoples and would impinge on Indigenous veterans' re-establishment.

Sometimes, circumstances peculiar to Indigenous peoples required additional legislation or programs. This was especially evident in relation to the sometimes complex and distinct legal status and administration of Indigenous lands. For example, the New Zealand rehabilitation guide cited above went on to advise:

provision for the further development of Native lands, including tribal lands offered to the Board for Maori settlement, will have to be made. The Board has

[92] A. O. Neville to the Minister for Native Affairs, 18 April 1947, SRO WA, 135-47.
[93] R. Scott Sheffield, "Canadian Aboriginal Veterans and the Veterans' Charter After the Second World War," in *Aboriginal Peoples and Military Participation*, 80.

conferred with the Native Department, which administers Maori development measures, and it is anticipated that these measures, with appropriate modifications, will provide agricultural rehabilitation of Native ex-servicemen, within the rehabilitation framework.[94]

The complexities of Māori land title, and the generally uneconomic small blocks into which it had been divided through the Maori Land Court system, created extensive delays for Māori ex-servicemen seeking re-establishment on the land. Even as late as 1949, 214 Māori veterans, some 4.3 per cent of all Māori veterans who had been graded 'A', were stuck in limbo awaiting farms. Understandably, 'trained farmers got sick of waiting for farms and took up unskilled work, even though this sometimes cost them their "A" grade qualification'.[95]

In Canada, too, the legal standing of Indian reserve lands, which were held in trust by the Crown for the collective use of a particular Indian band, proved problematic for agricultural re-establishment. As a result, individuals could not own a plot in fee simple, nor could banks seize lands or chattels in forfeiture of an unpaid debt from a reserve. In practice, this meant that financial institutions refused to provide credit for any resident of an Indian Reserve. The Veterans Land Act (VLA) required a veteran to have clear title to a plot of land and be suitable for credit, which made the VLA untenable on reserves. While veterans might opt to apply for a standard VLA settlement outside their reserve, the Director of Indian Affairs acknowledged they would face serious impediments:

The average Indian veteran may be confronted with a practical difficulty in seeking qualification papers from the responsible committees set up for the purpose, who may be expected to feel some diffidence about qualifying an Indian for establishment on the land on a debt basis. In other words it is feared that few Indians could qualify under the conditions set by the Act.[96]

During the research for the report, *A Search for Equity*, Canada's Department of Veterans' Affairs could find virtually no evidence of Status Indians qualifying for VLA off reserve. To make some VLA support available on reserves, the Canadian government passed an amendment, which gave Status Indian veterans access to a grant up to $2,320, equivalent to the grant portion of the $6,000 loan/grant under a standard

---

[94] The Serviceman's Guide to Demobilization and Rehabilitation, 23, ANZ, WAII 1 DA550-1-1.

[95] Thomson, "The Rehabilitation of Servicemen of World War II in New Zealand, 1940–1954," 319.

[96] To all Indian Agents, Inspectors and the Indian Commissioner for BC, from R.A. Hoey, 3 March 1945, LAC, RG 10, vol. 10712, file #43/39-6, pt. 1.

VLA settlement.[97] Though a much lower sum, Indian Affairs argued that the difference was balanced 'by the "more favourable conditions" that existed on reserve'.[98] First Nations veterans rarely found reserve conditions 'favourable' and struggled to translate VLA support into a successful agricultural re-establishment.

Native American veterans faced similar disadvantages accessing loan provisions within the GI Bill because reservations were held in trust. Under the Dawes Act, veterans could sometimes obtain patents in fee for an allotment of reserve land, which they could put up as security for a loan. The fact that requests for patents in fee quadrupled during the 1946–50 years suggest many Native American veterans sought to do so. Ironically, they found themselves working against the Indian New Deal agenda that sought to end alienation of tribal lands. Thus bureau officials initially resisted veterans' requests for patents, fearing they might later sell the lands and permanently reduce tribal territories. The BIA was nevertheless forced to respond and revised some of its internal restrictions on individuals accessing some monetary value of trust lands for collateral. They even redirected tribal credit funds towards individual veterans unable to access commercial credit.[99] These ad hoc measures helped but never fully levelled the playing field for Native American veterans seeking GI loans.

Some hints of special re-establishment programs being developed for Aboriginal veterans can be gleaned in Western Australia state records, where ideas were floated in 1947 and again in 1950.[100] The Acting Commissioner of Native Affairs in 1947 was sceptical about the reported numbers of Aboriginal servicemen and dismissive of any utility of special programs:

Any rehabilitation course of training for native ex-servicemen is considered unnecessary because of the very small numbers involved, and further, the scheme which provides for white ex-servicemen is quite capable of dealing with any native cases. Native soldiers upon discharge were fully informed of the benefits to which they were entitled, but very few displayed any great interest as they preferred to return to their home districts and resume the occupations they followed prior to enlistment.[101]

---

[97] The Order-in-Council that created Section 35A was P.C. 5932, 7 September 1945, LAC, RG 10, vol. 452-32, p.2.
[98] RCAP, *Report of the RCAP, Vol. 1: Looking Forward, Looking Back*, Chapter 12 (1996), 33.
[99] Bernstein, *American Indians and World War II*, 142–144.
[100] See SRO WA, 135-47 Re-establishment Training Scheme for Natives.
[101] A/Commissioner of Native Affairs to K. W. Growcott, Ministry of Post-War Reconstruction, 1 September 1947, SRO WA, 135-47.

This suggests that access to regular veterans' support was available, though also that some veterans may not have availed themselves of it. The official's negative assessment of the value of special programs appears to hinge on his belief in Aboriginal incapacity. The subsequent paragraph demonstrates the fatalism that underlay such assumptions of Indigenous inferiority:

It is my considered opinion that the majority of the adult natives in this State are not capable of any form advanced training and that this is due to their, more or less, complete lack of education in the past. I feel that these people because of their nomadic tendencies and disregard to responsibility are not suitable for inclusion in a scheme which might envisuage [sic] their total absorption into the Community as equal citizens.[102]

Views of this sort were not uncommon amongst Indigenous administrators in all of these settler states, which was problematic for returning Indigenous veterans who would find these officials increasingly involved in their veterans' re-establishment.

All four countries developed separate policy structures and administrative processes to handle the cases of Indigenous veterans. Invariably, veterans' re-establishment officials sought advice and support from the Canadian Indian Affairs Branch, United States Bureau of Indian Affairs, Department of Maori Affairs or Australian state Aboriginal agencies, or these agencies insinuated their agendas into the administration of Indigenous veterans' cases. As a result, Indigenous veterans fell into a sometimes hazy jurisdictional overlap between Indigenous and veterans administrations, as the following circular letter from Canada's Indian Affairs to its field staff reveals: 'The Indian Affairs Branch is not responsible for veteran legislation or administration excepting administration of grants made under Section 35A of the Veterans' Land Act. The Branch, however, has everything to do with Indians...'[103] In New Zealand, Māori could opt for regular Pākehā re-establishment channels or separate Māori alternatives. For those accessing the latter, Maori Affairs and the Rehabilitation Board established a joint Rehabilitation Finance Committee which 'controls the Rehabilitation of Maoris', with all the powers of the Board of Native Affairs and of the Rehabilitation Board 'in expending money made available by the Treasury for loans other than the expenditure on land'.[104] The office manual of the Rehabilitation Department laid out the nature of the relationship:

[102] Ibid.
[103] Report – Welfare Division - Indian Veterans' Affairs, 1946, LAC, RG 10, vol. 8927, file 68/39-1.
[104] Office Manual – Administration and Organization – Rehabilitation Department, p. A/3, ANZ, WAII 21 68a cn121 part 2.

The Native Department acts as the agent of the Board in the majority of cases where rehabilitation assistance is afforded to Maori ex-servicemen by way of loans ... the Maori ex-serviceman, if fully qualified, is offered the choice of proceeding with his application for any form of rehabilitation assistance provided by the Board either through the standard procedures or through special channels in the Native Department designed to meet any peculiar need or problem. The choice of one or other methods does not in any way affect the extent of assistance forthcoming, and in all respects, the same rehabilitation benefits are available to Maori as pakeha ex-servicemen. The services of the Native Department are utilized in all cases where land settlement involves clarification of title and taking of title to Native land, a procedure which entails considerable specialized knowledge than is required in the case of European-owned land.[105]

While this implies a smooth joint system of administration, differences in philosophy and belief in Māori capacity led to some disagreements in the execution of programs like trade training and employing Māori graduates building homes.[106]

Despite the repeated claims of equality in both regular and Māori channels of re-establishment, special policies did distinguish and at times disadvantage returning Māori servicemen and women. The specific venues for Māori farm training, for instance, were:

- 'on blocks or farms operated or controlled by the Native Department'.
- '*in special cases*' where no Native land is available, on the land development blocks controlled by the Lands Department'.
- 'At Agricultural Colleges'.
- 'On Rehabilitation Board training farms'.
- 'With private farmers, under subsidy'.[107]

The fact that Māori access to Land Department development blocks was only 'in special cases' limited Māori to the often marginal and uneconomic blocks of remaining Māori lands. What is more, once they had completed agricultural training, Māori veterans were graded differently from Pākehā veterans:

Where a Maori was a competent farmer and capable of farming in a wide area, irrespective of whether there were other Maoris there or not, he received an 'A' grade certificate for that area without any qualification. On the other hand, if it is felt that he could satisfy the same conditions only within the boundary of the Maori Land Court district in which he normally resided, his grading was limited to that district. If it was considered that a Maori applicant was up to 'A' grade standard except in respect of ability to manage his finances to obtain the best results, the grading certificate indicated this by the endorsement 'subject to

---

[105] Ibid.
[106] Thomson, "The Rehabilitation of Servicemen of World War II in New Zealand, 1940–1954," 313–314.
[107] *Rehabilitation Handbook*, pp. 23–24, ANZ, WAII 1 DA550.1.1, emphasis added.

supervision from the Department of Maori Affairs', and the department maintained supervision of the ex-serviceman's affairs after settlement until such time as the settler, in the opinion of the Maori Rehabilitation Finance Committee, was capable of assuming full control.[108]

The trouble with this structure was widespread Pākehā assumptions of Māori financial improvidence. For example, one member of the Whangarei Rehabilitation Committee 'considered that 97 per cent of Maori applicants for farm settlement were unable to handle their own finances, and added that after thirty-three years working among Maoris he had still to meet a Maori farmer who would succeed if left to his own resources'.[109] In a similar vein, Māori applicants could opt for regular rehabilitation or special Māori channels except where 'the applicant was living in a Maori community or where his application involved the occupation or acquisition of Maori land or of land through Maori channels, or where the use of any other facilities provided by the Department of Maori Affairs was required'.[110] These caveats would have funnelled a large proportion of Māori applicants through the department whether they wished it or not.

It is possible the separate administrative regimes for Indigenous veterans operated as efficiently as normal veterans' programs, but there are reasons to suspect otherwise. The case in Canada has received the most attention. For First Nations veterans, the onus for managing their re-establishment was shifted from the veteran to the local Indian agents. During Wilfred Westeste's demobilisation, an officer or non-commissioned officer was advising men of where to go to learn about options for university, vocational or agricultural training options. Westeste recalls the adviser saying, 'oh by the way, he said, you Indian boys here, he says, you don't go to any of these, he said, you go back to the reserve, and the Indian Agent will look after you.'[111] This left Westeste and other First Nations veterans almost entirely dependent on their Indian Agent for accurate information, appropriate counselling, completing and submitting applications and often a positive recommendation. Mistakes or problems in any of these categories could undermine the veteran's re-establishment.

Despite theoretical equality of access, the final report of the National Round Table on First Nations Veterans Issues concluded that in practice First Nations veterans confronted systemic problems accessing

[108] War History of Rehabilitation in NZ, 1939–65, p. 179, ANZ, WAII 21 79a-cn129.
[109] John Parkin to Director, 14 February 1944, ANZ, Re 10/1, cited in Thomson, "The Rehabilitation of Servicemen of World War II in New Zealand, 1940–1954," 317.
[110] War History of Rehabilitation in NZ, 1939–65, p. 177, ANZ, WAII 21 79a-cn129.
[111] Wilfred Westeste, quoted in Sheffield, *A Search for Equity*, 51.

information and application advice. Furthermore, the extra bureaucratic layer of the Indian Affairs Branch and the Indian Act meant: 'the result for many First Nations veterans was an unequal access to the Veterans Charter, and a steeper climb to successfully re-establish themselves than that faced by most Canadian veterans ... in the crucial ten years after 1945'.[112] Indian Agents sometimes failed to inform veterans of all their options or dissuaded veterans from options the agent felt beyond their capacities, such as education and training opportunities. The Indian Affairs Branch also used the Veterans Land Act grants to subsidise their branch's overstretched welfare budget for on-reserve housing. But while making a house available to a veteran may have improved their quality of life, it was not the purpose of such programs, which were intended to help veterans re-establish themselves in a livelihood that provided long-term stability.[113]

All too often, the insinuation of state Indigenous administrators into the re-establishment of veterans brought a reassertion of traditional paternalism. Benefits potentially placed substantial sums of money in the hands of ex-servicemen and women, something that many settler administrators viewed as counterproductive to Indigenous people's well-being. In New Zealand, one of the primary responsibilities of the Department of Maori Affairs was what the official history euphemistically termed, 'post-settlement supervision'.[114] Veterans often resented such patronising intervention, as did the following Māori veteran who recalled that 'you have to borrow money from Maori Affairs, and they send a broken-down bloody Pakeha contract painter to administer your finances. You're not even allowed to write your own cheques to pay for your bills ... Some firms were notified that they were to send the bills directly to the farm adviser.'[115]

In Canada, financial control extended into the post-war re-establishment of veterans as well. One veteran recalled, 'Once again I had to abide by the wishes of the Indian Agent and Farm Instructor. The cattle I bought with my $2320.00 was branded with the Indian Department brand I.D. [and] I could not sell one or kill one for my families [sic] consumption without his approval'.[116] During a fascinating discussion in 1955 about the potential liability of the Commonwealth to pay benefits to veterans of the Torres Strait Islander units under the Repatriation Act and the Re-establishment and Employment Act, it was made clear that

[112] Ibid., viii.
[113] Ibid., 49.
[114] War History of Rehabilitation in NZ, 1939–65, p. 177, ANZ, WAII 21 79a-cn129.
[115] Quoted in Soutar, *Nga Tama Toa*, 373.
[116] Howard Anderson, in Sheffield, *A Search for Equity*, 53.

pensions for Torres Strait Islander veterans were paid to the Queensland Director of Native Affairs.[117] An Attorney General report on the matter raised doubts about the legality of dispensing pensions in this manner but recommended a distinct arrangement that would enable the same effect.[118] The overall pattern for the returned servicemen and women is one of separate structures and little direct access to their benefits or control of their post-war re-establishment.

Those who did manage to access benefits tended to be those ex-servicemen or women who, either willingly or otherwise, were participating in post-war assimilation agendas. This is because assimilation was often explicitly woven into the access or execution of veterans programs. From Australia, Reg Saunders is a great example of this. Saunders appeared in assimilation propaganda throughout the 1950s and was shown (not always accurately) as an Aboriginal man who was succeeding living in white Australia.[119] In the United States, many Native American veterans moved off the reservations to urban areas to attain the educational opportunities afforded by the GI Bill. Their moves foreshadowed the relocation policies of the 1960s–70s, which encouraged Native Americans to move to urban areas as part of a wider assimilation agenda.[120] There is a key distinction to make here between the veterans' agency versus government agendas. Whilst officials may have *interpreted* these veterans as assimilating, often the veterans were learning new skills but without surrendering their Indigenous cultures.

However problematically, those who actually received benefits were the lucky ones, as not all Indigenous service personnel even received veterans' status and the standard array of benefits, which flowed from that identity. This was particularly the case in Australia, where two groups of Indigenous people that had served during the war were either provided a separate and significantly less generous re-establishment package or shut out altogether by the quasi- or unofficial-nature of their military service. The first instance refers to the post-war experience of Torres Strait Islanders. The same philosophical rationales about Indigenous improvidence and lower cost of living, which had underpinned the low wartime wages they received, were extended to veterans' benefits. A 1953 Treasury report noted that in 1944: 'Having regard for the cost of living of the Torres Strait Islanders, the Cabinet fixed the pension rates at, on the

[117] G. F. Wooten, Chairman, Repatriation Commission to the Secretary, Prime Minister's Department, 27 July 1955, NAA, A463, 1956/1096.
[118] L. D. Lyons, Attorney General's Department, memorandum for the Secretary – Repatriation Commission, 3 May 1955, NAA, A463, 1956/1096.
[119] Riseman, "Aboriginal Military Service and Assimilation," 163–168.
[120] Fixico, *Termination and Relocation*.

average, one-third of the equivalent Repatriation pension. In defending this, the Cabinet attached great weight to the views of the Queensland Director of Native Affairs.'[121] Rather than grant access to regular benefits, cabinet deemed that 'the natives applied for and received such benefits as were made available under the Act of Grace Schemes which were decided upon. These benefits were, of course, far less than those available under the Repatriation and Re-establishment and Employment Acts.'[122] It was not until 1971 that officials attempted to put Torres Strait Islander veterans' benefits on an equal footing with other ex-service members when their benefits were to be shifted from the Native Members of the Forces Benefits Act to the Repatriation Act.[123]

Even reduced rates were denied to those Aboriginal Australians across the threatened north of the country who had served in quasi-official or ad hoc capacities and whose service was deemed insufficient to qualify them as veterans. Men who conducted patrols around mission airfields like Bathurst Island or Groote Eylandt, capturing enemy and saving Allied airmen, or even those individuals enlisted by Donald Thomson in the NTSRU, were largely shut out of compensation. Residents in the region were frustrated and bitter at their lack of recognition and compensation when the war ended.[124] According to Yolngu wartime participant, Gerry Blitner, 'I didn't come out with no bars on my shoulder, no ribbons on my chest, no money in my pocket, no deserved [reserved] pay, no land to go back to and say this is my land.'[125] Along Canada's threatened west coast, the more than 15,000 unpaid volunteers of the Pacific Coast Militia Rangers, including the substantial First Nations membership, ended the war with nothing more the right to keep their uniform and purchase their rifle for the nominal fee of five dollars – if they had served at least ninety days.[126] The status of Indigenous members of the Alaska Territorial Guard formed during the Second World War vis-à-vis post-war support appears similarly doubtful as well, though the literature is quiet on this.[127]

Given all the issues raised thus far, was it reasonable to believe that veterans' benefits could really have made a difference in the lives of Indigenous returned service personnel? The mythology and popular

[121] Report, Assistant Secretary to the Treasurer, 17 March 1953, NAA, A1308, 762/2/135.
[122] G. F. Wooten, Chairman, Repatriation Commission to the Secretary, Prime Minister's Department, 27 July 1955, NAA, A463, 1956/1096.
[123] R. Kelly to the Director-General, 27 January 1971, NAA, A884, A6931.
[124] Riseman, *Defending Whose Country?* 95–97.
[125] Gerry Blitner, in *No Bugles, No Drums.*
[126] Lackenbauer, "Guerrillas in our Midst," 65.
[127] Charles Hendricks, "The Eskimos and the Defense of Alaska," *Pacific Historical Review* 54 (August 1985): 271–295.

memory that enshrouds veterans' re-establishment in all four countries suggests that it could and should have been a difference maker.
Yet it did not automatically translate into as successful a post-war re-
establishment, as was the norm amongst settler veterans. The addition of
state Indigenous agencies into Indigenous benefits administration led to
greater frustrations to qualify or apply for programs or to interminable
bureaucratic delays. Veterans who had survived the war and undergone
profound personal transformation as a result of their war service grew
disillusioned with heavy-handed, paternalistic and stifling administration
of their benefits.

More fundamentally, even if Indigenous veterans did have access to
benefits and qualified for comparable amounts, the bevy of programs
developed to smooth veterans' transition to civilian life, while quite
diverse and flexible, were predicated on building upon an individual's
pre-war foundation of work experience, education, skills and capital/land.
The marginal economic and social space occupied by many Indigenous
people in these four settler societies during the interwar years, combined
with widespread Indigenous land insufficiency and generally poor access
to education and healthcare, meant that the bulk of Aboriginal, Torres
Strait Islander, Māori, First Nations and Native American veterans
lacked some or all of that foundation. The Australian Deputy-Director,
Re-establishment Division saw few possibilities:

... for normal training under the [Re-establishment and Employment Act]
Scheme owing to the general lack of educational qualifications and it is felt that
the practical assistance which could be rendered would be in the form of financial assistance to enable the purchase of necessary equipment such as boats, nets,
etc., for fisherman, rabbit traps, means of transportation for rabbiters, etc. Any
purchases of the nature indicated should be effected [sic] by the Department
of Native Affairs in preference to making the money available direct to the
aborigine.[128]

New Zealand administrators likewise noted the discrepancy and sought
to overcome the shortfall in part through special emphasis on trade
training, which Māori veterans were nearly four-times' more likely to
choose than the national average, and which Jane Thomson dubs 'the
one conspicuous success story in Maori rehabilitation'.[129] More typically,
without the pre-war foundation, Indigenous veterans struggled to translate their re-establishment programs and benefits into long-term economic stability. Far from closing the gap between themselves and their

---

[128] H. T. Glover to the Director, Re-establishment Division, 4 June 1947, NAA, MP513/
A1684 Part 2.
[129] Thomson, "The Rehabilitation of Servicemen of World War II in New Zealand, 1940–
1954," 312.

non-Indigenous comrades-in-arms, the successful glow these provisions retain in the popular memory of Americans, Australians, New Zealanders and Canadians suggests the gap may even have widened.

## Conclusion

The immediate transition to peace in these four settler societies revealed diverging expectations for the future between Indigenous communities and Indigenous veterans. The existing literature largely overlooks this in favour of a narrative of hopeful aspirations, warm homecomings, veterans' benefits and Indigenous policy reform. Yes, there were hopes for a better future amongst Indigenous peoples; some veterans did experience warm homecomings and benefited from veterans' programs. Even in cases where reforms to secure Indigenous rights did not come to fruition for decades, that aspect of hope for returning veterans and their families looms large in the dominant narratives. Crucially, such accounts fail to address the difficulties, variability and ambivalence of these historical processes and the resulting diversity of responses from Indigenous societies.

Despite the ambiguities in the process, both the literature and this examination suggest the transition to peace was an important evolutionary, if not revolutionary, moment in time for Indigenous peoples and their relationship with settler societies. In the American context, Kenneth Townsend interprets this period as a proverbial crossroads for Native Americans:

Unlike their fathers, these men did not plan to resume automatically the lives they surrendered for military service. This generation of Native American veterans expected to exercise free choice in determining their future – the right of self-determination. The inclusion that Indians found in the armed forces and the racial equality that seemed so sincere and all-pervasive suggested an American society open for Indian assimilation ... At the same time, pre-war reservation development – the extension of health care, educational services and, tribal self-government, along with a redirection in reservation economics – all hinted that Indians could opt for a more traditional existence.[130]

Townsend is right that these Native American veterans returned from war expecting more choices to determine their futures. These ideas applied transnationally to other Indigenous peoples, but the situation was more complex than a binary choice between assimilation or tradition. Indeed, Joshua Nelson argues that the dichotomy between assimilation(ism)/traditionalism represents a false binary because 'both are oriented toward

---

[130] Townsend, *World War II and the American Indian*, 215.

the support of community cohesion, collective values, and basically making people's lives better ... they similarly respond to ongoing change by drawing from various existing strategies, borrowing strategies from other groups, or inventing new ones.'[131] Ultimately, when we look past structural analyses of (false) dichotomies, what we are left with is Indigenous people seeking greater acceptance and autonomy, which did not necessarily fit neatly within these two categories.

Finally, in terms of the intersection of Indigeneity and veteran-ness in the post Second World War years, it is clear that the badge of belonging embodied by military service sustained some of its inclusive magic into the post-war years. Veterans' benefits were designed to accommodate as many individual needs and aspirations as possible and in all four countries offered powerful rhetoric of equality of access. Thus many Indigenous veterans were able to access some benefits and programs in most jurisdictions, giving a little credence to the rhetoric of equality so hard won through military service. For some the benefits provided life-changing opportunities, and, for most, the funds and programs enhanced veterans' quality of life in the wake of the conflict. Nevertheless, the colonial structures of each settler state remained intact at war's end; indeed, as the next chapter makes clear, these structures were reinvigorated and reasserted post-war. The rehabilitation of assimilationist systems was evident in the involvement of Indigenous administrations in the reestablishment procedures and special provisions developed for Indigenous veterans. More often than not, Indigeneity trumped veteran-ness, to the detriment of returned Indigenous service personnel.

---

[131] Joshua Nelson, *Progressive Traditions: Identity in Cherokee Literature and Culture* (Norman: University of Oklahoma Press, 2014), 26.

# 9 Rehabilitating Assimilation

## Post-War Reconstruction and Indigenous Policy Reform

War's end was a time for soul-searching, renewal and new opportunities for societies and states just as much as for individuals. All four countries in this study undertook major programs of post-war reconstruction designed to rehabilitate civil societies and economies that had been buffeted by sixteen years of depression and war. The planning for reconstruction began long before the war itself was over: Australia's Department of Post-War Reconstruction was established in 1942, while the Canadian government created its initial Committee on Demobilization and Re-Establishment in December 1939, only three months after it declared war. In each country, these agencies examined the complex processes that they would face during the transition from war to peace: the demobilisation of military personnel, the shift from wartime to peacetime economy, the dismantling of wartime state controls and taxation and the development or expansion of social welfare systems.

Importantly though, for everyday Australians, Americans, New Zealanders and Canadians, far removed from the policy considerations of those in government, looking forward to a post-war era was invested with weighty emotional and psychological expectations. People's visions of the future were burdened by their past and present: they sought not only an end to the sacrifice and suffering of the war but also to avoid any repeat of the socio-economic pain of the Great Depression. Many also recalled the end of the First World War in 1918 and the difficult years that followed, determined that, this time, they would win the peace. In each country, the anxieties and hopes for the future were articulated in the notion of building a 'New Order' out of the chaos and pain of war and depression.

For twenty-first century audiences, there might not at first appear a clear and direct connection between the Second World War, the post-war reconstruction agenda and settler state administration of Indigenous peoples. For Canadians, Americans, Australians and New Zealanders in 1945 though, the connection was evident, sometimes glaringly so. As one prairie newspaper noted, 'some 3000 Canadian Indians were serving in the armed forces, a fact that has injected the problem of Indian policy directly into the field of post-war plans'.[1] It was principally the military service and wartime contributions that Indigenous peoples had made on behalf of the state that underscored the connection. Cynthia Enloe notes that subject minorities who served in colonial militaries subsequently could 'claim the right to participation and influence on the basis of having defended the nation-state'.[2] The result was an upswing of public interest in and discussion of Indigenous peoples, the perceived 'problem' they represented and what their future relationship should be with(in) these settler societies. Pressure on governments made them revisit and revise Indigenous policies and legislation, particularly in North America. Indigenous leaders added their own voices to these debates, working hard to consolidate or gain from their wartime contributions. Their ability to be heard or to shape the conversations, let alone the policy reforms, was uncertain and varied widely across and within these four countries. The post-war years carried possibilities for both Indigenous peoples and their settler neighbours. The shape of that future would need to be negotiated, but the groundwork laid would powerfully influence the lives of Indigenous peoples and their relationships with all four settler societies through the latter half of the twentieth century.

## Indigenous Politicisation and Activism at War's End

As the two previous chapters have made clear, Indigenous people and communities, through the war years and into the peace, faced an array of challenges as well as opportunities. Responding to these provoked a trend of political organisation and activism, which would continue during the early post-war years. At community, regional and increasingly national levels, new and long-standing Indigenous political organisations entered into dialogue in media and government halls. The end of the conflict presented both fresh prospects for positive reform as well as assimilationist threats, with widely varying circumstances across the four settler states. Fittingly then, Indigenous peoples articulated diverse aspirations during post-war debates, ranging from wishing to be left alone, to gaining acceptance, citizenship rights and even autonomy or sovereignty.

Wartime circumstances for many Indigenous peoples demanded collective action, evident from prominent national organisations that emerged during the war: in New Zealand, the Maori War Effort Organisation was

---

[1] "The Canadian Indian," *Saskatoon Star-Phoenix*, 25 September 1944, 9.
[2] Enloe, *Ethnic Soldiers*, 78. See also Young, *Minorities and the Military*; Krebs, *Fighting for Rights*.

created in 1942; in Canada, the North American Indian Brotherhood (NAIB), born in 1943, was the first Indigenous political organisation with legitimate national aspirations; the National Congress of American Indians (NCAI) formed in the United States in November 1944 with a diverse group of Native American leaders. Australia proved an anomaly in this setting, where the Aboriginal political organisation, which had waxed during the interwar years, waned somewhat during the war. The politicisation escalated during the transition from war to peace, especially in North America, and not only amongst Indigenous elites. One Canadian Indian Agent complained to his superiors about the 'marked feeling of unrest among the Indians of Tyendinaga Reserve, which, in part, can be attributed to a participation in the activities of the North American Indian Brotherhood and other Indian organizations'.[3] Even in Australia, where politicisation was less noticeable, it is noteworthy that the first strikes by Aboriginal pastoral workers occurred in the Pilbara region of Western Australia in 1946 and in Darwin in 1947.[4] Bernstein argues that in the United States a new generation of activists emerged in the shadow of the war. The extraordinary levels of interaction with the white world heightened their own awareness of their American Indian identities. They saw, often for the first time, the contrasting socio-economic standards for whites versus Native Americans on reservations, and they became more conscious of the control exerted over their lives through the law and the Bureau of Indian Affairs.[5] In this climate, the NCAI formed as a national forum to channel Native American voices when addressing federal Indian policy and laws.[6]

In New Zealand, too, the Māori Parliamentarian Paraire Paikea had told the Prime Minister that, 'In the minds of the Maori people, the establishment of the Maori War [Effort] Organization is the greatest thing that has happened in the history of the Maori people, since the signing of the Treaty of Waitangi. They feel that in the organization lies

---

[3] Agent's Report for the Quarter ending 31 December 1945, A. D. Moore Indian Agent, LAC, RG 10, vol.6811, file 1/1-2-16, pt. 1. See also Sheffield, *Redman's on the Warpath*, 138.

[4] Mahli Nielson, "Hiatus or Catalyst? The Impact of the Second World War on Aboriginal Activism and Assimilation, 1939–1953" (BA [Honours] Thesis, Australian National University, 2008), 62–64; Kay Saunders, "Inequalities of Sacrifice: Aboriginal and Torres Strait Islander Labour in Northern Australia During the Second World War," *Labour History* 69 (November 1995): 131–148; Graham Alcorn, *The Struggle of the Pilbara Station Hands for Decent Living Standards and Human Rights* (Stockton, NSW: Max Brown, 2001).

[5] Bernstein, *World War II and the American Indians*, 171.

[6] Thomas W. Cowger, "'The Crossroads of Destiny': The NCAI's Landmark Struggle to Thwart Coercive Termination," *American Indian Culture and Research Journal* 20, No 4 (1996): 121–122.

the future prosperity, development and happiness of their people.'[7] He and other Māori parliamentarians fought for the MWEO to continue not just through the end of the war but into peacetime as well. Indeed, as Richard Hill writes, the 'extra tasks that they encouraged it to take on, in fact, increasingly included preparations for peacetime relationships and organisation of Maori'.[8] One observer had 'been to numerous Maori tribal and their executive committee meetings, and their work in the past few months has had nothing to do with the war'.[9]

Given the central role of Indigenous military service to the propitious post-war climate, it would be logical to assume that Indigenous veterans were at the heart of the post-war politicisation. While some returning veterans became engaged early on as political leaders and activists for their communities, most noticeably in the United States, this appears to be the exception rather than the norm in the immediate post-war era. For instance, in New Zealand, some of the senior officers from the Maori Battalion, including Rangi Royal, as well as Lt. Colonels Keiha, Awatere and Henare, took up prominent roles as Maori Welfare Officers. Sir Charles Bennett remarks:

after the war, when we came back and settled down into civilian life, a lot of the men who were in the Māori Battalion wanted to continue their service to the Māori people. Then came the 1945 *Social and Economic Advancement Act* and the formation of our tribal committees and executives and welfare officers. I think many of the men of the battalion felt that this was a niche, a place for them to continue to serve the people, as they had during the war. A lot of the welfare officers and administrative officers in the organisation were men of the 28th Māori Battalion.[10]

These individuals clashed with the Pākehā bureaucrats of the Maori Affairs Department over who controlled their activities. These welfare officers pressed for Māori autonomy via local and regional committee structures from the MWEO. After the National Party came to government in 1949, the bureaucracy successfully halted these welfare officers' advocacy.[11]

In Canada, the famous First Nations veteran, Thomas Prince, was asked to join the Manitoba Indian delegation as its spokesman before the Special Joint Parliamentary Committee on the Indian Act in 1947.[12] The

[7] Paikea to War Cabinet, 3 April 1943, ANZ, Walter Nash Papers 2067.
[8] Hill, *State Authority, Indigenous Autonomy*, 198.
[9] *Hawk's Bay Herald Tribune*, 11 April 1945, quoted in Angela Ballara, *Iwi: The Dynamics of Māori Tribal Organisation from c. 1769 to c. 1945* (Wellington: Victoria University Press, 1998), 318.
[10] Sir Charles Bennett, in *Early Stories from Te Tīmatanga Tātau Tātau*, 316.
[11] Gardiner, *Te Mura O Te Ahi*, 180–181.
[12] *SJC*, Minutes and Proceedings no. 19, 8 May 1947.

most striking cases of Indigenous veterans taking leading roles appears to be in the campaign for the state franchise in Arizona and New Mexico, where Native American veterans trying to vote in 1947 sparked court cases that overturned state barriers to Indigenous exercise of the franchise.[13] These notable figures aside, more often in the immediate postwar years the veterans' impact lay in being potent symbols employed by more senior and experienced Indigenous political leadership, rather than as dynamic leaders themselves. Throughout the literature on Indigenous war service, the notion of their return to positions of importance in their own communities is common, perhaps because, as Robert Innes writes, it 'fits nicely with the poetic image of the victorious warrior on the battlefield continuing the fight for freedom at home. However, to link Indian postwar political activities to Indian veterans' wartime experience without any substantiation is not justified.'[14]

Most veterans were still wrestling with the challenges of the transition to civilian life, such as Reg Saunders in Australia. He felt a great responsibility to become engaged as a spokesman for Aboriginal rights and better treatment and did undertake some speeches.[15] He later noted:

[There] were no great jobs like there are for Aborigines today in public life. If you were involved in Aboriginal affairs in those days you paid your own way and I had a wife and four or five kids. They had to be fed, so I just couldn't get away ... couldn't spare the time to do those sorts of things that I would like to have done.[16]

Innes argues that in Canada, the majority of returning First Nations veterans were still young and politically inexperienced. While they could speak of battle experience, the majority had left as teenagers and did not yet have the skills or sometimes social capital to assume leadership roles within their Bands. Instead, they began to attend meetings, listening and learning from the Elder leaders as a form of 'political apprenticeships'. Some anomalies aside, the bulk of Indigenous veterans came into their own politically, primarily, in the later 1950s and 1960s. For instance, during the 1960s, all leaders of the Federation of Saskatchewan Indians were Second World War veterans.[17] Reports suggest the pattern Innes observed in Canada was paralleled in the experience of Native American, Māori, Aboriginal and Torres Strait Islander ex-servicemen and women. Many of the leaders of Indigenous political organisations that drove the

[13] Bernstein, *American Indians and World War II*, 138–139.
[14] Innes, "I'm On Home Ground Now. I'm Safe," 709.
[15] Ramsland and Mooney, *Remembering Aboriginal Heroes*, 193.
[16] Reg Saunders, in Hall, *Fighters from the Fringe*, 97. See also Riseman, "Aboriginal Military Service and Assimilation," 164–166.
[17] Innes, "I'm On Home Ground Now. I'm Safe," 711–712.

revival and protests of the late 1960s across all four countries were veterans of the Second World War, and, by the 1970s and 1980s, Korea and Vietnam veterans, too, were active in Indigenous affairs.[18]

Those future battles for rights and policy change were still far away; in the immediate post-war years what is striking is how different were the particular constellations of opportunity and threat that Aboriginal and Torres Strait Islanders, First Nations, Native Americans and Māori faced. The first thing that Indigenous leaders sought to do was to capitalise on the generally positive images and feelings generated by their wartime contributions amongst settler societies and governments. Claudia Orange has suggested that 'Tirikatene no doubt hoped that the climate of opinion had been improved by Maori performance in the war effort; that there was a chance for the [Labour] government to convert wartime policy into the fulfilment of its earlier promise of mana Maori motuhake [autonomy], first made in a policy statement on Maori affairs in 1925.'[19] In Canada, Innes argues that the existing Indian leadership was still pushing the Indian rights issues. Yet, they recognised the shifting social attitudes and applied the veterans' contributions as part of their rhetorical strategy to influence change.[20] For Native Americans, as Russell Barsh argues, the wartime media coverage of Indians as good soldiers continued to influence public opinion about their contributions towards winning the war.[21] In Australia, the Victorian executive of the RSL argued 'the fact that an Aborigine has served his country in the Armed Forces should be sufficient to warrant his enjoying all the privileges of an Australian citizen.'[22] In this sense then, it seemed a propitious time for Indigenous people to press their claims and aspirations upon settler societies that might prove unusually receptive in the post-war climate.

Running as a countercurrent to the constructive potential of shifting settler society attitudes were a number of policy directions that Indigenous leaders viewed as threats. In Australia, and to a lesser extent in the other three settler states, Indigenous leaders faced stubborn indifference and racism that remained well-entrenched in spite of their

---

[18] See, for instance, Noah Riseman, "Ex-service Activism after 1945," in *Serving Our Country*, 261–281; Noah Riseman, "Indigenous Soldiers: Native American and Aboriginal Australian Service in Vietnam," in *New Perceptions of the Vietnam War: Essays on the War, the South Vietnamese Experience, the Diaspora and the Continuing Impact*, ed. Nathalie Huynh Chau Nguyen (Jefferson, NC: McFarland & Company, Inc., 2015), 214–218.

[19] Orange, "An Exercise in Maori Autonomy," 252.

[20] Innes, "I'm On Home Ground Now. I'm Safe," 686.

[21] Russell Lawrence Barsh, "War and the Reconfiguration of American Indian Society," *Journal of American Studies* 35 (2001): 380.

[22] CW Joyce, secretary, Victorian branch RSL, to JC Neagle, federal secretary, RSL, 28 March 1947, National Library of Australia, RSL papers, series 1, MSS 6609, Box 158, file 2248c.

wartime exploits. In the United States, the newly formed NCAI, the first successful national organisation controlled by Native Americans, found itself not only trying to capitalise on its successful war service but increasingly to battle the emerging Congressional interest in forcibly terminating federal relationships with tribes. Indeed, the NCAI embarked on an unprecedented campaign to stop or amend the emerging termination policies.[23] Māori leaders, particularly in Parliament, found themselves manoeuvring to consolidate their wartime gains in the face of a Pākehā government determined to reverse wartime concessions to Māori autonomy. Māori MPs organised four major conferences of their leaders to highlight Māori desires for a new direction in administration and especially the place of Native Affairs Department.[24] The particular mix of challenge and possibility combined with long-standing aspirations and debates around the place of Indigenous peoples to shape the goals of Indigenous politicisation and activism in the post-war period.

The aspirations to which Indigenous leaders directed their efforts were of necessity, and in keeping with the tremendous diversity across Indigenous peoples, remarkably varied. At one end of the spectrum, most evident in Canada, were some Indigenous leaders who sought simply to be left alone. This theme permeates several of the 411 written briefs submitted to the Canadian Special Joint Parliamentary Committee (hereafter SJC) to examine the Indian Act between 1946 and 1948. The SJC would sit for two years, gathering evidence from witnesses and written briefs, including First Nations representatives for the first time appearing in high-level policymaking. One First Nations chief wrote simply:

> I want to remain an Indian.
> I do not want to pay taxes.
> I want to remain on the old Indian Act.
> I have nothing against any school.
> I do not want white people on our reserve.[25]

The St. Regis Iroquois expressed similar sentiments:

We want to remain Indian in this fast changing world. We have seen the results of the white man's way of life. We think it better to remain a good Indian than a poor imitation of a white man! We want to live our own life on our reservations, without interference from outside sources, and governed by our own chiefs appointed in our own way ... In plain English we want our treaties to be respected and lived up to![26]

---

[23] Cowger, "The Crossroads of Destiny," 122.
[24] Orange, "An Exercise in Maori Autonomy," 250.
[25] *SJC*, Minutes and Proceedings no. 5, 20 March 1947, 164.
[26] *SJC*, Minutes and Proceedings no. 33, 12 June 1947, 1745.

Even if this meant preserving the status quo, it did not constitute an endorsement of settler policies per se but rather reflected wariness that any reforms could actually worsen the socio-political status for First Nations.

At another extreme were Indigenous leaders and activists who argued for outright sovereignty, free from settler society control. Amongst the most vocal of these were the Six Nations nationalists in the United States and Canada who had agitated throughout the war against conscription on the grounds that the settler governments in Washington and Ottawa had no authority to compel Six Nations people to serve.[27] Hauptman notes that in New York State, 'as newspapers announced congressional intentions to "free Indians" from government supervision, the Iroquois became even more assertive in their calls for tribal sovereignty and the retention of "time-honored" treaty rights'.[28] North of the border, in their submission to the SJC, the Community from Lake of Two Mountains (also known as Oka or Kanesatake) opened bluntly:

We hereby resolve not to subject to amendment to the Indian Act. As we are resolved to abolish the Indian Act, by virtue of our ancient treaties; that by virtue of our treaty rights Indians of the Six Nations are not liable to any federal or provincial laws within our territories; that by virtue of our treaty rights Indians of the Six Nations are not liable for payment of taxes to either Dominion or provincial governments. That by right of our treaty rights we demand of the Canadian Government the recognition and respect of our sovereign rights and privileges as a Nation.[29]

Of course, it is worth remembering that for many Indigenous communities in more remote regions with limited or intermittent contact with the settler state, the post-war transition raised barely a ripple on the surface of their worlds. In Arnhem Land east of Darwin, the end of the war even amounted to a resumption of inter-clan warfare which had been going on in the 1930s among rival Yolngu leaders.[30]

Much more common were Indigenous spokespeople who tried to parley military service into expanded social and economic opportunity and enhanced rights, often articulated within the only rights paradigm available at that time – citizenship rights. Cherokee woman Ruth Muskrat Bronson had long been an activist for Native American unity

---

[27] Sheffield, *Redman's on the Warpath*, 145; Hauptman, *The Iroquois Struggle for Survival*, 4–9.

[28] Hauptman, *The Iroquois Struggle for Survival*, 49.

[29] *SJC*, Minutes and proceedings, no. 33, 12 June 1947, 1794–1795.

[30] Phyllis Batumbil, Australian Institute for Aboriginal and Torres Strait Islander Studies, RISEMAN_N01.

and self-determination since meeting with President Calvin Coolidge as part of the Committee of One Hundred in 1923.[31] In 1944 Bronson published *Indians are People, Too*, in which she outlined the historic policies and practices of assimilation that had disempowered Native Americans and hindered their social and economic opportunities. Significantly, Bronson explicitly invoked Native American men and women's participation in the war effort, both in the services and on the home front, to argue their capacity if granted the opportunity to participate as equals in American society and in control of their own destinies. She drew on the language of Franklin Roosevelt's Four Freedoms – freedom of speech, freedom of religion, freedom from want and freedom of fear – and his calls for self-determination for colonised peoples. Bronson argued that Native Americans deserved the same considerations: 'For surely the people of America would not knowingly permit Indian children and older Indian people of America, unable to provide for themselves, to live in extreme want while under the guardianship of a nation strong enough and generous enough to stretch out its arms to the ends of the world to help those of other nations who are helpless.'[32]

In Canada, Chief Nanawin from Poplar River similarly queried before the SJC in 1947: 'Why could Indians not share equal Benefits as the white people in fishing, in agriculture, in social affairs. I[t] would drive a white man crazy if he only had sixty dollars coming to him after hard work.'[33] The brief submitted by the Aboriginal Natives of the Fraser Valley and Interior Tribes of British Columbia claimed that:

the time has come for the recognition of us Natives as people with equal intelligence and integrity, eligible to exercise equal status of full citizenship privileges [while] maintaining all our traditions, aboriginal rights, interests and benefits, a system identical to that granted to the Maori Indians of New Zealand, viz. Representation in Parliament, and in the administration of the Natives General Affairs.[34]

Other Canadian First Nations disagreed regarding citizenship rights; many would have sided with the Abenaki delegation to the SJC, who stated that the 'right to vote and the responsibility to pay taxes do not interest us at all'.[35]

---

[31] Gretchen Harvey, "Cherokee and American: Ruth Muskrat Bronson, 1897–1982" (PhD Thesis, Arizona State University, 1996), 50.
[32] Ruth Muskrat Bronson, *Indians Are People, Too* (New York: Friendship Press, 1944), 15–16.
[33] *SJC*, Minutes and Proceedings, no. 2, 11 March 1947, 58.
[34] *SJC*, Minutes and Proceedings, no. 2, 11 March 1947, 52.
[35] *SJC*, Minutes and Proceedings, no. 33, 12 June 1947, 1741.

In the United States, it was veterans' legal action that resolved the final vestiges of restrictions on citizenship rights.[36] Arizona and New Mexico, along with Maine, were the only American states which had not granted voting rights between the 1924 Indian Citizenship Act and the American entry into the Second World War. Frank Harrison, a Mohave Apache veteran, tried to vote in 1947 in Arizona's Maricopa County, but the country recorder refused to register him, citing a 1928 decision that Indians were legally 'persons under guardianship' and therefore disqualified. In New Mexico, the case *Trujillo v. Garley* revolved around a different issue. Miguel Trujillo, a Pueblo ex-Marine, was denied the right to vote because the state constitution considered Indians a people 'not taxed'. Judges' decisions in both cases struck down state constitutional barriers and opened up the franchise to Native Americans.

Alongside enhanced rights, the most prevalent line of Indigenous advocacy was for various degrees of autonomy and freedom. This could take different forms in different constituencies, even within each country. For example, in the United States, many Indigenous leaders and veterans argued for the freedom to choose their future path in life, whether that meant a traditional cultural path on a reservation or a more integrated life within settler society, an option that the wartime decrease in prejudice promised as a possibility. This became the official line for the NCAI, which was composed of many voices speaking for both alternatives; Townsend describes the NCAI as a 'national mouthpiece for Indians, regardless of tribal affiliation: a single, vocal force in pursuit of equality, freedom of choice, and non-discrimination'.[37] Some Indigenous voices articulated decidedly assimilationist, or at least integrationist views. For example, Joseph Bruner, national president of the American Indian Federation, in a letter to a congressman in 1945, asked rhetorically, 'Don't you think World Wars I and II, alone entitle him to the enjoyment of FREEDOM at HOME from government supervision and direction by people less capable than himself, and a final settlement with his guardian-government?'[38] Amongst such diversity, many Americans heard only those pronouncements that aligned with their own views on the future of Native Americans.

In New Zealand, Māori were very concerned by war's end about sustaining, solidifying and even expanding the autonomy, or rangatiratanga that the Pākehā state had conceded to the Maori War Effort Organisation.

---

[36] Franco, *Crossing the Pond*, 190–202; Bernstein, *American Indian and World War II*, 138–40.

[37] Townsend, *World War II and the American Indian*, 208.

[38] Joseph Bruner to William Stigler, 3 September 1945, University of Oklahoma, Western History Collections, Box 22, William G. Stigler papers, quoted in Fixico, *Termination and Relocation*, 14.

Tirikatene declared that Māori control of their own affairs was 'the most vital matter being discussed both generally and politically on every Maori marae in New Zealand at the present time'.[39] Pairare Paikea and, after his death in 1943, other Māori parliamentarians, initially envisioned establishing a new Ministry of Maori Welfare that would operate in parallel with, or even supplant, the existing Ministry of Native Affairs. Paikea and his followers eventually backed away from a distinct ministry because their allies in the governing Labour Party baulked. Such a degree of autonomy as Māori attained was unimaginable for Aboriginal and Torres Strait Islander Australians, First Nations or Native Americans at that time, but representatives of these groups agitated for greater measures of self-governance and autonomy and a loosening of controls in various ways. In Canada, this meant both enhancing the powers of local community leaders and band councils and reducing the authority of the Indian Agent and Superintendent General of the Indian Affairs Branch in Ottawa. The Lower Kootenay Band articulated this in their brief to the SJC:

We want our reserve to have a good chief and councilmen and to have them make rulings on the reserve. We want our chief to stand in front, not next to the Indian Agent. The Indian Agent has too much to say; the Indian Agent has too much power over the chief on our reserve. We want the Indian Agent to be set back a step behind the chief.[40]

In Australia, there was minimal Indigenous activism before the late 1950s, as the war significantly disrupted the fledgling activism of the 1930s. For instance, Melbourne's Australian Aborigines' League lost much of its momentum after the death of leader William Cooper in 1941. Moreover, because of the nature of the states' control over Indigenous livelihoods, much of the demands of the 1930s activists seem modest when compared to the other settler nations. While they did advocate for citizenship rights such as the vote, at the most basic level Indigenous people were demanding the right to be freed from the restrictions imposed by the state protection boards. In this, they did achieve some placating reforms during the war. New South Wales reforms to Aboriginal affairs included the protection board being reconstituted as the Aborigines Welfare Board in 1940. More significantly, from 1943 the Welfare Board included two elected Aboriginal representatives. Other states would eventually adopt similar reforms in the 1950s. Over time these elected representatives, such as Aborigines' Progressive Association founder William Ferguson and secretary Pearl Gibbs, would grow disenchanted at the

---

[39] Hill, *State Authority, Indigenous Autonomy*, 203.
[40] *SJC*, Minutes and Proceedings no. 21, 13 August 1946, 865.

Board's obstinate commitment to assimilation and disinterest in self-determination. Even so, in the immediate post-war period, the cosmetic reforms – appearing to give Indigenous people a voice – as well as continuous Aboriginal mobility and the generally improved economic situation, defused activism.[41]

Whether they were advocating to be left alone, for sovereignty or for citizenship rights, there was a key commonality among the desires of Indigenous leaders: self-determination. Most were rejecting assimilationist assumptions of settler societies, instead advocating the right to choose the manner and terms of engagement with settler society, framed within the context of historical treaties where relevant. Indigenous veterans were also seeking their own economic opportunities and rights to practice their culture in ways that suited their identities as modern Indigenous people. In essence, Indigenous people across the four settler nations were pushing for much the same thing, but the historical, political and legal parameters in each country determined how limited were their demands, and their ability to achieve them in the post-war climate.

### Settler Attitudes towards Indigenous Peoples

Amongst the most remarkable phenomena to emerge from this transnational and comparative examination was settler societies' shared engagement in policy and legislative review and reform vis-à-vis Indigenous people between 1945 and 1953. All four countries would see widespread calls for reform of Indigenous policy and/or enhanced rights for Indigenous populations from diverse sources, including veterans' groups. In settler societies where, in the first half of the twentieth century, public perspectives of Indigenous peoples were characterised more by indifference than any other adjective, this was profoundly unusual. At its core, what generated the attention was the surprisingly high degree of publicity and propagandistic utilisation of Indigenous military service and wartime contributions in the mass media of each settler state. This was particularly noticeable in North America and New Zealand while in Australia media coverage focused primarily on particular individuals such as Reg Saunders. Publicity was only one cause of the heightened awareness. Wartime conditions led to a huge expansion of interactions between settlers and Indigenous people, whether in military service, through settler invasion of previously sheltered Indigenous territories, or Indigenous movement into urban centres. The result ensured that Americans, New Zealanders, Canadians and even Australians were thinking about Native

[41] Goodall, *Invasion to Embassy*, 262.

Americans, First Nations, Māori, Aboriginal and Torres Strait Islander people to an unprecedented degree at war's end.

This phenomenon was perhaps most profound among Americans, who had been barraged with images and information about Native Americans in the war effort. Mary Weston argues that overwhelmingly:

Indians who served in World War II were portrayed in the press as the quintessential braves on the warpath. The old image of the bloodthirsty savage transformed into that of a noble warrior for the Allied cause ... Indians' homefront contributions to the war were portrayed in a positive light that made them out to be unswervingly patriotic and loyal to the American cause.[42]

Such extensive and positive press combined with propaganda use of individuals like Ira Hayes to raise the profile of Native Americans dramatically in the minds of Americans. More than this, the positive nature of the coverage combined with the wartime setting to generate both sympathy and admiration amongst settler society.[43] These divergent images, deemed 'warped' by Lawrence Hauptman, would underpin a transformative period in US Indian policy. Popular assumptions, grafted onto a limited understanding of the historical, legal and political status of Native American peoples, led many Americans to endorse Indians' participation in American society.[44] A widely read article in Reader's Digest by O. K. Armstrong, who claimed to have interviewed Native Americans across the country, assured Americans that Native Americans who had served would demand 'a greater share of American freedom'. Those who had 'tasted economic opportunity for the first time' would not be content to 'live in a shack and loaf under a blanket'.[45]

Where the Indian Reorganization Act had pitted liberals and conservatives against one another since the 1930s, the post-war era would bring both progressively together in a bipartisan desire to 'reward' Native American loyalty and ability by getting the government off the back of the Indian. From the liberal perspective, the goal was to provide more rights and essentially treat Native Americans as equals without distinction, even if that meant severing their Indigenous rights. From the conservative perspective, severing Native Americans' special status would save money otherwise spent servicing reservations through the BIA. Thus began the march, 'shrouded in liberalism and morality', as Tom Holm puts it, to the termination of the federal government's trust relationship

---

[42] Mary Ann Weston, *Native Americans in the News: Images of Indians in the Twentieth Century Press* (Westport, CT: Greenwood Press, 1996), 94.

[43] Franco, *Crossing the Pond*, 144.

[44] Hauptman, *The Iroquois Struggle for Survival*, 2.

[45] O. K. Armstrong, "Set the American Indians Free!" *Reader's Digest* 47 (August 1945): 47–48, in Holm, "Fighting a White Man's War," 76.

with many Native American tribes.[46] While the ideologies underpinning termination came to the fore in the shadow of the war, it took time to formulate such ideas as policy, which ultimately came to fruition from 1953. Of course, lost among both liberals and conservatives was the perspective and wishes of Native Americans themselves.

Canadians were similarly much affected by Indigenous contributions to the national war effort. This had begun before the guns fell silent, with the House Committee on Reconstruction and Re-establishment in May 1944 dedicating several sessions to the conditions of the First Nations population. One letter sent to that committee conveyed a prevalent sentiment: 'there are Indian men and boys in the Services who will not want to come home to Reserves. They are making sacrifices on a par with the "Whites" for Freedom, they are fighting for a freedom they never had. One of the first places where we could well begin to dispense the "Four Freedoms" is right in our midst: to the Indians.'[47] So clear was that link for many Canadians that the 'Indian Problem', as it was usually termed, was hitched to the considerable momentum of the national post-war reconstruction agenda.

Interestingly, while First Nations' wartime contributions had forced some Canadians to re-evaluate their positions, as the transition to peace began, settler society increasingly turned the scrutiny inwards upon itself and its treatment of Indigenous peoples. What they saw did not impress; a 1945 *Kamloops Sentinel* article noted:

> The truly sad picture these Indians present today is a direct reflection of our unjust administration. They are wards of the government in the fullest sense of the word, and we, the citizens are responsible for the actions of our government. What the Indian is today we have made him through neglect ... [and] in criticizing the Indians, we are but criticizing ourselves.[48]

Canadian Indian policy and administration, which had for decades largely gone about its business without any but the most cursory and laudatory interest from the general public, suddenly came under scathing attack. The critique extended to Canadian society itself, as Canadians' gaze upon the marginalisation of First Nations made them reflect on their country's own failures to live up to the ideals of equality, freedom and democracy.[49] Many Canadians were sufficiently moved to write or otherwise register their dissatisfaction with the responsible government

---

[46] Ibid., 79. See also Fixico, *Termination and Relocation*.
[47] Winifred Paris to the Committee on Reconstruction and Re-establishment, 6 August 1944, LAC, RG 10, vol. 8585, file #1/1-2-17.
[48] "Champions Native Indians," *Kamloops Sentinel*, 4 April 1945.
[49] Sheffield, "Rehabilitating the Indigene," 349.

agencies and to debate Indian policy in the press. The result was a rare and vibrant public debate about the current and future place of First Nations people in Canada.

Strikingly, while Pākehā were increasingly discussing Māori and their future as the war drew to a close, there was little of either the potent attack on the existing administrative regime such as the American public undertook, or the self-reflection so evident in Canada. Instead, amidst assumptions of assimilation (rarely explicitly articulated) was a strong self-congratulatory current. A 1947 *Dominion* article expressed such sentiments common amongst Pākehā:

> In no other country of the British Commonwealth of Nations is there greater freedom for its original inhabitants to go forward in harmony with others towards the full development of its resources. Maori and pakeha mingle and co-operate in local and national service, in employment, in sport and indeed, in all departments of our social life.[50]

The inattention to Pākehā's own role in the future relationship with Māori conveys their underlying confidence and complacency regarding race relations in New Zealand. What also highlights this was the focus on what Pākehā perceived to be the one remaining flaw among Māori that was inhibiting their final achievement of assimilation. Pākehā usually articulated this as responsibility, initiative or self-reliance, and Pākehā were enthused that the war, and especially the Māori war effort, seemed to have at long last unleashed or revealed this precious trait.[51] As one Pākehā church representative, speaking before a conference of Māori leaders in late 1944, claimed:

> it was his experience that the Maori did not want to be regarded as a race to be humoured, but to be invested with responsibility. It was his experience that the Maori could assume responsibility, and if there was anything that preserved the democratic way of life it was the self-reliance of the individual, the family and the race. That self-reliance must be aspired to, attained and held.[52]

New Zealanders then conceptualised the Maori War Effort Organisation narrowly as the very embodiment of 'responsibility' they hoped would continue into the future, enabling Māori to complete their journey to full assimilation.

One potential anomaly in the pattern of heightened settler awareness of both Indigenous peoples and their relationship with the settler state during the transition to peace is Australia. Much of the awareness in the other three countries was predicated on extensive wartime publicity.

---

[50] "Maintenance of Maori Culture," *Dominion*, 12 June 1947.
[51] Sheffield, "Rehabilitating the Indigene," 354–355.
[52] "Welfare of Maori – 30 Tribes Represented at Conference," *Dominion*, 19 October 1944.

Robert Hall has argued that in Australia during the war there was an intentional suppression of Aboriginal stories in the major newspapers. He notes a tailing off of media coverage of Aboriginal subjects in Sydney papers, with serious implications for Aboriginal and Torres Strait Islander peoples after the war.[53] Notwithstanding Hall's point about media coverage, there is also evidence that some white Australians wrestled with the same symbolic challenge that Indigenous wartime contributions represented in the other three settler societies. For instance, poet and Sapper, 'Bert' Beros, made famous for penning the verse 'The Fuzzy Wuzzy Angels' about Papua New Guinean carriers on the Kokoda Trail, also wrote a less well-known poem entitled, 'The Coloured Digger':

> He came and joined the colours
> When the War God's anvil rang,
> He took up modern weapons to replace his boomerang,
> He Proved he's still a warrior, in action not afraid,
> He faced the blasting red-hot fire
> From mortar and grenade;
> One day he'll leave the Army,
> Then join the League he shall,
> And he hopes we'll give a better deal
> To the Aboriginal.[54]

Certainly, many soldiers who either served alongside Aboriginal or Torres Strait Islander comrades or who worked with Aboriginal labourers appear to have been engaged by the incongruity, as were three men serving in the Northern Territory whose thoughts on the matter were each published in an article entitled 'The Case for the Original Australian'. Sergeant W. Smith suggested that the 'Atlantic Charter, like charity, must begin at home'; Second Pte D. R. Pearce argued that given Aboriginal contributions in the war, the '"new world" planned for tomorrow must include a policy of advancement and betterment for the original Australians'; and Sgt V. C. Hall hoped that some 'day, some time, the story of the Australian native's service to his country will be written ... Let us hope that the white man's gratitude for the native's efforts will be more enduring than the cold ashes of the camp fires Jacky helped them build.'[55] Beyond these few quotations were many other examples, including press clippings, indicating that a diverse range of Australians were indeed aware of Aboriginal and Torres Strait Islander service and were making conceptual connections similar to those seen in other settler

---

[53] Hall, *The Black Diggers*, 191.
[54] Sapper Bert Beros, "The Coloured Digger," in *The Fuzzy Wuzzy Angels and Other Verses* (Sydney: F.H. Johnston Publishing Company, 1943), 25.
[55] "The Case for the Original Australian," *Salt* 11, no. 7 (1945): 34–37.

societies. Such individuals, groups and organisations included churches, veterans' organisations, academics, the Women's Christian Temperance Union, the Premier of South Australia, unionists, politicians of various stripes, teachers groups, the British Empire Union, the Australian Communist Party, the Canberra Citizens' Rights Committee and the Federal Pacifist Council of Australia.[56]

## Post-War Reform

All four states would see varying degrees of governmental review, new legislation and policy regimes for Indigenous populations. Some of these, such as the American establishment of its policy of termination or the Australian adoption of assimilation, were dramatic new policy directions that had major implications for the Indigenous population. In New Zealand and Canada by contrast, new legislation, in the Maori Social and Economic Advancement Act (1945) and the Indian Act (1951) respectively, produced more limited change, though both were important nonetheless for what they did and did not do. The post-war patterns, viewed in comparison, are revealing about the impact of the war, as well as about the place of Indigenous minorities in settler societies.

Perhaps most pertinent to the issue of Second World War service was the question of how each nation would henceforth consider Indigenous people in their defence forces. In Canada and the United States, where First Nations and Native Americans had been the least singled out under wartime policies, the status quo would continue in the post-war era: Indigenous people could continue to serve without official restriction. In the United States, the most significant change post-war was the 1948 directive to desegregate black and white troops. It would not be until the 1970s, after racial tensions between black and white soldiers witnessed in Vietnam, that the US military would adopt education programs to combat racism within its ranks.[57] Meanwhile, Native Americans have continued to be disproportionately represented in the American armed forces, and many of the stereotypes of the martial race continued to follow them in conflicts such as Korea and Vietnam.[58] The same cannot be said for Canada where, after anecdotally strong First Nations service percentages in Korea, Indigenous service declined well below their proportion of population by the twenty-first century.

---

[56] See correspondence in NAA, A431, 1950/597.
[57] See James Westheider, *Fighting on Two Fronts: African Americans and the Vietnam War* (New York: New York University Press, 1997).
[58] Holm, *Strong Hearts, Wounded Souls*; LaDuke, *The Militarization of Indian Country*.

The biggest transformations, at least as far as policy was concerned, were in New Zealand and Australia. In New Zealand, there were divisions over whether to continue to allow Māori to serve in their own unit, or to integrate them entirely across the forces. This was a complex debate where ideas about Māori nationalism, integration and assimilation all intersected, dividing opinions among both Māori and Pākehā. Veterans of the Maori Battalion were the most prominent advocates for a separate unit, arguing that it would be the most efficient way to mobilise a unified Māori force, as well as to preserve their cultural identity. Authorities argued for integration, claiming it would provide more career and educational opportunities for Māori within the armed forces. As New Zealand became involved in conflicts such as Korea, Malaya and Vietnam, having a mixed force proved beneficial when interacting with local communities who saw no racial segregation. By the 1960s, there was a generation gap between veterans of the Maori Battalion who still consistently called for a separate unit while the younger generation of Māori soldiers generally expressed satisfaction with the interracial dynamics of New Zealand's military.[59] Even so, while the official policy of the time described the military reforms as integration, it did align with a wider assimilationist push to end separate Māori institutions and bring them into the mainstream. It was not until the 1990s that the New Zealand Defence Force adopted a genuinely bicultural approach, embedding aspects of Māori knowledge and cultural practice across the services.[60]

Upon war's conclusion, the Australian forces reinstated the rules barring enlistment of people 'not substantially of European origin or descent'. Yet, there was a pushback from both Aboriginal and non-Indigenous veterans who sent letters to the press protesting this discrimination. Reg Saunders argued that 'soldiers he had met in the army were not colour conscious towards the aboriginal, and he felt sure that they would never agree with this discrimination.'[61] In 1948, Australian Military Regulations and Orders 177 removed references to enlistees needing to be of European origin or descent, opening the door for Aboriginal people to join the Army. The RAAF and Navy continued to restrict enlistments until 1951 amendments to the Defence Act removed the exemptions for non-Europeans from compulsory call-up during peacetime. Even so,

[59] Corinne David-Ives, "Integration Politics and the New Zealand Army: The Fate of the Maori Battalion in the Wake of the Second World War," in *War Memories: Commemoration, Recollections, and Writings on War*, ed. Stéphanie A. H. Bélanger and Renée Dickason (Montreal: McGill-Queen's University Press, 2017), 373–87.

[60] Debbie Hohaia, "In Search of a Decolonised Military: Māori Cultural Learning Experiences in the New Zealand Defence Force," *Kōtuitui: New Zealand Journal of Social Sciences Online* 11, no. 1 (2016): 47–58.

[61] *The Daily News* (Perth), 26 March 1946, 6.

there would continue to be exemptions and inconsistencies in Australia's approach to the newly implemented national service scheme.[62] One driving force behind Australia's changed approach to military service was assimilation. In Australia, magazines, newspapers, government pamphlets and even some branches of the RSL promoted military service as a site of assimilation.[63] In this sense, the Australian armed forces were also reflecting wider assimilationist pushes in settler-Indigenous relations across all four settler states.

In terms of broader post-war reform, New Zealand would see its first legislative shot fired at an altered peacetime Māori-state relationship shortly before war's end in 1945. A central concern in the minds of Pākehā, when considering post-war directions for Māori, was how to sustain the energy and dynamism unleashed by the Māori war effort.[64] The Rehabilitation Handbook, in seeking to reassure Māori veterans, concluded that every 'effort is being made to enable him to return to civil life and take his part in the post-war reconstruction of New Zealand with the same drive and initiative that have characterised his services in the War'.[65] Much of the focus was on the MWEO, which had mobilised 17,000 males to enlist and an additional 10,000 men and women into the war workforce, for a combined total of roughly 30 per cent of the Māori population.[66] Eruera Tirikatene and the other Māori MPs worked through 1944–5 on potential architecture for a new ministry of Māori welfare that would build on the MWEO structure with enhanced powers and resources. They proceeded cautiously for fear that such an entity might fall too much under the sway of their Pākehā bureaucrat rivals in the Ministry of Native Affairs, and elsewhere in government, who viewed Māori autonomy as problematic and retrogressive.

Unable to push through a new and separate ministry, Tirikatene effectively fought a rear-guard action to salvage any of the gains Māori had accrued during the war. His draft Maori Social and Economic Reconstruction bill sought to replicate the MWEO within the Department of Native Affairs but with 'wide scope for flax-roots influence on decision making'.[67] The Minister of Native Affairs, H. G. R. Mason, vetoed the Māori proposal. In its place, he produced a new draft incorporating aspects of the MWEO structure within his department, though without any Māori authority beyond the local committee level. The New Zealand

[62] Riseman and Trembath, *Defending Country*, 20–21.
[63] Ibid., 27–32; Riseman, "Aboriginal Military Service and Assimilation," 155–178.
[64] Sheffield, "Rehabilitating the Indigene," 341–360.
[65] Rehabilitation Handbook, 24, ANZ, WAII 1 DA550-1-1.
[66] Belich, *Paradise Reforged*, 476.
[67] Hill, *State Authority, Indigenous Autonomy*, 203–210.

Labour Government opted for Mason's bill, now named the Maori Social and Economic Advancement Act, reflecting Pākehā assimilationist aspirations, and it came into effect 1 April 1946.

Hill suggests that the Act was essentially a victory for the bureaucracy. The new system retained some aspects of MWEO, but fundamentally the tribal committees within the Native Department would lack significant power. In fact, the committees were limited to influencing 'Maori wellbeing and perpetuating Maori culture', reducing the power Māori had previously attained.[68] Subsequently, despite Māori MPs' pleas to buy into the structure, many Māori chose instead to disengage, and some local and executive committees shut down or withered. Angela Ballara argues that Māori allegiance to the MWEO during the war had been conditional and contested, with executive councils and state-appointed Māori officials of the MWEO sometimes perceived as government agents intruding on local hapu autonomy.[69] If so, these hapus' withdrawal may have reflected the end of the wartime crisis as much as a specific judgement on the Act. The Maori Social and Economic Advancement Act did produce some improvements in access to social welfare, removing long-standing benefit disparities for Māori for instance.[70] In the end, Hill concludes that the legislation required the Native Department at least to consider Māori views. Moreover, the Māori committees at least laid the possibility for future self-government, meaning there were potential long-term benefits of the new structures established within Māori communities.[71] Māori had paid what Apirana Ngata had termed the 'price of citizenship', but the immediate post-war pay-off seemed at best ambivalent.

Canadians' self-examination in the wake of media coverage of First Nations issues led to widespread calls through 1944 and 1945 for a major governmental review of the Indian Act, reform of Canadian Indian policy generally, and the extension of citizenship rights. Such calls arose not only from educated elites but from a broad swath of the population: veterans associations, labour unions, town councils, churches, youth groups, provincial legislatures, civil rights organisations, homemakers clubs and Indigenous rights advocates, to name just a few.[72]

The Liberal Government finally responded to pressure in May 1946 and announced the formation of the aforementioned SJC to investigate

---

[68] Ibid., 213–214.
[69] Ballara, *Iwi*, 317–318.
[70] Melanie Nolan, "Constantly on the Move, But Going Nowhere? Work, Community and Social Mobility," in *The New Oxford History of New Zealand*, ed. Giselle Byrnes (Melbourne: Oxford University Press, 2009), 409.
[71] Richard Hill, "Maori and State Policy," in *The New Oxford History of New Zealand*, 528.
[72] Sheffield, *The Red Man's on the Warpath*, 95–96; 131–132.

the Indian Act.[73] As already highlighted, this post-war review sparked a wave of politicisation amongst Indigenous communities across the country. All told, the SJC held 128 meetings, heard 122 witnesses, received 411 written briefs and amassed over 3,200 pages of evidence. It was a wide-ranging and thorough review by a group of fairly sympathetic and dedicated parliamentarians. Its functioning, though, still privileged state and settler society assumptions about the appropriate future for First Nations in Canada. The final SJC report recommended the revision, replacement or removal of virtually every clause in the Indian Act, articulating a program that would 'make possible the gradual transition of Indians from wardship to citizenship'.[74] While dressed in the garb of liberal democracy suitable to Canadians' New Order, the overall thrust of the SJC was, in fact, a reaffirmation of assimilation that grew from the settler assumptions about the meaning of Indigenous wartime participation. Innes notes that the government, for the first time, was publicly recognising First Nations people's adaptability, but they misconstrued the context. The Canadian government interpreted First Nations participation in the war as marking a new desire within their communities to assimilate.[75]

Translating the SJC report into a new Indian Act was delayed until 1950 when Bill 267 was introduced to the House of Commons without any First Nations consultation. The proposed bill stepped back from most of what contemporary observers viewed as the more progressive SJC recommendations and left most of the arbitrary powers of the Indian Affairs Branch, and thus the status quo, intact. The resulting storm of protest from Indigenous leaders, opposition MPs from the Conservative Party and Cooperative Commonwealth Federation, as well as the media, led the Minister of Citizenship and Immigration to retract the bill and promise a replacement and consultation with Status Indian leaders the following year. A new Indian Act passed in 1951, an evolutionary rather than revolutionary document. The legislation removed some of the more oppressive powers of the government and Indian Agents, slightly enhanced band council powers, rescinded Indigenous alcohol restrictions and the infamous ban on cultural practices like the potlatch and Sun Dance. Status Indians still did not have the federal franchise and would not until 1960. As in New Zealand, Canadian First Nations' 'reward' for their wartime contributions was decidedly mixed.

---

[73] Ibid., 149, and Chapters 6 and 7 more generally; Laurie Majer Drees, "Citizenship and Treaty Rights: The Indian Association of Alberta and the Canadian Indian Act, 1946–1948," *Great Plains Quarterly* 20 (Spring 2000): 141–158.

[74] *SJC*, Minutes and Proceedings no. 5, 13 April to 21 June 1948, 187.

[75] Innes, "I'm on Home Ground Now, I'm Safe," 698–699.

The United States and Australia were somewhat slower to pull the trigger on post-war policy change, though the scope of change in both countries proved far greater. In the United States, the political battle over the Indian Reorganization Act (1934), between Collier and other Indian New Deal supporters on the one hand and assimilationist members of Congress on the other, had intensified during the war. The war and shifting public opinions on Native Americans emboldened elements in Congress who launched repeated attacks against the Indian New Deal program at the same time as the BIA lurched from crisis to crisis. According to Holm, 'fighting the White man's war gained sympathy for American Indians but it also fuelled a fire that they did not want and eventually found difficult to extinguish'.[76] Collier fought vigorously to defend the Indian Reorganization Act and the BIA, with some success, while gradually surrendering ground to an integrationist approach. Yet, doing so wore him out, and he retired in January 1945. With Collier gone, American officials of diverse political stripes were already taking steps on the path towards massive policy change.

The Senate in 1946 demanded from the BIA a list of those tribes considered most 'ready' to sever their special trust relationship, as well as the financial savings to the federal government for each tribe so terminated. Congress passed legislation in 1946 to establish an Indian Claims Commission (ICC) as well, intended to settle all outstanding Indigenous monetary claims against the settler state within a decade and hasten assimilation. Tribes had five years to submit their claims, grounded principally in treaty violations, to the ICC, with all cases meant to be settled by 1957. The reality proved more complicated than initially envisioned. By the deadline, 370 petitions had been submitted, with 852 specific claims, and the ICC's work would eventually be extended until 1978 before its dissolution. Most commentators have been critical of its purpose, record and legacy.[77] With the ICC in place from 1946, the federal government could now (falsely) claim that it had redressed injustices towards Native Americans, and it was now time to move forward, with termination as the best way to do so.

The steps to termination operated through the late 1940s, with Native American children increasingly integrated into state schooling systems, BIA services transferred to other federal agencies or state

[76] Holm, "Fighting A White Man's War," 79.
[77] See Fixico, *Termination and Relocation*, 21–44; Bernstein, *American Indians and World War II*, 162; Townsend, *World War II and the American Indian*, 223–224; Harry Kersey, Jr., "Indigenous Sovereignty in Two Cultures: Maori and American Indians Compared," *Occasional Paper Series*, Number 1 (Wellington: Treaty of Waitangi Research Unit, 2000), 16.

jurisdictions, and symbols of subordinate status like liquor and fire-arms restrictions removed. President Truman appointed Dillon Myer as BIA Commissioner in 1950, the first pro-termination commissioner, and he would oversee the high-water of the termination tide. Myer had headed the Wartime Relocation Authority, which was responsible for the internment of the Japanese-American population. He was determined to end government administration of Indians, both for the 'freedom' of Native Americans and to reduce federal expenditures. With little or no consultation with Native American communities affected, and in the face of opposition from the NCAI who loudly opposed its implementation, Congress endorsed termination legislation in 1953.[78]

Australia is an interesting case, where relatively little policy change resulted immediately following the war. There was one notable excep-tion: the extension of the federal franchise to Aboriginal and Torres Strait Islander veterans. The Commonwealth Electoral (War-time) Act 1940, by covering all service personnel, had inadvertently extended the franchise to Indigenous servicemen and women while enlisted and for six months thereafter. It was actually the RSL that led the charge to enfranchise Indigenous veterans permanently. Sub-branches and mem-bers, especially from Victoria, sent letters to the government as well as to newspapers. Other smaller associations, such as the Fighting Services Association in Perth, sent letters to authorities. A March 1946 letter to the Western Australia Department of Native Affairs stated:

My Association's first concern is the future welfare of all Ex-Service men and that of our aboriginal and half-caste men makes a special problem. They have in the Army associated on equal terms with their fellow Australians and no doubt have learned many things useful to them in the future. Some have given their lives, others permanently injured. These, of course, will get all due consideration from Army authorities. It is their future as civilians that we are concerned with.[79]

Such interventions were effective at securing action; amendments to the Commonwealth Electoral Act in 1949 granted the federal vote to all Indigenous veterans or serving Defence members. In the early 1950s, the RSL continued occasional advocacy for citizenship rights, such as extending the franchise in states where it was still denied, as well as for the lifting of restrictions on alcohol. By the mid-1950s, though, the RSL's role advocating for Indigenous citizenship rights was waning, as it entered a long period more hostile to notions of Indigenous rights.[80]

---

[78] Fixico, *Termination and Relocation*, 63–133.
[79] M. Lambert, to the Under Secretary, 15 March 1946, SRO WA, Acc 993 529–40.
[80] Riseman and Trembath, *Defending Country*, 39–55.

While the franchise represented an important gain for Aboriginal and Torres Strait Islander veterans, it also was not irreconcilable with the Commonwealth and states' radical transition to official assimilation in the early 1950s. Unlike the American experience, where the literature is unanimous in linking the war and its affects to termination, Australian historians are divided over the impact of the Second World War on Aboriginal and Torres Strait Islander policy. Some, such as Tim Rowse, point to the heightened settler democratic sentiments and Indigenous labour and military participation as catalysts advancing the case for assimilation.[81] Mahli Neilson likewise makes a case for the war's influence at inspiring greater politicisation, activism and radicalism amongst Aboriginal Australians.[82] Others such as Bain Attwood have dismissed the war as 'something of an interregnum for Aboriginal reform'.[83] Those who have examined the war most closely, including Robert Hall, Kay Saunders and Noah Riseman, suggest little, if any, change, though Hall and Saunders at least see the potential for the war to provoke reform.[84] Riseman's work argues that the war left the edifice of colonialism virtually undented in Australia, bringing his work into line with two other recent studies that cover Australian Aboriginal policy in the post-war years: Russell McGregor's, *Indifferent Inclusion: Aboriginal People and the Australian Nation* and Anna Haebich's, *Spinning the Dream: Assimilation in Australia, 1950–1970*.[85]

Haebich begins her study in 1950 and argues that the new international discourse of equality and human rights, as well as a newfound humanitarian interest within Australia, led policymakers to embrace assimilation.[86] McGregor takes a longer trajectory than Haebich and does explicitly examine the war and its impact, which he sees encapsulated in the almost total disinterest in Aboriginal issues on the part of the Commonwealth Department of Post-War Reconstruction. For McGregor, any impact of the war was indirect via broader cultural and social shifts in settler society that followed the war. In his words, 'shortly after the war the Australian nation changed in ways conducive to a greater inclusiveness of Aboriginal people', and he points to factors like the United Nations, the slow demise

[81] Tim Rowse, *White Flour, White Power: From Rations to Citizenship in Central Australia* (Cambridge: Cambridge University Press, 1998), 8.
[82] Neilson, "Hiatus or Catalyst?"
[83] Bain Attwood, *Rights for Aborigines* (Crows Nest, NSW: Allen & Unwin, 2003), 118.
[84] Hall, *The Black Diggers*; Saunders, "Inequalities of Sacrifice," 131–148; Riseman, *Defending Whose Country?*
[85] McGregor, *Indifferent Inclusion*; Anna Haebich, *Spinning the Dream: Assimilation in Australia, 1950–1970* (Fremantle, WA: Fremantle Press, 2008).
[86] Haebich, *Spinning the Dream*, 11.

of the White Australia Policy, increased immigration from southern and eastern Europe, the anthropologist A. P. Elkin's citizenship push and the gradual awakening among Australians to appreciate Aboriginal people and culture.[87] Riseman similarly argues that, in significant contrast to the interwar activists' claims for citizenship rights, 'In the post-Second World War era, military service did not feature so heavily in Indigenous claims to rights. In the 1950s and 1960s, the arguments for equal citizenship rights were primarily grounded in international discourses of human rights and drew heavily on strategies and rhetoric from the Black American Civil Rights Movement.'[88] Beyond the franchise, the weight of the historiography is against any significant policy consequences arising from either the Second World War or Aboriginal and Torres Strait Islander roles in that conflict (aside from veterans becoming activists), making Australia an anomaly amongst these four settler states.

Two factors help explain the apparent disconnect between Aboriginal and Torres Strait Islander wartime contributions and Indigenous policy reform in post-war Australia. Firstly, Australia's fragmented jurisdiction over Aboriginal affairs between the various state governments, something that stands in sharp contrast to the other settler states whose Indigenous administrations were highly centralised, worked to deflect and divide the growing calls for reform. For instance, in response to a veterans' group resolution asserting that Aboriginal ex-servicemen's 'subsequent treatment as civilians is not in keeping with the high regard the general public has for their services in war time',[89] the Secretary of the Prime Minister's Department offered the following:

I desire to inform you that the Commonwealth Government has been giving consideration to the question of the welfare of the aboriginal population of Australia in general and intends as soon as practicable to implement a progressive policy for the amelioration of their conditions. As you are no doubt aware the Commonwealth controls aborigines only within Commonwealth Territories, that is within the Northern Territory, Australian Capital Territory, and the Wreck Bay Aboriginal Station. Advice from the Department of the Interior indicates that there are no aboriginal ex-servicemen domiciled in these areas.

The Secretary went on to clarify that the 'Administrator of the Northern Territory has advised that a number of aborigines actually worked for the Army in the Territory, but they were employed under conditions prescribed by the Aborigines Ordnance and were not enlisted in the Forces. Half-castes who were enlisted already enjoy full citizen rights in

[87] McGregor, *Indifferent Inclusion*, 57.
[88] Riseman, "Ex-service Activism after 1945," 263.
[89] Letter, J. A. K. Wicks to F. Strahan, 17 April 1946, NAA, A431, 1946/1357.

the Northern Territory.'[90] This neglected entirely those Aboriginal people who had served in quasi-official and unofficial military units and roles and overlooked Aboriginal men or women who had formally enlisted with the Australian forces.

Military service had been a national experience, and a mark of serving the nation, but it could not spark a national reform of Aboriginal policy because public concerns were redirected to a handful of state administrations, each with distinct corporate cultures and policy structures. Even the notion of citizenship, as distinct from citizenship rights, is complicated in Australia. Before 1948, there actually was no concept of Australian citizenship, as all Australians were seen as British subjects. The first creation of Australian citizenship was under the 1948 Nationality and Citizenship Act, which, technically, made Aboriginal and Torres Strait Islander people citizens. Yet in Australia, the usual rights of citizenship (e.g., the vote, the right to drink, custodianship of their children) operated independently of citizenship status and, therefore, Aboriginal and Torres Strait Islander people continued to be denied the rights of citizenship until the state and federal governments passed legislation extending such rights.[91] Similar situations existed in the United States and Canada where pre-civil-rights-era segregation laws and the disenfranchisement connected to Status, respectively, meant that Indigenous citizenship did not necessarily mean equality.

Some state governments responded to wartime pressures with new policy or legislation. Most notable was Western Australia with its Natives (Citizenship Rights) Act 1944, which created a status of 'state citizenship' for Aboriginal people. The provisions of this act were not dissimilar from other states' welfare provisions granting citizenship rights to those men and women who could show 'good character'. Aboriginal residents could apply for an exemption certificate from the restrictions imposed by the Aborigines Act. Under this legislation the exemption was called a Certificate of Citizenship; across Australia Aboriginal people colloquially referred to these exemptions as dog tags. The Western Australian legislation was the only one specifically to reference someone who 'served in the Naval, Military or Air Force of the Commonwealth and has received or is entitled to receive an honourable discharge' as eligible to apply.[92] The Commissioner of Native Affairs described the act as bringing in 'an enlightened policy [which] was desirable in respect of those natives

---

[90] F. Strahan, Secretary, to the Assistant Secretary, RSS & AILA, 1 August 1946, NAA, A431, 1946/1357.
[91] John Chesterman and Brian Galligan, *Citizens Without Rights: Aborigines and Australian Citizenship* (Cambridge: Cambridge University Press, 1997), 119–120.
[92] Western Australia, Native (Citizenship Rights) Act 1944, section 4(2)(a).

who, by reason of character, standards of intelligence and development were deserving of consideration in connection.'[93] Some Aboriginal veterans did obtain citizenship certificates, though they considered the entire process demeaning. Gloria Brennan described her father suffering the 'indignity of getting a citizenship rights card so as to be able to walk into a hotel to have a drink with the same men he fought side by side with. That really got his pride.'[94] Given the restrictive covenants associated with state citizenship, like exemption certificates in other states, many other eligible Aboriginal people did not take up the scheme. Instead, they would fight for equal rights as the norm rather than an 'exemption' granted on a case-by-case basis.

The second causal factor to consider was the still-potent racism and racialist ideas that persisted, despite the war, throughout much of settler Australian society. As McGregor phrases it, wartime 'attitudinal shifts were somewhat shallow'.[95] As such, ideas about racial superiority persisted into the post-war era. State laws were still quite prescriptive about whom they defined as Aboriginal, with mixed-descent people considered Aboriginal in some locales (such as Queensland) but defined as white in other places (such as Tasmania or Victoria).[96] Indeed, sometimes Indigenous people were simultaneously fighting to be recognised as Aboriginal whilst concurrently wanting the removal of the restrictions such recognition imposed. North American parallels included those not on tribal rolls fighting for recognition in the United States or the nebulous situation for Non-Status Indians and Métis people in Canada.[97] Western Australia's 1944 Annual Report of the Aborigines Department, responding to calls for reform and equality, was frank and bleak about the societal realities faced on the ground:

Social Fusion is spoken of glibly, but there is a colour prejudice in Australia, and whilst many detribalised natives might become educated and desire to live as whites, they are not accepted socially by whites, and this means that they mainly live as a class unto themselves. Many people speak of social equality and justice in civics for the natives, and criticise native administrations, but with few exceptions whites are hostile to social equality or to marriage with their own kin, or to

---

[93] Tamara Hunter, "The Myth of Equality: The Denial of Citizenship Rights for Aboriginal People in Western Australia," *Studies in Western Australian History* 22 (2001): 77. See also Chesterman, *Civil Rights*, 125–134.

[94] Kevin Gilbert, *Living Black: Blacks Talk to Kevin Gilbert* (Melbourne: Allen Lane, 1977), 79.

[95] McGregor, *Indifferent Inclusion*, 56.

[96] See Australia, Human Rights and Equal Opportunities Commission, *Bringing Them Home*.

[97] Ellinghaus, *Blood Will Tell*; Jacqueline Peterson and Jennifer Brown (eds.), *The New Peoples: Being and Becoming Métis in North America* (St. Paul: Minnesota Historical Society Press, 2001).

social association with the natives in this deepest and sincerest sense; therefore we must deal with this matter with no misgivings as to its effects, or final results in practice.[98]

Deep-seated settler ideologies of race were evident in all four settler societies, where they contested the war-related philosophical challenges, prompting reformist calls. Such fundamental beliefs remained too strong in Australia. When augmented by the longstanding connection between 'whiteness' and Australian citizenship, rewarding Aboriginal war service with equality and citizenship proved a hard sell. The combination of limited publicity, fragmented state responsibility for Aboriginal populations and stubborn social antipathy to the acceptance of blacks on equal terms explains more fully the Australian anomaly.

## Conclusion

One of the fascinating themes arising in all four settler nations was just how much attention was directed to Indigenous issues post-war. As the evidence shows, there was a substantial upswing in politicisation and activism amongst Native Americans, First Nations, Aboriginal and Torres Strait Islander Australians and Māori, who all added their views to the post-war dialogue. In New Zealand and Canada, Indigenous politicians and representatives actively participated in the policymaking process, albeit on the margins. Nevertheless, their overall volume within the post-war discussions around Indigenous people, rights and place in society was relatively muted by the cacophony of settler voices. Most of the talking, and much of the impetus for reform post-war, actually originated within settler society. Effectively, what Americans, Australians, New Zealanders and Canadians were mulling over was what they should do about the perceived 'problem' that Indigenous populations represented to them. Clearly not only Indigenous populations, leaders and veterans felt the meaning and significance of the war; so, too, did settler societies and governments.

The well-spring for settler engagement and reformist ideas in the immediate post-war period appears to have been twofold. The first, and arguably most significant, was settlers' latent guilt for the dispossession and neglect of Indigenous populations, fanned into a blaze by wartime

---

[98] Annual Report of the Aborigines Department, Western Australia, 1944, cited in Christine Choo, *Mission Girls: Aboriginal Women on Catholic Missions in the Kimberley, Western Australia, 1900–1950* (Crawley: University of Western Australia Press, 2004), 288.

circumstances. The symbolism and poignancy of marginalised people – often bereft of the rights or the genuine reality of citizenship – serving, fighting and sacrificing in their soldiers' ranks, and pitching in to the collective crusade at home, proved difficult to ignore. For settler societies, the juxtaposition of Indigenous wartime participation against pre-war neglect, oppression, maladministration, injustice and lack of rights proved especially uncomfortable. The result spawned urges to correct past injustices, improve quality of life, loosen state control and reward Indigenous societies. The painful self-examination evident in post-war discourse around the Indigenous 'problem' was often an exercise in self-flagellation. Reformers regularly entwined imagery of Indigenous sacrifice in war with state oppression and societal racism in their rhetorical strategies calling for change. The same concepts made their way into both sides of the debates between Indian New Dealers and assimilationists in the United States during and after the war, though the latter appear to have scored more points by doing so. The interesting anomaly here is New Zealand, where Pākehā actually exhibited almost no signs of guilt. Instead, they remained smugly complacent that Māori, in their view the best, and best treated, savage race on the planet, were happily progressing on the road to complete assimilation.

The second root of post-war reform impulses was the desire to identify, capture and sustain into the future what settlers saw as the previously absent characteristics revealed or enabled in Indigenous societies by the war: usually articulated as energy, initiative, responsibility, and/or civic-mindedness. In order to make permanent the potential demonstrated by Indigenous military service, US officials felt compelled to get the government off the backs of the Indian, assuming that only separate legal status and treaties had impeded genuine equality and citizenship (and cost money) before the war. In Canada, the optimistic post-war reform process sought to realise the 'potential Indian citizen' that war service seemed to promise. In New Zealand, the public and governmental debate focussed obsessively on the perceived revelation of the Māori war effort – the discovery by Māori of what Pākehā termed initiative or a sense of responsibility. Pākehā saw this as the sole missing ingredient in Māori's final assimilation. Australia might not have been as prominent on this score due to a profound presumption of inferiority of Aboriginal people amongst white Australians; they simply could not imagine that Aboriginal people were capable. When Commonwealth and state officials did adopt assimilation policies from 1951, the promise of equality for Indigenous Australians met a significant obstacle: the attitudes of everyday white Australians and how they would interact with Indigenous Australians.

A final crucial parallel across all four settler societies in the immediate post-war years is that uniformly, reform took the paths desired by settler society. Whether moved to question the 'problem' of Indigenous peoples because of guilt or the desire to bottle wartime Indigenous energy, the New Zealand, Canadian, American and Australian governments all seemed to come to the same final answer: assimilation. The relative salience of Indigenous voices and involvement in the process, from direct governmental representatives in New Zealand to almost complete marginalisation in Australia, does not appear to have greatly altered the result. The doctrine of assimilation was extremely malleable and moulded in different ways in each country to match legal, economic and political conditions. For instance, in New Zealand, the outcome of reform was a reassertion of state control over Māori and a rejection of the relative autonomy and *rangatiratanga* conceded to the MWEO during the war. 'Assimilationism's last stand' was how James Belich described the Maori Social and Economic Advancement Act (1945).[99] By contrast, in the United States, assimilationist ideology pushed officials towards the removal of state controls over Native Americans and the termination of any special relationship between the state and Indigenous tribal communities. Canada's parliamentary review and new Indian Act (1951), despite the democratic window dressing and stripping away of coercive overtones, marked a return to the nation's long-standing policy of paternalistically encouraging assimilation. By the 1950s, settler administrators were also increasingly turning to urbanisation as the panacea to further the assimilation of Indigenous populations.[100]

[99] Belich, *Paradise Reforged*, 477.
[100] Bryan Gilling, "Paddling Their Own Waka or Rowing the Government's Boat? The Official System for Maori Socio-Economic Development in the Post-1945 Period," *Rangatiratanga Series*, Number 15 (Wellington: Treaty of Waitangi Research Unit, 2008), 3; Hill, *State Authority, Indigenous Autonomy*, 206–207; Bernstein, *American Indians and World War II*, 168–169; Franco, *Crossing the Pond*, 94; Hugh Shewell, *"Enough to Keep Them Alive": Indian Welfare in Canada, 1873–1965* (Toronto: University of Toronto Press, 2004); Anna Haebich, "Nuclear, Suburban and Black: Middleton's Vision of Assimilation for Nyungar Families," in *Contesting Assimilation*, ed. Tim Rowse (Perth: API Network, 2005), 201–220; Corinne Manning, "'If aborigines are to be assimilated they must learn to live in houses': Victoria's Transitional Housing Policy," in *Contesting Assimilation*, 221–235.

# Conclusion

After the guns of the Second World War fell silent and the post-war flurry of homecoming and policy reform had run their course, the Indigenous participation in the conflict largely faded from the collective memories of settler societies and even many Indigenous communities. While that conflict lived on as the 'good war' of the 'greatest generation' for Americans, Australians, New Zealanders and Canadians, the Indigenous experiences, excepting perhaps the Maori Battalion, were rarely woven into that historical myth-making. Through the subsequent decades, Indigenous peoples and political leadership wrestled with settler governments, which were again pursuing assimilationist agendas, leaving little space and energy for remembrance and recognition of Indigenous war service. New battles for self-determination and civil rights consumed the attention of Indigenous communities. Many Indigenous veterans were active in these movements and assumed leadership positions among the proliferation of Indigenous organisations that emerged in the 1960s–70s. Yet, their contributions to the war effort at home and abroad remained on the periphery of Second World War histories. Given this, it is worth exploring what was accomplished, what it meant to those involved, and what, if any, legacies lingered.

The seemingly simple question of why thousands of Indigenous men and women signed up for military service and fought with settler militaries lends itself to diverse, complex and sophisticated responses. We should not be surprised that there is no one big answer to this 'why' question, for whether an individual chose to enlist or engage in the war effort drew substantially on situational evaluations, based on multiple criteria. Sometimes Indigenous people's actions had much in common with settler society: searching for a steady job, patriotism, seeking adventure or succumbing to societal or conscription pressures. In other cases, the criteria, motivations and meanings were distinct and arose from Indigenous cultures, localised economies, politics or histories. A comparable decision-making process also occurred collectively in Indigenous communities. Whether a community pitched in, volunteered, donated funds, remained aloof or actively resisted wartime pressures depended on diverse factors and the specifics of the situation, threat or opportunity as the community leaders assessed it. Communities continuously re-evaluated their responses to the war depending on the nature of the issue at hand, the broader context of the war, or shifting internal politics. One marked example was the Six Nations in southern Ontario resisting the lease of land for an airfield in early 1940 and then, after the fall of France, offering another piece of property for only nominal rent as a patriotic gesture. On the surface, such strategies could appear contradictory, erratic or capricious, but balancing the volunteerism, sacrifice and patriotism alongside the protests, resistance and efforts at self-determination reveals that Indigenous peoples were seeking control over their own engagement with the war. Underlying the wartime experience were Indigenous peoples fighting for both the right to inclusion and the autonomy to define themselves and their futures for themselves.

There was no singular form of Indigenous war service. In the respective armed forces, the servicemen and women could perform differentiated service shaped by their Indigeneity, or identical service to that of non-Indigenous comrades. Indigenous personnel – including women – served in every branch of their nation's services and in every theatre of war to which they were posted. The vast majority served integrated into regular settler military units, and this was simultaneously an acculturating, empowering and egalitarian experience for the bulk of service personnel. For women, in particular, it represented an opportunity not only to learn new skills but also to challenge some of the masculine warrior traditions within their own cultures. Some segregation of Indigenous service personnel occurred, sometimes at their own request such as in the case of New Zealand's Maori Battalion. The segregated units also reflected settler military desires to capitalise on the Indigeneity of these people: their knowledge, language, location and/or martial capacity. These were thus aligning agendas where settler militaries provided a framework that drew on Indigenous knowledge, but Indigenous people were active agents shaping the deployment of that knowledge. In assessing both integrated and segregated examples of Indigenous military service, it is important to consider them alongside their comrades in arms. Indigenous experiences were not entirely distinct and different; rather, their experiences and reactions, in diverse situations, had much in common with the broader soldiers' psychological and physiological experiences of modern war. Having said this, each man or woman brought his or her own cultural lens to their experience, and for many Indigenous service personnel, this could mean some nuanced differences in how they perceived and responded in particular circumstances.

Beyond those enlisted in the armed forces, the war wove its way into many facets of Indigenous peoples' everyday lives. The war infiltrated community politics, ceremonial practices, interpersonal dealings with non-Indigenous people, relations with the settler state and both community and individual endeavours. Sometimes Indigenous people joined settler society home front campaigns supporting the war effort while in other instances they developed their own organisations, fundraisers, celebrations and commemorative practices. Women were often at the forefront of these efforts, whether they be in rural, Indigenous lands or newly forming urban Indigenous communities. The war witnessed the diminishment of prejudice, both in the forces and at home, as the wartime spirit of solidarity helped to ease settler prejudice and fostered an environment more open to Indigenous people and cultural practices. Indigenous people became 'us' against the new enemy 'others': the Japanese, Germans and Italians. Whether serving together on a frontline trench in Libya, or women sharing in a common barracks in Brisbane, or working together on a factory line in Montreal or together patrolling a remote part of Alaska, the many wartime needs opened up more opportunities for cross-cultural engagement and exchange.

The wartime economy boomed in all four settler states, opening new opportunities for Indigenous men and women alike – particularly as more Indigenous and non-Indigenous people joined the armed forces. The resulting labour shortages meant that people, usually marginalised economically, suddenly found numerous options for gainful employment. This was especially evident in urban areas but also in rural Indigenous communities and even in many remote regions. The war witnessed expanded agricultural production from Indigenous lands, industrial jobs in wartime factories, expansion of traditional resource extraction industries and employment in military facilities established on or near Indigenous lands. The war thus represented a brief period where most Indigenous families and communities were financially secure, even prosperous, something unseen in previous eras. Unfortunately, these conditions, all directly linked to the war, largely receded with the return to peacetime conditions. In rural and remote areas especially, some of the promises of development, foreshadowed by the war, would take decades to implement.

Through all these efforts, Indigenous peoples paid what Māori MP Apirana Ngata termed the 'price of citizenship', but as these societies transitioned into peace, it remained uncertain whether the rewards would be commensurate. Undeniably, the war and Indigenous participation in the conflict had left an impression on settler societies and governments. Arguably the single most important impact of the war was building the misguided confidence that Indigenous populations deserved, desired and were capable of making good on opportunities to assimilate – full stop. In this context, it is understandable why scholars in each country have generally painted the war's end as a pivotal moment in the history of settler-Indigenous relations. Widespread post-war policy and legislative changes underscore such interpretations. American historian Kenneth Townsend argues that the war represented a 'crossroads' for both Native Americans and also Indian Affairs policy: they could continue the Indian New Deal push to revitalise Indian communities and cultures, or they could renew the push for assimilation.[1] Townsend's assessment could in many respects apply to Canada, Australia and New Zealand, though he overlooks an important point by painting this as a crossroads. The war experience both reaffirmed the value, efficacy and emotional importance of Indigenous identities, cultures and languages while also promising the offer of inclusion and respect within settler societies – it was not a question of either/or but rather of both/and. Indigenous peoples sought respect and acceptance without having to sacrifice their sense of self. As Cherokee activist Ruth Muskrat Bronson argued in 1944, 'Now, when we are concerned for the freedom of mankind everywhere, it seems not unreasonable to hope that the people of America will accept into even greater national fellowship these once-conquered Indians who are living within the heart of the nation.'[2] Indigenous people had proven that they were assets to the state and society, as culturally distinct entities that had paid the price of citizenship on their own terms.

Sadly, though the war produced conditions for a genuine re-evaluation of the relationship between Indigenous peoples and settler states, it fundamentally did not break down enough of the underlying structures of colonialism shared across all four countries. These structures resurfaced to dominate the resulting shifts of policy direction, whether subtle or substantive. Settler societies saw in the war experience and Indigenous participation what they wanted to see, and they interpreted the actions and underlying motivations in ways that meshed with their ideological assumptions, assuaged their anxieties or fed into their aspirations for the future. Thus, even where Indigenous peoples managed to win a hearing, they were not genuinely heard by settler society. Policy reform affecting Indigenous peoples during post-war reconstruction was very much about rehabilitating assimilation in newfound and newly damaging ways.

The Second World War, nevertheless, had offered Indigenous men and women, both in the services and on the home front, a glimpse of equality.

[1] Townsend, *World War II and the American Indian*, 3.
[2] Bronson, *Indians Are People, Too*, 15.

The economic advances, combined with newfound education and skilled employment opportunities, produced critical conceptual changes that provided the groundwork of values, expectations and rights that were precursors to the civil rights movements of the 1960s–70s. All four settler societies, and many Indigenous communities, conceptually reconfigured their constructions of Indigeneity in both contemporary and positive ways strengthening the connection between citizenship and Indigenous people. Such altered understandings were an essential precondition before states could even consider accepting Indigenous grievances and conceding a role for them in policy reform. Indeed, much of the civil rights movements of the 1960s grew from settler governments' failure to consult and work with Indigenous people: who now expected, and could credibly demand, to be seen as equal citizens, endowed with particular rights by virtue of their Indigeneity and claims to sovereignty.

As Indigenous people reacted to new policies of the post-war period, another factor would emerge in both government justifications as well as Indigenous claims-making: international discourses and doctrines of human rights. The language of the 1948 Universal Declaration of Human Rights particularly gained traction, first through the civil rights movement in the United States and then echoing in other settler states. Indigenous veterans across all four societies would adopt this language and use the knowledge and moral leverage they acquired through military service to champion a variant of human rights for themselves and their people, setting the stage for the next fight for Indigenous rights. Considered in this way, the Second World War produced short-term change, some of it substantial, but its larger impact is only discernible in a longer view. The war, directly and indirectly, helped establish the post-war arena within which on-going negotiations and conflicts regarding Indigenous peoples' place in these settler societies would be considered. This process has continued through to the present. This is why there is still political resonance to the memory of Indigenous military service and veterans today, and why Indigenous organisations and leadership mobilise such tropes to pursue broader agendas with settler governments.

Local Indigenous veterans groups emerged in New Zealand in 1960, then in the United States and Canada in the 1970s. These organisations initially focused on particular units, nations or regions, such as the 28th Māori Battalion Association, the Navajo Code Talkers Association or Saskatchewan Indian Veterans' Association. Such groups represented an opportunity for veterans to gather, remember old times and support one another. Since the mid-1980s, though, there has been a shift in these organisations' agendas, as well as numerous new groups, aiming to recover and honour the experience and sacrifice of Indigenous service personnel within the national narratives. Other associations have actively campaigned on specific grievances. This process was partly a parallel of the global 'memory boom' since the early 1980s and resurgence of memory of Second World War veterans who are ageing and passing away.[3] When looking at Indigenous military service, in particular, there is also an alignment with the reconciliation agendas of the 1990s and beyond; what better way of showing the coming together of Indigenous and non-Indigenous peoples than through shared acts of sacrifice and patriotism to defend the country.[4]

Most significantly, across all four settler societies, it has been Indigenous communities themselves that have driven these campaigns for Indigenous service recognition. Interestingly, the children of the Second World War generation have often injected new energy or even led these campaigns – themselves often having served in conflicts such as Korea, Vietnam, peacekeeping missions or in the post-war women's services. In Canada, Indigenous veterans' grievances over benefits provoked two major government reports in the 1990s, a National Round Table resolution to veterans grievances (2001), a subsequent apology for the inequity in accessing veterans' benefits, a $39 million dollar compensation package (2002), a National Aboriginal Veterans Memorial unveiled in Ottawa in 2001 and extensive inclusion in local and national acts of remembrance. There were sporadic local initiatives in Australia to honour Indigenous veterans in the 1980s–90s, but really it has been in the new millennium that organisations have emerged in most states to commemorate Indigenous military service. Commemorative activities include annual ceremonies honouring Indigenous service during Reconciliation Week, Aboriginal Anzac Day marches and memorials being constructed in several capital cities.

New Zealand and the United States have, paradoxically, been simultaneously the most inclusive and exclusive at incorporating Indigenous service into national narratives of the good war for freedom and democracy. The story of the 28th Maori Battalion is rightly celebrated and forms a significant part of Aotearoa/New Zealand's dominant memory of the Second World War. Lost in the narrative, however, are the contributions of the thousands more Māori who served in integrated units, not

---

[3] See Winter, *Remembering War*; Bart Ziino, "Introduction: Remembering the First World War Today," in *Remembering the First World War*, ed. Bart Ziino (Abingdon, Oxon; New York: Routledge, 2015), 1–17.

[4] See Noah Riseman, "Evolving Commemorations of Aboriginal and Torres Strait Islander Military Service," *Wicazo Sa Review* 32, no. 1 (2017): 80–101; Riseman, "The Rise of Indigenous Military History," 901–911.

to mention the experiences of Māori servicewomen. Since the 1990s, the story of the Navajo Code Talkers has permeated many school lessons about the Second World War and is also the subject of a Hollywood film and numerous works of juvenile fiction. The Navajo and other code talkers have received numerous presidential and congressional medals, honouring their distinct feats in the war.[5] Yet, the thousands of Native American men and women who did not use their language as a code remain on the periphery of national commemorations and memories of the war.

Perhaps symbolic of the growing importance of recognition, memory and commemorations is the fate of the 28th Māori Battalion Association. The association had its genesis in 1958 and then staged reunions biennially until 2006. By then the number of veterans had dwindled, so the organisation shifted to annual reunions. In 2012, there were only twenty-six surviving veterans of the Maori Battalion, less than half of whom were able-bodied; those members voted to wind up the association that year.[6] The end of the 28th Māori Battalion Association marks the passage of the Second World War from the era of memory to post-memory, shifting the onus to younger generations to learn about, understand and commemorate the legacies of Indigenous contributions to the Second World War.[7] We hope this book has contributed to meeting that obligation.

[5] Meadows, "An Honor Long Overdue," 91–121.
[6] Monty Soutar, booklet at closure of 28th Māori Battalion Association, 1 December 2012.
[7] Marianne Hirsch, "Family Pictures: Maus, Mourning, and Post-Memory," *Discourse* 15, no. 2 (1992): 3–29.

# Bibliography

## Manuscript, Archival and Library Collections

*National Archives of Australia*

### Canberra

A431 1946/1357.
A431 1949/822.
A431 1950/597.
A463 1956/1096.
A659 40/1/858.
A659 1939/1/129.
A659 1945/1/1563.
A884 A6931.
A1308 762/2/135.
A1608 AG45/1/12.
A2653 1940 M214.
A2653 1943 M2.
A2671 145/1944.
A6006 1941/01/24.
A11116, CA693 PART 1, Item barcode 31172567.
A13977, 326, 31405912.
A13977, 431, 31406010.
A14039, 7866, 31750481.
AA1978/215, item 24.
AA1978/215, item 33.
B356 54.
E791, D357/1/11, Item barcode 5387420.

### Melbourne

MP431/1, 929/19/912.
MP508/1, 50/703/12.
MP508/1, 82/710/2.
MP508/1, 82/712/1310.

MP508/1, 275/701/556.
MP508/1, 275/750/1310.
MP508/1, 323/723/972.
MP513, A1684.
MP729/6, 16/402/111.
MP729/6, 29/401/618.
MP729/6, 29/401/626.
MP742/1, 94/1/915.

*Australian War Memorial*

AWM 834/1/1.
AWM 1187.
AWM F00519.
AWM, series 54, item 628/1/1B.
AWM, series 54, item 741/5/9, Part I.
AWM F04051.
AWM P01066.001.
AWM P02522.016.
The Blamey Paper (3DRL 6643).
Private Records Collection: Mr Don Cameron MHR (PR 87/78).
Keith Murdoch Sound Archive.

*National Library of Australia*

RSL Papers: 1, MSS 6609, box 158, file 2248c.

*State Records Office of Western Australia*

File 135-47 Re-establishment Training Scheme for Natives.
Acc 993 38-1940.
Acc 993 529-40.

*Archives New Zealand*

AD1 226-19-7, vol. 1, 1935–1941.
AD1 319-1-9, vol. 1.
AD1 319-1-21.
AD1 344-3-30.
AD1 1117 209-3-57.
AD1-1265 300.1.2.
AIR 1 762 33-20-4.
EA 1 Box 394, 81-1-11.

MA 1 19-1-411.
MA 1 19-1-452.
MA 1 W2459 19-1-239.
N1 308 13-3-1.
N1 309 13-3-1.
WAII 21 62C-CN115.
WAII 21 68a cn121.
WAII 21 79a-cn129.
WAII 1 DA550-1-1.

*Alexander Turnbull Library, Wellington, New Zealand*

Bennett, Sir Charles. Interviewed by Jim Sullivan. 31 March and 1 April 1993. Alexander Turnbull Library Oral History Centre. OHColl-0217-1. Available from www.28maoribattalion.org.nz/audio/charles-bennett-discusses-tribal-formation-battalions-companies.

Edwards, Patira, Ngāpuhi (1919–2005). Interviewed by Megan Hutching. 27 November 2000. *Second World War Oral History Project – Crete.* Alexander Turnbull Library Oral History Centre. OHInt-0729-08. Available from www.28maoribattalion.org.nz/audio/patira-edwards-first-encounter-with-germans.

Eric Ramsden Papers, MS-0196-275. Available from www.28maoribattalion.org.nz/memory/rangi-logan-writes-home.

Glover, Tautini (Tini), Te Aitanga-a-Hauiti. Interviewed by Megan Hutching. 16 August 2003. Alexander Turnbull Library Oral History Centre, OHInt-0748-02. Available from www.28maoribattalion.org.nz/audio/tini-glover-describes-being-attacked-italy and www.28maoribattalion.org.nz/audio/tini-glover-describes-going-battle.

Ngata Family Papers, MS-Papers-6919-0788. Available from www.28maoribattalion.org.nz/node/15335.

Parkinson, Jerome (Maiki or Jules) (1924–2006). 23 March 2004. Interviewed by Megan Hutching. *Second World War Oral History Project – North Africa.* Alexander Turnbull Library Oral History Centre. OHInt-0798-12. Available from https://28maoribattalion.org.nz/audio/maiki-parkinson-recalls-a-stuka-attack-el-alamein.

Walter Nash (Nash Papers).

*Libraries and Archives Canada*

RG 10, vol. 11289, file #'214-5.
RG 10, vol. 6763, file #'452-5.
RG 10, vol. 6764, file #'452-6.
RG 10, vol. 6765, file #'452-6-17.
RG 10, vol. 6768, file #'452-20.
RG 10, vol. 6769, file #'452-20-3.

RG 10, vol. 6769, file 452-20-10.
RG 10, vol. 6767 file 452-15.
RG 10, vol. 6770, file 452-26.
RG 10, vol. 6770, 452-26.
RG 10, vol. 6772, file 452-42.
RG 10, vol. 8585, file 1/1-2-17.
RG 10, vol. 10712, file 43/39-6.
RG 10, vol. 11289, file 214-5.
RG 10, vol. 6811, file 1/1-2-16, pt. 1.
RG 10, c-8513, vol. 6769, file #452-20-3.
RG 24, vol. 3302, file # 280-1-2 v.2.
RG 24, vol. 3307, no. H.Q. 282-1-2 v.2.
RG 24, vol. 9801, 2/IND RTcomm/1.
RG 85, 1005-2-3.

*Department of National Defence, Directorate
of History and Heritage (Canada)*

75/347, 25-04-139.
112. 3H1.009/D293.
N.S. 30-2-12.
Historical Section Army H.Q. Report no. 71.
S.2-1-2.
113, 3A2009/D2.
169. 009(D77).
169. 009(D94).

*National Archives and Records Administration (USA)*

RG 75, Records of the Bureau of Indian Affairs, Scrapbook of Newsclippings Relating to World War II, 1944, Box 1, Entry 998A.
RG 457, Special Research Histories. SRH-120: Utilization of American Indians as Communication Linguist. Box 34, folder 020.
RG 457, Special Research Histories. SRH-120: Utilization of American Indians as Communication Linguist. Box 34, folder 042.

*Library of Congress: American Folklife Center*

Akee, Dan. Interview with Carol Fleming and Warren C. Salomon. AFC/2001/001/52555. 24 July 2004. Tuba City, AZ.
Bailey, Roy Daniel. Interview with Kurt Ainslie, Kyle Ainslie and John Ferrick. AFC/2001/001/44446. 26 February 2005. Sitka, AK.
Byrd, Lawrence Leslie. Interview with Patricia McClain. AFC/2001/001/00666. No date. Salem, IN.

Clarkson, Leonard. Interview with Bonnie Kipp. AFC/2001/001/61307. 19 January 2008. Michigan.

Draper, Sr., Teddy. Interview with Carol Fleming and Warren C. Salomon. AFC/2001/001/52556. 10 December 2003. Chinle, AZ.

Goodwin, Oscar Alvin. Interview with Shawn Milam. AFC/2001/001/56155. No date or place.

Hawthorne, Roy O. Interview with Carol Fleming and Warren C. Salomon. AFC/2001/001/52528. 9 December 2003. Lupton, AZ.

Horn, Sr., Gilbert. Interview with Josephus Nelson. AFC/2001/001/24257. 9 July 2004. Fort Belknap, MT.

Irons, William D. Interview with David Farley, Krystal Osburn and Gary Stone. AFC/2001/001/17531. 26 April 2004. Reno, NV.

Le Beau, Marcella Ryan. Interview with Maarja Vigorito. AFC/2001/001/24202. 9 July 2004. Unknown location.

McClung, Earl Ervin. Interview with Sherlan Marrott. AFC/2001/001/34734. 2 December 2003. Pueblo West, CO.

Mzhickteno, Leroy 'Mickey'. Interview with Gale Beal. AFC/2001/001/38223. 31 March 2005. Mayetta, KS.

Sandoval, Merril. Interview with Patricia Steelman. AFC/2001/001/14223. 27–30 May 2004. Washington, DC.

### Government Documents and Legislation

Australia. Defence Act (1909).

Australia. Human Rights and Equal Opportunity Commission, National Inquiry into the Separation of Aboriginal and Torres Strait Islander Children from Their Families. *Bringing Them Home: Report of the National Inquiry into the Separation of Aboriginal and Torres Strait Islander Children from Their Families.* Sydney: Human Rights and Equal Opportunity Commission, 1997.

Canada. Indian Act, 1876.

Canada. Parliament. *Special Joint Committee of the Senate and House of Commons Appointed to Examine and Consider the Indian Act.* Minutes and Proceedings of Evidence. Ottawa: 1946–8.

Canada. Parliament. Senate. Standing Senate Committee on Aboriginal Peoples. *The Aboriginal Soldier after the Wars.* Ottawa: 1995.

Canada. Royal Commission on Aboriginal Peoples (RCAP). *Report of the RCAP. Vol. 1: Looking Forward, Looking Back.* Ottawa: Supply and Services, 1996.

Canada, *The Final Report of the Truth and Reconciliation Commission of Canada,* Canada's Residential Schools: The History, Part I – Origins to 1939, vol. 1. Montreal and Kingston: McGill-Queen's University Press, 2015.

New Zealand. Sir Apira Ngata, to PM Fraser. 30 March 1943. Available from www.28maoribattalion.org.nz/node/15348. Accessed 9 August 2017.

United States Commission on Wartime Relocation and Internment of Civilians. *Personal Justice Denied: Report of the Commission on Wartime Relocation and Internment of Civilians.* Washington, DC: Government Printing Office, 1983.

Western Australia. Native (Citizenship Rights) Act 1944.

*Other Interviews*

## Australia

Batumbil, Phyllis. Interview with Noah Riseman. Mata Mata, Northern Territory. 29 September 2005. Australian Institute for Aboriginal and Torres Strait Islander Studies. RISEMAN_N01.

Pike, Betty. Interview with Noah Riseman. Melbourne. 12 April 2011. Available from Serving Our Country, http://ourmobserved.anu.edu.au/yarn-ups/yarn-participants/betty-pike

Quakawoot, Mabel. Interview with Noah Riseman. Mackay, QLD. 5 June 2011. Available from Serving Our Country, http://ourmobserved.anu.edu.au/yarn-ups/yarn-participants/mabel-quakawoot

## New Zealand

Palmer, John, Ngāti Raukawa, Ngāti Toa Rangatira, Ngāti Tūwharetoa (1918–2011). Interviewed by Mathew Devonald. Family collection. Available from www.28maoribattalion.org.nz/audio/john-palmer-discusses-trying-find-m%C4%81ori-battalion-greece

## United States

Begay, Thomas. Interviewed by Sally McClain. August 1992. Sally McClain collection. Navajo Nation Tribal Museum.

Billison, Sam. Interviewed by Sally McClain. 31 May 1993. Sally McClain collection. Navajo Nation Tribal Museum.

Maker, Marie. Interviewed by Leonard Maker. 20 June 1969. Western History Collections, University of Oklahoma. OK, T-407.

Rexroat, Ola Mildred. Interviewed by Patricia Jernigan. 8 September 2006. Women Airforce Service Pilots Oral History Project. The Woman's Collection, Texas Woman's University.

Sarracino, Nellie. Interviewed by Elizabeth Castle. 12 April 2005. Rosie the Riveter World War II American Homefront Oral History Project. Regional Oral History Office, The Bancroft Library, University of California, Berkeley.

Traversie, Faith. Interviewed by Elizabeth Castle. 19 February 2005. Rosie the Riveter World War II American Homefront Oral History Project. Regional Oral History Office, The Bancroft Library, University of California, Berkeley.

*Media Sources*

## Australia

*Argus* (Melbourne)
*Australian*
*Australian Broadcasting Corporation (ABC)*
*Daily News* (Perth)
*National Times Magazine*
*Salt*
*Special Broadcasting Service* (SBS)

*Weekly Review*
*West Australian* (Perth)
*Zero Post*

## Canada

*Brantford Expositor*
*Brockville Recorder and Times*
*Calgary Herald*
*Cardston News*
*Globe and Mail*
*Kamloops Sentinel*
*Lethbridge Herald*
*Maclean's*
*Regina Leader-Post*
*Saint John Telegraph-Journal*
*Saskatoon StarPhoenix*
*Saturday Night*
*Vancouver Province*
*Vancouver Sun*

## New Zealand

*Dominion Post*

## United States

*Lawrence Journal-World*
*National Home Monthly*
*The Beaver*
*The New York Times*

## Unpublished Theses

Arrowsmith, Emily. 'Fair Enough? How Notions of Race, Gender, and Soldiers' Rights Affected Dependents' Allowance Policies Towards Canadian Aboriginal Families During World War II'. PhD Thesis, Carleton University, 2006.

Barry, Amanda. 'Broken Promises: Aboriginal Education in South-eastern Australia, 1837–1937'. PhD Thesis, University of Melbourne, 2008.

Boxer, Elise. 'Citizen Soldiers: Fort Peck Indian Reservation's Company B, 1940–1945'. MA Thesis, Utah State University, 2004.

Close, Kirstie. 'Invisible Labourers: Cape Bedford (Hopevale) Mission and the "Paradox" of Aboriginal Labour in the Second World War'. Master's Thesis, University of Melbourne, 2009.

Davison, Janet F. 'We Shall Remember Them: Canadian Indians and World War II'. Masters Thesis, Trent University, 1992.

Harvey, Gretchen. 'Cherokee and American: Ruth Muskrat Bronson, 1897–1982'. PhD Thesis, Arizona State University, 1996.

Jones, Lloyd. 'Images of Maori in the Pakeha Press: Pakeha Representations of Māori in the Popular Print Media, 1935–1965'. Master's Thesis, University of Auckland, 1998.

Leslie, John. 'Assimilation, Integration or Termination? The Development of Canadian Indian Policy, 1943–1963'. PhD Thesis, Carleton University, 1999.

Muir, Kristy. 'The Hidden Cost of War: The Psychological Effects of the Second World War and Indonesian Confrontation on Australian Veterans and Their Families'. PhD thesis, University of Wollongong, 2003.

Neilson, Mahli. 'Hiatus or Catalyst? The Impact of the Second World War on Aboriginal Activism and Assimilation, 1939–1953'. BA (Honours) Thesis, Australian National University, 2008.

Ross, Angela M. 'The Princess Production: Locating Pocahontas in Time and Place'. PhD thesis, University of Arizona, 2008.

Sheffield, R. Scott. '"… in the same manner as other people": Government Policy and the Military Service of Canada's First Nations People, 1939–1945'. Master's Thesis: University of Victoria, 1995.

Steeves, Kerry Ragnar. 'Pacific Coast Militia Rangers, 1942–1954'. Master's Thesis, University of British Columbia, 1990.

Thomson, Jane R. M. 'The Rehabilitation of Servicemen of World War II in New Zealand, 1940–1954'. PhD Thesis, Victoria University of Wellington, 1983.

Toomey, Roy. 'Canadian Indians and the Second World War: The Pivotal Event of the 20th Century for Canadian Indians and Canadian Indian Policy?' MA Thesis, University of Northern British Columbia, 2006.

Willis, Brian. 'Aborigines and the Defence Forces in Western Australia in World War II'. MA Thesis, University of Western Australia, 1995.

### Documentaries

*Ka-wayawayama: Aeroplane Dance*. Produced and directed by Trevor Graham. 58 minutes. Film Australia, 1994. DVD.

*No Bugles, No Drums*. Produced by Debra Beattie-Burnett. Directed by John Burnett. 49 minutes. Seven Emus Productions in association with Australian Television Network, 1990. Videocassette.

*Thomson of Arnhem Land*. Produced by Michael Cummins and John Moore. Directed by John Moore. 56 minutes. Film Australia, in association with John Moore Productions, 2000. Videocassette.

## Books, Book Chapters and Journal Articles

Aaseng, Nathan. *Navajo Code Talkers: America's Secret Weapon in World War II*. New York: Walker and Co., 2002.

Adair, John and Evon Vogt. 'Navaho and Zuni Veterans: A Study in Contrasting Modes of Cultural Change'. *American Anthropologist* 51, no. 4 (October–December 1949): 547–561.

Adams, David Wallace. *Education for Extinction: American Indians and the Boarding School Experience, 1875–1928*. Lawrence: University Press of Kansas, 1995.

Alcorn, Graham. *The Struggle of the Pilbara Station Hands for Decent Living Standards and Human Rights*. Stockton, NSW: Max Brown, 2001.

Allen, Gwenfread. *Hawaii's War Years 1941–1945*. Honolulu: University of Hawaii Press, 1950.

Altschuler, Glenn C. and Stuart M. Blumin. *The G.I. Bill: A New Deal for Veterans*. Oxford and New York: Oxford University Press, 2009.

Anderson, Atholl. 'Origins, Settlement and Society of Pre-European South Polynesia'. In *The New Oxford History of New Zealand*, edited by Giselle Byrnes, 21–46. South Melbourne: Oxford University Press, 2009.

Armitage, Andrew. *Comparing the Policy of Aboriginal Assimilation: Australia, Canada and New Zealand*. Vancouver: University of British Columbia Press, 1995.

Attwood, Bain. *Rights for Aborigines*. Crows Nest, NSW: Allen & Unwin, 2003.

Attwood, Bain and Andrew Markus. *Thinking Black: William Cooper and the Australian Aborigines' League*. Canberra: Aboriginal Studies Press, 2004.

Awatere, Hinemoa Ruataupare. *Awatere: A Soldier's Story*. Wellington: Huia, 2003.

Ballara, Angela. *Iwi: The Dynamics of Māori Tribal Organisation from c.1769 to c.1945*. Wellington: Victoria University Press, 1998.

   *Taua: 'Musket Wars', 'Land Wars', or Tikanga? Warfare in Māori Society in the Early Nineteenth Century*. Auckland: Penguin, 2003.

Banivanua-Mar, Tracey. *Decolonisation and the Pacific: Indigenous Globalisation and the Ends of Empire*. Cambridge: Cambridge University Press, 2016.

Banner, Stuart. *Possessing the Pacific: Land, Settlers, and Indigenous People from Australia to Alaska*. Cambridge, MA: Harvard University Press, 2007.

Barman, Jean, Yvonne Hébert and Don McCaskill. *Indian Education in Canada, Volume I: The Legacy*. Vancouver: University of British Columbia Press, 1986.

Barrington, John. *Separate but Equal? Māori Schools and the Crown 1867–1969*. Wellington: Victoria University Press, 2008.

Barsh, Russel Lawrence. 'American Indians in the Great War'. *Ethnohistory* 38, no. 3 (Summer 1991): 276–303.

   'War and the Reconfiguration of American Indian Society'. *Journal of American Studies* 35, no. 3 (2001): 371–410.

Bayly, C. A., Sven Beckert, Mathew Connelly, et al. 'AHR Conversation: On Transnational History'. *American Historical Review* 111, no. 5 (December 2006): 1440–1464.

Begay, Agnes. 'History – Munitions Plant Work During World War II'. In *Navajos and World War II*, edited by Keats Begay and Broderick H. Johnson, 47–50. Tsaile, AZ: Navajo Community College Press, 1977.

Begay, Keats and Broderick H. Johnson, eds. *Navajos and World War II*. Tsaile, AZ: Navajo Community College Press, 1977.

Belcourt, Herb. *Walking in the Woods: A Métis Journey*. Nanoose Bay, BC: Brindle & Glass, 2006.

Belich, James. *Making Peoples: A History of the New Zealanders*. Auckland: Penguin Books, 1996.

   'Myth, Race and Identity in New Zealand'. *New Zealand Journal of History* 31, no. 1 (1997): 9–22.

   *Paradise Reforged: A History of the New Zealanders*. Auckland: Allen Lane, 2001.

*Replenishing the Earth: The Settler Revolution and the Rise of the Anglo-World,* *1783–1939.* New York: Oxford University Press, 2009.

Bell, Stephen. 'The 107th "Timber Wolf" Battalion at Hill 70'. *Canadian Military History* 5, no. 1 (Spring 1996): 73–78.

Benally, Dan. 'Ex-Prisoner of War, European Theater, World War II'. In *Navajos and World War II,* edited by Keats Begay and Broderick H. Johnson, 64–85. Tsaile, Navajo Nation, AZ: Navajo Community College Press, 1977.

Benn, Carl. *The Iroquois in the War of 1812.* Toronto: University of Toronto Press, 1998.

Bennett, Mary. 'Meskwaki Code Talkers'. *Iowa Heritage Illustrated* 84, no. 4 (Winter 2003): 154–156.

Berndt, Ronald and Catherine Berndt. *End of an Era: Aboriginal Labour in the Northern Territory.* Canberra: Australian Institute of Aboriginal Studies, 1987.

Bernstein, Alison. *American Indians and World War II: Toward a New Era in Indian Affairs.* Norman: University of Oklahoma Press, 1991.

Beros, Sapper Bert. *The Fuzzy Wuzzy Angels and Other Verses.* Sydney: F. H. Johnston Publishing Company, 1943.

Bioletti, Harry. *The Yanks Are Coming: The American Invasion of New Zealand, 1942–1944.* Auckland: Century Hutchison, 1989.

Bixler, Margaret. *Winds of Freedom: The Story of the Navajo Code Talkers of World War II.* Darien, CT: Two Bytes Publishing Company, 1992.

Blondin, George. 'When the World Was New: Stories of the Sahtú Dene'. In *Out of the Background: Readings in Canadian Native History,* 2nd edn., edited by Kenneth Coates and Robin Fisher, 245–278. Toronto: Irwin Publishing, 1998.

Bodfish, Sr., Waldo. *Kusiq: An Eskimo Life History from the Arctic Coast of Alaska.* Fairbanks: University of Alaska Press, 1991.

Bongiorno, Frank. 'Anzac and the Politics of Inclusion'. In *Nation, Memory and Great War Commemoration Mobilizing the Past in Europe, Australia and New Zealand,* edited by Shanti Sumartojo and Ben Wellings, 81–97. Oxford: Peter Lang AG, 2014.

Booth, George. *33 Days.* Elwood, VIC: Greenhouse Publications, 1988.

Brawley, Sean and Chris Dixon. 'Jim Crow Downunder? African American Encounters with White Australia, 1942–1945'. *Pacific Historical Review* 71, no. 4 (2002): 607–632.

Briscoe, Gordon. *Racial Folly: A Twentieth Century Aboriginal Family.* Canberra: ANU Press and Aboriginal History Incorporated, 2010.

Britten, Thomas. *American Indians in World War I: At Home and at War.* Albuquerque: University of New Mexico Press, 1997.

Brodie, Nick. *1787: The Lost Chapters of Australia's Beginnings.* Richmond, VIC: Hardie Grant Books, 2016.

Brokaw, Tom. *The Greatest Generation.* New York: Random House, 2004.

Bronson, Ruth Muskrat. *Indians Are People, Too.* New York: Friendship Press, 1944.

Brookes, Barbara. *A History of New Zealand Women.* Wellington: Bridget Williams Books, 2016.

Brooking, Tom. '"Busting Up" The Greatest Estate of All: Liberal Maori Land Policy, 1891–1911'. *New Zealand Journal of History* 26, no. 1 (1992): 78–98.

Broome, Richard. *Aboriginal Victorians: A History since 1800*. Crows Nest, NSW: Allen & Unwin, 2005.

*Aboriginal Australians: A History since 1788*, 4th edn. Crows Nest, NSW: Allen & Unwin, 2010.

Brown, Cozy Stanley. 'Code Talker: Pacific Theater, World War II'. In *Navajos and World War II*, edited by Broderick H. Johnson, 51–63. Tsaile, Navajo Nation, AZ: Navajo Community College Press, 1977.

Buchowska, Zuzanna. *Negotiating Native American Identities: The Role of Tradition, Narrative and Language at Haskell Indian Nations University*. Poznañ, Poland: Uniwersytetu im. Adama Mickiewicza w Poznaniu, 2016.

Byrnes, Giselle, ed. *The New Oxford History of New Zealand*. Melbourne: Oxford University Press, 2009.

Caccia, Ivana. *Managing the Canadian Mosaic in Wartime: Shaping Citizenship Policy, 1939–1945*. Montreal: McGill-Queen's University Press, 2010.

Cadzow, Allison. 'North West Mobile Force'. In *Serving Our Country: Indigenous Australians, War, Defence and Citizenship*, edited by Joan Beaumont and Allison Cadzow, 282–303. Sydney: NewSouth Publishing, 2018.

Campbell, Maria. *Halfbreed*. Lincoln and London: University of Nebraska Press, 1973.

Carlson, Keith Thor, ed. *You Are Asked to Witness: The Stó:lō in Canada's Pacific Coast History*. Chilliwack, BC: Stó:lō Heritage Trust, 1997.

Carroll, Al. *Medicine Bags and Dog Tags: American Indian Veterans from Colonial Times to the Second Iraq War*. Lincoln & London: University of Nebraska Press, 2008.

Chandonnet, Fern, ed. *Alaska at War 1941–1945: The Forgotten War Remembered*. Fairbanks: University of Alaska Press, 2008.

Chesterman, John. *Civil Rights: How Indigenous Australians Won Formal Equality*. St. Lucia: University of Queensland Press, 2005.

Chesterman, John and Brian Galligan, *Citizens without Rights: Aborigines and Australian Citizenship*. Melbourne: Cambridge University Press, 1997.

Choo, Christine. *Mission Girls: Aboriginal Women on Catholic Missions in the Kimberley, Western Australia, 1900–1950*. Crawley: University of Western Australia Press, 2004.

Clark, Mavis Thorpe. *The Boy from Cumeroogunga: The Story of Sir Douglas Ralph Nicholls, Aboriginal Leader*. Sydney: Hodder and Stoughton, 1979.

Clarke, Banjo. *Wisdom Man*. Camberwell, VIC: Penguin Books, 2003.

Clendinnen, Inga. *Dancing with Strangers*. New York: Cambridge University Press, 2005.

Coates, Kenneth. *A Global History of Indigenous Peoples: Struggle and Survival*. Basingstoke: Palgrave Macmillan, 2004.

Coates, Ken and William Morrison. *Land of the Midnight Sun: A History of the Yukon*. Carleton Library Series. Montreal and Kingston: McGill-Queen's University Press, 2005.

Cody, Joseph Frederick. *28 (Maori) Battalion*. Wellington: War History Branch, Dept. of Internal Affairs, 1956.

Cole, Douglas and Ira Chaikin. *An Iron Hand upon the People: The Law against the Potlatch on the Northwest Coast*. Vancouver: Douglas & McIntyre, 1990.

Connor, John. 'Traditional Indigenous Warfare'. In *Before the Anzac Dawn: A Military History of Australia before 1915*, edited by Craig Stockings and John Connor, 8–20. Sydney: NewSouth Publishing, 2013.

Cook, Tim. *Vimy: The Battle and the Legend.* Toronto: Allen Lane, 2017.

Cowger, Thomas. '"The Crossroads of Destiny:" The NCAI's Landmark Struggle to Thwart Coercive Termination.' *American Indian Culture and Research Journal* 20, no. 4 (1996): 121–124.

Crawford, John, ed. *Kia Kaha: New Zealand in the Second World War.* Melbourne: Oxford University Press, 2002.

Crosby, R. D. *The Musket Wars: A History of Inter-Iwi Conflict 1806–1845*, 2nd edn. Auckland: Reed, 2001.

Curthoys, Ann. 'Does Australian History Have a Future?' In *Challenging Histories: Reflections on Australian History, Australian Historical Studies* 33, special issue no. 118 (2002): 145–146.

*Freedom Ride: A Freedom Rider Remembers.* St. Leonards, NSW: Allen & Unwin, 2002.

Darian-Smith, Kate. *On the Home Front: Melbourne in Wartime 1939–1945*, 2nd edn. Carlton, VIC: Melbourne University Press, 2009.

'Pacific Partners: Gendered Memories of the US Marines in Melbourne, 1943'. In *Gender and the Second World War: Lessons of War*, edited by Corinna Peniston-Bird and Emma Vickers, 135–150. London: Palgrave, 2017.

David-Ives, Corinne. 'Integration Politics and the New Zealand Army: The Fate of the Maori Battalion in the Wake of the Second World War'. In *War Memories: Commemoration, Recollections, and Writings on War*, edited by Stéphanie A. H. Bélanger and Renée Dickason, 373–387. Montreal: McGill-Queen's University Press, 2017.

Davis, Fiona. *Australian Settler Colonialism and the Cummeragunja Aboriginal Station: Redrawing Boundaries.* Brighton, UK: Sussex Academic Press, 2014.

de Lee, Nigel. 'Oral History and British Soldiers' Experience of Battle in the Second World War'. In *Time to Kill: The Soldier's Experience of War in the West*, edited by Paul Addison and Angus Calder, 359–368. London: Pimlico, 1997.

Dempsey, L. James. 'Alberta Indians and the Second World War'. In *For King and Country: Alberta and the Second World War*, edited by Ken Tingley, 39–52. Edmonton: Provincial Museum of Alberta, 1995.

Dempsey, L. James. *Warriors of the King: Prairie Indians in World War I.* Regina: Canadian Plains Research Centre, 1999.

Denoon, Donald. 'Understanding Settler Societies'. *Historical Studies* 18 (1979): 511–527.

Dickason, Olive Patricia. *Canada's First Nations: A History of Founding Peoples from Earliest Times*, 3rd edn. Don Mills, ON: Oxford University Press, 2002.

*A Concise History of Canada's First Nations*, 4th edn. Toronto: Oxford University Press, 2006.

Drees, Laurie Meijer. 'Citizenship and Treaty Rights: The Indian Association of Alberta and the Canadian Indian Act, 1946–1948'. *Great Plains Quarterly* 20 (Spring 2000): 141–158.

Dunlay, Thomas. *Wolves for the Blue Soldiers: Indian Scouts and Auxiliaries with the United States Army, 1860–90.* Lincoln and London: University of Nebraska Press, 1982.

Dye, Bob, ed. *Hawai'i Chronicles III: World War Two in Hawai'i, from the Pages of Paradise of the Pacific*. Honolulu: University of Hawai'i Press, 2000.

Edmonds, Penelope. *Urbanizing Frontiers: Indigenous Peoples and Settlers in 19th-Century Pacific Rim Cities*. Vancouver: University of British Columbia Press, 2010.

*Settler Colonialism and (Re)conciliation: Frontier Violence, Affective Performances, and Imaginative Refoundings*. Basingstoke: Palgrave Macmillan, 2016.

Edwards, Mihi. *Mihipeka: Early Years*. Auckland: Penguin Books, 1990.

Egan, Ted. *Justice All Their Own: The Caledon Bay and Woodah Island Killings 1932–1933*. Carlton, VIC: Melbourne University Press, 1996.

Ellinghaus, Katherine. *Taking Assimilation to Heart: Marriages of White Women and Indigenous Men in the United States and Australia, 1887–1937*. Lincoln: University of Nebraska Press, 2006.

*Blood Will Tell: Native Americans and Assimilation Policy*. Lincoln: University of Nebraska Press, 2017.

Ellis, John. *At the Sharp End: The Fighting Man in World War II*. Newton Abbot, UK: David & Charles, 1980.

'Reflections on the "Sharp End" of War'. In *Time to Kill: The Soldier's Experience of War in the West*, edited by Paul Addison and Angus Calder, 12–18. London: Pimlico, 1997.

Enloe, Cynthia. *Ethnic Soldiers: State Security in a Divided Society*. New York: Penguin, 1980.

*Police, Military and Ethnicity: Foundations of State Power*. New Brunswick, NJ: Transaction Books, 1980.

Evans, Julie, Patricia Grimshaw, David Philips and Shurlee Swain. *Equal Subjects, Unequal Rights: Indigenous Peoples in British Settler Colonies, 1830–1910*. Manchester: Manchester University Press, 2003.

Faulkner, Samantha and Ali Drummond. *Life B'long Ali Drummond: A Life in the Torres Strait*. Canberra: Aboriginal Studies Press, 2007.

Fixico, Donald. *Termination and Relocation: Federal Indian Policy, 1945–1960*. Albuquerque: University of New Mexico Press, 1986.

Fleras, Augie and Jean Leonard Elliott. *The Nations within: Aboriginal-State Relations in Canada, the United States, and New Zealand*. Toronto: Oxford University Press, 1992.

Ford, Ruth. 'Lesbians and Loose Women: Female Sexuality and the Women's Services During World War II'. In *Gender and War: Australians at War in the Twentieth Century*, edited by Joy Damousi and Marilyn Lake, 81–104. Cambridge: Cambridge University Press, 1995.

Forsyth, Hannah and Altin Gavranovic. 'The Logic of Survival: Towards an Indigenous-Centred History of Capitalism in Wilcannia'. *Settler Colonial Studies* 8, no. 4 (2018): 464–488.

Franco, Jeré Bishop. *Crossing the Pond: The Native American Effort in World War II*. Denton: University of North Texas Press, 1999.

Fredrickson, George. 'From Exceptionalism to Variability: Recent Developments in Cross-National Comparative History'. *Journal of American History* 82, no. 2 (1995): 587–604.

Fyfe, Judith and Gaylene Preston, eds. *War Stories Our Mothers Never Told Us*. Auckland: Penguin, 1995.

Gaffen, Fred. *Forgotten Soldiers*. Penticton, BC: Theytus Books, 1985.

Gagnon, Mélanie and Iqaluit Elders. *Inuit Recollections on the Military Presence in Iqaluit*. Iqaluit: Nunavut Arctic College, 2002.

Gardiner, Wira. *Te Mura o Te Ahi: The Story of the Maori Battalion*. Auckland: Reed, 1992.

Garfield, Brian. *The Thousand-Mile War: World War II in Alaska and the Aleutians*. Anchorage: University of Alaska Press, 1969.

Garton, Stephen. *The Cost of War: Australians Return*. Melbourne: Oxford University Press, 1996.

Gilbert, Kevin. *Living Black: Blacks Talk to Kevin Gilbert*. Melbourne: Allen Lane, 1977.

Gilling, Bryan. 'Paddling Their Own Waka or Rowing the Government's Boat? The Official System for Maori Socio-Economic Development in the Post-1945 Period'. *Rangatiratanga Series*, Number 15. Wellington: Treaty of Waitangi Research Unit, 2008.

Gilling, Tui. *The Crown, Rangatiratanga and the Māori War Effort in the Second World War: A Preliminary Survey*. Wellington: Treaty of Waitangi Research Unit, Stout Research Centre for New Zealand Studies, 2005.

Golodoff, Nick. *Attu Boy: A Young Alaskan's WWII Memoir*. Fairbanks, AK: University of Alaska Press, 2015.

Goodall, Heather. *Invasion to Embassy: Land in Aboriginal Politics in New South Wales, 1770–1972*. St. Leonards, NSW: Allen & Unwin and Black Books, 1996.

Gordon, Harry. *The Embarrassing Australian: The Story of an Aboriginal Warrior*. Melbourne: Landsdowne Press, 1962.

Gould, Ashley. 'From Taiaha to Ko: Repatriation and Land Settlement for Maori Soldiers in New Zealand after the First World War'. *War & Society* 28, no. 2 (2009): 49–83.

Gouveia, Grace Mary. '"We Also Serve": American Indian Women's Role in World War II'. *Michigan Historical Review* 20, no. 2 (1994): 153–182.

Green, Rayna. 'The Pocahontas Perplex: The Image of Indian Women in American Culture'. *The Massachusetts Review* 16, no. 4 (1975): 698–714.

Grey, Jeffrey. *A Military History of Australia*, 3rd edn. Cambridge and Port Melbourne: Cambridge University Press, 2008.

Grimshaw, Patricia and Hannah Loney. '"Doing Their Bit Helping Make Australia Free": Mothers of Aboriginal Diggers and the Assertion of Indigenous Rights'. *Provenance: The Journal of Public Record Office Victoria* 14 (2015): 3–16.

Haake, Claudia. *The State, Removal and Indigenous Peoples in the United States and Mexico, 1620–2000*. New York & London: Routledge, 2007.

Haebich, Anna. *For Their Own Good: Aborigines and Government in the South West of Western Australia, 1900–1940*. Nedlands: University of Western Australia Press, 1998.

 'Nuclear, Suburban and Black: Middleton's Vision of Assimilation for Nyungar Families'. In *Contesting Assimilation*, edited by Tim Rowse, 201–220. Perth: API Network, 2005.

 *Spinning the Dream: Assimilation in Australia, 1950–1970*. Fremantle, WA: Fremantle Press, 2008.

Hall, Robert. *The Black Diggers: Aborigines and Torres Strait Islanders in the Second World War*. Sydney: Allen and Unwin, 1989.

*Fighters from the Fringe: Aborigines and Torres Strait Islanders Recall the Second World War*. Canberra: Aboriginal Studies Press, 1995.

Hallinan, Chris and Barry Judd. 'Duelling Paradigms: Australian Aborigines, Marn-Grook and Football Histories'. In *Indigenous People, Race Relations and Australian Sport*, edited by Chris Hallinan and Barry Judd, 61–72. London and New York: Routledge, 2014.

Harawira, Padre. December 1941 broadcast. Available from www.28maoribat talion.org.nz/audio/libyan-campaign-part-4-padre-harawira. Accessed 9 August 2017.

Harman, Kristyn. '"The Families Were … Too Poor to Send Them Parcels": The Provision of Comforts to Aboriginal Soldiers in the AIF in the Second World War'. *Aboriginal History* 39 (2015): 223–244.

Hauptman, Laurence. *The Iroquois Struggle for Survival: World War II to Red Power*. Syracuse: Syracuse University Press, 1986.

Hemingway, Albert. *Ira Hayes: Pima Indian*. New York: University Press of America, 1988.

Hendricks, Charles. 'The Eskimos and the Defense of Alaska'. *Pacific Historical Review* 54 (August 1985): 271–295.

Henty-Gebert, Claire. *Paint Me Black: Memories of Croker Island and Other Journeys*. Canberra: Aboriginal Studies Press, 2011.

Hill, Richard. *State Authority, Indigenous Autonomy: Crown-Maori Relations in New Zealand/Aotearoa, 1900–1950*. Wellington: Victoria University Press, 2004.

'Maori and State Policy'. In *The New Oxford History of New Zealand*, edited by Giselle Byrnes, 513–536. Melbourne: Oxford University Press, 2009.

'Maori Urban Migration and the Assertion of Indigeneity in Aotearoa/New Zealand, 1945–1975'. *Interventions* 14, no. 2 (2012): 256–278.

Hirsch, Marianne. 'Family Pictures: Maus, Mourning, and Post-Memory'. *Discourse* 15, no. 2 (1992): 3–29.

Hohaia, Debbie. 'In Search of a Decolonised Military: Māori Cultural Learning Experiences in the New Zealand Defence Force'. *Kōtuitui: New Zealand Journal of Social Sciences Online* 11, no. 1 (2016): 47–58.

Holbrook, Carolyn. *Anzac: The Unauthorised Biography*. Sydney: NewSouth Publishing, 2014.

Holm, Tom. 'Fighting a White Man's War: The Extent and Legacy of American Indian Participation in World War II'. *Journal of Ethnic Studies* 9, no. 2 (1981). 69–81.

'Culture, Ceremonialism, and Stress: American Indian Veterans and the Vietnam War'. *Armed Forces & Society* 12, no. 2 (Winter 1986): 237–251.

'Patriots and Pawns: State Use of American Indians in the Military and the Process of Nativization in the United States'. In *The State of Native America: Genocide, Colonization, and Resistance*, edited by M. Annette Jaimes, 345–370. Boston: South End Press, 1992.

*Strong Hearts, Wounded Souls: Native American Veterans of the Vietnam War*. Austin: University of Texas Press, 1996.

Holmes, Richard. *Acts of War: The Behavior of Men in Battle*. New York: The Free Press, 1985.

Howard, Ann. *You'll be Sorry!* Sydney and Melbourne: TARKA Publishing, 1990.
*Where Do We Go from Here?* Sydney: TARKA Publishing, 1994.

Huggonson, David. 'Aboriginal Diggers of the 9th Brigade, First AIF'. *Journal of the Royal Australian Historical Society* 79, no. 3–4 (1993): 214–223.

Hughes, Karen. 'Mobilising across Colour Lines: Intimate Encounters between Aboriginal Women and African American and Other Allied Servicemen on the World War II Australian Home Front'. *Aboriginal History* 41 (2017): 47–70.

Hunter, Tamara. 'The Myth of Equality: The Denial of Citizenship Rights for Aboriginal People in Western Australia'. *Studies in Western Australian History* 22 (2001): 69–82.

Hutchinson, Dave, ed. *Remembrances: Metis Veterans*. Regina, SK: Gabriel Dumont Institute of Native Studies & Applied Research, 1994.

Innes, Robert. '"I'm On Home Ground Now. I'm Safe": Saskatchewan Aboriginal Veterans in the Immediate Postwar Years, 1945–1946'. *American Indian Quarterly* 28, no. 3&4 (2004): 685–718.

Iverson, Peter. *Diné: A History of the Navajos*. Albuquerque: University of New Mexico Press, 2002.

Jackomos, Alick and Derek Fowell. *Forgotten Heroes: Aborigines at War from the Somme to Vietnam*. South Melbourne: Victoria Press, 1993.

Jacobs, Margaret. *White Mother to a Dark Race: Settler Colonialism, Maternalism, and the Removal of Indigenous Children in the American West and Australia, 1880–1940*. Lincoln: University of Nebraska Press, 2009.
*A Generation Removed: The Fostering and Adoption of Indigenous Children in the Postwar World*. Lincoln: University of Nebraska Press, 2014.

James, Jan 'Kabarli.' *Forever Warriors*. Perth: Scott Print, 2010.

Janowitz, Morris. 'Military Institutions and Citizenship in Western Societies'. *Armed Forces and Society* 2, no. 2 (1976): 185–204.

Jevec, Adam. 'Semper Fidelis, Code Talkers'. *Prologue: Quarterly of the National Archives and Records Administration* 33, no. 4 (Winter 2001): 270–277.

Johnson, Miranda. *The Land Is Our History: Indigeneity, Law and the Settler State*. New York: Oxford University Press, 2016.

Johnson, Murray and Ian McFarlane. *Van Diemen's Land: An Aboriginal History*. Sydney: University of New South Wales Press, 2015.

Johnston, Philip. 'Indian Jargon Won Our Battles'. *The Masterkey for Indian Lore and History* 38, no. 4 (1964): 130–137.

Junger, Sebastian. *Tribe: On Homecoming and Belonging*. London: HarperCollins Publishers, 2016.

Kersey, Jr., Harry A. 'Indigenous Sovereignty in Two Cultures: Māori and American Indians Compared'. *Occasional Paper Series*, Number 1. Wellington: Treaty of Waitangi Research Unit, 2000.

Keshen, Jeff. 'Getting it Right the Second Time Around: The Reintegration of Canadian Veterans of World War II'. In *The Veterans' Charter and Post-War Canada*, edited by Peter Neary and J. L. Granatstein, 62–84. Montreal & Kingston: McGill-Queen's University Press, 1998.

Kidd, Rosalind. *Trustees on Trial: Recovering the Stolen Wages*. Canberra: Aboriginal Studies Press, 2006.

King, Michael. *Te Puea: A Biography*. Auckland: Hodder and Stoughton, 1977.

*The Penguin History of New Zealand*. Auckland: Penguin Books, 2003.

*Te Puea: A Life*, 4th edn. Auckland: Reed, 2003.

Kirtland, John C. and David F. Coffin, Jr., eds. *The Relocation and Internment of Aleuts during World War II*. Anchorage: Aleutian-Pribilof Islands Association, 1981.

Krebs, Ronald. *Fighting for Rights: Military Service and the Politics of Citizenship*. Ithaca, NY and London: Cornell University Press, 2006.

Kruger, Alec and Gerard Waterford. *Alone on the Soaks: The Life and Times of Alec Kruger*. Alice Springs, NT: IAD Press, 2007.

Kulchyski, Peter. 'A Considerable Unrest: F.O. Loft and the League of Indians'. *Native Studies Review* 1, no. 1–2 (1988): 95–117.

Labrum, Bronwyn. '"Bringing Families Up to Scratch": The Distinctive Workings of Maori State Welfare, 1944–1970'. *New Zealand Journal of History* 36, no. 2 (2002): 161–184.

Labumore, Elsie Roughsey. *An Aboriginal Mother Tells of the Old and the New*. Fitzroy, VIC: McPhee Gribble Publishers Pty Ltd, 1984.

Lackenbauer, P. Whitney. 'The Irony and the Tragedy of Negotiated Space: A Case Study of Narrative Form and Aboriginal Government Relations during the Second World War'. *Journal of the Canadian Historical Society* 1, no. 15 (2004): 177–206.

*Battle Grounds: The Canadian Military and Aboriginal Lands*. Vancouver: University of British Columbia Press, 2007.

'Guerrillas in Our Midst: The Pacific Coast Militia Rangers, 1942–45'. *BC Studies* 155 (December 2007): 95–131.

'"A Hell of a Warrior": Remembering Sergeant Thomas George Prince'. *Journal of Historical Biography* 1 (Spring 2007): 27–78.

'"A Hell of a Warrior": Sergeant Thomas George Prince'. In *Intrepid Warriors: Perspectives on Canadian Military Leaders*, edited by Colonel Bernd Horn, 95–138. Kingston, ON: Canadian Defence Academy Press, 2007.

*The Canadian Rangers: A Living History*. Vancouver: University of British Columbia Press, 2013.

'Race, Gender, and International "Relations": African Americans and Aboriginal People on the Margins in Canada's North, 1942–48'. In *Dominion of Race: Rethinking Canada's International History*, edited by Laura Madokoro, Francine McKenzie and David Meren, 112–138. Vancouver: University of British Columbia Press, 2017.

'At the Crossroads of Militarism and Modernization: Inuit-Military Relations in the Cold War Arctic'. In *Roots of Entanglement: Essays in Native-Newcomer Relations*, edited by Myra Rutherdale, P. Whitney Lackenbauer and Kerry Abel, 116–158. Toronto: University of Toronto Press, 2018.

Lackenbauer, P. Whitney and Ryan Shackleton. 'Inuit-Air Force Relations in the Qikiqtani Region during the Early Cold War'. In *De-Icing Required: The Canadian Air Force's Experience in the Arctic*, edited by P. W. Lackenbauer and W. A. March, 73–94. Trenton: Canadian Forces Air Warfare Centre, 2012.

Lackenbauer, P. Whitney, John Moses, R. Scott Sheffield and Maxime Gohier. *A Commemorative History of Aboriginal People in the Canadian Military*. Ottawa: Department of National Defence, 2010.

Lackenbauer, P. Whitney and R. Scott Sheffield. 'Moving Beyond Forgotten: The Historiography of Native Peoples in the World Wars'. In *Aboriginal People and the Canadian Military: Historical Perspectives*, edited by Craig Leslie Mantle and Whitney Lackenbauer, 209–232. Kingston: CDI Press, 2007.

LaDuke, Winona. *The Militarization of Indian Country*. East Lansing: Makwa Enewed, Michigan State University Press, 2013.

Lake, Marilyn and Henry Reynolds. *Drawing the Global Colour Line: White Men's Countries and the Question of Racial Equality*. Carlton, VIC: Melbourne University Publishing, 2008.

*What's Wrong with Anzac? The Militarisation of Australian History*. Sydney: University of New South Wales Press, 2010.

Lamilami, Lazarus. *Lamilami Speaks: The Cry Went Up: A Story of the People of Goulburn Islands, Northern Australia*. Sydney: Ure Smith, 1974.

Lloyd, Clem and Jacqui Rees. *The Last Shilling: A History of Repatriation in Australia*. Melbourne: Melbourne University Press, 1994.

Lovett-Gardiner, Aunty Iris. *Lady of the Lake: Aunty Iris's Story*. Melbourne: Koorie Heritage Trust, Inc., 1997.

Lutz, John Sutton. *Makúk: A New History of Aboriginal-White Relations*. Vancouver: University of British Columbia Press, 2008.

MacDonald, Peter with Ted Schwarz. *The Last Warrior: Peter MacDonald and the Navajo Nation*. New York: Orion Books, 1993.

Macintyre, Stuart. *Australia's Boldest Experiment: War and Reconstruction in the 1940s*. Sydney: NewSouth Publishing, 2015.

Madden, Ryan. 'The Forgotten People: The Relocation and Internment of Aleuts during World War II'. *American Indian Culture and Research Journal* 16, no. 4 (1992): 55–76.

Magee, Gary and Andrew Thompson. *Empire and Globalisation: Networks of People, Goods and Capital in the British World, c. 1850–1914*. Cambridge: Cambridge University Press, 2010.

Manning, Corinne. '"If aborigines are to be assimilated they must learn to live in houses": Victoria's Transitional Housing Policy'. In *Contesting Assimilation*, edited by Tim Rowse, 221–235. Perth: API Network, 2005.

Marika, Wandjuk, as told to Jennifer Isaacs. *Wandjuk Marika: Life Story*. St. Lucia: University of Queensland Press, 1995.

Marston, Muktuk. *Men of the Tundra: Eskimos at War*. New York: October House Inc., 1969.

Maynard, John. '"Let us go" … it's a "Blackfellows War" – Aborigines and the Boer War'. *Aboriginal History* 39 (2015): 143–162.

'On the Political "Warpath": Native Americans and Australian Aborigines after the First World War'. *Wicazo Sa Review* 32, no. 1 (2017): 48–62.

'The First World War'. In *Serving Our Country: Indigenous Australians, War, Defence and Citizenship*, edited by Joan Beaumont and Allison Cadzow, 74–93. Sydney: NewSouth Publishing, 2018.

McCarthy, James. *A Papago Traveler: The Memories of James McCarthy*. Tucson: Sun Tracks and the University of Arizona Press, 1985.

McClain, Sally. *Navajo Weapon: The Navajo Code Talkers*. Tucson: Rio Nuevo Pub., 2002.

McGibbon, Ian, ed., with Paul Goldstone. *The Oxford Companion to New Zealand Military History*. Auckland: Oxford University Press, 2000.

*New Zealand and the Second World War: The People, the Battles and the Legacy.* Auckland: Hodder Moa Beckett, 2004.

McGinness, Joe. *Son of Alyandabu: My Fight for Aboriginal Rights.* St. Lucia: University of Queensland Press, 1991.

McGrath, Ann. *Born in the Cattle: Aborigines in Cattle Country.* Sydney: Allen & Unwin, 1987.

*Illicit Love: Interracial Sex & Marriage in the United States and Australia.* Lincoln: University of Nebraska Press, 2015.

McGregor, Russell. *Indifferent Inclusion: Aboriginal People and the Australian Nation.* Canberra: Aboriginal Studies Press, 2011.

McLeod, John. *Myth & Reality: The New Zealand Soldier in World War II.* Auckland: Reed Methuen, 1986.

Meadows, William. *Kiowa, Apache, and Comanche Military Societies: Enduring Veterans, 1800 to the Present.* Austin: University of Texas Press, 1999.

*The Comanche Code Talkers of World War II.* Austin: University of Texas Press, 2002.

'North American Indian Code Talkers: Current Developments and Research'. In *Aboriginal Peoples and Military Participation: Canadian & International Perspectives,* edited by P. Whitney Lackenbauer, R. Scott Sheffield and Craig Leslie Mantle, 161–213. Kingston, ON: Canadian Defence Academy Press, 2007.

'"They Had a Chance to Talk to One Another ...": The Role of Incidence in Native American Code Talking'. *Ethnohistory* 56, no. 2 (2009): 269–284.

'An Honor Long Overdue: The 2013 Congressional Gold and Silver Medal Ceremonies in Honor of Native American Code Talkers'. *American Indian Culture and Research Journal* 40, no. 2 (2016): 91–121.

'Native American "Warriors" in the US Armed Forces'. In *Inclusion in the American Military: A Force for Diversity,* edited by David E. Rohall, Morten G. Ender and Michael D. Matthews, 83–108. Lanham, MD: Lexington Books, 2017.

Miller, Carman. *Painting the Map Red: Canada and the South African War, 1899–1902.* Montreal and Kingston: Canadian War Museum and McGill-Queen's University Press, 1993.

Miller, James Roger. *Skyscrapers Hide the Heavens: A History of Indian-White Relations in Canada,* 3rd edn. Toronto: University of Toronto Press, 1991.

*Shingwuak's Vision: A history of Native Residential Schools.* Toronto: University of Toronto Press, 1996.

*Compact, Contract, Covenant: Aboriginal Treaty Making in Canada.* Toronto: University of Toronto Press, 2009.

Miller, Jen. 'Frybread'. *Smithsonian Magazine* (July 2008). www.smithsonian mag.com/arts-culture/frybread-79191/.

Milloy, John S. *A National Crime: The Canadian Government and the Residential School System, 1879–1986.* Winnipeg: University of Manitoba Press, 1999.

Montgomerie, Deborah. 'Beyond the Search for Good Imperialism: The Challenge of Comparative History'. *New Zealand Journal of History* 31, no. 1 (1997): 153–168.

*The Women's War: New Zealand Women 1939–1945.* Auckland: Auckland University Press, 2001.

Moore, John Hammond. *Over-Sexed, Over-Paid, and Over Here: Americans in Australia, 1941–1945*. St. Lucia and New York: University of Queensland Press, 1981.

Moremon, John. 'After "the Girls" Came Home: Ex-Servicewomen of Australia's Wartime Women's Auxiliaries'. In *When the Soldiers Return: November 2007 Conference Proceedings*, edited by Martin Crotty and Craig Barrett, 203–211. Melbourne: RMIT Publishing in association with the School of History, Philosophy, Religion and Classics, University of Queensland, 2009.

Morgan, Cecilia. *Building Better Britains? Settler Societies within the British Empire 1783–1920*. Toronto: University of Toronto Press, 2016.

Morgan, George. *Unsettled Places: Aboriginal People and Urbanisation in New South Wales*. Kent Town, SA: Wakefield Press, 2006.

Morgan, Sally. *Wanamurraganya: The Story of Jack McPhee*. Fremantle, WA: Fremantle Arts Centre Press, 1989.

Moriarty, John. *Saltwater Fella*. Ringwood, VIC: Viking, 2000.

Morrison, William and Kenneth Coates. *Working the North: Labor and the Northwest Defense Projects 1942–1946*. Fairbanks: University of Alaska Press, 1994.

Morrow, Dan. 'Tradition and Modernity in Discourses of Māori Urbanisation.' *Journal of New Zealand Studies* 18 (2014): 85–105.

Moses, John, with Donald Graves and Warren Sinclair. *A Sketch Account of Aboriginal Peoples in the Canadian Military*. Ottawa: DND Canada, 2004.

Murray, Paul. 'Who Is an Indian? Who Is a Negro? Virginia Indian in the World War II Draft'. *Virginia Magazine of History and Biography* 95, no. 2 (1987): 215–231.

Myers, Sarah. 'Battling Contested Airspaces: The American Women Airforce Service Pilots of World War II'. In *Gender and the Second World War: Lessons of War*, edited by Corinna Peniston-Bird and Emma Vickers, 11–33. London: Palgrave, 2017.

Nash, Gerald A. *The American West Transformed: The Impact of the Second World War*. Bloomington: Indiana University Press, 1985.

Neary, Peter and J. L. Granatstein, eds. *The Veterans Charter and Post-World War II Canada*. Montreal and Kingston: McGill-Queen's University Press, 1998.

Nez, Chester and Judith Schiess Avila. *Code Talker: The First and Only Memoir by One of the Original Navajo Code Talkers of WWII*. New York: Berkley Caliber, 2011.

Ngata, Apirana. *The Price of Citizenship*. Wellington: Whitcombe & Tombs Limited, 1943.

Nolan, Melanie. 'Constantly on the Move, but Going Nowhere? Work, Community and Social Mobility'. In *The New Oxford History of New Zealand*, edited by Giselle Byrnes, 357–387. South Melbourne: Oxford University Press, 2009.

Oliver, Dean. 'Awaiting Return: Life in the Canadian Army's Overseas Repatriation Depots, 1945–46'. In *The Veterans Charter and Post-World War II Canada*, edited by Peter Neary and J. L. Granatstein, 32–61. Montreal & Kingston: McGill-Queen's University Press, 1998.

Orange, Claudia. *The Treaty of Waitangi*. Wellington: Allen & Unwin in association with Port Nicholson Press, 1987.

'An Exercise in Maori Autonomy: The Rise and Demise of the Maori War Effort Organization'. In *Aboriginal Peoples and Military Participation: Canadian and International Perspectives*, edited by P. Whitney Lackenbauer, R. Scott Sheffield and Craig Leslie Mantle, 237–266. Kingston, ON: Canadian Defence Academy Press, 2007.

Osborne, Elizabeth. *Torres Strait Islander Women and the Pacific War*. Canberra: Aboriginal Studies Press, 1997.

Pascoe, Bruce. *Dark Emu: Black Seeds, Agriculture or Accident?* Sydney: Magabala Books, 2014.

Paul, Doris. *The Navajo Code Talkers*. Pittsburgh: Dorrance Publishing Company, 1973.

Peniston-Bird, Corinna and Emma Vickers, 'Introduction'. In *Gender and the Second World War*, edited by Corinna Peniston-Bird and Emma Vickers, 1–8. London: Palgrave, 2017.

Perkins, Charles. *A Bastard Like Me*. Sydney: Ure Smith, 1975.

Peters, Evelyn J. '"Our City Indians": Negotiating Meaning of First Nations Urbanization in Canada'. *Historical Geography* 30 (2002): 75–92

Peterson, Jacquline and Jennifer Brown, eds. *The New Peoples: Being and Becoming Métis in North America*. St. Paul: Minnesota Historical Society Press, 2001.

Pierson, Ruth Roach. *They're Still Women after All: The Second World War and Canadian Womanhood*. Toronto: McClelland & Stewart, 1986.

Potts, Eli Daniel and Annette Potts. *Yanks Down Under, 1941–45: The American Impact on Australia*. Melbourne: Oxford University Press, 1985.

Poulin, Grace. 'Invisible Women: Aboriginal Servicewomen in Canada's Second World War Military'. *Aboriginal Peoples and the Canadian Military: Historical Perspectives*, edited by P. Whitney Lackenbauer and Craig Leslie Mantle, 137–169. Kingston, ON: Canadian Defence Academy Press, 2007.

*Invisible Women: World War II Aboriginal Servicemen in Canada*. Thunder Bay: Ontario Native Women's Association, 2007.

Powell, Alan. *The Shadow's Edge: Australia's Northern War*, Rev. edn. Darwin, NT: Charles Darwin University Press, 2007.

Pratt, Rod. 'Queensland's Aborigines in the First Australian Imperial Force'. In *Aboriginal Peoples and Military Participation: Canadian & International Perspectives*, edited by P. Whitney Lackenbauer, R. Scott Sheffield and Craig Leslie Mantle, 215–236. Kingston, ON: Canadian Defence Academy Press, 2007.

Pugsley, Chris. *Te Hokowhitu a Tu: The Maori Pioneer Battalion in the First World War*. Auckland: Reed Publishing, 1995.

Ramsland, John and Christopher Mooney. *Remembering Aboriginal Heroes: Struggle, Identity and the Media*. Melbourne: Brolga Publishing Pty Ltd, 2006.

Rangihau, John. 'Being Maori'. In *Te Ao Hurihuri: Aspects of Maoritanga*, edited by Michael King, 165–175. Auckland: Reed, 1992.

Rechniewski, Elizabeth. 'Remembering the Black Diggers: From "the Great Silence" to "Conspicuous Commemoration"?' In *War Memories: Commemoration, Recollections, and Writings on War*, edited by Renée Dickason and Stéphanie A. H. Bélanger, 388–408. Montreal: McGill-Queen's University Press, 2017.

Reese, Roger R. *Why Stalin's Soldiers Fought: The Red Army's Military Effectiveness in World War II.* Lawrence: University Press of Kansas, 2011.

Reynolds, Georgeanne L. 'Introduction.' In *Alaska at War 1941–1945: The Forgotten War Remembered,* edited by Fern Chandonnet, ix–xiv. Fairbanks: University of Alaska Press, 2008.

Reynolds, Henry. *Fate of a Free People.* Ringwood, VIC: Penguin Books Australia, 1995.

*The Other Side of the Frontier: Aboriginal Resistance to the Europeans Invasion of Australia.* Sydney: University of New South Wales Press, 2006.

*Unnecessary Wars.* Sydney: NewSouth Publishing, 2016.

Richards, Jonathan. *The Secret War: A True History of Queensland's Native Police.* St. Lucia: University of Queensland Press, 2008.

'"What a Howl There Would Be If Some of Our Folk Were So Treated by an Enemy": The Evacuation of Aboriginal People from Cape Bedford Mission, 1942'. *Aboriginal History* 36 (2012): 67–98.

Rintoul, Stuart. *The Wailing: A National Black Oral History.* Port Melbourne, VIC: William Heinemann Australia, 1993.

Riseman, Noah. 'The Stolen Veteran: Institutionalisation, Military Service and the Stolen Generations'. *Aboriginal History* 35 (2011): 57–77.

*Defending Whose Country? Indigenous Soldiers in the Pacific War.* Lincoln, NE: University of Nebraska Press, 2012.

'The Curious Case of Mervyn Eades: National Service, Discrimination and Aboriginal People'. *Australian Journal of Politics & History* 59, no. 1 (2013): 63–79.

'Aboriginal Military Service and Assimilation'. *Aboriginal History* 38 (2014): 155–178.

'Enduring Silences, Enduring Prejudices: Australian Aboriginal Participation in the First World War'. In *Endurance and the First World War: Experiences and Legacies in New Zealand and Australia,* edited by David Monger, Sarah Murray and Katie Pickles, 178–195. Newcastle upon Tyne, UK: Cambridge Scholars Publishing, 2014.

'The Rise of Indigenous Military History'. *History Compass* 12, no. 12 (December 2014): 901–911.

'Escaping Assimilation's Grasp: Aboriginal Women in the Australian Women's Military Services'. *Women's History Review* 24, no. 5 (2015): 757–775.

'Indigenous Soldiers: Native American and Aboriginal Australian Service in Vietnam'. In *New Perceptions of the Vietnam War: Essays on the War, the South Vietnamese Experience, the Diaspora and the Continuing Impact,* edited by Nathalie Huynh Chau Nguyen, 203–228. Jefferson, NC: McFarland & Company, Inc., 2015.

*In Defence of Country: Life Stories of Aboriginal and Torres Strait Islander Servicemen and Women.* Acton: ANU Press, 2016.

'Evolving Commemorations of Aboriginal and Torres Strait Islander Military Service'. *Wicazo Sa Review* 32, no. 1 (2017): 80–101.

'Ex-service Activism after 1945'. In *Serving Our Country: Indigenous Australians, War, Defence and Citizenship,* edited by Joan Beaumont and Allison Cadzow, 261–281. Sydney: NewSouth Publishing, 2018.

Riseman, Noah and Richard Trembath. *Defending Country: Aboriginal and Torres Strait Islander Military Service since 1945.* St. Lucia: University of Queensland Press, 2016.

Robbins, Rebecca. 'Self-Determination and Subordination: The Past, Present, and Future of American Indian Governance'. In *The State of Native America: Genocide, Colonization, and Resistance,* edited by M. Annette Jaimes, 87–121. Boston: South End Press, 1992.

Rogers, Anna and Mīria Simpson, eds. *Te tūmatanga—tātau tātau: Te Rōpū Wāhine Māori Toko i te Ora = Early stories from founding members of the Māori Women's Welfare League.* Wellington: Māori Women's Welfare League – Bridget Williams Books Limited, 1993.

Rose, Deborah Bird. *Hidden Histories: Black Stories from Victoria River Downs, Humbert River and Wave Hill Stations.* Canberra: Aboriginal Studies Press, 1991.

Rowse, Tim. *White Flour, White Power: From Rations to Citizenship in Central Australia.* Cambridge: Cambridge University Press, 1998.

Russell, Lynette, ed. *Colonial Frontiers: Indigenous-European Encounters in Settler Societies.* Manchester, UK: Manchester University Press, 2001.

Saunders, Kay. 'Inequalities of Sacrifice: Aboriginal and Torres Strait Islander Labour in Northern Australia during the Second World War'. *Labour History* 69 (November 1995): 131–148.

Scheiber, Harry and Jane Scheiber. *Bayonets in Paradise: Martial Law in Hawai'i during World War II.* Honolulu: University of Hawai'i Press, 2016.

Scott, Duncan Campbell. 'The Canadian Indians and the Great World War'. In *Canada in the Great War – Vol III: Guarding the Channel Ports,* 285–328. Toronto: United Publishing of Canada Ltd., 1919.

*1919 – Report of the Deputy Superintendent General for Indian Affairs: The Indians and the Great War – House of Commons Sessional Paper No. 27.* Ottawa: King's Printer, 1920.

Seal, Graham. *Inventing Anzac: The Digger and National Mythology.* St. Lucia: University of Queensland Press in association with the API Network and Curtin University of Technology, 2004.

Shannon, James A. 'With the Apache Scouts in Mexico'. *Journal of the United States Cavalry Association XXVII,* no. 114 (April 1917): 539–557.

Sheffield, R. Scott. '"Of Pure European Descent and of the White Race": Recruitment Policy and Aboriginal Canadians, 1939–1945'. *Canadian Military History* 5, no. 1 (1996): 8–15.

*A Search for Equity: A Study of the Treatment Accorded to First Nations Veterans and Dependents of the Second World War and the Korean Conflict. The Final Report of the National Round Table on First Nations Veterans' Issues.* Ottawa: Assembly of First Nations, May 2001.

*The Red Man's on the Warpath: The Image of the 'Indian' and the Second World War.* Vancouver: University of British Columbia Press, 2004.

'Rehabilitating the Indigene: Post-War Reconstruction and the Image of the Indigenous Other in Anglo-Canada and New Zealand, 1943–48'. In *Rediscovering the British World,* edited by Phillip Buckner and R. Douglas Francis, 341–361. Calgary: University of Calgary Press, 2005.

'Canadian Aboriginal Veterans and the Veterans' Charter after the Second World War'. In *Aboriginal Peoples and Military Participation: Canadian & International Perspectives*, edited by P. Whitney Lackenbauer, R. Scott Sheffield and Craig Leslie Mantle, 77–98. Kingston, ON: Canadian Defence Academy Press, 2007.

'Fighting a White Man's War? First Nations Participation in the Canadian War Effort, 1939–1945'. In *Canada and the Second World War*, edited by Geoffrey Hays, Michael Bechthold and Matt Symes, 67–91. Waterloo: Wilfrid Laurier University Press, 2012.

'Indigenous Exceptionalism under Fire: Assessing Indigenous Soldiers and Combat during the Second World War'. *Journal of Imperial and Commonwealth History* 45, no. 3 (2017): 506–524.

'Veterans' Benefits and Indigenous Veterans of the Second World War in Australia, Canada, New Zealand and the United States'. *Wicazo Sa Review* 32, no. 1 (Spring 2017): 63–79.

'Canadian First Nations and the British Connection during the Second World War'. In *Fighting with the Empire: Canada, Britain and Global Conflict, 1867–1947*, edited by Steven Marti and Tyler Turek. Vancouver: University of British Columbia Press, in press.

Sheffield, R. Scott and Hamar Foster. 'Fighting the King's War: Harris Smallfence, Verbal Treaty Promises and the Conscription of Indian Men, 1944'. *University of British Columbia Law Review* 33, no. 1 (1999): 53–74

Sheftall, Mark. 'Mythologising the Dominion Fighting Man: Australian and Canadian Narratives of the First World War Soldier, 1914–1939'. *Australian Historical Studies* 46, no. 1 (March 2015): 81–99.

Shewell, Hugh. 'Jules Sioui and Indian Political Radicalism in Canada, 1943–4'. *Journal of Canadian Studies* 34, no. 3 (1999): 211–242.

Simon, Judith, ed. *Nga Kura Maori: The Native Schools System 1867–1969*. Auckland: Auckland University Press, 1998.

Simon, Judith and Linda Tuhiwai Smith, eds. *A Civilizing Mission? Perceptions and Representations of the New Zealand Native Schools System*. Auckland: Auckland University Press, 2001.

Skocpol, Theda and Margaret Somers. 'The Uses of Comparative History in Macrosocial Inquiry'. *Comparative Studies in Society and History* 22, no. 2 (April 1980): 174–197.

Smaal, Yorick. *Sex, Soldiers and the South Pacific, 1939–45*. Basingstoke: Palgrave Macmillan, 2015.

Soutar, Monty. *Nga Tama Toa: The Price of Citizenship: C Company 28 (Maori) Battalion*. Auckland: David Bateman, 2008.

Stabler, Hollis. *No One Ever Asked Me: The World War II Memoirs of an Omaha Indian Soldier*. Lincoln & London: University of Nebraska Press, 2005.

Standfield, Rachel, Ray Peckham and John Nolan. 'Aunty Pearl Gibbs: Leading for Aboriginal Rights'. In *Diversity in Leadership: Australian Women, Past and Present*, edited by Joy Damousi, Kim Rubenstein and Mary Tomsic, 53–67. Canberra: ANU Press, 2014.

Stanley, Peter. *Invading Australia: Japan and the Battle for Australia, 1942*. Camberwell, VIC: Viking, 2008.

Stasiuk, Glen. '"Warriors then … Warriors still": Aboriginal Soldiers in the 20th Century'. *Journal of Australian Indigenous Issues* 7, no. 3 (2004): 3–13.

Stasiulis, Daiva and Nira Yuval-Davis. 'Introduction: Beyond Dichotomies – Gender, Race, Ethnicity and Class in Settler Societies'. In *Unsettling Settler Societies: Articulations of Gender, Race, Ethnicity and Class*, edited by Daiva Stasiulis and Nira Yuval-Davis, 1–38. London: Sage Publications, 1995.

Stephenson, Maxine. 'Closing the Doors on the Maori Schools in New Zealand'. *Race Ethnicity and Education* 9, no. 3 (September 2006): 307–324.

Stevenson, Michael. 'The Mobilisation of Native Canadians during the Second World War'. *Journal of the Canadian Historical Association* 7, no. 1 (1996): 205–226.

Streets, Heather. *Martial Races: The Military, Race and Masculinity in British Imperial Culture, 1857–1914*. Manchester: Manchester University Press, 2010.

Summerby, Janice. *Native Soldiers Foreign Battlefields*. Ottawa: Ministry of Supply and Services Canada, 1993.

Talbot, Robert. '"It Would Be Best to Leave Us Alone": First Nations Responses to the Canadian War Effort, 1914–1918'. *Journal of Canadian Studies* 45, no. 1 (Winter 2011): 90–120.

Tallberg, Teemu and Johanna Valenius. 'Men, Militaries and Civilian Societies in Interaction'. *norma: Nordic Journal for Masculinity Studies* 3, no. 2 (2008): 85–98.

Tate, Michael L. 'From Scout to Doughboy: The National Debate over Integrating American Indians into the Military, 1891–1918'. *The Western Historical Quarterly* 17, no. 4 (1986): 417–437.

Tennant, Paul. *Aboriginal People and Politics: The Indian Land Question in British Columbia, 1849–1989*. Vancouver: University of British Columbia Press, 1990.

Thomson, Alistair. *Anzac Memories: Living with the Legend*, 2nd edn. Clayton, VIC: Monash University Publishing, 2013.

'Anzac Memories Revisited: Trauma, Memory and Oral History'. *Oral History Review* 42, no. 1 (2015): 1–29.

Thornell, Harold, as told to Estelle Thompson. *A Bridge Over Time: Living in Arnhemland with the Aborigines 1938–1944*. Melbourne: J. M. Dent Pty Limited, 1986.

Titley, E. Brian. *A Narrow Vision: Duncan Campbell Scott and the Administration of Indian Affairs*. Vancouver: University of British Columbia Press, 1986.

Tobias, John L. 'Protection, Civilization, Assimilation: An Outline History of Canada's Indian Policy'. In *As Long as the Sun Shines and the Water Flows: A Reader in Canadian-Native Relations*, edited by Ian A. L. Getty and Antoine Lussier, 39–55. Vancouver: University of British Columbia Press, 1983.

Townsend, Kenneth. *World War II and the American Indian*. Albuquerque: University of New Mexico Press, 2000.

Tucker, Margaret. *If Everyone Cared: Autobiography of Margaret Tucker M.B.E.* Sydney: Ure Smith, 1977.

van de Logt, Mark. *War Party in Blue: Pawnee Indian Scouts in the United States Army, 1864–1877*. Norman: University of Oklahoma Press, 2010.

Vance, Jonathan. *Death So Noble: Memory, Meaning, and the First World War*. Vancouver: University of British Columbia Press, 1997.

Veracini, Lorenzo. *Settler Colonialism: A Theoretical Overview*. Basingstoke: Palgrave Macmillan, 2010.

'"Settler Colonialism": Career of a Concept'. *The Journal of Imperial and Commonwealth History* 41, no. 2 (2013): 313–333.

Verass, Sophie. 'The Fascinating Life of WWI's only Serving Indigenous Woman, Marion Leane Smith'. *National Indigenous Television.* 25 April 2017. www.sbs.com.au/nitv/article/2017/04/25/fascinating-life-wwis-only-serving-indigenous-woman-marion-leane-smith

Vogt, Evon. *Navaho Veterans: A Study of Changing Values. Papers of the Peabody Museum of American Archaeology and Ethnology, Harvard University.* Cambridge, MA: The Museum, 1951.

Wadham, Ben. 'Brotherhood: Homosociality, Totality and Military Subjectivity'. *Australian Feminist Studies* 28, no. 76 (2013): 212–235.

Walker, Franchesca. '"Descendants of a Warrior Race": The Maori Contingent, New Zealand Pioneer Battalion, and the Martial Race Myth, 1914–1919'. *War & Society* 31, no. 1 (March 2012): 1–21.

Walker, Ranginui. *He Tipua. The Life and Times of Sir Apirana Ngata.* Auckland: Viking, 2001.

    *Ka Whawhai Tonu Matou. Struggle without End,* Rev. edn. Auckland: Penguin, 2004.

Walker, Richard and Helen Walker. *Curtin's Cowboys: Australia's Secret Bush Commandos.* Sydney: Allen & Unwin, 1986.

Wanhalla, Angela and Erica Buxton. 'Pacific Brides: US Forces and Interracial Marriage during the Pacific War'. *Journal of New Zealand Studies* 14 (2013): 138–151.

Wanhalla, Angela and Kate Stevens. '"I Don't Like Maori Girls Going Out with Yanks": Māori-American Encounters in New Zealand'. In *Mothers' Darlings of the South Pacific: The Children of Indigenous Women and US Servicemen, World War II,* edited by Judith Bennett and Angela Wanhalla, 202–227. Dunedin, New Zealand: Otago University Press, 2016.

Ward, Mathew. '"The European Method of Warring Is Not Practiced Here": The Failure of British Military Policy in the Ohio Valley, 1755–1759'. *War in History* 4, no. 3 (1997): 247–263.

Watson, Bruce. 'Jaysho, moasi, dibeh, ayeshi, hasclishnih, beshlo, shush, gini. (World War II voice code)'. *Smithsonian* 24, no. 5 (August 1993): 34–43.

Westheider, James. *Fighting on Two Fronts: African Americans and the Vietnam War.* New York: New York University Press, 1997.

Weston, Mary Ann. *Native Americans in the News: Images of Indians in the Twentieth Century Press.* Westport, CT: Greenwood Press, 1996.

White, Richard. *The Middle Ground: Indians, Empires, and Republics in the Great Lakes Region, 1650–1815,* 2nd edn. Cambridge: Cambridge University Press, 2010.

Winegard, Timothy. *For King and Kanata: Canadian Indians and the First World War.* Winnipeg: University of Manitoba Press, 2012.

    *Indigenous Peoples of the British Dominions and the First World War.* Cambridge: Cambridge University Press, 2012.

Winter, Jay. *Remembering War: The Great War between Memory and History in the Twentieth Century.* New Haven, CT: Yale University Press, 2006.

Wolfe, Patrick. 'Nation and MiscegeNation: Discursive Continuity in the Post-Mabo Era.' *Social Analysis: The International Journal of Social and Cultural Practice,* no. 36 (October 1994): 93–152.

*Settler Colonialism and the Transformation of Anthropology: The Politics and Poetics of an Ethnographic Event.* London; New York: Cassell, 1999.

'Land, Labor, and Difference: Elementary Structures of Race'. *The American Historical Review* 106, no. 3 (2001): 866–905.

'Settler Colonialism and the Elimination of the Native'. *Journal of Genocide Research* 8, no. 4 (December 2006): 387–409.

*Traces of History: Elementary Structures of Race.* London; Brooklyn: Verso, 2016.

Young, Warren. *Minorities and the Military: A Cross-National Study in World Perspective.* Westport, CT: Greenwood Press, 1982.

Ziino, Bart. 'Introduction: Remembering the First World War Today'. In *Remembering the First World War,* edited by Bart Ziino, 1–17. Abingdon, Oxon; New York: Routledge, 2015.

## Unpublished Sources

'Historical Population Estimates Tables'. *Stats NZ Tatauranga Aotearoa.* Available from www.stats.govt.nz/browse_for_stats/population/estimates_and_projec tions/historical-population-tables.aspx. Accessed September 2016.

'History of Native American Military Service'. C-SPAN 3. www.c-span.org/ Events/History-of-Native-American-Military-Service/10737426478/. Accessed 4 March 2013.

Lackenbauer, P. Whitney. 'Indigenous Peoples and the Defence of Remote Regions in Canada, Alaska, and Australia', paper delivered at the Native American and Indigenous Studies Association conference, University of Saskatchewan, 15 June 2013.

'Māori and the Second World War: Page 3 – Achievements'. *New Zealand History.* Available from www.nzhistory.net.nz/war/maori-and-the-second-world-war/ achievements. Accessed 23 December 2017.

'Objectives and Methods'. GENCIMIL – *Gender Perspectives on Civil-Military Relations in Changing Security Environment.* Available from http://blogs.hel sinki.fi/civmil/objectives-and-methods/. Accessed 30 June 2015.

Sheffield, R. Scott. *Canada's Veterans' Charter and Métis Veterans of the Second World War and Korea.* Unpublished Report, Métis National Council, 2012.

Soutar, Monty. Booklet at Closure of 28th Māori Battalion Association. 1 December 2012.

# Index

Printed in the USA
CPSIA information can be obtained
at www.ICGtesting.com
CBHW070339031224
18343CB00005B/299

9 781108 440745